More Praise for *No Place Like Utopia*

"[Blake's] memoir of the people, the time and the places has an authentic and yet a relaxed tone. (It helps, too, that the author can be very funny.) Blake tells us much about the politics of architectural fame. . . . But perhaps his book's most winsome attributes are the affectionate, though hardly uncritical, portraits of people he knew well. . . . A very lively, intelligent read. . . . At his very best he's a sophisticated, perceptive, and gentle appreciator of architecture, architects, and other life forms."

—Benjamin Forgey, *Washington Post*

"This vivid, delightfully opinionated memoir is a scathing critique of the co-optation of modern architecture by the super rich who lack taste. . . . [Peter Blake's] personal insider's history is replete with candid close-ups of Philip Johnson, Frank Lloyd Wright, Jackson Pollock, Le Corbusier, Bertrand Russell, Buckminster Fuller, and many others."

—*Publishers Weekly*

"A book of permanent significance, a source for the historians of the future . . . Blake was one of the best editors who ever ran an architectural magazine. He was daring, personal, vital, intelligent, experimental, and alive to the need for ethics and values and vision in architecture." —Robert Campbell, *Boston Globe*

"Blake's half-century association with the Museum of Modern Art and the *Architectural Forum* placed him in the perfect position to observe, work with, and comment on the great figures of 20th-century architecture. . . . Insightful and illuminating."

—*Library Journal*

"I haven't read a single book on architecture written with such moral intelligence and skill." —Patwant Singh

"Peter Blake has been everywhere, seen and understood (almost) everything about those halcyon days when Modernism was more a moral mission than an aesthetic movement. . . . *No Place Like Utopia* is never dull and almost always charming; it is guaranteed to astonish and to offend almost every reader interested in the politics of postwar American architecture."

—Robert A. M. Stern

ALSO BY PETER BLAKE

Form Follows Fiasco
God's Own Junkyard
The Master Builders

NO PLACE LIKE UTOPIA

Modern Architecture and the Company We Kept

PETER BLAKE

W. W. NORTON   NEW YORK • LONDON

First published as a Norton paperback 1996
by arrangement with the author

Library of Congress Cataloging-in-Publication Data
Blake, Peter.
    No place like Utopia: modern architecture and the
    company we kept / by Peter Blake.—1st ed.
        p.   cm.
    Includes index.
    ISBN 978-0-393-31503-5
    1. Blake, Peter.—1920–   2. Architecture—United
States—Biography   3. International style (Architecture).
4. Architects—Psychology.   5. Architecture and society—
History—20th century.   I. Title.
NA737.B55A2   1993
720'.92—dc20
                                            [B] 92-27847
                                              CIP

Printed in the United States of America

W. W. Norton & Company, Inc.
500 Fifth Avenue, N.Y., N.Y. 10110
W. W. Norton & Company Ltd.
10 Coptic Street, London WC1A 1PU

1 2 3 4 5 6 7 8 9 0

THIS BOOK IS FOR MY SWEET FRIENDS
SUSIE, LILY, LIPPITY, AND COCONUSS

ACKNOWLEDGMENTS

■ So many people helped me in so many ways in the preparation of this book that it is virtually impossible to acknowledge them all.

So I won't try. I will mention only one—a lady whose sweetness, diligence, and wit encouraged me over a period of many months. Her name was Mary Lou Masey, and she was the wife of my friend Jack Masey. Mary Lou, a professional editor, read most of my manuscript, offered me her criticism and her suggestions, and encouraged me when I needed encouragement. She died, tragically, before I was able to supply her with my final chapters. It would have been a better book if she had lived; and those of us who knew and loved her would have had better lives if she had stuck around.

I received two grants, both of them welcome: one from the Graham Foundation for Advanced Studies in the Fine Arts; the other from the National Endowment for the Arts. The latter was a "Distinguished Designer Fellowship," and I appreciated that title almost as much as I appreciated the money that came with it.

—P. B.

PREFACE

■ When I was a boy, I went to school in the city of York, in northern England. One weekend, when I was about fourteen years old, my father came up from London to visit me and to have a Serious Talk about my future. The only thing one could do in York on weekends was to go for walks; and the best of those walks, especially if you wanted to impress a visitor from London, was the one on top of the massive stone walls that still ring the old town, with its medieval cathedral, the Minster. The walls are thick, and the path on top of those ramparts is generally wide enough for two people to walk side by side.

My father and I took our Sunday walk, clockwise around the city, and he came to the point almost immediately: "What do you want to be when you grow up?" I had given the matter some thought, and so I answered that I wanted to be a writer.

My father, a conservative corporate lawyer, was appalled. Writers, to him, were people roughly on a level with pimps, communists, and other deadbeats. He was sure that I would be poor for the rest of my life, and probably unshaven and immoral as well. Because he seemed so genuinely upset, I suggested an alternative: "What if I became an architect instead?" He seemed relieved, and grumped that this was probably all right.

As it turned out, I ended up both an architect and a writer. For reasons that may become clear in this book, I have alternated between practicing architecture, writing books and magazine articles, teaching architecture at schools and universities, and sometimes doing all these things more or less simultaneously. It has been a hectic life, but I recommend it highly: most people who pursue only one profession often seem to get bored with their lives. I have never had that problem, though I must confess that I might have been a better architect, or a better writer, or a better teacher if I had devoted all of my time to one of these arts, to the exclusion of the others. At least, I sometimes think so.

That, however, is not the point of this book. Because I found myself writing about architecture for so much of the time, as well as practicing it, I began to occupy one or two posts, in the years after World War II, from which it was possible to observe most of the action in architecture and the visual arts during a period when that action was intense. At an early age, even before I had graduated from a school of architecture, I was appointed curator of the Department of Architecture and Industrial Design at the Museum of Modern Art; shortly thereafter, I became an associate editor of the *Architectural Forum,* probably the best magazine of its kind in those years; and at the age of forty, I became its editor. Several years later, for reasons of no importance to this story, my entire staff and I left the *Architectural Forum* and started a new publication—*Architecture Plus*—which lasted for a mere two years but broke ground in a number of significant ways.

By lucky circumstance, therefore, I came to know most of the players in architecture and the other visual arts over a period of nearly forty years, and many of them became personal friends. I knew Wright, Mies van der Rohe, Gropius, Breuer, Le Corbusier, Tange, Aalto, Scharoun, Eero Saarinen, Eames, Rogers, Neutra, Lescaze, Buckminster Fuller, Yorke, Wells Coates, Chermayeff, and all the rest—some of them very well indeed, others merely as major figures in the Modern Movement whose work I published and whose ideas we debated. Since they were, by and large, one or two generations older than I—three generations older, I suppose, in the case of Wright—most of them did not consider me even remotely an equal; but I was close to many of them nonetheless.

And because much of the innovative development in the other visual arts—painting, sculpture, graphics, photography, and so on—took place in New York and its environs in the years after

Alexey Brodovitch, ca. 1962, in the Art Department at Harper's Bazaar. *Printer's proof of a jacket he had designed for a book of mine is pinned up on his notice board. (Courtesy, Andy Grundberg)*

World War II, I was drawn into that milieu as well. Jackson Pollock and his wife, Lee Krasner, became close friends; and through them I met most of the artists who were their contemporaries and became involved with them and their problems and ideas long before the art establishments discovered them. Finally, because my mother was a fashion illustrator, I met many people in the New York fashion world, and became a close friend of the now legendary Alexey Brodovitch, long the art director of *Harper's Bazaar,* and the teacher and mentor of almost all the American fashion photographers who made their appearance in the late 1940s and early 1950s. Brodovitch and I collaborated on a book (which he designed), and he designed the jacket of another book for me. Of all the products of my collaborations with graphic designers, these two efforts continue to stand out, many years after the fact.

I list these credentials only to lay the foundation for what follows. This book will not be about me, but about the men and women who shaped my time in the areas that interest me most. It will deal with their works and their ideas, and with the ideals that motivated them. It will also, as nearly as possible, tell the truth.

I will come back to "the truth" at various points in my story—not because telling the truth interests me especially (Frank Lloyd Wright, who lied like a trooper, would have been a bore if he had stuck to the facts), but because those outside my profession of architecture should, perhaps, be given the facts, since they (the outsiders) not only consume architecture, as it were, but also pay for it. Architecture critics in the U.S., at least, have been singularly reluctant to tell the truth in the years I plan to cover; most of the critics, in fact, have served as flacks for cliques of friends in the profession—and I have been guilty of some of the same flackery myself. So "telling the truth" is one theme of this book.

It is not the only one, and not the principal one. Initially, the title of this book was to have been *When Utopia Was Young*, and that title was to have implied a decline in modern architecture and modern art over the past fifty years or so. Or a decline in the idealism that motivated so many of us when we started out. For various reasons I decided to change that original title—but the original message, alas, has remained unchanged.

I have written about the failures of the Modern Movement elsewhere—at least, the failures as I saw them. The loss of idealism that concerns me in this book is perhaps more fundamental. It seems to me that the generation of young architects who, like myself, came out of World War II, was motivated by certain passions: we were determined to change the world, nothing less. We realized that mankind was faced by all sorts of predictable disasters—population explosion, hence wars, disease, poverty, and so on. We believed, quite sincerely, that modern architecture could do something about all these things—especially about housing the poor, and about creating viable, healthy, democratic (and, incidentally, beautiful) communities. We believed that we could slay the automobile, defeat fascism, and abolish disease. We were starry-eyed, and beautifully naïve.

Today, most of this idealism seems to be gone. Philip Johnson, a brilliant, scholarly, and utterly delightful charlatan, once told me that Henry Hobson Richardson, the great nineteenth-century architect who reinvented the Romanesque style, when asked what he considered to be the chief problem of architecture, liked to say: "To get the job!" Johnson probably invented the story and, in any case, surely improved on it; but this, today, seems to be the preoccupation of all of those who were once so starry-eyed, so idealistic.

There is no longer much talk about saving mankind; instead, there is a great deal of talk about how to get the job—how to manipulate the media, how to clobber the competition, how to make a buck. My generation once considered ourselves to be ombudsmen (and, I suppose, ombudswomen) for the environment; today, most of the horror which is man-made America was and is being created by architects—sometimes by the very same people who once dedicated themselves to the creation of a more humane and more beautiful future.

If there is one event, one specific date, that marks the turning point, it was the design and construction of the Pan Am Building in 1963, in the center of Manhattan. A firm known for its schlock architecture had proposed a scheme for this tower (not a bad one, in retrospect), and the developer, a businessman with a Medici complex, decided that he needed to cosmeticize the proposed design. So he invited Walter Gropius and Pietro Belluschi to consult, and these two—both of them winners of Gold Medals proffered by the American Institute of Architects—became responsible for the tower as it was ultimately built: a massive monstrosity that blocks the flow of Park Avenue and defaces the heart of Manhattan.

Why did they do it? Why did they accept the commission? The argument advanced in such cases has always been: "If we don't do it, just think who will!" It is a convenient argument, and admittedly a compelling one. I recall a conversation with Paul Rudolph at the time. Rudolph had been a student of Gropius at Harvard, and was appalled that this man—this personification of integrity and of idealism—could lend his name to such an abomination. I asked Rudolph if he thought he could have turned down so large, so significant a commission if it had been offered to him. He was silent for a moment, and then he said: "No, I couldn't have accepted it. You see, I have to face all those students."

Rudolph was then chairman of the Department of Architecture at Yale, and he knew that he could not let his students down—at least, not so blatantly. Gropius, it should be remembered, had been head of the Department of Architecture at Harvard, and Belluschi was dean of the School of Architecture at MIT. The example they set with the Pan Am Building, more than any other one event, became the turning point in the motivation of architects in the U.S. and, to a lesser extent, elsewhere.

There was another shift, less visible but equally significant. When I studied architecture at the University of Pennsylvania and at Pratt Institute, we were told, in courses on "Professional Practice," that the architect's position, ethical and legal, vis-à-vis the client and the general contractor, in the event that disputes arose over the design or construction of a project, was that of an impartial arbiter, whose prime responsibility was to the quality of the environment, natural as well as man-made—that is, to architecture.

Today, an architect's sole responsibility, in the U.S. and elsewhere, is clearly to the client—to the person who pays the bills. And much of the quality of our cities, our suburbs, and our countryside has suffered dramatically as a result.

I am not sure this will soon change, given the priorities of a capitalist society. In 1960, the American Institute of Architects held its annual convention in Miami Beach, about as bizarre a man-made environment as has been created outside Las Vegas. The keynote speaker was Sir Nikolaus Pevsner, the distinguished British architectural historian; and Sir Nikolaus, with hardly a reference to the grotesque setting to which he had been transported, spoke about the decline in the quality of architecture's clients.

Today's clients, in a capitalist society, fall into three categories: those who want to make a fast buck; those who want to memorialize themselves; and those who want to do good, so they can go to heaven. The first category is almost beyond retrieval: although the architectural magazines frequently publish articles attempting to prove that "good architecture is good business," this is generally false. Good architecture always costs more than schlock architecture, and is never, therefore, very good business—unless you can charge the extra cost of a building to advertising. This may be a convincing argument in a few cases, such as the AT&T Building by Philip Johnson in midtown Manhattan, which probably brought in a great deal of free publicity for the Telephone Company. Most of the time, the argument doesn't stand up.

The second category of today's clients—those who wish to memorialize themselves—consists of politicians, university presidents, and donors of art collections, etc.; and these clients can sometimes be persuaded to commission good architecture. But the motivation is not especially noble, and, in any event, is fairly far removed from the kinds of ideals that motivated generations of modern architects prior to, roughly, 1950.

The third category of clients—those who want to do good so they can go to heaven—overlaps with the second. But, since belief in the hereafter seems to be waning, these potential clients are few and far between, and getting rarer.

In any case, architects who pander to these categories of clients either do so tongue in cheek, or to make a fast buck, or both. They are rarely concerned with the quality of our environment or the future of mankind. By 1970 or thereabouts, any connection that may have once existed between modern architecture and a commitment to humanity seemed to have evaporated: a large California firm of architects and engineers, well known for its rather handsome modern industrial structures, had taken on commissions to build for the U.S. war effort in Vietnam, and was believed to have designed and constructed some of the notorious "tiger cages" to hold prisoners of the South Vietnamese secret police. Only twenty-five years earlier, some of us—and presumably some of those who would later design those "tiger cages"—had argued whether or not it was proper for a dedicated modern architect to do work for big corporations that engaged in unfair labor practices, or manufactured products that might be harmful to living things. But by 1970, the story of the California firm and its "tiger cages" was ignored by all the professional magazines, including my own. (Our attorneys thought we'd be in trouble if we published the story, since none of the employees of the firm—architects of my own generation—was willing to supply details in support of the charge!)

Perhaps the connection between modern architecture and a certain commitment to humanity was never very strong, and perhaps those of us who believed it existed were simply naïve. Philip Johnson liked to say that the only reason Mies van der Rohe left Nazi Germany was that Hitler didn't like flat roofs (a typically devastating Johnsonian *mauvais mot*); and it is quite true that modernists in Italy happily designed buildings for Mussolini, and modernists in the Soviet Union would have been delighted to work for Stalin, had he not preferred wedding-cake classicism.

But we (the young ones, fresh out of World War II uniforms, or fresh out of school, or both) thought there was at least an undercurrent of political and social idealism to all the things that we believed in as architects, and planned to do when we started to build what we had designed. And some of us became political radicals, believing that the new society that we hoped to construct would have to be socialist.

There was one last flash of this radicalism in 1968, when the student rebellions on U.S. campuses took place, almost invariably sparked by strikes, lockouts, and other demonstrations at the local school of architecture. Those who led those uprisings were often misguided and seemed, at times, faintly demented; but their wild enthusiasm made our hearts beat faster: they reminded us of an earlier time, long before Gropius and Belluschi had sold out with the Pan Am Building, a time when it was radical and, indeed, revolutionary to commit yourself to architecture, and when you had no doubts at all about your mission in life. They reminded us—if only for a fleeting moment—of our youth. For, not long thereafter, Nixon put an end to compulsory military service, and the peace movement on U.S. university campuses fell apart overnight. I remember being at Yale shortly after Nixon abolished the draft, in 1973, and talking to Vince Scully, the architectural historian who had been a leader in the movement. "It's all over now," he said sadly. "When Nixon ended the draft, the peace movement just collapsed."

As this is written, almost twenty years later, my students seem very far removed from the rebels who took over Avery Hall at Columbia in 1968. My students are career-oriented, and they seek to acquire marketable skills. They look just like the young men and women who took over Avery, except for being somewhat more clean-shaven and having somewhat shorter hair. They are very nice, and very much worried about getting a job once they graduate. They are not at all interested in politics, radical or otherwise, and they wonder what all the shouting was about thirty or forty or fifty years ago.

Well, dear friends and students, there was a time, not so very long ago, when Utopia was young. . . .

PETER BLAKE
Washington, D.C.
Spring, 1993

No Place Like Utopia:
Modern Architecture and the Company We Kept

CHAPTER ONE

■ When I was twelve years old, my family stopped being rich. Gone overnight were the chauffeur, his wife, the cook, the maid, the English governess, and the gardener. One of the two cars followed shortly thereafter, as did the villa in which we lived.

Let me try to explain: My father's family had lived, for many generations, in the small and beautiful Hanseatic town of Stralsund, on the Baltic. My father was born there, and went to a nearby university to study law, after which he practiced his profession on the nearby island of Rügen, defending chicken thieves and poachers.

At the outbreak of World War I he closed his law office and, like the good Prussian he was, joined the Kaiser's army, serving as an infantry sergeant. Late in 1914, during the battle of Tannenberg in East Prussia, his unit came under attack from Cossack cavalry, and his men, deciding that discretion was the better part of valor, took off into the nearest woods. He, trying to set an example of some sort, remained to fight with his saber and was virtually massacred: he suffered five bayonet wounds, and a fierce gash from a sword across his head which came within a millimeter or two of splitting his skull. He was left on the battlefield for dead.

Twenty-four hours later the area was recaptured by German troops, and my father was found, miraculously still alive. It took a year of intensive hospitalization to bring him back to operating condition, after which he volunteered for combat service again, having obviously lost his marbles. His rather mindless heroism was rewarded by Field Marshal von Mackensen, his commanding officer, with the Iron Cross, and he was made a lieutenant. After the war, he married my mother, moved to Berlin, went into corporate law, became head of a large public utility company, and pursued his work and his conservative politics until 1933.

That year, the freely elected Nazi government further rewarded him for his mindless heroism at the battle of Tannenberg: because he was of Jewish origin, he was kicked out of his job and put (briefly) in jail, his family was thrown out of its home, all the family's property was stolen, he was put on trial on trumped-up charges (which were finally quashed—not even a Nazi court could make them stick), and he and his family (my mother, sister, and I) were kicked out of our country. We were permitted to leave with the clothes on our backs and with ten marks each in our pockets. Of our relatives who remained behind in that beautiful Hanseatic town, most were subsequently murdered by the Nazi government.

So much for that.

Six years later, I was living in the Bloomsbury section of London, subletting part of a cold-water flat from a South African painter and his actress friend. (Actually, I slept on a mattress placed inside an inoperative bathtub.) I was working as an office boy for an architect, studying at night at the Regent Street Polytechnic, and subsisting primarily on fish-and-chips, which, in those days, were sold wrapped in pieces of newspaper—Lord Beaverbrook's *Evening Standard,* as I recall. I had virtually no money and a perfectly wonderful time. Still, I would not necessarily recommend poverty as a shortcut to happiness; it forces you to waste an awful lot of time earning money to pay the rent.

I mention all this only because I suspect that, if my family had continued to be rich, I might not have become interested in certain aspects of architecture. Not many rich children have occasion to notice that other children are poor; and even fewer feel that they ought to pay some attention to the way such children, and their parents, live.

In the years immediately preceding World War II, the traditional profession of architecture in Europe and in America was still largely an elitist pursuit: architects designed and built houses for the rich, and grand palaces for corporations and for governments. In some instances, they designed and built monuments to prop up fascist and communist dictatorships—and their projects and buildings were remarkably similar to those being promoted currently by postmodern "name architects."

By contrast, most of the *modern* architects between the two World Wars seemed concerned with the creation of a democratic, egalitarian social order: they were concerned with problems of housing for everyone, with problems of planning humane and healthy communities for all, with sheltering a human family that was about to burst at its seams. *Of course* they were also concerned with artistic issues, and some modern architects were highly sophisticated in these matters. But art came second to the basic concerns that dealt with problems of the real world: economic and social justice, overpopulation, poverty, disease. While traditionalists—like their postmodern offspring half a century later—concerned themselves with symbolism and imagery, often in the service of dictatorships, banks, and other ruling establishments, radical modern architects hoped to improve the human condition in an egalitarian society.

Admittedly, many modern architects, in order to be able to build at all, accepted commissions to design villas for the rich. But even when they did, they tended to use those commissions to seek solutions of broader applicability, solutions that could be translated into buildings for everyone. Le Corbusier, especially, had a single-minded sense of dedication to such broader objectives: when, for example, he designed the Villa Savoye in 1929, for a wealthy family on an estate in Poissy-sur-Seine, near Paris, he did indeed produce a very elegant residence, complete with a gatehouse and other appurtenances; but, much more important, he built a large-scale diagram of a new kind of city—a city of structures raised off the ground to permit free pedestrian circulation at street level; a city topped with roof gardens that would create a communal, urban space open to the sky. In short, the Villa Savoye was a diagram for the kind of vertical city he had described in innumerable projects beginning with his Ville Radieuse of 1922, and would continue to refine into his final work as a practicing architect. Similarly, when he designed the luxurious Villa for Gertrude Stein's brother Michael at Garches, a couple of years earlier, he explored these same urbanistic principles, plus certain notions of creating multistory apartment units—*villas superimposées*—first explored in 1922, and realized thirty years later in his Unité d'Habitation at Marseilles.

Not much of this has been understood by recent critics and practitioners who have attempted to interpret and to copy what they seem to regard as a sort of cubist "style." Some have even discovered certain parallels between the Villa Savoye and some of Andrea Palladio's villas around Vicenza—a comparison which, I am certain, would have come as a considerable surprise to Le Corbusier. And some postmodern decorators, especially in the U.S., have adopted Le Corbusier's details, forms, and even his occasional mistakes, to create a "Style Le Corbusier" to satisfy the weekly or monthly need, on the part of home fashion editors and magazines, for something new and sexy and hence marketable. But the creation of a "style" for the amusement of home fashion magazines was not exactly what Corbu had in mind.

Nor was it in the minds of young people, like myself, in the late 1930s, when I was living in that bathtub in Bloomsbury. Modern architecture in those years was not fashionable at all. Most people, certainly in England, thought that modern architects were rather scruffy foreigners, and probably communists. Evelyn Waugh's fictitious Professor Otto Silenus in *Decline and Fall* was obviously patterned after Walter Gropius, who was at about that time living in London and doing some very un-British houses in partnership with Maxwell Fry. (Alec Waugh says that Evelyn never met Gropius, to the best of his knowledge; but the caricature is devastating and—like all of Waugh's characterizations—vastly entertaining.) Although Silenus was not especially scruffy, he was unmistakably foreign and ideologically baffling; and that was what most English people, in the 1930s, thought of modern architects.

Prior to going to London to work in and study architecture, I had spent several years at a British "public school" in the beautiful medieval city of York. The school was not exactly typical of those "public schools" that were designed to educate the children of the upper classes. It was a Quaker school; and while its students and teachers were not in the least bit stuffy, they took their Quakerism very seriously. For example, there were no Boy Scouts at *this* school (because Quakers were against uniforms); all of us were expected to be "doing good" in one way or another, but nobody ever talked about it; we were assumed to be pacifists, and rather expected to become conscientious objectors in the likely event that war would shortly break out in Europe; we were assumed to be leftish in our political views—Labour, at the very least—and to be anti-establishmentarian in general.

None of this was ever spelled out in so many words; but we all grew up in an atmosphere of socialist euphoria. Instead of spending our summer holidays on some rich man's exotic beach or yacht—as boys from Harrow or Eton were likely to do—we spent them working in depressed mining villages in South Yorkshire, living with the families of miners disabled or killed in mining accidents, and working, in daytime, on the rocky, barren "allotments" that Conservative governments had given disabled and unemployed miners to grow vegetables on. (These allotments were virtually untendable, especially if you were severely incapacitated, as many of those unemployed miners were; and so we spent weeks digging up the hard soil, hacking away at enormous clumps of rocks and roots, and turning the allotments into arable vegetable gardens.)

The active miners, at the end of these summers, would take us down into one of their shafts—a special treat that was accorded hardly anyone outside the mining profession itself, and not even to the miners' families. These trips down into a mine were terrifying beyond anything I ever experienced even during combat in World War II. We would descend a thousand feet or more in a vertical shaft, in a lift that seemed to be engaged in some sort of "free fall," hurtling down at breakneck speed into the bowels of the earth; then, when we had reached a level somewhere near China, the lift—a primitive wooden crate—would pull up sharply, and let us off at the level of a tunnel that went off horizontally into total blackness.

We staggered down this tunnel, slightly crouched, each of us carrying a miner's lamp. Soon, the spindly wooden props holding up the rocks and coal above would give way to . . . nothing. And then the tunnel would become a low-ceilinged tube, hardly high and wide enough to contain a single person crawling on his stomach toward the "face" of the mineshaft, where the coal was hacked out of the rock. We crawled through this tube on our bellies, pushing the lamps ahead of us to see what there was to see—nothing but unrelieved blackness. I was more frightened than I have ever been before or since. Aside from the sounds of our own heavy breathing, and the scraping sounds of our bodies crawling through this rocky tube, there was the horrifying sound of creaking and cracking, of

Students from Bootham School, in York, England, getting ready to descend into a coal mine near Pontefract, ca. 1937. I (second from left) was the smallest boy in the group, and the most frightened.

the rocks and the coal and the earth above us shifting and rumbling and crunching.

Our hosts, the workers in these small mining villages, experienced this horror day after day, for thirty or forty years, until they were forced to retire. The lives of some of them were cut short, for those dark satanic mills of Yorkshire and Wales were giant death traps that would burn, explode, and cave in regularly, killing and maiming men who were forced to eke out a living for their families in these dreadful hellholes south of Doncaster and Maltby.

We lived with the miners' widows and orphans, in nineteenth-century houses that were very properly and touchingly furnished (especially the parlor, which was used only on very special occasions). There were no indoor toilets—the outhouses were way in back, at the far end of the dried-up gardens. We—presumptively rich boys from a private school up in York—had (inexplicably) decided to spend our holidays in these impoverished villages; and our hosts at first thought we were either crazy or hideously condescending, or both. But, gradually, as they watched us hard at work, day after day, the miners and their families began to accept us. Our days were spent hacking away at those rocky allotments; our evenings, if we were not too tired, at the local miner's club or at some lively party thrown by one of the miners' families. We grew extremely fond of these people, and when we left at the end of the summer there were scenes that pass for emotion in England. (Even working-class people, in England, think that emotions are what foreigners show, and the Irish.)

Ever since those summers in the Yorkshire mining villages, such terms as "working class" and "exploitation" and "hunger" and "unemployment," and so on, have held a special meaning for those of us who lived with those pale and undernourished and incredibly tough people. We didn't find out about poverty and injustice from pamphlets and books; we lived with it for many weeks, and the memory of those weeks has never faded.

CHAPTER TWO

■ In 1938, having graduated from the school in York, I went to London to find a job in an architect's office. That summer I had spent a few weeks in Normandy, near Caudebec and Les Andélys, doing some perfectly awful paintings of castles and streets and landscapes, in the manner (I thought) of Utrillo. The paintings were done with palette knives, and the thick paint never quite dried on the canvas.

However, the paintings were among the few "samples" of my work that I could present to a potential employer; and so I rolled up the canvases and proceeded to my first job interview, which happened to be with Serge Chermayeff—one of the very best of the new, modern architects in England.

There were about a dozen of these "modernists," most of them in London—but three of them stood out: Maxwell Fry, F. R. S. (Kay) Yorke, and Chermayeff himself. After Hitler came to power in Germany and modern architecture was banished, several practitioners of the latter emigrated to Britain. Among them were Walter Gropius, the founder of the new, post–World War I Bauhaus, who came to London and associated with Max Fry; Marcel Breuer, who had been head of the Bauhaus Furniture Workshop (and a leading architectural practitioner at that school and elsewhere), who joined forces with Kay Yorke; and Erich Mendelsohn, perhaps the principal non-Bauhaus "modernist" in Weimar Germany, who had gone into partnership with Chermayeff.

Gropius, who had known my father in Berlin, had been kind enough to write to Chermayeff from Harvard (where both Gropius and Breuer had gone to settle and teach earlier that year) and suggest that I might be worth taking on as an apprentice; and so Chermayeff agreed to see me.

His office was located in a stately townhouse on Grosvenor Place, overlooking Buckingham Palace Gardens; and Chermayeff—by that time separated from Mendelsohn, who had gone to work in what was still Palestine—occupied the top floor of this elegant building, with four or five draftsmen/designers in white smocks sitting at long, expansive drafting tables.

Although Serge, as I discovered later, was quite radical in his politics and in his artistic preferences, his appearance was one of upper-class elegance: he had won the World's Tango Competition at the Palladium in 1927, and had kept the figure of a tall and (one assumed) irresistible gigolo. His English—enunciated with the perfection and precision of which only aristocratic Russians were capable—was Harrovian. (He had come to Britain from tsarist Russia at the age of thirteen, and gone to Harrow as a youngster.) His suits were clearly made in Savile Row, and his manner was imperial (and imperious). He seemed like an improbable fraud on first, and possibly second, sight; he turned out to be one of the most brilliant teachers I, or anyone else, could possibly have encountered at the beginning of an architectural career.

Serge Chermayeff (left) and Philip Johnson arguing heatedly at the Museum of Modern Art, ca. 1950. (Norman McGrath)

Serge unrolled my Normandy canvases and instantly smeared great streaks of paint all over his Savile Row sleeve. I was mortified, but he merely snorted—whether at the quality of my work or the stains on his sleeve I shall never know. In the end—largely, I suspect, because Gropius had recommended me—he agreed to let me stay on. There was no salary, needless to say; and my duties, initially, would consist of doing errands, making coffee for the office, and fetching sandwiches at lunchtime.

It was the lowliest of all lowly jobs, but I was in heaven: here, in this rather small office, all the avant-garde action in architecture and the visual arts in Britain seemed to converge. Serge and his assistants—especially Whitfield Lewis, a Welshman, who later became chief architect for the London County Council, and Eastland Fortey, a gifted interior designer—were generous with their time and their invitations; and so I met most of the leading modern architects in Britain, attended their meetings and exhibits, listened to their discussions, and met many of their friends.

In these final months before the outbreak of World War II, the London art scene was a very lively place: all the artists and architects and designers who made up the so-called "Modern Movement" in England knew one another and formed a tightly knit group. People like Henry Moore, Ben Nicholson, Barbara Hepworth, Max Fry and Jane Drew, Wells Coates, Berthold Lubetkin, Kay Yorke, Ashley Havinden, McKnight Kauffer, Misha Black, Nikolaus Pevsner, and a handful of others—including, very prominently, Serge Chermayeff himself—knew each other well, worked together, and considered us kids to be, if not on a par, certainly part and parcel of the avant-garde. The so-called "MARS Group"—a British branch of CIAM (Congrès Internationaux d'Architecture Moderne) that had been formed by Le Corbusier, Siegfried Giedion, and others on the Continent—was actively engaged in promoting the Modern Movement. The beautiful and sophisticated monthly magazine *Architectural Review* published some of the finest work done by members of the Modern Movement in Britain and on the Continent; and a quarterly, called *Focus,* whose emphasis was rather more on urban planning than on architectural design, published three or four issues that formulated a kind of ideological program for the leading members of the MARS Group. "The birth of a new socialized society may be complicated, painful, and dangerous," declared an editorial in the summer 1939 issue of *Focus,* "but it is as inevitable in the natural course of events as the birth of a child. . . . Our capitalist society . . . has now reached a stage at which it is no longer appropriate or useful. . . . This is something which most of us are ready to admit, and something of which we are all continually conscious as architects or town planners."

In the spring of 1939, Frank Lloyd Wright had come to London as a guest of the Royal Institute of British Architects, and he gave four talks about his work in the auditorium of the RIBA Building, on Portland Place. The auditorium was jammed as Wright made his way to the stage on those evenings, looking very much like a Victorian character actor, or, more ominously, like Richard Wagner, with his flowing white locks and billowing cape. He spoke about a new world of space and freedom expressed in a language of organic forms, and he put on a terrific show.

But he clearly had not the remotest sense of the mood of Western Europe in 1939, or the ideas and ideals that moved those of us

Frank Lloyd Wright, at Taliesin West, in Scottsdale, Arizona, ca. 1950. (P. E. Guerrero)

who were likely, very soon, to become cannon fodder in the predictable fascist war. He spoke to us with that arrogance of ignorance that one had come to expect from some Americans: it was quite clear to us that Wright thought he was visiting some pre–twentieth century Britain; that he was quite unaware of the meaning, to us, of such events as the surrender at Munich, the Anschluss, the news of the Nazi concentration camps, or of the increasing realization, among some of my friends, that the seeming promise of the Soviet Union had turned out to be a total fallacy. And, finally, it was quite clear that he was hardly aware of the fact that the Spanish Republic—that place that had occupied so many of our thoughts and dreams—had finally fallen to the fascists. All this, and more, seemed to be a matter of total unconcern to the euphorious visitor from the New World. In his summer resort in Spring Green, Wisconsin, and his winter resort in Scottsdale, Arizona, there were no wars, no revolutions, no assassinations; there was no poverty, no pollution, no disease, no unemployment; and when Mr. Wright graced the British Isles with his presence, six weeks after our spiritual brethren in the trenches of Madrid had surrendered to Franco's troops, Frank Lloyd Wright—as one of his critics put it a few days later—offered us images of paradise. "Like Marie Antoinette," this critic said, "he offered us cake."

The critic was Naum Gabo, the Russian Constructivist sculptor, who had left the Soviet Union in the early 1920s and had lived, since then, in Weimar Germany, Paris, and London. (He would later move to the U.S., where he died in the 1970s.) After Wright's performance at the RIBA, the Architectural Association, or AA, held an informal discussion of what the visitor from across the ocean had said, and what, if anything, it meant to young artists and architects in Britain. (The AA in those years was the antiestablishmentarian opposition to the very established RIBA; it ran an excellent school, which graduated some of the finest British architects to emerge after World War II; and it was viewed as decidedly "modern" in its orientation—as opposed to the stuffy upper-class orientation of the RIBA.)

Gabo began by saying that he remembered his days as a student at the Polytechnic, in Munich, in 1911, when he and others first heard about Wright and his work. "The excitement and delight that was suddenly amongst us is unforgettable. What especially impressed us was his open and revolutionary spirit, his clear mind towards the future and clear criticism of architecture." Gabo had gone to all of Wright's four lectures. He continued: "I did not expect it of Wright that he would change so fundamentally. . . . Architecture is something more than building a villa, and Wright knows it. To build a villa for anybody who can afford it, who has money and leisure and the chance to go into the country, is now quite irrelevant. . . . even if we can afford to live like that, even then we will not be happy so long as men, women, and children are living in the most scandalous conditions, suffocating in towns. So long as these millions of people are living in that state, nobody can be happy. . . . Wright's ideas are inorganic; they are conservative, escapist. It is not a solution to leave the town and go to the country. He forgets that just over the river is Peckham Rye." To read this, some fifty years later, is refreshing indeed: it is an extraordinarily pointed indictment of the yuppie architecture that flourished in America during the insouciant reign of Ronald Reagan.

The Modern Movement, during the last days of the twenty-year-long armistice between the two World Wars, was a political movement, not a "style" as Philip Johnson, Henry-Russell Hitchcock, and Alfred Barr had it when they presented it at New York's Museum of Modern Art in 1932. It was politically left, anticapitalist, and dogmatically so. Whether its proposed solutions to urban blight made sense and were, in fact, responsive to the needs of the people who needed help is today more than a little in doubt—and will be discussed in later chapters. But the concern was overwhelmingly there, and those of us who decided, in those tense years before World War II, to become architects knew what this meant: it was a commitment to help change the world, nothing less. The idea that we would become architects in order to create a new style would have struck us as obscene. It still strikes me that way today.

Although Gabo and others expounded a radical, anticapitalist line, not all the new architects and artists lived in a proletarian mode. Serge, his wife, Barbara, and his two young sons, Ivan and Peter, together with assorted servants, lived in a beautiful country house in Sussex, which Serge had designed. It was a house I got to know very well, for the Chermayeffs were extremely generous in letting me stay on weekends, and on at least one occasion invited my mother to come and stay on one of her visits from the Continent.

The house was one of the most accomplished works of modern domestic architecture I had ever seen. It was neatly framed in painted timber posts and beams (quite unusual for a house in England), with the repetitive, structural bays filled with glass or wood siding, and neatly expressed. Although the main body of the house was two stories in height, various one-story wings extended out into the landscape to form entrance courts and terraces. A reclining figure by Henry Moore (now in the collection of the Museum of Modern Art, in New York) was placed at the end of one of the terraces. The landscaping (done by Christopher Tunnard, who later went on to teach at Yale) was almost imperceptibly merged with the natural site. Everything about the house was delicate, understated, and accomplished with flawless taste.

Several people had mentioned to me that Serge had learned a great deal from his former associate Erich Mendelsohn, and this may be true. But in comparing Serge's relatively few completed buildings with the large number of structures built by Mendelsohn in Germany, England, the U.S., and in Israel, it is clear to me that Chermayeff's work was invariably more elegant and more delicate than Mendelsohn's, and that the latter, in his later work, had learned a great deal from the former.

Serge was a marvelous teacher, not only through his own work and the sure way in which he combined all the elements of architecture—structure, detail, function, spatial organization, color, and flawless taste—but also in the way he opened my eyes to all the other arts and disciplines. He had been a first-rate industrial and furniture designer in the early 1930s, and I learned to understand the intimate relationship between architecture and those design disciplines long before that was a routine experience for young architects. He was a talented artist—much influenced by the work of his friend John Piper—and I learned a great deal from his paintings. (He was so accomplished that for a while he liked to "copy" well-known canvases by Picasso, Léger, and others—"improving" a detail here and there if he thought the originals lacked some refinement. In fact, he and Barbara had bought a small Picasso in the 1930s, which was stored in a warehouse during the years of the blitz. In one of the German firebombings, the Picasso was badly damaged, and Picasso's signature was burned off, together with much of the rest of the painting. After the war, Serge repainted the damaged portions of the painting and showed the massively "restored" work to Picasso himself. Picasso thought it was excellent—an improvement on the original, in fact—and decided to sign the work with his own name! Undoubtedly, some future restorer or forgery expert will be driven mad trying to unravel this minor mystery.)

Unhappily for Serge and all those close to him, he had a monstrous temper and delighted in reducing everyone—his wife, his friends, his employees, his students—to quivering jelly by verbally demolishing them, preferably in public. All of us who admired him and loved his family found his vituperative outbursts distressing beyond belief; and to visit the Chermayeffs became an increasingly hazardous enterprise.

One of the results of his unfortunate temper tantrums was that he almost invariably fought with potential or actual clients, and so very few Chermayeff buildings were ever built. Yet the few that were continue to be among the finest works of the 1930s; they combined all the discipline of Mies van der Rohe's work with the functional practicality that much of Mies's work tended to lack. Compared to the work of most of his contemporaries in England, Serge's buildings continue to look self-assured and thoroughly professional. One of the projects in his office while I was running errands around the place was a complex of research laboratories for the Imperial Chemical Industries (ICI) in Manchester. These laboratories were quite complex in their requirements—not only was the usual modular flexibility present throughout, but there was also an intricate system of mechanical services that separated noxious fumes from routine air circulation, and so on. And the resulting buildings were so neatly organized, and so well detailed, that they were subsequently copied (without credit) by lesser architects elsewhere.

Admittedly, the ICI laboratories did not dramatize the presence of "service systems" as Louis Kahn's spectacular Richards Labs at the University of Pennsylvania, or his equally beautiful Salk Labs in La Jolla, California, did some twenty years later; but they did a better job, efficiently, elegantly, and with technical assurance. (Most architecture critics paid little attention, for Serge's buildings, oddly enough, were extremely understated, whereas Lou Kahn's Richards Labs were wonderfully expressive of their functions, and even of some functions that were, in fact, nonexistent. The critics couldn't help but notice the drama of Richards and Salk, whereas they hardly noticed, or understood, Serge's more efficient buildings for ICI.)

Serge had started his career as a designer and painter, and his facility as an artist never left him—not even in his later years, when he was severely crippled by arthritis and living in painful retirement in Wellfleet, Massachusetts, growling, grumping, cursing, but still painting. His paintings were abstract, derived from Braque's early cubist work, from the canvases of Serge's friend John Piper, and from the work of others; they were sometimes derided as being "too graphic," but they were dazzling in boldness and color. He was given a one-man show at the Tate in his later years, and his older son, Ivan—who has become one of the finest graphic designers in the U.S.—clearly absorbed much of *his* facility from his father.

Ivan and his younger brother, Peter (who later became an important architect in his own right), were a few years younger than I, but we became friends during those weekends at Halland, in Sussex, and continued our friendship after the Chermayeffs left Britain in 1940 and settled in the U.S. Sometime in the 1960s, Serge and I were having lunch in New York and I asked him to explain how two sons of Serge Chermayeff, of all people, could have turned out so splendidly. He drew himself up to his full six feet something and said, in his most "subacid" tone: "I will tell you my secret—it is studied neglect!" He told me that shortly after the Chermayeff family arrived in the U.S. in early 1940, he and Barbara had decided to buy a station wagon and to drive across the continent to get a feel for the place. The family was loaded into the car, and their first stop was a motel near Paoli, Pennsylvania, just outside Philadelphia. At this point, Serge decided that to make such a trip with two teenage boys in tow might be a little tiresome, and so he simply parked Ivan and Peter with the motel owners—a couple totally unknown to the Chermayeffs until that morning—and arranged to have the boys picked up after a few months, when the parents had completed their reconnaissance. It all worked out splendidly: "studied neglect" had left no visible psychological scars; in fact, the boys rejoined their parents rather reluctantly when the time came.

I mention all this only to point out that Serge was not the proverbial caring, warmhearted parent or (in my case) parent substitute—though Barbara was all of that and much, much more. As already noted, he was often unspeakable in his brutality toward friends and family alike; but he was so devastatingly articulate, so elegant, so capable of enormous charm (if and when called for), so brilliant, so amusing (when not his more frequent, foul-tempered self) that I for one, and a few others, found it not too difficult to forgive him his monstrous temper tantrums. He simply knew more than anyone else around about the nature and essence of modern art and design, and he had a critical eye so sharp, so sure, so deadly in its accuracy, that I never stopped marveling at his visual intelligence.

Serge considered himself politically radical, but his radicalism was clearly more rhetorical than real. He lived very well, despised roughly ninety-nine percent of the human race, and treated them with disdain. Since this ninety-nine percent included a fair number of the poor, poorly educated, and poorly housed and nourished, he could hardly claim to be a champion of the common man—though I am sure he thought he was.

There was in Britain in those years a very vocal intellectual elite which favored something like social and economic democracy, but really couldn't bear the sight, sound, or smell of the lower classes. Serge unquestionably belonged to that elite. Yet, if anyone had asked him about his political convictions in those years, I am sure he would have defined himself as a Marxist revolutionary.

Which would have been ridiculous on the face of it. Still, in his work as an architect he certainly concerned himself with problems and solutions that were and are part of the socialist catechism: decent housing for all; healthy communities, replete with all the amenities a welfare state could and should provide; and a technology (and resulting aesthetic) that facilitated mass production of shelter that was affordable by all. To Serge, and to all of us who subscribed to those ideals, an architectural language of neoclassicism was synonymous with fascism (though, curiously enough, not with Stalinism or New Dealism, both of which practiced it just as consistently), and, hence, to be rejected out of hand.

In any event, I didn't get whatever radicalism I may have acquired in those days from Serge or from any other *Salon Kommunisten* to be found in the local avant-garde. What I did get from Serge was a lesson or two on how to use my eyes. He had a sure eye for detail, for finish, for graceful elegance in everything he designed and made. And a very broad range as well: Mies, from whom I would learn a great deal in later years, and who possessed an equally sure touch in everything he created, had a very narrow range in his work: aside from architecture and furniture and his own delicate drawings, and possibly his own, very elegant clothes, he had no recognizable "style." His collection of paintings (most of them by his old friend Paul Klee) was flawless but curiously limited: as in all his work, he seemed to have explored every possible alternative, selected the one he thought best, refined it to perfection, and lived with it for the rest of his life.

With Serge, there seemed to be a constant search for alternative ideas and for new images. While Mies was absolutely certain in his direction as an architect—so certain, in fact, that he really changed very little in the last twenty-five years or so of his life—Serge was capable of going off in all kinds of directions, and simultaneously: while he was, in fact, an extremely elegant designer and an accomplished painter, he loved to denigrate aesthetic decisions and judgments with snorts of contempt, claiming (in his articulate essays and lectures) that aesthetic concerns were the playthings of the rich, and that he for one was concerned with the needs of common men, women, and children. Ivan, his older son, once said to me that "Serge can argue on both sides of any given issue, with equal passion and simultaneously."

In a way, it was this special multifaceted quality of creative madness that made him such a good teacher. I learned from him to look at everything from all possible points of view and simultaneously.

In the summer of 1939, when it became clear that Hitler was about to start his war in Europe, work in architectural offices in London dried up; and Serge decided to join forces with Wells Coates, the Tokyo-born Canadian architect and engineer who had done some of the finest modern high-tech work in England in the thirties and was one of the founders of the MARS Group. Wells's studio and apartment were located in a charming little townhouse on Yeoman's Row, in Knightsbridge; and that is where we moved the office, lock, stock, and barrel, to cut everybody's overhead in half. Wells had gutted the little house and rebuilt it into a combination split-level apartment and design studio—too small, really, to house two architectural offices; but then, there was practically no work to be done anyway, and so everyone seemed to manage.

On the day war was declared, I happened to be in Dublin, working on a small competition with a young Irish architect who had left Serge's office a few weeks earlier. After finishing our drawings, I returned to London, registered as an "enemy alien" (since I was technically a German citizen), collected my gas mask from the local air raid protection office, and decided I had better try to join the British Army, Quakerism notwithstanding. (I believed, and still do, that the issues between Good and Evil were fairly clearly drawn in World War II—as they had not been in World War I—and that declaring oneself a conscientious objector, as most of my former schoolmates did, meant giving some support, however minor, to Hitler's side.) Alas, the British government thought that I had the wrong passport and wouldn't accept me for military service; and so I decided to join my family, by then assembled in New York. My father had written to Harvard, and the Graduate School of Design (with Gropius as chairman for architecture) offered me a full scholarship—if I could get to Cambridge, Massachusetts, without delay.

Unfortunately, all American transatlantic passenger ships were fully booked by U.S. citizens trying to get home before all hell broke loose in Europe; considering these circumstances, I was fortunate to get a berth on something called the *American Farmer*, departing Southampton for New York at the end of the year—by which time the Harvard scholarship had been awarded to the next applicant in line.

I left England and all my friends, and a great deal more: a place so civilized, so unbelievably decent, so delightfully incompetent, so clearly (it seemed) marked for disaster. A couple of weeks later the *American Farmer* docked at one of New York's Hudson River piers. It was late in the evening, and the skyline of Manhattan was brightly lit. (London, needless to say, had been blacked out for months.) The first sounds I remember were those of several police cars, sirens going full blast, careening about under the West Side Highway, their occupants (and their prey) firing shots at each other and into the night.

It was exactly what I had expected America to be like. In London, now four months into the war, I had never heard a shot fired in anger (or, for that matter, in joy). The only sounds in the night were those occasional whines of air raid sirens—and, of course, the sounds of my friends carousing in the darkened streets along King's Road in the weeks before all hell did, in fact, break loose and many of them went off to war.

CHAPTER THREE

■ For the next nine months or so, I lived in Manhattan, waiting to be admitted to the School of Architecture at the University of Pennsylvania, which had offered me a scholarship. Those nine months were more than a little bizarre: in daytime, I worked as a packer in a warehouse, filling crates with samples of various kinds of junk designed for sale in South America. (I remember earning $13.50 a week doing this—enough to be able to rent my own pad in Greenwich Village.) At night, I'd hang out with young artists and architects in various bars around 8th Street, talking politics, art politics, and architecture politics. Sometimes I'd rent a dinner jacket and sneak off to some improbable nightclub like El Morocco to hobnob with fancy friends of some fancy London friends. But the next morning, at the crack of dawn, I'd be back in the warehouse packing those crates and taking them down to the post office on a pushcart.

Every now and then, I'd get a free-lance job as a draftsman; and one of these jobs was an assignment to redraw the plans of several rather undistinguished airport buildings, for publication in a professional magazine called the *Architectural Forum*. The *Forum* (as it was universally known) had its rather glamorous editorial offices on the top floor of the then Time-Life Building, in Rockefeller Center. The magazine's art director was a charming man called Paul Grotz, who had been born in Stuttgart and had managed somehow to get out of Germany, with the help of his American wife, around the time Hitler came to power.

Paul's assistant was a very shy lady called Madeleine Thatcher, whose voice hardly ever rose above a whisper; the managing editor was George Nelson—rather laconic, witty, clever, and knowledgeable about architecture and design; and the editor in chief and publisher was a large, amiable bear of a man called Howard Myers, who had sold his publication to Henry Luce several years earlier and stayed with it, as part of Time Inc., turning the *Forum* into the most avant-garde magazine of its kind anywhere in the world—and into one of the leading champions of modern architecture in America.

I don't know what those four people and their various associates thought of the scruffy young free-lance draftsman who seemed to take a dim view of the architectural quality of the buildings he was hired to depict. Some years later, Howard told me that I would come into the editorial offices every morning, shake hands with everyone in sight, sit down and do my drawings, and then shake hands with everyone at the end of the day before departing for Greenwich Village. They were totally nonplussed by this display of Old World courtesy, especially coming from this rather seedy-looking bohemian. (They didn't know about El Morocco.) If anyone in those days had suggested that I might end up as editor of the *Forum* some twenty years thence, he or she would have been laughed out of court—and I myself would have been among the laughers: I was tremendously impressed by these suave, sophisticated people and considered myself enormously fortunate to have been called in to help out in their Art Department, in however menial a position.

Despite this, I found the people at the *Forum* more than a little baffling. Their commitment to modern architecture seemed to have nothing at all to do with any political ideology. In fact, I knew that Henry Luce's Time Inc. was basically conservative in orientation, and the *Forum*'s editors seemed to feel that modern architecture—or something someone had labeled the International Style—was simply an appropriate "look" for twentieth-century buildings and cities. Howard, in fact, seemed most impressed if and when he managed to win over some leading captain of industry or other capitalist bigwig to the modern cause; there seemed to be no special interest in the Modern Movement as part and parcel of some ideal socialist community.

Paul Grotz, as photographed ca. 1934 by his friend Walker Evans. (Courtesy, Dorothy Grotz)

On the other hand, some of the key people on the *Forum's* editorial staff were distinctly leftist in their political preferences—fellow travelers or actual members of the Communist Party; but for some reason which I did not understand, their political orientation did not seem to extend to architectural or urban theories. In fact, some of the most outspoken Stalinists or Stalinoids on the magazine's editorial staff were quite *anti*modern in their architectural convictions—or at least anti–International Style: they tended to oppose the likes of Gropius, Mies van der Rohe, Le Corbusier, and other International Stylists, and to prefer Frank Lloyd Wright (whose politics, if any, were a random mixture of pro-Stalinism and profascism, or whatever seemed most useful in the service of Wrightism); or they would prefer neoclassicism, which had become the official party line of the Soviet Union when Stalin wiped out the so-called Russian Constructivist movement and many of its idealistic protagonists of the first decade of the new Soviet state.

It was all very confusing and I decided that these people were naïve in their political and cultural commitments, and that they simply didn't understand what was going on in Europe and elsewhere, in politics, architecture, or, for that matter, in very much else. Even those of my European friends and relatives who had felt sympathetic toward the Soviet Union in their youth had been disillusioned by the Stalin purges of the late 1930s, and ultimately turned off by the Hitler-Stalin Pact of 1939. Yet here, among many intellectuals in New York, the Soviet Union still seemed to represent some sort of twentieth-century nirvana, and the dimwitted rules laid down by the Communist Party (U.S.A.) seemed to represent a dependable guide to all decisions, including issues of cultural or stylistic preference.

Howard Myers, I suspect, was innocent in all these matters, and unaware of what motivated some of his associates. He was probably a liberal Republican by conviction—if, indeed, he harbored any political convictions at all. And his dedication to the Modern Movement was probably more journalistic than anything else: while traditionalists were likely to produce the same old stuff—in buildings, sculpture, painting, graphics, and all the rest—"modernists" were likely to produce new and startling ideas and images at frequent intervals, and hence dependably produce the one sine qua non of journalism—that is, *news*. Because Howard had a surprisingly keen eye for interesting new images, he was almost un-

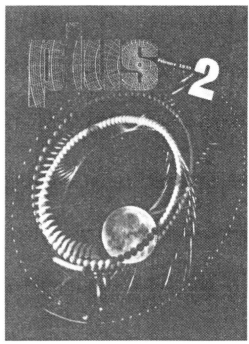

failing in his journalistic pursuits: he recognized Frank Lloyd Wright's genius at a time when Wright was largely ignored by the American media; and he persuaded the editors of *Life* (the biggest of the *Forum*'s sister publications) to devote unprecedented coverage to Wright's new Johnson Wax Headquarters in Racine, Wisconsin—and followed this with a special *Architectural Forum* issue, in January 1938, devoted entirely to Wright's work.

That special issue is today a collector's item, apparently worth several thousand dollars. It was designed by Wright himself, with the help of Paul Grotz, the *Forum*'s art director; and it, together with the publicity generated by the article in *Life,* in effect rescued Wright's career at a time when he was bankrupt, despondent, and generally at the end of his rope. Wright never forgot this; and the *Architectural Forum,* for better or worse, remained his chosen medium through which to speak to the rest of the world. Moreover, Wright took a special liking to Paul Grotz; so that, even after Howard's death in 1948, a special relationship continued between Taliesin and the *Forum,* primarily via Paul.

Unlike many other partisans of Wright, Howard Myers was

LEFT: *Cover of the December 1938 issue of* PLUS, *designed by the Swiss graphic artist Herbert Matter. The colors were red and black.*
RIGHT: *Cover of the February 1939 issue of* PLUS, *also designed by Matter. The photograph of the golfer, a multiple-flash exposure by H. E. Edgerton, was used to illustrate an article on Alexander Calder by James Johnson Sweeney. The colors were black and yellow.*

quite unorthodox in his artistic preferences. In 1938 he decided that what the *Forum* needed was a quarterly supplement that would be designed by the farthest-out avant-gardists of the day, and contain some of the farthest-out articles on architecture, art, design, and related matters then being discussed by Howard's friends. This quarterly supplement was named *PLUS,* and it came out four times, starting in December 1938, before paper shortages and other problems related to the outbreak of war in Europe put an end to it.

Those issues of *PLUS* were designed by a young, then virtually unknown Swiss graphic designer called Herbert Matter: and its contributors included Fernand Léger, James Johnson Sweeney, Laszlo Moholy-Nagy, Alvar and Aino Aalto, Amédée Ozenfant, and other members of the international avant-garde. In its graphic design, *PLUS* antedated some of the most distinguished "little magazines" in the visual arts produced fifty years later; in its content, *PLUS* resembled some of the even littler magazines produced in the 1920s by the Bauhaus, by the de Stijl movement, by Italian Futurists, and by Russian Constructivists—publications then almost totally unknown in the U.S., and barely remembered in Europe. In short, *PLUS* was that most daring of journalistic endeavors—a publication addressed not to some demographically defined average readership, but to perhaps a hundred or so of the editor's friends, or to those whose intelligence and judgment the editor admired most, in the hope that the other 29,900 readers of the publication might be stimulated and challenged by whatever that minority of one hundred found stimulating and challenging.

For the editor of a successful building industry publication, whose advertisers sold things like asphalt tile and porcelain lavatories, to enter into such a journalistic undertaking was truly astonishing. Although it probably didn't do much to elevate the level of the American cultural discourse in 1939, the brief existence of *PLUS* set the *Forum* apart from all its competitors in the U.S., and in most other industrialized countries. There were at least three so-called "professional" architectural publications in the U.S. in those years, but they were roughly on the intellectual level of a hardware catalogue; nobody remembers what, if anything, they published then (or for several decades to come), until the *Forum* finally ceased publication, in the early 1970s, and these publications tried to fill the void.

Not all of this was due to Howard Myers's perceptiveness and courage, though most of it was. For example, he realized as early as 1940 that there was a new profession called "industrial design," and that architects were very much involved in it; so he published a special issue entitled "Design Decade," wholly devoted to this new profession. One reason he was so aware of all aspects of the designed environment was that he knew all the key players and was very close to them: Henry Dreyfuss, who practically invented the industrial design profession in America, was a friend; and Hans Knoll, who almost single-handedly introduced modern furniture to the U.S., was another friend (and became one of my closest friends after Howard introduced us). Howard seemed to know all the leading artists, from Alexander Calder to Jackson Pollock, and he clearly admired their work, often long before most museum curators and gallery owners did. He was open to new ideas, to new visions, and to the young people who held these ideas and visions. And he gave these new people a "forum" from which to address the rest of the world when no one else was willing to take such chances.

During the war years he published special issues devoted to the opportunities of the postwar years, as he saw them; and these special issues (labeled 194x) contained specially commissioned projects by people like Mies van der Rohe and Eero Saarinen, as well as such lesser-known designers and architects as Charles Eames—whose talent was recognized by Howard, but by very few others. And at the instigation of Henry Wright, who served as co–managing editor with George Nelson, Howard published major stories on energy conservation in buildings and related matters—some twenty-five years before the significance of such issues was recognized.

Howard was not especially sophisticated in his tastes and preferences, and certainly not in the least ideological. He just seemed to sense that there was something absolutely terrific going on in the visual arts and in the applied arts, and that—whatever it was (and he wasn't entirely sure)—it made for great "copy." He was also bright enough, and generous enough, to hire some first-rate people to work for him—people like George Nelson, Paul Grotz, Henry Wright, James Marston Fitch, Walter McQuade, Christopher Tunnard, and one or two others who would later emerge at the tops of their professions; and he would listen to them and support them in their ideas even if he didn't quite understand what they were trying to do. As a result, the *Forum* was an extraordinarily happy place for all those who worked there, and the magazine that was produced by the people whom Howard had discovered and hired was by far the most exciting publication of its kind and of its time.

CHAPTER FOUR

■ In the fall of 1940 I moved to Philadelphia to enroll at the School of Architecture at Penn. I don't know what I expected to find there; but all of my limited previous experience and education had been in modern architecture: apprenticeship in Serge Chermayeff's office in London; encounters with some of the radical young leaders of the MARS Group in London, and with artists like Ben Nicholson, Henry Moore, John Piper, and others; the brief experience in the art department of the *Architectural Forum* in New York; and meetings with radical, idealistic young architects and artists in Greenwich Village and environs. I assumed, without giving the matter much thought, that a School of Architecture in so modern and progressive a nation as the United States would be equally modern and progressive, especially since Walter Gropius and Marcel Breuer had completely transformed the Graduate School of Design at Harvard a couple of years earlier, Mies van der Rohe had done the same at the Armour Institute in Chicago at about the same time, and Laszlo Moholy-Nagy had resurrected the Bauhaus as the Institute of Design, in Chicago. I realized that Penn was probably a little farther behind what was happening elsewhere in the U.S., but I did not expect to find what I did.

To begin with, there was the building itself: a Victorian, vaguely

Collegiate-Gothic pile of bricks that had been built in the 1870s to serve as the School of Dentistry and was transformed into the School of Architecture some fifty years later, without any noticeable alteration in its form, plan, spaces, or anything else (including, possibly, its faculty and its student body). It was dark (except for the upstairs studios, presumably designed originally to ennoble the teaching of orthodontia), dingy, and generally dilapidated—in short, a rather wonderful place in which to absorb almost anything except, possibly, the theories and practice of modern architecture.

The faculty was headed by a seemingly ancient dean who (like most of his fellow professors) had been trained at the École des Beaux-Arts in Paris, or in its traditions at some École-oriented school in the U.S. Until recently, the school had been led by a distinguished French-born graduate of the École named Paul Cret, whose best-known works, in the U.S., had been the Pan-American Union Building and the Folger Shakespeare Library, both in Washington, D.C. Cret was a conventionally neoclassicist architect whose work has recently been rediscovered by postmodernists in search of godfathers and/or respectability. Cret himself had retired from teaching because of illness, but his influence was everywhere, perpetuated by squads of rather less interesting former Cret associates or disciples.

There existed something in New York called the Beaux-Arts Institute, whose principal function was to draw up programs for design projects to be handed out to students in the schools of architecture that subscribed to the principles of the Beaux-Arts Institute—i.e., traditional styles, traditional plans, traditional methods of presentation, traditional methods of teaching—the "traditions" being those of the original École, in Paris. (The student projects would be judged nationally by Beaux-Arts juries assembled in New York.) Virtually all U.S. schools of architecture at one time belonged to the Beaux-Arts Institute, and in 1940 most schools still did—in spite of Gropius and Breuer at Harvard, Mies at Armour Institute, Moholy at the Institute of Design, Wright at his own idiosyncratic Taliesin, and one or two others. The University of Pennsylvania's School of Architecture most definitely belonged to the Beaux-Arts Institute.

To convey some of the flavor of this system, as it appeared to a very young, unsuspecting modern-architecture student dropped into this odd teaching and learning environment, let me describe a typical design problem presented to us in one of those majestic halls of dentistry shortly after my arrival at Penn: the challenge was to design a building for an American Legion post in a medium-sized American town. The structure was to be Greek Revival in style, symmetrical in plan (naturally), and presented on a tightly stretched parchment—the plans, elevations, and sections to be rendered in washes of india ink, with large-scale details of the Greek Revival entablature presented with all shades and shadows properly in place.

Well, this wasn't exactly what I had had in mind when I decided to study architecture; and so I proceeded to develop my own plans, elevations, and sections for a building of this sort, following the functional requirements of the program, but translating them into what I thought was a more appropriate, entirely "modern" building for that site. My fellow students were astounded, the studio professors (or "critics") were infuriated, and my project earned me a so-called H.C., or *hors de concours*—the Beaux-Arts term for disqualification. (French terms and phrases from the original Beaux-Arts studios were in use throughout the school and continue to be, to some extent, in the U.S. architectural profession: for example, the term *charrette*—an abbreviation of *en charrette*—continues to stand for some sort of crash effort in completing an architectural project. The derivation is from a Beaux-Arts tradition, according to which students continued to touch up their presentation drawings while these were already en route, on a pushcart, or *charrette,* to the École, to be judged in its stately halls. One gathers that the students would run next to those pushcarts applying finishing touches—hence they and their work were *en charrette.*)

An H.C. at Penn was the equivalent of a "fail," and enough H.C.'s would mean that you had flunked the course. So the only way to pass without selling your soul was to present *two* solutions for each design problem offered in the studio: a Beaux-Arts solution and a "modern" solution. This is what I did; and though one or two fellow students joined me, most of them clearly thought I was out of my mind. They were probably right, especially since I had to hold down a part-time job on the side to support myself. Somehow I managed, though there was very little time for nightclubbing or any other form of socializing.

Still, I continued to be enormously lucky: Serge had given me a generous letter of recommendation "To Whom It May Concern" just before I left London for the U.S., and the letter got me a part-time job in one of the very few "modern" architectural offices in Philadelphia—that of Oskar Stonorov and his junior partner, a then unknown and very odd pixie named Louis Kahn. Stonorov & Kahn had a small office in an old, two-story carriage house not far from Rittenhouse Square, a lovely, rather English-looking part of the city.

There were only a couple of others in the office when I was hired: a young Danish architect called Abel Sorensen, who was later to play a significant part in the development of the UN Headquarters complex in Manhattan; and a German-born architect, some ten years older than I, named Wilhelm Viggo von Moltke, who had been trained in his native Germany, left the country shortly after Hitler came to power, worked in Sweden (for Gunnar Asplund) and in London, and had ended up in the U.S. when the war started in Europe.

Von Moltke, who was known to all as "Willo," was an extraordinarily talented designer and draftsman—enormously sensitive in his drawings, and in his aesthetic and humanistic concerns. There was no problem Willo could not handle with infinite patience and tact, and there was no one who could produce more exquisite drawings. Realizing that I was a mere beginner with very little use-

Willo von Moltke at work in the City Planning Commission in Philadelphia, ca. 1961.

ful, practical knowledge in design or in the development of technical details or "working drawings," Willo decided to take me on as his personal apprentice, and before long he and I became close friends—a friendship that was to last for some forty-five years, until his death from cancer in 1987.

Stonorov was a brusque, bustling, impatient operator—a rather heavy-handed designer, and better, perhaps, as a politician of architecture and planning and as a job-getter. He was not very close to any of us in the office, though I think he was really a more sensitive and sophisticated artist than we thought at the time: one day, many years later, when Lou Kahn and I reminisced about those early days (Oskar had died in an airplane crash a couple of years earlier), I turned to Lou and said: "You know, I have been thinking about that SOB lately, and I hate to say it but he really taught me one hell of a lot." Lou stared at me with his mouth open and said: "I have been thinking exactly the same thing: Oskar was a bastard much of the time, but I learned more from him than from almost anyone else." Lou Kahn by that time was one of America's two or three leading architects—a man considered to be on a par with Mies and others of that caliber—and while he was extremely generous toward others, he was also quite frankly critical in his judgments . . . so this was high praise indeed!

But in the fall of 1940, Lou Kahn was—in our eyes—a sweet, romantic, hopelessly impractical, and slightly incomprehensible dreamer. His drawings were charming and romantic; his designs were barely "modern"—they resembled a kind of modernized vernacular, not unlike Pennsylvania Dutch stone-and-wood barns endowed with vaguely "modern" glass gable-ends. His buildings were tasteful, intelligent, somewhat reminiscent of the *folklorique* drawings done by Le Corbusier in his early years. Lou was clearly a very talented designer and draftsman; but if anyone had told us that he would soon—within ten years or so—emerge as one of America's most influential modern architects, we would have thought the prophecy was simply absurd.

Yet we were enormously fond of him. His home life, so far as any of us could tell (he never discussed it) seemed less than happy, and so he stayed on in the office every night until all hours of the morning, and spent many hours at his drawing board on weekends as well. So his schedule and mine tended to coincide, since I had to spend most daytime hours, on weekdays, at school and worked in the Stonorov & Kahn office only at night and on weekends. On

Louis Kahn, in the 1950s.
(Hans Namuth)

most evenings, all of us—Willo, Abel, Lou, assorted friends and associates, and I—would go out for dinner to some cheap, gregarious pub in the middle of town, and Lou would entertain us with his charmingly naïve reminiscences and occasionally, if there was a piano available, by playing loudly and passionately, and rather randomly—his repertoire ranging roughly from Chopin's polonaises to Gershwin and Irving Berlin.

One Sunday evening several of us were driving around Philadelphia in a large convertible with the roof down. Philadelphia in those days was dead every weekday evening, and totally dead on weekends. At a traffic light another convertible pulled up next to ours, and I asked the driver, a massive, prosperous-looking businessman, if he knew of a place where we could get a drink in this town on a Sunday evening. He pulled out his card and wrote down an address—that of, I think, the Sixth Ward Republican Club or some such place—and told us to mention his name. "It'll cost you a dollar to join but it's worth it," he said. I thanked him and we proceeded to a rather dingy walk-up establishment, off Broad Street, signed up, and became members of the Sixth Ward Republican Club, as instructed.

The place was empty, but there was an upright piano on a small stage at the end of the bar and Lou made a beeline for it. His favorite tune that night was Gershwin's "Rhapsody in Blue," and he performed it with enormous energy and verve. After a few minutes of this, there was a call from a hotel across the street telling the club to ask the pianist to pipe down—a hotel guest, it seems, was receiving the last rites of the Catholic Church. Lou, a man of very gentle persuasions, immediately reduced the decibel count of his performance to a mere tinkle. Then, after a while, he got up and phoned the hotel to find out how the hotel guest was making out. The report was not encouraging, and Lou reduced the decibel count still further. This continued for another hour or so—Lou was quite indefatigable on the piano—and then the news came that the guest had passed away and the priest was leaving. Lou, without a moment's hesitation, returned to the keyboard and finished his rendition of the Gershwin "Rhapsody" with an appropriate crescendo and with much feeling.

Although he was small and seemingly frail, Lou was in fact enormously strong: a handshake from him could crush the strongest bones. Because of a childhood injury which left half his face scarred and disfigured by acid burns, he seemed to wear a permanent half-crooked grin. And yet, with all his disfiguring scars, he was one of the most beautiful men I have ever known. He had a kindness and a puckish wit that transformed his face into a landscape of endless fascination. That, together with his increasingly incomprehensible way of speaking of architecture—his personal poetry—completely mesmerized his students (and clients) in later years; but when I first met him he was straight, clear, uncomplicated, and without any mystery whatsoever. He simply loved architecture, and music, and beautiful women. As for politics, he had no special enthusiasms that I can recall.

In those last months just before Pearl Harbor, the only work for architects in the U.S. was in so-called "Defense Housing." All over the country, on suburban land located not far from "Defense Industries," communities usually consisting of about 300 to 400 apartments arranged in low-rise buildings or townhouses would be planned and built roughly along the lines of those pleasant garden cities pioneered by a handful of planners in the days of the New Deal and earlier in Europe. These communities would usually consist of a peripheral road with secondary, cul-de-sac streets arranged like spokes of a wheel radiating inward toward a pedestrian parklike village green, and outward toward a peripheral parklike greenbelt that would separate the community from its neighbors.

The pattern that was followed had been established in the U.S. in communities like Radburn, New Jersey; Greenbelt, Maryland; and Baldwin Hills, near Los Angeles; and Oskar, who was friendly with many of those early New Deal architects and planners like Henry Wright (father of the Forum's Henry Wright) and Clarence Stein, was very competent in the planning and design of those miniature garden cities.

While Oskar would plan these "Defense Housing" projects and their individual units, Lou was usually brought in to design the few buildings in those projects that offered some opportunity for more variety: kindergartens, schools, and community centers. These small, communal buildings would be located near the centers of the village greens, surrounded by public parks and accessible, on foot, to those who lived in the houses and apartments built along the cul-de-sacs.

While the pattern I have described did not offer many opportunities for Grand Designs, it did suggest an alternative to suburban sprawl that was novel for the U.S.—and was promptly abandoned after the end of World War II. For whatever reasons—narrow stupidity on the part of postwar mortgage bankers who in effect designed American postwar suburbs down to the smallest deplorable details; or ingrained rugged individualism on the part of would-be suburbanites—the American suburb, as planned and built by free enterprise, returned to the traditional pattern of tacky little houses on tacky little private and individual lots as soon as that war was over. The idea of having communally owned and maintained village greens or miniparks apparently smacked of socialism or worse; and so the patterns established by "Defense Housing" projects in the greenbelts around Philadelphia and other U.S. cities were abandoned almost instantly.

But for a couple of years, while such small communities were being planned and built with federal government money and by architects working in the traditions of European housing of earlier years, there was a serious effort to introduce a new and more humane pattern for suburban living into the American scene. Oskar Stonorov probably knew more about ways and means of creating those patterns than most other American architects active in those years, and he was dedicated to exploring new ways of creating communities of a quality equal to that of older, more prosperous suburbs.

Frankly, the creation of suburban housing communities was not a subject that lent itself to very significant architecture; and so Oskar was pretty much alone in his enthusiasms—at least in his own office. Most of us were more interested in the modest architectural experiments being carried on by Lou Kahn and by a few others around the country who were creating new theoretical communities for some distant and ideal tomorrow.

None of us in those days seriously questioned the very concept of "housing," the very concept of "planning." If you were a card-carrying Modern Architect—and though I was still very much at school, I certainly considered myself one—then you believed in "housing" and "planning" and in other keystones of the modern dogma; or else you were clearly suspect. The suspicion that the very notion of "housing" and of "housing projects" was inimical to life and liveliness in cities or, for that matter, in suburbs did not arise until some twenty years later, when Jane Jacobs began to speak and write about the "Death and Life of Great American Cities." And the thought that "planning" was, just possibly, antithetical to life in a free enterprise society, and antithetical to the kind of colorful chaos that seemed to characterize cities in an egalitarian democracy—well, that thought never crossed our minds. In fact, the few people who occasionally questioned our absolute certitudes were thought to be hopelessly reactionary, and beyond the pale.

Among those who seemed at least somewhat reactionary was a very patrician Philadelphian called George Howe, who had been the partner of the Swiss-born architect William Lescaze in the design and construction of the Philadelphia Savings Fund Society (PSFS) skyscraper on Market Street, done in 1931. The PSFS Building was and is one of the most remarkable entirely "modern" buildings of its time and of this century; it antedated the first buildings of Rockefeller Center by four or five years, and it contained none of the flashy appliqué streamlining that characterized such "modernistic" skyscrapers as the Empire State and Chrysler buildings, now considered, by some revisionists, to be works of avantgarde significance.

There was almost nothing about the PSFS Building that was not clean, strong, self-assured, clearly articulated as to function and structure. It was designed with masterful sophistication by someone who was obviously familiar with everything from De Stijl composition to Bauhaus typography, from Russian Constructivist experiments to Eric Mendelsohn's visionary drawings and buildings of the 1920s in Weimar Germany.

Although Howe & Lescaze were the architects of record, it was quite clear to me that William Lescaze's hand was the one that shaped that building. Lescaze had done a number of impressive modern structures prior to PSFS and was thoroughly familiar with the idiom; Howe had done almost nothing but elegant, traditional, often palatial residences on Philadelphia's Main Line for his and his family's wealthy friends. And while Howe, after the experience of PSFS, became a "modern" architect (if one were to stretch the term rather tautly), Lescaze had never, to the best of anybody's knowledge, done anything but "modern" buildings, in Europe or in the U.S.

However, the record has been fudged, and for good reason: Lescaze, whom I got to know quite well after World War II, was not an especially likable person. Those who worked for him, in his New York office or in Philadelphia, on the PSFS skyscraper, thought of him as a rather ruthless operator; whereas George Howe, with all his conservative politics (he was a right-wing Republican, so far as I could tell), with all his elitist tastes, with all his almost grotesquely patrician upbringing, education, World War I service, and bearing, was a gentleman of enormous sophistication—a man so extraordinarily open and intelligent and witty that one simply could not resist his charm. "Let me tell you something about George," Lou Kahn said to me, years later, after Howe had died. "He would take me for lunch to that club of his, the Union League Club, that would have never admitted me, a Jew, if I was the last living human in Philadelphia; and he would introduce me to all those stuffy Mainline neighbors of his, whom he really couldn't stand, and he'd tell them that I was the most talented architect in America . . . and then, later, in 1950, when George had become dean of architecture at Yale, he saw to it that Yale gave me my first real commission to do a big building. He believed in me, more than anyone else." And Lou said, looking away, "You know, I really loved that man."

At some point in the early 1940s, George Howe, Oskar Stonorov, and Lou Kahn decided to join forces, and the firm became Howe, Stonorov & Kahn. George and Lou had collaborated on one or two projects before and had developed a very close and very compatible working relationship. So things looked quite promising—although, especially after Pearl Harbor, there was precious little work for architects in Philadelphia or anywhere else.

Soon after the new partnership was formed, George was appointed supervising architect for the Public Buildings Administration, in Washington—the highest governmental post in U.S. architecture—and he spent virtually all his time there or in New York, and with a very pleasant lady, a painter named Clara Fargo Thomas who had a great old studio and townhouse near Gramercy Park and a beautiful, Howe-designed summer house in Maine. So there was very little change in the office: Oskar was off trying to solicit work—planning work, mostly—from such potential and real clients as the United Automobile Workers in Detroit, and from Ed Bacon (who was beginning to orchestrate his career as Philadelphia's chief city planner); George Howe was in Washington or New York or in Maine; and the office was being run, in effect, by Lou. There were some other changes: I was sent out to work in the construction trailer on the site of a housing project in North Philadelphia, checking shop drawings and contractor performance, and spent less and less time in the office; and the office itself moved from the small carriage house off Rittenhouse Square into the Philadelphia Bulletin Building, next to City Hall—a building that had been rather indifferently remodeled by George Howe a few years earlier. And Willo von Moltke, my closest friend in the office, went up to Harvard to get a proper American professional degree by studying under Gropius and Breuer at the Graduate School of Design.

CHAPTER FIVE

■ Shortly after arriving in Philadelphia in the fall of 1940, I had spent a weekend with some friends in Paoli, at the end of the Mainline; and on Saturday evening several of us had gone to a square dance being held at a local village hall. There I met a young English woman who had been left stranded in the U.S. when the war started in Europe, and had found herself unable to return home since there was no passenger transport available to her. She was working as a combination secretary-housekeeper for an English family living nearby; and the family, it turned out, was that of Bertrand Russell and his wife, Patricia (Peter) Spence, and their little boy, Conrad, then only three or four years old. My new friend, Pam, introduced me to them. There was a pump house on the property the Russells had rented, and I started using it as my second home.

I had a rough idea of who Russell was and what he had done. I knew he was considered one of the most influential philosophers of his time; that he was a socialist (and a convinced anti-Stalinist); that he had been a leading British pacifist during World War I and had gone to prison for that (although he had been too old to serve in the military and could have escaped imprisonment if he had simply kept quiet); that his views on education and premarital sex were considered fairly radical by most people and outrageous by the Catholic Church, which had banned his books; and that he had been a friend of everyone who had been active in socialist and otherwise (to me) enlightened pursuits in Britain: of the Webbs, of D. H. Lawrence, of Joseph Conrad (Russell's young son was named after the writer), of G. B. Shaw, of the Huxleys—Aldous and Julian—and of everyone else who, to people of my generation, seemed almost sainted and barely real. I also knew that Russell had recently gone through hell in New York, where the Catholic Church, the Hearst press, and several opportunistic politicians had ganged up to deny him a position at City College by going to court and blocking his appointment at CCNY on the grounds that his mere presence on the campus would corrupt the mind and hence the morals of a youthful lady student who, it turned out, wouldn't even be enrolled in any of his courses.

Russell had given up other teaching appointments in order to move to New York with his family. He was now almost destitute: none of his limited British funds could be converted into dollars because of wartime restrictions; and he could not return to Britain because Nazi U-boats had put an end to transatlantic passenger shipping.

Fortunately, his friend the American philosopher John Dewey was able to help: Dewey was much admired by one Dr. Albert C. Barnes, an eccentric collector of art and writer on art and related subjects, who had established a foundation in Merion, Pennsylvania, on the Mainline, which admitted students to attend lectures by Dr. Barnes and by others invited by him. The Barnes Foundation was an extraordinary place—its founder had collected some remarkable early works by Picasso, Matisse, and others, and mixed them up with other works of art and of crafts that, to him, seemed relevant and related; and when Barnes, who delighted in thumbing his nose at anyone and anything that smacked of establishment mores or politics, invited Russell at Dewey's suggestion to move to Pennsylvania, Russell accepted with pleasure or, in any event, with considerable relief. A few weeks later Russell (known as "Diddy" to his family), Peter, Conrad, and Pam moved to Little Datchet Farm near Paoli; and I turned up a few months after that.

I knew enough about Russell to be absolutely terrified of meeting so grand a person: Diddy was in his seventies by then, and rather intolerant of anyone he considered to be very far beneath him intellectually; but Peter, thank God, was about forty years younger—and Diddy's two children by an earlier marriage, John and Kate, would show up now and then between stints at their American universities. Although there was a fairly steady stream of intimidating visitors, like Julian Huxley, Sidney Hook, Freda Utley, and others, most of the people at Little Datchet were close to Pam's age and mine; and except for occasional and fairly horrendous marital tensions, which ultimately led Peter and Diddy to divorce, life there was not at all intimidating.

Diddy himself, though very grand when he wanted to be, was utterly charming *en famille:* every night he would tell Conrad a long bedtime story, made up on the spur of the moment and dealing with one of the seemingly endless and varied adventures of one Captain Niminy Piminy, a famous explorer who had been sent to deepest Africa to catch some exotic animal for Uncle Julian's zoo. (Sir Julian Huxley was the director of the London Zoo in those days—a fact which gave him very special cachet in Conrad's eyes.) Conrad was completely mesmerized by these stories—as were we—partly because Diddy was able to draw upon his encyclopedic knowledge of geography, biology, zoology, astronomy, and everything else to embellish the bedtime fables, and to add vast credibility to every detail of the captain's exploits.

When Diddy was not composing his stories about Captain Niminy Piminy's travels, he would recite Hilaire Belloc's *Cautionary Verses.* All of us, in short order, learned those verses by heart, and found them applicable to almost any situation likely to arise in the course of a day—in fact, almost indispensable in dealing with ordinary as well as extraordinary daily problems. I am sure that visitors were often convinced that they had strayed into some rather exclusive madhouse whose inmates addressed each other with mysterious references to people like John Vavassour de Quentin Jones (who was very fond of throwing stones), or Henry King (whose chief defect was chewing little bits of string). Since Belloc, according to Diddy, was a raving anti-Semite, we made a point of ignoring his occasional excesses in that regard; but we found the "morals" of his alphabetic verses absolutely essential in carrying on any intelligent (or, for that matter, unintelligent) conversation: "Decisive action, in the hour of need/ Denotes the Hero, but does not succeed," still seems to me about as good a way of dealing with the crushing defeats of everyday life as any I can imagine.

Diddy was the first "pragmatist" I had ever met: if one were to pin him down to explain exactly what he really felt strongly about (and it would have never occurred to me to ask so presumptuous a question), I think he might have said that he would do almost anything to help prevent or reduce cruelty on earth.

This seems like an obvious sort of answer; but Diddy was quite cold-blooded about preventing cruelty: for instance, he was quite supportive of the notion of some kind of American Empire after the explosion of the first atomic bombs, explaining that the only hope for the survival of the human race was to have the United States impose disarmament on the Soviets and on anyone else potentially capable of making atomic weapons. When the United States failed to impose its imperial power on the rest of the world while it still possessed a monopoly of atomic weapons, Diddy thought this failure was almost criminally stupid; and when the Soviets developed their own bombs, Diddy felt that the *only* hope then for the survival of the human race was for everyone to disarm—or, even for the West to disarm unilaterally. He had no illusions as to what might happen to Western Europe, say, if Stalin's troops were to take over; but he was sure that, whatever might happen to some or many people in reasonably free countries, it would not be as bad as what would surely happen to *all* of humanity in the event of a nuclear war.

Many people did not understand his logic at all, feeling that one could not be anti-Stalinist (as he was) and advocate a political course that would probably lead to gulags for all of Diddy's friends and relatives, and for Diddy himself. Yet, given the pragmatic clarity with which he liked to approach all issues—political as well as personal—his changing positions seemed to me to make eminently good sense, considerably more sense than the inflexible catechisms that were being bandied about by dogmatists of every stripe, be it in politics, religion, or, for that matter, in architecture. Although the issues that my fellow architects and I confronted were hardly as earthshaking as those of war and peace, I learned to look at my portion of the world in a very different way the longer I thought about Diddy's unconventional beliefs.

On Sundays, at Little Datchet, young couples—philosophy professors or students from CCNY—would arrive from Manhattan to express their solidarity with Diddy. On one such occasion, as a young, adoring couple bade him farewell at the door of Little Datchet, we overheard the wife saying, "Lord Russell, it was so wonderful to bask in your light!" Ever after, we would remind Diddy, come Sunday, that some people were expected for lunch "to bask in your light"—a prospect that did not amuse him quite as hugely as one might think. (One Sunday, when the usual visitors arrived, Diddy could not be found, and Peter sent me off to look for him; I found him sitting in a tree, quite far up, fully and properly dressed, puffing away at his pipe and looking out at the Pennsylvania Dutch landscape. "Diddy, come down! They've come to bask in your light!" He said "Damn them" and that he didn't quite know how to get down from his perch. I lent him a hand, while he grumbled.)

It was, for me, the best of times. Although neither Diddy nor Peter showed much interest in architecture or city planning, the ways in which they approached any issue, in whatever field, taught me more than a dozen learned lectures at Penn. On one occasion, Diddy said that he sometimes played a game with himself: "I assume that everything I have always known to be absolutely true is, in fact, not true at all—that the very opposite is true. Most of the time, of course, the result is utter nonsense. But sometimes I find it opens up some very interesting new perspectives." On another occasion, when we were talking about the possibility of building entirely new towns to accommodate population increases and so on, Diddy and Peter said they thought those new towns sounded absolutely awful—and proceeded to advance the kinds of arguments that would be advanced, many years later, by Jane Jacobs and by Lewis Mumford.

Much of the talk had to do with politics and the war. Diddy had turned passionately anti-Communist after seeing the cruelty of the Soviet regime at first hand in the early 1920s, and after experiencing, secondhand, through some of his close friends, like Freda Utley, the brutality of Stalin's purges. Still, even after the Soviet Union had been attacked and had become an ally against Hitler, Diddy felt that one could not be a pacifist in this war—that, in this case, it *would* make a difference whether Hitler won or our side won. (He didn't think the difference would be very considerable, but he did think it was there.)

One weekend I brought Willo out to Little Datchet, and everyone liked him instantly: both Diddy and Peter had known several young anti-Nazi Germans in England in the 1930s, when a number of them, including Adam von Trott zu Solz, had studied briefly at Oxford and Cambridge. Willo's brother, Count Helmuth James von Moltke, was a close friend of Adam von Trott, so the Russells knew all about Willo's family.

Helmuth, who was a lawyer and an expert in international law, had decided to stay on in Nazi Germany and to join the German Foreign Office, hoping to be able to oppose the regime's plans more effectively from within. Willo knew only that his brother was working in Berlin—he assumed that Helmuth was part of some secret opposition movement, but had no detailed knowledge of this until much later. But he had long agonized over his own decision to leave Germany instead of staying with Helmuth and helping him fight the Nazi regime.

Willo and his brothers and sister were half British South African, but the name von Moltke carried with it an aura that the Nazis found most attractive; and my guess is that Willo, if he had stayed, could have become Hitler's "staff architect." I don't think he and I ever discussed that possibility—he would have laughed uproariously at the thought. He could never, under any circumstances, have imagined himself as part of the Nazi establishment; yet he adored his oldest brother and worried about him throughout the war years. When Helmuth finally met his dreadful end—the Nazis had him hanged, and filmed the execution—Willo was, I think, utterly crushed by sorrow as well as a sense of guilt. I don't believe he was ever sure that he had done the right thing in leaving Germany when he did.

But in the early 1940s we could only worry and talk and hope. Both Willo and I would soon be drafted into the U.S. Army, and all of us seemed to be losing control over events in our lives. There was virtually no work in architectural offices anywhere in the U.S., and Willo went back to Harvard to finish his studies. I had decided to leave Penn: despite the fact that I had learned a good deal in the nuts-and-bolts areas of building, the Beaux-Arts orientation of the school seemed to become increasingly irrelevant. While working for people like George Howe, Oskar Stonorov, and Lou Kahn, and living—much of the time—with that extraordinary family at Little Datchet, I did not think I needed what Penn had to offer.

In the meantime, problems had arisen between the Russells and Dr. Barnes. It all started innocently enough, with a walk that Willo and I took down a country road near Little Datchet one Sunday morning. As we ambled along, a small, rather decrepit truck overtook us and pulled up ahead. It was driven by a tall, burly gent whom we took for a local farmer—he was wearing a pair of battered old bluejeans, and a checkered shirt even more battered. "You guys need a ride?" he asked. We said "sure," and hopped in. "I guess you're students," said the farmer. "We're studying to be architects," Willo answered. The farmer perked up. "Is that right? Are you interested in pictures?" We said we were.

The "farmer," of course, turned out to be Dr. Albert C. Barnes, and he invited us over to his "place" to look over his "stuff." Once we realized who he was, we accepted eagerly. Dr. Barnes took us to his house, and to his gallery in Merion, and proceeded to show us around, obviously pleased as punch to have picked up some very ordinary kids who seemed overwhelmed by what they saw. He took us from one Matisse to another, from a Picasso to a Cézanne, always pointing out that the strange assortments of Pennsylvania Dutch wrought iron that hung next to the paintings somehow related to what the painter had been trying to do. Our heads were spinning. After two hours of this, we suddenly saw Diddy coming out of one of his lectures. He waved to us, and came over. "I think we'd better go—we're expected for dinner." Dr. Barnes did not appreciate the interruption; he turned abruptly and walked away. He had been irritated by Peter a few days earlier—while attending one of Diddy's lectures, she had engaged in knitting a sweater for Conrad—and Diddy's innocent interruption was the last straw. He canceled Diddy's contract; and the Russells prepared to move to Princeton, where there seemed to be some teaching opportunities, thanks to Albert Einstein, who had long been one of Diddy's friends.

I knew that my draft number would soon come up, and I decided to return to New York. Around Christmas of 1942, I sent a note to George Nelson, then managing editor of the *Architectural Forum,* explaining my situation and adding "Christmas is here—give!," which was the slogan of a nationwide charity drive that year. Nelson was amused by the appeal and asked me to come to work for him as a junior writer—at least until my draft number was up. So I moved back to New York and went to work at a typewriter.

CHAPTER SIX

■ A story used to make the rounds in journalistic circles that Harold Ross, the founding editor of *The New Yorker,* liked to start off incoming junior writers by appointing them to some exalted position, like managing editor—perhaps on the theory that managing editors, unlike incoming junior writers, didn't have to know how to type. Fortunately for all concerned, this policy did not prevail at the *Architectural Forum* (and may never have prevailed at *The New Yorker* either); so, despite the fact that I did not know how to use a typewriter (and after fifty years still don't), nobody offered me the job right away. Instead, I was assigned to doing what all incoming junior writers do, that is, writing product reviews, forging "Letters to the Editor" (when there weren't enough real ones to fill the columns between the ads), and doing the obituaries. Now and then I might be asked to review a book or an inconsequential exhibit; but, to be perfectly frank, my assignments, by and large, were not of the sort to win any Pulitzer Prizes.

I was at the *Forum* for only six or eight months before my draft number came up, and I remember only a few specific events that stood out from what was otherwise a pleasant but fairly routine experience. The most memorable of them involved my first, rather dramatic encounter with Frank Lloyd Wright.

Sometime during my first week at the *Forum,* somebody—I still cannot imagine who—gave me a copy of Mr. Wright's *An Autobiography,* a massive piece of work, 560 pages long, and just then published in its first edition with an introduction by Fritz Gutheim. (Fritz was a regular contributor on architecture and planning to the *New York Herald Tribune.*) Mr. Wright's *An Autobiography* was clearly a major literary event not merely in our specialized field, but in the field of modern American cultural history as well. It was not a book that one would ask a virtual apprentice to review—especially if one was the editor of the magazine that Mr. Wright had made his own—a magazine which, in turn, had invested very large sums of money in buttering up the old egomaniac in the manner to which he had become accustomed. (Incidentally, no one, with the exception of his immediate family, ever referred to him as anything but *Mr.* Wright.)

So, here it was, all 560 pages of fairly pompous prose, and I took it home with me to read at leisure and without distraction.

Before very long, certain aspects of the *Autobiography* began to jar: first, there were some extraordinarily mean-spirited anti-Semitic diatribes in the first "book" out of the five that made up the *Autobiography.* Next came thinly veiled pro-German (possibly pro-Nazi?) comments, praise for Charles Lindbergh's America First/pro-Nazi stance, apologias for Japan's entry into the war on the side of Hitler and Mussolini, and—incredibly—a sort of "Ode to Stalin," written after a 1937 visit to the USSR and culminating in the considered judgment that "if Comrade Stalin . . . is betraying the revolution . . . I say he is betraying it into the hands of the Russian people."

In retrospect, these assertions seem so obviously silly that my angry reaction at the time may appear overdone. Still, the time was 1943; most of us knew, by then, that some form of mass murder of Jews was under way in Europe; everyone knew that Stalin had engaged in his own campaign of mass murder in the 1930s, and was likely to continue along the same lines if and when he ended up on the winning side of the war he had helped to start; and everyone knew that the Japanese military, far from being the defenders of a great civilization as Mr. Wright seemed to see them, had engaged in mass murder throughout the Far East.

Moreover, quite a few members of my generation had already died as a result of Hitler's war, and more of us would surely die before we were through. To read, in 1943, Mr. Wright's obscene account of a fight he had had with someone in the office of Dankmar Adler and Louis Sullivan, where he was working as a junior draftsman, was more than startling. Here is a sample: "I laid down my pencil," he wrote in 1943, "swung around on the stool and looked at him. He sat at his table, a heavy-bodied, short-legged, pompadoured, conceited, red-faced Jew, wearing gold glasses. His face, now red as a turkey-cock's wattles. 'I think I've had enough of you,' I said. I got up and walked slowly over to him and without realizing he was wearing glasses, or hesitating, struck him square, full in the face with my right hand, knocking him from his stool to the floor, smashing his glasses. I might have blinded him.

"With a peculiar animal scream . . . he jumped for the knife, a scratcher-blade with a long handle, lying by his board. Half-blinded, he came at me with it.

"I caught his head under my arm as he came. . . . I wound my right hand in the back of his collar and . . . hurled him away from me. He went staggering, toppling backward. . . . He got up on his feet again and with that same curious animal scream grabbed the knife and came on—a blood-thirsty little beast. Quick as a flash, as he came toward me, I grabbed the long, broad-bladed T-square on my board by the end of the long blade, swung it with all my might, catching [him] with the edge of the blade beside his neck just above the collar. . . . He wilted, slowly, into a senseless heap on the floor. . . ." And later, after the antagonist had come to: "It was good to see him move, for I thought I had killed him. . . . He went without ever coming back to the office."

This was the kind of prose that made *Der Stürmer* a favorite journal among Nazi sadomasochists. Had I known then how badly Mr. Wright needed to assert his manhood—how he had retouched his hairline on published photographs in the *Forum,* and how he insisted on being photographed on horseback (since he was, in fact, rather short)—I might have laughed this off as an unintentionally revealing self-portrait of the artist as an ambulant inferiority complex; but as it was, I wasn't terrifically amused.

And so I sat down at my typewriter and typed out, one-finger-fashion, a review that would (I thought) put this little bigot in his place. I left the review on George Nelson's desk and went out to lunch.

While both George and I were gone, Mr. Wright himself decided to grace the *Architectural Forum* with his presence. He liked to drop in unexpectedly and walk around the editorial offices, hoping to encounter a friend who would take him out to lunch. If no one was to be found, as on this inauspicious day, Mr. Wright would start snooping around, picking up letters, copy, books, and other interesting tidbits to keep himself amused. He rather liked snooping around George Nelson's office, I discovered later, and on this occasion he sat down at George's desk and picked up the nearest piece of copy—which happened to be my review. I don't know exactly what came next, but when I returned from lunch there seemed to be a certain commotion on the premises: Paul Grotz, our kindly art director, who was Mr. Wright's ex officio ambassador to the *Forum*'s editorial staff, was pale-faced and distraught; George Nelson was resigned and faintly amused; and the editor and publisher, Howard Myers, was closeted in his office, apparently trying to reach Mr. Wright by phone.

What had happened was this: When George returned from lunch, he found my copy on his desk, and scrawled across it in red crayon (Mr. Wright's personal, imperial color) the words: "George—I always thought you were a son of a bitch, but now I know!" Signed, with inimitable flourish, "F.LL.W." Implied, but not spelled out, was that Mr. Wright had severed his connections with the *Architectural Forum*. Clearly, he had assumed that the review had been written by George; in any case, had he seen my name on the copy sheet, it would have meant absolutely nothing to him.

I imagine that the most junior writer on the editorial staff might have been forgiven one or two transgressions of a minor sort during his first week on the job; but my admittedly unintentional faux pas looked anything but minor: Mr. Wright, as I mentioned earlier, was the most valuable editorial "property" the *Forum* could boast; and the magazine had invested considerable sums of money in publicizing his work in one, memorable special issue, and was planning to publish more such special issues as soon as paper shortages and related wartime restrictions were a thing of the past. All of these plans, it seemed, might now be imperiled.

Fortunately for all concerned, Howard's skillful diplomacy and other written and spoken apologies to the Great Man saved the day; and it seems that he did not demand the scalp of the villain as part of his price; all he did demand, and get, was a laudatory review of *An Autobiography*, this one written by George Nelson himself, and duly published. George's review was fair, serious, and reasonable; it overlooked the Master's little peccadilloes that had so enraged me—

and if George felt any qualms about having caved in to the Master's ire, he never let on. My guess is that George, a very likable cynic, probably felt that this sort of incident was part of the price one paid for success, and that, in any case, it might make an amusing story if and when the time came.

For some reason, which still escapes me, the question of my continued employment on the *Forum*'s staff never arose at all. In retrospect, I suspect that others on the editorial staff, from Howard Myers on down, were just as amused as George Nelson may have been. I did not find the incident nearly so amusing. I wish I could claim that possible violations of the First Amendment and other issues of press freedom bothered me—but this was not the case. The fact is that I liked this new job very much and was terrified of getting fired.

In retrospect, my aborted review of Mr. Wright's *An Autobiography* should have dealt with another aspect of this man and his work. Unlike some of the modern architects with whose work I had become familiar in Europe, Mr. Wright seemed less concerned with the fate of the human race in an industrialized mass society than with the fate of one of its members—that is, of Mr. Wright. He had clearly come to believe that he (or He) was Architecture, and Architecture was Wrightian or it was nothing at all. And not only American Architecture: he seems to have become convinced, over decades of growing egomania, that *all* modern architecture, to be valid, *had* to be Wrightian. He had evolved a kind of theory of Manifest Architectural Destiny which seemed to suggest that only Mr. Wright's version of the future held within it valid answers to the problems of an urbanized world.

Since he hated cities and had very little interest in their problems, this theory of Manifest Architectural Destiny was based very largely on ignorance—and Mr. Wright had that "arrogance of ignorance" that Chesterton liked to blame for many of the world's ills. He really did not understand building technology very clearly—his notions of structure and skin were delightfully poetic, but not especially helpful in the real world of construction; and he did not understand the problems and potentials of industrialized mass production. In fact, his efforts, in later years, to design "prefabricated" buildings or building systems were charming but totally inept. He simply did not know: how mass-produced housing, for example, might be made efficient; what aspects of such housing could be most usefully standardized, and what aspects could not; and how such factors as land use, financing, labor practices, distribution, etc., affected the final product.

There was no particular reason why Mr. Wright should have had the answers to all or even some of these complex problems—except that he claimed to have them, denounced those who were trying to find rational (rather than mystical) solutions to them, and frequently misled clients or potential clients who were charmed by his fraudulent protestations and found themselves in dire financial straits because they trusted his judgment in such things as cost, practicality, and structural stability.

Actually, since most of his house clients were fairly wealthy, they usually managed to survive their architect's extravagance. (Mr. Wright's anti-Semitic tirades, incidentally, seemed to evaporate in the later "books" of his *Autobiography*—perhaps because some of his most receptive clients turned out to be Jews.) Unlike Le Corbusier, Mies, Gropius, and others who had their share of wealthy house clients, Mr. Wright never seems to have used his residential commissions as laboratory tests that might produce prototypes for broader application to, for example, the solution of low-cost housing and related problems. He was designing mansions for the wealthy, and his proposals for the American City were, in effect, to build vast agglomerations of mansions for affluent Americans. He called his favorite proposal for suburban sprawl "Broadacre City," and it reads like a prescription for turning all of America into one vast, gold-plated Grosse Point, in which everyone would have at least one 1940 Lincoln Continental (Mr. Wright's favorite car) in his or her garage—or, preferably, two or three.

His solution for America's and the world's urban problems—the problems of Calcutta, Mexico City, America's urban ghettos, and all the rest—was to have everyone move to the country and live in a villa on a one-acre plot. He had not the remotest understanding of the monumental problems of urban congestion in a world of six billion people by the year 2000, or of providing shelter for these billions, many of whom would seek jobs in cities; and if these horrendous figures did, occasionally, penetrate his consciousness, he clearly put them aside very quickly.

Whatever notions he did advance regarding some sort of City of Tomorrow made Le Corbusier's Ville Radieuse seem like a romantic little village by comparison. Mr. Wright's most megalomanic urban proposal was a "Mile High" tower, to be built near the Chicago lakefront. (A building a mile high would be about four to five times the height of New York's Empire State Building!) This structure would stand in a park, thus presumably providing vast parking facilities below ground to accommodate the thousands upon thousands of vehicles that would serve it. The park presumably would be created by wiping out dozens of existing city blocks, with their residential, commercial, and institutional structures—all of which, one assumes, would be incorporated into Mr. Wright's 5,280-foot-tall monolith. Vertical transportation within this vast tower would be by high-speed elevators that would use up a very large portion of the floor area on each of the building's 400-odd floors. (Even with stacked elevator shafts, that height would require a dozen or more transfer points at various levels within the monolith; and the trip from the ground to the rooftop would take half an hour or more.) What this piece of projected megalomania might do to the rest of the city is almost mind-boggling: the influx into and outflow from the "Mile High" tower each morning and each evening would probably paralyze the rest of the city for several hours every working day.

None of this seemed to concern Mr. Wright very much—he would be living in Spring Green, Wisconsin, or in the Arizona desert while this daily madness destroyed the city he detested and its inhabitants, whom he seemed to despise. And yet, in this *Autobiography,* he had written at great length about the problem of automobile traffic, which, he suggested, was at least partly due to "tyrannical super-building in cities." He was using this sort of argument in trying to deflate Le Corbusier's notion of the Ville Radieuse—a proposal to replace today's congested cities with a new kind of urban pattern consisting of tall (but certainly not 5,280 feet tall) buildings spaced far apart and interspersed with large parks, playgrounds, and other recreation areas. "Enormous exaggerations of avenues of traffic is [sic] suggested but making all intercommunication utterly impractical because the actual nature of circumstances is surely making such exaggeration entirely unnecessary," Mr. Wright wrote, somewhat incoherently. He had learned at least one lesson from American intellectuals of his time: nothing succeeds like gobbledygook—and rhetoric can take care of reality any day!

With supreme insouciance he predicted that our traffic problems would soon be solved, and that the highway and the automobile were a sort of nirvana in which his "Usonian" society would flourish. "Complete mobilization of our American people is one natural asset of the machine, fast approaching," he announced. "Even now, a day's motor journey is becoming something to be enjoyed in itself—enlivened, serviced, and perfectly accommodated *en route*. No need to get tangled up in spasmodic stop-and-go traffic in some wasteful stop-and-go trip to town. . . . These common highway journeys may soon become the delightful modern circumstance, an ever-varying adventure within reach of everyone. Already, as Cervantes said, the Road is always better than the Inn." Well . . .

The fact of the matter is that Mr. Wright probably didn't know how to drive! He invariably had one of his apprentices drive his regal or imperial Lincoln Continental while the Master and his guests were enjoying one of those "delightful modern circumstances." His apparent inability to handle an automobile did not prevent him from issuing directions to all concerned regarding its use, and indeed redesigning it in his drawings for Broadacre City. He was absolutely certain that he had the answers to everything: architecture, cities, health, the future, the past, mechanization, arts, crafts, war, and peace. As for his judgment of his fellow men and women, this was governed by a very simple rule of thumb: those who paid obeisance to Mr. Wright were the salt of the earth; those who didn't were beneath contempt. On the occasion, in 1938, when Mies van der Rohe was installed as head of the school of architecture at the Armour Institute, in Chicago, Mies asked Mr. Wright to come and speak at the official ceremonies. The Master consented, and this, in full, is what he had to say:

"Ladies and Gentlemen, I give you Mies van der Rohe. But for me there would have been no Mies—certainly none here tonight. I admire him as an architect and respect and love him as a man. Armour Institute, *I* [his italics] give you my Mies van der Rohe. You treat him well and love him as I do." With that, Mr. Wright stepped down from the dais and walked out.

In retrospect, it is difficult to understand how intelligent, civilized, self-respecting scholars and critics could have accepted this megalomaniac for anything other than an embarrassment. His dress (that of an elderly Shakespearean actor, by the time I met him), his language (pseudo-Whitman), his Weltanschauung (Wagnerian), and his stance vis-à-vis his fellow men and women (ill-concealed contempt) all added up to a fairly embarrassing Portrait of the Artist as a Joke.

And all this, in retrospect, is true. Except . . . except for the fact that behind this ludicrous facade, this monumental arrogance, this overbearing ignorance, there was a talent simply unequaled in this century, and in much of the architecture of the past.

If one were to define what makes architecture great, one might start with such two- or possibly three-dimensional qualities as proportion, elegance of detail and craftsmanship; with effortless logic in functional planning; with a facility in massing, in the use of colors and of textures; and with the combining of all of these in a single harmonious whole. All these are qualities that can be defined in drawings or in written specifications; and while not everyone can master them, they are not beyond the reach of people with a degree of talent.

And then there are two or three qualities in great architecture that are simply beyond the reach of anyone but a person almost divinely gifted. They have to do with the way spaces in and around buildings can be shaped by such means as light and sound and other elusive devices; the way buildings can be formed by and in relation to the landscape; and the way all these mysterious and poetic effects can be achieved in varying degrees, at different times of the day and the night and the year.

I remember once, several years later, spending some time in a modest little house that Mr. Wright had designed in 1908, in Rochester, New York. The house had been painstakingly restored by its new owners, in precisely the manner in which the architect had originally built it. It was a sunny day, and light streamed in through the stained-glass windows and washed across the paneled walls and wooden floors. But as the morning wore on, the patterns of light and shadow began to change, slowly, imperceptibly at first, but finally transforming the house and its spaces into something quite different from what they had been when I first walked in.

Moreover, the sources of light were quite mysterious: some of the light streamed in through large and visible windows; elsewhere, the light seemed to sneak into the house, through strips of clerestory windows hidden within some sort of roof overhang or ceiling cove; and in still other areas, the light was reflected off interior and exterior wall surfaces, in ways that seemed quite magical.

What made all this so impressive was not only the manner in which the wandering sun had been made to animate and transform the interior spaces as if by some supreme skill of stagecraft; what made it impressive, to me, was that I *knew*, as a (by then) fully trained and practicing architect, that there was simply no way in which these effects of stagecraft could have been "drawn" or "specified" by conventional means of draftsmanship or written outline. This magic that was being performed before our eyes, that was transforming the spaces within the house every minute of the day, was something that could only be generated in the architect's imagination and then translated into reality by various sleights of hand that are not taught at any schools I had ever attended. What Mr. Wright had done here—and in literally dozens of buildings which I would get to know well in later years—was to perform a series of acts of supreme genius: he had used the ephemeral tools of light and time and motion, and with those tools transformed our more pro-

Taliesin West. Much of the furniture was designed by Wright himself, to echo the geometry of the architecture. He admitted that most of it was uncomfortable. (George Cserna)

saic materials (wood, stone, brick, and glass) into elements of performing art.

I have not seen many buildings that made this transition from the mundane to the ethereal. Mies van der Rohe's 1928 Barcelona Pavilion, which I went to see in 1987 after it had been precisely reconstructed on its original site, made that transition: it made space move and transformed it into pure magic. And I have seen buildings of the past in which dazzling light and dazzling stained glass transformed grand interiors into magic spaces and adorned them with jeweled reflections. But I have seen very few buildings in which light created spaces in motion, and guided you, irresistibly, from one room into the next.

That was one thing. The other aspect of Mr. Wright's work that set him apart from most other architects had to do with the manner in which he was able to relate his buildings to the landscape.

Guest room at Taliesin East, in Spring Green, Wisconsin. Sunlight from many windows and skylights enlivened all of Wright's interior spaces. (Ezra Stoller)

Dome house in Cave Creek, Arizona, designed by Mark Mills and Paolo Soleri and built in 1951. The roof consists of two half-domes of glass that can be rotated inside one another, thus opening part of the house to the sky. (Julius Shulman)

Most architects, when given a site for a new building, would be inclined to *occupy* that site, in some fashion, with their structures. Mr. Wright did that on various occasions, especially when building in cities.

But in most of his buildings that I came to know he performed acts of truly uncharacteristic deference: he would look at the site, its contours, its views, its vegetation, its colors, its orientation— and, if he liked it, he would preserve it by, in effect, moving his building as far as possible to the edge of the land, leaving the landscape undisturbed; or he would make it his principal concern to enhance the natural site, rather than turn it into a platform for the architecture.

I found in working on some of my own buildings in later years that this was a remarkably sensitive lesson: not many new buildings leave their sites better places than they were before the architect imprinted his or her own permanent mark. Mr. Wright, I suspect, never violated the face of the earth. It is a lesson that not many of his fellow architects, at least in the U.S., seem to have absorbed.

In recent years, some of Mr. Wright's buildings or parts of buildings have been shipped off to museums, to be displayed to visitors like specimens under glass. The Metropolitan Museum in New York, for example, acquired the living room of Mr. Wright's 1913 Francis W. Little house, originally built on a spacious site in Wayzata, Minnesota. The idea seemed about as absurd as exhibiting the Matterhorn in a giant cake of aspic in some museum of natural history: the room, in itself, is interesting; but it was undoubtedly built to come alive in different kinds of light, and in relation to the landscape of which it became a part. Plonked down inside the galleries of an urban museum, it is merely a specimen removed from its all-important context. Elsewhere, well-intentioned people have "saved" houses designed by Mr. Wright from some new highway project by moving the buildings to another site— thus amputating the houses from their sites and leaving both half-crippled.

Admittedly, the special qualities that Mr. Wright was able to give his buildings are nontransferable; and his former students and apprentices have rarely been able to match their master's work. Two who did match it were a couple of young men named Paolo Soleri and Mark Mills—and Mr. Wright, always jealous of any talent he thought might threaten his own reputation, kicked them out of Taliesin when they completed a stunning small "dome house" at Cave Creek, Arizona, in 1951.

I wasn't aware that they had been banished from the Imperial Presence; and so one day in the early 1950s, after I had finally returned to the *Forum*, I showed some beautiful photographs of the house to Mr. Wright, who happened to be visiting our Art Department. "Look at what we just got of a house two of your 'boys' built in the desert," I said, quite innocently. (He had either forgotten my book review or never made the connection in the first place.) Mr. Wright glanced at the photos, and—without a moment's hesitation—announced, "Oh, yeah, it's by those two ——, Soleri and Mills. I had to kick them out. And you know what?" This was followed by a series of obscenities too boring to repeat. Mr. Wright was sometimes not a very nice man.

CHAPTER SEVEN

■ Although most of the people I associated with in the early 1940s were artists or architects or crtics of art and architecture, all of us were deeply involved in politics as well. We could hardly help it. Some of us had experienced the confrontations—physical and ideological—of the 1930s, in Germany, Italy, the USSR, Spain, and elsewhere; others had been touched by these confrontations more indirectly while they were growing up. All of us, in one way or another, felt involved: some of my acquaintances were Stalinists, others were Trotskyites, still others were conventional socialists, a few were fascists—or, rather, ex-fascists, like Philip Johnson, whose fling with Nazism was largely over by the time of Pearl Harbor.

In retrospect, some of these political disputes seem less significant today than they did at the time. Young Americans—like older Americans—were often ignorant of the Stalin purges and other aspects of the Soviet state; and some of my acquaintances in New York and Philadelphia considered me an extreme reactionary for equating Stalin with Hitler. Some of the younger architects of the time, many of whom are today among the leading lights in our profession in America, were probably members of the Communist Party; others were what Dwight Macdonald called "Stalinoids"— followers of the party line in almost every respect, but perhaps not actual members of the CPUSA. (It really made little difference, since these bright young "progressives" faithfully toed the Communist line, supported others who did, and attempted to make life difficult for all those who did not.) And some of my friends were simply naïve.

In the 1950s, when witch-hunts became increasingly common in America and the likes of Martin Dies, Richard Nixon, Joe McCarthy, and others promoted their own political careers by literally destroying the lives of many people to the left of them, those of us who favored a more egalitarian social order began to come together; and the scars of the 1930s and 1940s began to heal.

But during the early 1940s, especially, the lines were drawn very sharply; the Stalinists agitated, around the clock, for nonintervention in the European war (which, to their embarrassment, had of course been triggered by the Hitler-Stalin Pact); but on the day after Hitler invaded the Soviet Union, in June 1941, they became impassioned interventionists, and the "imperialist war" in Europe was transformed into an antifascist people's crusade.

In retrospect, our preoccupation—perhaps, more precisely, my preoccupation—with these factional battles may seem strange: all the political lines have been redrawn in the past forty years or so, and none of us who passionately believed that we should confront tyranny, of whatever stripe, could help but reassess those simplistic beliefs after Hiroshima and Nagasaki. My own exposure to Diddy and his friends would make me realize, in the years after the end of World War II, that the issues were no longer as clearly definable: if the only alternatives were compromise or the end of all life on earth, compromise, even with dictatorships, seemed not only preferable but inevitable. This gentle and fairly inoffensive notion, however, was quite unacceptable to right-wing zealots in the years after World War II—except, of course, where the dictatorships were right-wing also.

The five years prior to the end of World War II were the last years of the preatomic age, and many of us, on the left as well as the right, felt free to risk confrontation—if not on any battlefield less than 3,000 miles away, then certainly on the printed page and at New York cocktail parties. A quaint case in point of that period was a small publication produced by students at Harvard's School of Architecture (and other, nearby architectural think tanks) in 1941. The magazine was named *Task* (in proper Politburo lingo), and its contributors included some fairly big as well as little guns then emplaced on the local scene: Walter Gropius, Christopher Tunnard, William Lescaze, Laszlo Moholy-Nagy, Joseph Stein, Edward Larrabee Barnes, and my good friend Willo von Moltke, and others equally innocent, politically speaking.

Behind this apolitical facade, however, there raged a fierce battle between left/liberal students on the one hand, who wanted to produce an idealistic publication dedicated to such traditionally "modern" issues as decent housing, good planning, neat and clean modern buildings, and all the rest; and a small group of Stalinist or Stalinoid students who wanted to turn the little magazine into a propaganda organ first for peace and, after June 1941, for war; and who also followed the Stalinist line in the visual arts—which meant Socialist Realism in painting and sculpture, and neoclassical Revivalism in architecture.

When I look back on this little tempest in a Cambridge teapot, the whole affair looks more than a trifle absurd; but the fact is that even here, in fields seemingly far removed from issues of left-wing politics, the Stalinists were busy trying to take over and to displace anyone who stood in their way. Many artists who did not toe the party line were not exhibited or, if exhibited, not reviewed; many writers were not published or, if published, went similarly unreviewed; and in almost every other field with which I was familiar, those of us who opposed the party line, for whatever reason, found themselves in various degrees of trouble.

For most of us, this absurdly partisan confrontation in matters of less than earthshaking significance was simply an irritation; for some of my friends, however, it meant a loss of jobs or of other creative opportunities. Obviously, the vendetta waged by Stalinists against left/liberals was never even remotely as serious a matter as the sort of thing one had learned about from veterans of the Spanish Civil War, and would hear about later from survivors of Nazi concentration camps in which communist "trusties" had made common cause with the SS guards and had seen to it that noncommunist prisoners, who represented a potential postwar threat, were given exceptionally brutal assignments or worse.

What seemed odd to me, in the early 1940s, was that these battles were still being fought in the U.S. After the Stalin purges of 1937, after the betrayals of socialists and other noncommunists on the antifascist side in the Spanish Civil War, and after the Hitler-Stalin Pact and the subsequent division of Eastern Europe among Nazis and Soviets, not many of my friends in Western Europe harbored any illusions about Stalin's USSR. True, Arthur Koestler's shattering works had not yet been written, and one did not know too many details of Stalin's gulags (or, for that matter, about Hitler's concentration camps); but it was hard to believe that presumably intelligent, compassionate, fair-minded people dedicated to humanistic concerns and living in a free society would voluntarily form alliances with one of the most brutal cults on the face of the earth. Some of those who fell prey to Stalinist dogma were undoubtedly looking for a safe ideological haven—as were many young Germans, for that matter, when they joined the Hitler Youth. But it seemed unforgivable that young people presumably dedicated to a humanistic art would ally themselves, actually or philosophically, with a bunch of thugs.

Among those who formed such an alliance were a number of young architects who would later become widely known and admired for their devotion to certain admirable causes—and who shall here remain nameless. They included two men who were to become very prominent spokesmen for historic preservation and historicist causes in general; another who became a prime advocate of energy conservation and other environmental concerns; still another who became a significant innovator in the design of medical facilities; several others who became leading U.S. city planners and experts in public housing design; and one who became best known, in later years, for (of all things) his designs for corporate headquarters and other Temples of Capitalism!

Many of these people had talent, and they deserved their later professional success. But many of them, also, engaged in fairly ruthless intrigues to shunt aside some of their fellow architects and designers who happened not to share their Stalinist convictions.

I had become familiar with the sort of intrigue carried on by the Stalinists in the 1930s and 1940s: among the Russells' closest friends was Freda Utley, an Englishwoman who looked like everybody's favorite, slightly dotty maiden aunt, but turned out in fact to have been one of the leading British members of the Communist International, had gone to live in the USSR to practice what she preached, married a fellow Communist, had a son with him, and saw her husband arrested during the Stalin purges and taken off to a gulag, where he perished. Freda had managed to get out of the USSR with her son, thanks in part to Diddy's intervention with the Soviets, and had turned vehemently anti-Communist. Her stories, based on her experiences in Moscow, London, and elsewhere, were full of firsthand reports of the sort of Stalinist intrigue that I was seeing, on a very minor scale, in the New York and Boston art and architecture world. My uncle the poet and writer Hans Sahl, who had once been a Communist, and subsequently undergone the same sort of disillusioning experience that Koestler would undergo in France and elsewhere, confirmed Freda's horror stories—as did people like Dwight Macdonald, the wonderfully energetic and idealistic ex-everything, whom I met through my uncle, and for whose Trotskyite, or pacifist, or socialist, or Veblenesque magazine *Politics* I wrote a few things about postwar Germany after returning from overseas Army service after the war. In short, most of the people I knew in New York and Philadelphia, outside my immediate circle of artists and architects, were intellectuals who had experienced Stalinist intrigue and worse in the arts, and who felt, even after the Nazi invasion of Russia, that an Allied victory over Hitler was only the lesser of two evils now that Stalin was the most powerful of America's allies; and that Stalin's agents in the West and elsewhere were motivated as much by postwar scenarios (i.e., how to outmaneuver their likely postwar rivals) as they were by the necessity of winning the war.

In retrospect, it may seem that we overestimated the intelligence and influence of the Stalinists, and that we turned slightly paranoid in our concerns. I don't really think so. It should be remembered that it was not uncommon in the 1930s and 1940s for Stalin's enemies outside the USSR to be assassinated by GPU agents, or kidnapped, or smeared and otherwise ruined personally and professionally. It was not uncommon for people who opposed the Stalinist line to be blackballed for jobs in literature and the arts, for academic appointments, and for similarly innocent pursuits. Conversely, it was very common for Stalinists and their fellow travelers to be appointed, routinely, to jobs in the media, ranging from the most mundane to the most exalted. We were quite aware of this, and some of my friends had become aware of it through bitter personal experience; and the horror stories reported to us by ex-Communists were entirely credible.

Today, it is hard to believe that agents of the Comintern would be asinine enough to try to infiltrate and dominate a student publication on architecture and planning—and the whole thing is of course more than a little ridiculous. But it really did happen—and it happened on every level, and in virtually every field even remotely related to policy-making or to the shaping of public opinion. Some of my friends of those early 1940s—specifically the Fletchers, the McMillens, the Harknesses, and other liberal or left/liberal architects who would later join Walter Gropius to form The Architects Collaborative (TAC) in Cambridge, Massachusetts—these lovely, idealistic, innocent people couldn't believe what hit them: neither they nor I could honestly believe that Stalinists and their fellow travelers would waste their time trying to undermine the Harvard Graduate School of Design, of all places, for God's sake! Yet all of us knew that it was happening, and that we children were the targets. (I don't recall what ultimately happened in the momentous struggle for control of *Task;* I suspect the publication simply folded when paper rationing was established—but not until some ideological blood had been shed, and some of my friends and I had had our first, disillusioning baptism of power politics.)

It was all perfectly grotesque, of course; but it was also rather discouraging. My friends and I, in the U.S. as well as in Western Europe, had taken up Modern Architecture as a cause that would help solve the world's social and economic inequities and save mankind threatened by population explosion and the related threats of war. We really believed, most of us, that we could and would make a contribution to the salvation of the human race; and to find that some of our assumed friends and allies were, in fact, using that same cause—or at least its verbal trappings—to help impose tyranny on mankind was a shattering experience. It would not have surprised us to find advocates of an elitist, aristocratic neoclassicism supporting Hitler's fascism (as Albert Speer did); it did disillusion us to find seeming advocates of a humanistic architecture in support of Stalin's tyranny. It was not the last disillusionment we would encounter— but it was the first, and we were so deliciously innocent that it really seemed to hurt.

CHAPTER EIGHT

■ Everybody had a different war, and mine was not especially bloody: I did not have to shoot at anyone to the best of my knowledge, and was only shot at occasionally and by incompetents. On one occasion, an elderly German "home guard" draftee managed to miss me by several yards from about twenty feet away; on another, some shells from a Nazi 88mm gun dumped a great deal of plaster on my head—which was, however, protected by a very thick German feather bed; on still another occasion, a flight of B-17 bombers of the U.S. 8th Air Force, returning from a bombing raid on Berlin, decided to drop some of their cargo not far from us ("us" being a Combat Command in the U.S. Fifth Armored Division trying to catch some sleep on the ground and shaken up by all that racket)— but they missed.

In peacetime, you can create as private a life for yourself as you like—or as public and as gregarious a life. But in wartime you have no choice: you are with other people *all* the time; and you depend on them, and they on you. They are rarely people you would choose to spend much time with in civilian life, but you have no choice. It is a very interesting experience in egalitarian living, and it can be extremely discouraging, and boring.

I realized all of this within hours after being inducted into the

U.S. Army; and while there wasn't anything I could do to change that situation, I seemed to be incredibly fortunate once again: except for the usual contingent of interminably foulmouthed rednecks, the people with whom I was thrown together while in uniform were as interesting a collection of men as I have ever met anywhere in a comparable period of time. All of us may have been discouraged at times, and we were certainly shaken by the sights of war at other times; but we were never bored.

The U.S. Army, as many of us discovered, was an organization of predictable unpredictability: during the first twelve months of my service, I was given "basic training" in the Corps of Engineers, then transferred to some outfit known as "Airborne Engineers," which was to be deployed by air to enemy airfields, where we (and our accompanying bulldozers) were to emerge from crash-landed gliders to repair shell holes and other damage incurred on runways—all this while "our" paratroopers would be battling "their" defenders all around us. Fortunately for us, the bulldozers ordered by the Airborne Engineers to be transported in those gliders turned out to be a couple of inches too wide to fit into the planes—and so our unit was dissolved and we were reassigned.

Reassignment, in my case, meant a swamp in Florida, where I learned to be an aerial gunner—a skill that would require me to sit inside a tiny plastic gun turret, under, above, on the sides, or in the nose or the tail of a large U.S. bombing plane, firing two .50-caliber machine guns, in tandem, at attacking German (or Japanese) fighter planes. I got my gunner's wings; was told that the average life expectancy of an aerial gunner in actual combat situations was about two and a half minutes; and received my orders to go to North Africa, to report to a B-24 bomber base there.

A few hours before I was to have taken off for North Africa, my orders were rescinded and I was told to report to some outfit located at No. 1 Park Avenue, in New York City. This unit, it turned out, was charged with producing training manuals for the education of aerial gunners (like my recent self); and the Army Air Corps had assigned to it a dozen or so writers, photographers, and graphic artists, who, in their earlier, civilian incarnations had worked for various technical and popular journals. Among those who assembled at 1 Park Avenue were a former *Life* editor, a former *Fortune* editor, a former writer for the *New York Daily News,* a former architectural photographer, a former art director or two of *Fortune,* and myself—a very junior ex-writer of obituaries and other back-of-the-book filler material for the *Architectural Forum*. (The reason a person with my rather limited credentials was included in this illustrious group was that the officer in charge of us, an Army captain, was an architect by training and also a close friend of my friend Hans Knoll, the furniture maker. Hans had heard somehow that I was about to be sent to North Africa as cannon fodder and urged the captain to have me ordered to 1 Park Avenue instead.)

Although all of us, except for our commanding officer, were lowly enlisted men with one stripe at the very most on our sleeves, we lived rather well: every morning, at about 7 A.M., we had to report to the old armory at 34th and Park Avenue for an hour or so of close-order drill; but that was the extent of our strictly military service. After completing those drills, we would go across the street to our offices and act like any civilian group of writers, editors, art directors, and so on. The evenings were our own—we lived in modest apartments and spent our free time with family and friends.

New York in the mid-1940s was probably the best place in the world for anyone interested in the arts: many of the leading artists and architects had fled Paris when the Germans moved in, and had settled in Manhattan. The architect Pierre Chareau had come to town; and many of the leading Surrealists—poets, painters, writers, including André Breton, Yves Tanguy, André Masson, and numerous others—had settled in New York and begun to produce a publication called *VVV,* financed, I suspect, by the American artist Robert Motherwell. And the painters Fernand Léger, Piet Mondrian, and several others lived in New York—Mondrian just around the corner from my family's place, in an apartment he had furnished with homemade egg-crate furniture painted in typical Mondrianesque colors and patterns.

If Mondrian had ever been as severe or austere as his paintings suggested when he lived in Paris, New York seemed to loosen him up considerably. He loved American jazz and spent much time at the various clubs that flourished in Manhattan in those years. His paintings loosened up as well: *Broadway Boogie-Woogie,* which he finished in 1943, was a young man's painting—as was his *Victory Boogie-Woogie,* which was left unfinished when he died of pneumonia in 1944, aged seventy-two. He had willed much of the work he left behind to the American artist and critic Harry Holtzmann, who made a lovely little 8-mm film of Mondrian's flat and studio after his friend died, to document that extraordinary environment.

Mondrian, Léger, and other exiles from the Paris avant-garde joined such locals as Frederick Kiesler, José Lluis Sert, Alexander Calder, Hans Hofmann, Arshile Gorky, and others who had moved to New York in earlier years. And every Wednesday evening they would meet in a place called the Jumble Shop in Greenwich Village, and sit down at a large, rectangular table in one of the back rooms to talk, drink, smoke, and talk some more. Some of us starry-eyed youngsters—in and out of uniform—were sometimes invited to attend; and we would sit on chairs placed against the walls, watching and listening to the illustrious exiles seated around the long conference table in the middle of that room.

Since most of the conversation was in French, some of us had trouble understanding what was being discussed—but the general drift of the conversation was clear enough: it dealt, predictably, with news of the artists who had stayed behind, and their fate under Pétain and his Nazi bosses; with the discouraging war news from France and North Africa and the Soviet Union; and with the difficulty of making ends meet in a city that seemed to know little about the Paris art scene, and to care less—being preoccupied, at the moment, with more mundane issues. Some of the exiles learned to speak a word or two of English, but most of them did not: Léger, to the best of my knowledge, learned only two absolutely essential words—"Glasse birre!"—which he expleted at regular intervals in the general direction of waiters, and with relish. Others didn't even manage that.

Costantino Nivola in his garden in Amagansett, Long Island. (Ruth Nivola)

One of the young observers seated on the perimeter of the room was a Sardinian artist named Costantino Nivola, who had left fascist Italy and come to New York just before the war. There he began to work as art director for the magazine *Progressive Architecture,* and then for another one called *Interiors.* Tino was very small, but he had the powerful physique of an Italian peasant—which in fact he was. He had been born in Orani, a tiny place in Sardinia south of Sassari, the son of a master mason. After working for his father as a boy, he had won a scholarship to an art school on the Italian mainland and had done some elegant posters and other graphics for Olivetti, in Milan. Tino and his wife had settled in Greenwich Village, where they lived and worked in a small studio on 8th Street, just west of Fifth Avenue. Tino was probably the sweetest person I had ever met, or was ever likely to meet. His dazzling smile, his generosity and kindness were absolutely overwhelming; and I felt instantly drawn to him.

Through Tino, I got to know a number of extraordinary people who were his friends. One of these, several years later and after the war was over, was Le Corbusier. Corbu trusted virtually no one in the U.S., since he was convinced that all Americans were "gangsters" out to steal his ideas and to use them for their own profit—that is, virtually no one except Tino. And when Le Corbusier was appointed the French architect on the international panel assembled in New York after the war to design the UN Headquarters in Manhattan, he stayed in Tino's studio on 8th Street and painted innumerable canvases there while in residence.

The Nivolas by that time had bought and rebuilt an old farmhouse in Amagansett, Long Island, not far from Jackson Pollock's and Lee Krasner's house in The Springs, and moved there with their young children. And so Le Corbusier had the 8th Street studio to himself.

It was through Tino that I would meet Le Corbusier in the late 1940s; and through him I also got to know Saul Steinberg (who had originally studied architecture in Milan), Bernard Rudofsky, and dozens of others. Tino was, in a way, the heart of that small avant-garde world which had somehow coalesced in Manhattan in the 1940s. His dazzling smile was everywhere.

When I first met him in the Jumble Shop in Greenwich Village, his work was largely graphic, rather in the late-cubist manner of Le Corbusier himself, and of Léger at his more abstract. His drawings and paintings were not especially original, though they had a gutsiness that seemed to spring from Tino's own closeness to the materials of building—to stone, cement, bricks, and blocks—and from his closeness to the forms of nature in that rural landscape of his native Sardinia. I had a feeling that he was really an architect, and that massive concrete forms and sunlit spaces were his real métier. Although he was clearly a modern artist, he still spoke the earthy language of his native island—just as Luis Barragan, another very modern artist, unmistakably spoke the language of Mexico in all his beautiful spaces and forms. Tino rarely used words to describe his work; he let it speak for itself. There was art in everything he did: in the way he peeled a fruit; the way he cooked; the way he poured wine; the way he spoke, in his imperfect English, to his family and his friends; the way he touched the earth and plants and water and the walls he built to define them.

In later years, after the Nivolas had moved out to Amagansett (and he had managed to transform a perfectly ordinary American clapboard house and its grounds into a small Sardinian town), Tino developed an ingenious technique of making sculpture on the beach by scooping negative forms out of the wet beach sand and filling the formwork with plaster reinforced with burlap and chicken wire. The hardened plaster sculptures would retain the grainy surface of the beach sand, and Tino would take them back to his studio and sometimes paint portions of them in the bright pastel colors of his Mediterranean youth. In the late 1940s, when Corbu was in New York and living in that 8th Street studio, he would spend weekends in Amagansett, and Tino would introduce him to his beach sand sculptures. Needless to say, Le Corbusier instantly went to work casting his own pieces and decorating them in

Le Corbusier in Amagansett, Long Island, ca. 1950, painting a plaster sculpture he had cast in the sand along the beach. (Tino Nivola)

his own colors. But that, of course, came a good deal later, long after the war had ended.

The day the Army Air Corps decided to transfer me from that Aerial Gunnery School in Florida to 1 Park Avenue happened to coincide with the annual Christmas party organized by the editors of *Fortune* magazine in Rockefeller Center. A friend had asked me to meet him at that party, and that evening I made a beeline from the airport to the Time and Life Building still wearing my Florida "suntan" uniform, and shivering in the New York Christmas cold. I remember there were two elevators on the ground-floor level of the building, their doors open and beckoning. As I got into one of the two to go up to the *Fortune* floor, I saw that there was a young blonde in the elevator cab holding a glass of champagne—which she promptly offered me in the spirit of Christmas and of doing her bit for the boys in uniform. She had a very pleasant, very precisely articulated English voice, and her name, she said, was Rosalind Constable—a researcher at *Fortune* at the time.

Rosalind in those days held a fairly menial job at *Fortune* (Time Inc. being as male-chauvinist as everyone else in those years); but her intelligence, her wit, her charm, the authority of her judgments in all matters having to do with the visual arts and with literature— these were so impressive that no one ever ignored her. From the first day of our friendship, it was clear to me that she was a person of vast intelligence and of enormous decency, and that I would not meet many people even remotely like her.

The art world in New York during the early 1940s (and roughly until the end of the decade) was still almost exclusively Paris-oriented, and only one or two galleries had the nerve to show un-conventional, modern American art. The most interesting of these was the Wakefield Gallery, an adjunct to the Wakefield Bookshop. The director of the gallery was a woman called Betty Parsons, a close friend of Rosalind's; and I met Betty through her, and saw some of the exhibitions she mounted in that gallery—work by Saul Steinberg, Alfonso Ossorio, Theodoros Stamos, and others. Later, in 1946, when I was still overseas, Betty managed to open her own gallery, and I met her again when I returned from the Army a year later.

Rosalind was so fully aware of what was cooking in the arts— especially in the visual arts—that one could not find a better-informed observer of the art scene in New York. Although her critical judgment was extremely sharp, she considered herself a reporter, a person who could tell you, and would tell you, what was newsworthy in the arts at any given moment; and she was willing to grant any reasonably serious effort a hearing—so long as she thought that the artist involved was not a total charlatan.

Henry Luce, the editor in chief of Time Inc.—and a man of rather conservative and often limited vision—was bright enough to permit Rosalind, in 1948, to start an in-house newsletter on the avant-garde (or avant-gardes) designed to go to the top editors at all the Time Inc. publications so as to alert them to the most interesting new developments in the arts. The weekly *Constable Report* started with three pages but eventually grew to about fifteen; and it ran without interruption for twenty years, from 1948 to 1968, when Rosalind retired and moved to Santa Fe. It was a highly confidential publication, since it might (and frequently did) trigger important news stories in *Time* or *Life* about this painter or that sculptor and thus boost the market value of the artist's work overnight; and it was, for the twenty years of its existence, the most sought-after newsletter in the arts in New York. Luce, who was an extremely *intelligent* conservative, told people (including Rosalind) on several occasions that he considered her *Report* the best publication produced by Time Inc.—and he was quite right.

Having so knowledgeable a person as one's guide to the New York art world was an enormous blessing. Rosalind saw to it that I received her *Report* as soon as I joined Time Inc.'s *Architectural Forum* in 1950—and that I never stopped receiving it, although I was hardly one of the top editors in the first years of my tenure there. It was a valuable guide to me, and a charming, amusing, and surprising gift week after week. I sometimes wonder what might have happened to me if I had taken the other elevator.

During those evenings at the Jumble Shop and in the Greenwich Village studios inhabited by various artists and hangers-on, we thought and talked very little about what was likely to happen once the war was over. There was much conversation about artists and other intellectuals who had been caught by Nazi advances into Western Europe, and about others who had (one hoped) managed to escape to Switzerland, or Sweden, or Spain. There was increasing concern about those left in Nazi Germany who had been locked up in concentration camps, and there was some talk about small, isolated resistance groups that seemed to function in Nazi Germany, though seemingly with little effect.

Meanwhile, up on Park Avenue my editorial unit continued to function quite efficiently, producing one training manual after the other, each designed (by Army private Will Burtin, former art director of *Fortune*) and written and edited by other Army privates drafted from the editorial staffs of *Time* and *Life*. We were clearly doing something nonlethal, and possibly useful; but I thought the time had come for me to get serious about soldiering. The things that I thought I could do best might be related to military intelligence (since I spoke German fluently and one or two other languages reasonably well); and so I applied for transfer to a place called Camp Ritchie, in the Blue Ridge Mountains of Maryland. My application was granted.

According to a columnist known for his exposés of the military, Camp Ritchie, it seems, was the "Country Club of the U.S. Army." It certainly looked that way to anyone used to the typical basic-training establishments: its setting, among the Blue Ridge Mountains, lakes, and forests, was idyllic; its various "barracks" looked like the sort of thing you might find in a pleasant ski resort; and the service—provided, to a large extent, by rather friendly Italian prisoners of war—was excellent, as was the food. The trainees reinforced the resortlike atmosphere: among those whom I got to know well were the movie actor Peter Van Eyck, the architect Peter Harnden, and numerous others including writers, poets, musicians, and others not normally concentrated en masse in any military establishment.

All of us were put through all sorts of training exercises, including courses that dealt with German (or Japanese) military hardware, tactics, and tables of organization. We were trained in techniques of interrogation, in ways of identifying (or forging) enemy documents, in handling enemy weapons and other equipment, and in reading military maps and aerial photographs. We played "war games," full-scale and with live ammunition, that involved simulated (and sometimes frighteningly realistic) combat extending over several days; and we scared the living daylights out of the inhabitants of nearby Maryland villages—and out of each other. There was a company at Ritchie made up of American Indians, and these soldiers were expert at impersonating German or Japanese troops, as required—complete with German or Japanese uniforms, insignia, weapons, tanks, trucks, and artillery. They were very good at waking up the locals in the middle of the night, enacting what appeared to be a massive enemy assault upon their peaceful Maryland towns and villages.

When we were not playing at being spies, or commandos, we played at being playboys: there was a first-rate restaurant just outside the camp's gates, run by a Free French refugee who had apparently been set up in his establishment in the midst of the Blue Ridge Mountains by some zealous counterintelligence operatives interested in finding out how many drinks the would-be spies could swallow before they started to talk out of turn, and what sort of girlfriends we liked to import from New York on weekends to stay with us in the Frenchman's upstairs "bed-and-breakfast" facilities. (Van Eyck and Harnden won out, hands down.) Every eight days, we would get a weekend pass which would take us from "Campo Ricci," as our Italian POW friends called it, to "Baltimore" (pronounced to rhyme with *amore*)—a place they had never seen but imagined to be the closest thing to Nirvana, USA, or to some other incarnation of *la dolce vita*. Baltimore in the mid-1940s was in fact about as dismal a dump as any to be found this side of Gary, Indiana—but we never tried to disillusion our Italian friends.

Our training was not especially arduous, except for those simulated combat exercises; and after a few months of playing at being spies and commandos, we received our orders to go overseas. We were all brand-new second lieutenants and had not the slightest idea which way we were headed—except that our first stop would be Paris and our second stop some combat unit engaged in the final phase of the European war, the conquest of Nazi Germany.

A few weeks before we were supposed to be shipped overseas, I got married to a gentle and beautiful person called Martha Howard, whom I had met when she was a graphic designer in the *Forum's* art department. Martha had been born in Peking in the early 1920s, while her father was working as an eye surgeon at the Rockefeller Institute's hospital in the Chinese capital. She lived there for the first six years of her life—blond, blue-eyed, tall, and not looking very much like anyone else within sight. After that, her family returned to their hometown, St. Louis, and Martha made her way eventually to Radcliffe and Manhattan, where we met. Our marriage, like many wartime marriages, did not last—perhaps we were both too young. But we have remained close, united by (among other things) our admiration of a very remarkable daughter. . . .

The troopship that took Van Eyck and me and assorted other U.S. Army types across the Atlantic was the converted British liner *Mauretania*. This ship was believed by people in the know to be fast enough to outrun any U-boats that might try to intercept us. This meant that we would not be attached to any destroyer-protected convoy but would instead make a dash across the Atlantic without naval escort.

We were absolutely terrified; and since the sleeping quarters assigned to us were located several levels below the ship's waterline, we decided to spend the ten days it took to cross the Atlantic in an officers' lounge on one of the top decks—playing interminable games of poker and fantasizing about what we might do with ourselves once the war was over. In between card games and hallucinations about the future, we would nap in our chairs, half expecting the torpedoes to strike at any moment. Van Eyck, who was a fairly good amateur jazz pianist, whiled away some of the interminable hours on a dreadful upright piano, until he fell asleep—on the keyboard. "Where are you going to live after the war?" I heard Harnden ask him just before he, too, fell asleep. "I'm going to buy myself a decent baronial mansion on Lake Constance," Van Eyck mumbled. "And then I'm going to get some sleep." As fate would have it, Peter Van Eyck did in fact end up in just such a place on the Swiss side of Lake Constance—he had responded to Harnden in German, saying *"einen anständigen Herrensitz, am Bodensee"*—and lived there with his family for many years. Since he looked and acted very much like a Prussian nobleman—tall, incredibly white-blond, and sinfully handsome—a *Herrensitz* seemed precisely appropriate.

The *Mauretania* made it across safely enough, zigzagging rather wildly during the final twenty-four hours; and we disembarked at a British port, took off almost immediately for Le Havre, and ended up in a village outside Paris a few hours later. We were promptly arrested by some overzealous military police, to whom our various accents sounded highly suspicious: they were sure that Van Eyck was a Nazi spy (he looked and sounded exactly like a Hollywood interpretation of one), and that Harnden and I, with our vaguely mid-Atlantic accents, were Van Eyck's sidekicks. After we had been properly identified and reluctantly released by the MP's, we had one final bash, and then took off in different directions, dispersed to different combat units.

My own was to be the U.S. Fifth Armored Division, and I remained with it, as an intelligence officer in one of its three combat commands, until the war in Europe ended. Harnden, Van Eyck, and I lost touch for a while—private communications in combat situations were difficult—but I ran into Van Eyck one day, quite unexpectedly, on a country road somewhere near Hanover: I was riding in a jeep with some of my men, and we were all rumpled and covered with dust and mud, as was our vehicle. Suddenly I saw in our rear-view mirror that we were being followed by an immaculately polished jeep, carrying in it a driver and his equally immaculate officer-passenger. "Oh, Christ, it's Patton," I told my driver. "We're in trouble!" General Patton, a fierce spit-and-polish officer known for wearing a high-gloss steel helmet, flawlessly tailored uniforms, and so on, was also known for, among other things, cashiering junior officers in combat for not meeting his own spit-and-polish standards. As the shiny jeep and its occupants drew closer I recognized my narcissistic pal, who had somehow found time to go to Paris briefly to get an elegant U.S. Army officer's uniform custom-tailored for him by the French branch of Knize—and had got his driver to polish their jeep, helmets, weapons, and other gear to match. They made a splendid, spotless pair. We stopped our cars, jumped out, embraced, exchanged the latest news, and parted. My men, who had recognized Van Eyck from his performance in the film *The Moon Is Down* (in which, needless to say, he played the part of a Nazi officer) stood openmouthed, and for the first time treated me with a semblance of respect. I never discovered what Van Eyck was doing in our sector sightseeing in his Sunday finery. I didn't see him again for a year or so, when we met in West Berlin, where he was established in a splendid villa and living with an absolutely stunning blonde named Inge. By this time he was driving a Mercedes, and I forgot to ask.

Two or three weeks before the Nazis surrendered, the 5th Armored Division had reached the River Elbe. We were ordered to stop there to await the arrival of the Red Army—an arrangement that had been agreed upon at Yalta. While we sat and waited, German civilians by the hundreds came to us from Berlin (then bracing itself for the final assault by the Russians), begging us to proceed and to take the German capital—which, everyone agreed, would surrender to us, if not with pleasure, then certainly in preference to surrender to the Russians, whose widespread reputation for rape, murder, and other incivilities was well founded. Alas, there was no way: we had our orders. But when the Soviets finally did arrive on the east bank of the Elbe, around May 1, our commanding general ordered me and my driver to cross the river and to invite the commanding general of the Cossack Cavalry Division to have dinner that night at our headquarters.

We crossed the river in our jeep, on a motorized raft, and conveyed the general's invitation as instructed. Since it was still very early in the morning, I asked the Soviets if they had any objection to our driving into Berlin, which seemed to be about to surrender. They obviously thought that I was out of my mind, but wrote out a pass on a slip of paper, explaining that the pass probably wouldn't do any good. I asked my driver—a happy Chinese-American corporal from San Francisco—if he was game, and he seemed thrilled.

And so we headed east and became the first Americans to enter the German capital, several days before its official surrender. The trip, through tens of thousands of Red Army troops, tanks, German POW's, and over some fifty miles of bombed-out roads and bridges, took more than six hours—a nightmarish experience, especially once we had entered the burning and still embattled city. . . . The next morning, after we had managed, somehow, to return to our headquarters, I wrote a report to the commanding general predicting that the city could never be rebuilt. Forty years later, as one of several architects invited to design and build in West Berlin, I discovered that predicting was not my forte; for by that time, West Berlin was the most lively, the most exciting city in Western Europe—the place where all the action was in the arts, in theater, music, literature, film, and in just about everything else. I had been spectacularly wrong—but so was everyone else who saw Berlin in early May of 1945, when its buildings were burning and crashing into the streets, the Kurfürstendamm, where my grandparents used to live in a splendid apartment, was strewn with smashed German and Soviet tanks and guns, and Unter den Linden looked literally like the end of the world, and was.

· · ·

Those of us with ties to Germany had been aware for some time that there existed an anti-Nazi underground consisting of many different colorations: there was a Communist underground, about which one knew very little (it was highly disciplined, highly secretive in pursuing its own agenda, and tightly controlled by Moscow); there was a Protestant underground, whose most prominent leader was Pastor Martin Niemöller (since 1937 a prisoner in the Sachsenhausen and Dachau concentration camps, yet remarkably audible both inside and outside Nazi Germany); there was a Catholic underground, whose position was ambivalent, to say the least—the leaders of the Catholic Church seemed perfectly willing to deal with Hitler, while its more principled, younger priests and lay members were equally willing to risk arrest and worse; there was a liberal–social democratic underground, hardly organized at all and consisting basically of so-called "good Germans" of many backgrounds, who were united primarily by their loathing of Hitlerism—and who were willing, in some cases, to take great personal

May 3, 1945, Unter den Linden, Berlin. The steel-helmeted GI behind me is my Chinese-American driver, Corporal John Lee. The photo was taken by one of the Soviets, using my camera.

risks in protecting persecuted Jews, foreign slave laborers, escaped Allied prisoners of war, and others almost permanently on the run; and, finally, there was the "Establishment Underground"—a kind of upper-class family consisting of German aristocrats, their network of relatives, and their friends who found the Nazi regime equally loathsome, and who, by education, background, tradition, and conviction, subscribed to certain basic standards of decency that automatically placed them in opposition to the brutes who ran the Nazi state. These Establishmentarians ranged in conviction from extreme conservatism to liberalism and Fabian socialism; many of them belonged to what was known as the Junker class; and many of them had close ties to Britain and to other Western European nations (and to aristocratic cliques in the East as well).

Willo von Moltke's oldest brother, Count Helmuth James von Moltke, was one of the leading members of the Establishment Underground. His estate, in Kreisau, in Silesia, became the place where the Establishment Underground would meet and discuss plans for a possible takeover if and when the Nazi state began to disintegrate. Another member, as indicated earlier, was Adam von Trott zu Solz, who had been a close friend of the Russells when he studied at Oxford and lived in London in the 1930s. All through the months at Little Datchet Farm and later, the Russells would talk about Adam and his friends, and worry about his safety in wartime Berlin. And Willo, who was a very private person, would talk to me about Helmuth, and tell me of his fears for his brother's safety.

Our concerns were proven only too justified when, on July 20, 1944, an attempt was made by Colonel Count Claus Schenck von Stauffenberg to assassinate Hitler at his headquarters in East Prussia. The attempt failed and virtually all the conspirators were arrested, shot, or put on trial (and, more often than not, subsequently hanged). Helmuth von Moltke was actually under arrest already; in 1943, in his position as an expert on international law, he had received a top-secret memo, at the Nazi Foreign Office, detailing plans to round up all Jews in occupied Denmark and deport them to extermination camps in Poland. Without hesitation, Helmuth had gone to Copenhagen to warn the leaders of the Jewish community and to urge them to organize a mass exodus, by rowboat, to nearby Sweden, thus saving thousands of lives. Upon his return to Berlin, Helmuth was arrested, just as he expected to be (the top-secret memo had a limited circulation, and included his name); and when von Stauffenberg's bomb exploded, Helmuth was still being interrogated by the Gestapo.

After the 20th of July plot failed, the Gestapo rounded up all suspected conspirators—and it was found that most of them had one thing in common: they had been at Kreisau, and they knew Helmuth von Moltke. So Helmuth was put on trial for treason before a Nazi court, and hanged in February of 1945. Adam von Trott had been executed a month or two after the failed assassination attempt, and so had many others who were part of the Kreisau circle. To those of us on the Allied side who had kept in touch, however tenuously, with the situation in Germany, the assassination attempt and the subsequent massacre of the German Establishment Underground seemed to destroy all hope for a reasonable transition from Hitlerism to something acceptable, once the Nazis were defeated.

But aside from this discouraging realization, our principal concern was, of course, for those whose names had come to mean something to us—the Niemöllers, the Moltkes and Trotts, and their associates, and all the others who were now apparently being wiped out by the Gestapo. (Our concern for those who had already been shipped off to extermination camps in Eastern Europe and elsewhere was, of course, just as deep. But their fate seemed so predictable that most of us who had friends and relatives at Auschwitz and Dachau and elsewhere had long since given up all hope.)

From mid-1944 on, we watched the daily news of Allied advances toward Berlin, hoping against hope that "our" forces would somehow manage to get there in time, before Hitler had taken his revenge. Willo was stationed at Fort Knox, being trained to become an officer in a U.S. armored division; I was stationed at Camp Ritchie, being trained to be a spy. Our correspondence—full of German names and places—aroused the suspicions of the counter-intelligence censors at Ritchie (after all, here I was writing letters to and receiving letters from a bona fide von Moltke!); but, after months of snoopery, I gathered that I was cleared of whatever dark suspicions the sleuths had harbored.

Willo must have been in despair: every day the papers had more and more reports of Nazi atrocities, and of shootings and hangings of anti-Nazis caught by the Gestapo. Allied Intelligence was clearly getting desperate as well: as late as January 1945, a flight of fast RAF Mosquito bombers bombed the Berlin jail where Helmuth and others were held prisoner, in the frail hope that they might be able to escape in the ensuing turmoil; several months later, after Germany had surrendered, one of Helmuth's fellow prisoners, Fabian von Schlabrendorff, told me that the raid had almost succeeded— but not quite! Finally the news was broadcast from Berlin that Helmuth had been hanged. There was no reason to doubt the report.

A few weeks after the Nazis surrendered on May 7, 1945, my division was ordered to return to the U.S., presumably to be shipped out to the Pacific theater to join the final campaigns against Japan. The chief intelligence officer of our combat command, a feisty little cavalry major called Martin Philipsborn, was determined to stay in Europe and got himself assigned to the new U.S. headquarters in Frankfurt, to head a very hush-hush intelligence section that would produce a weekly, top-secret political intelligence review devoted to Western and Eastern Europe and addressed to the commanding officers of the U.S. Army contingents in Europe, and to the military government soon to be headquartered in West Berlin. He decided that he wanted to take me and one or two other junior officers from our division along with him to serve as his flunkies.

Martin was in fact an absolutely marvelous character. I had first met him, one dark night, in a blacked-out farmhouse in a north German village, while his headquarters were being bombarded, rather haphazardly, by a German eighty-eight. I was a fresh, inexperienced young second lieutenant straight out of Ritchie, and he was a veteran of the initial landings in North Africa and of the subsequent invasions of Normandy and Germany. I saluted smartly and reported to him, as they had told us to do at Camp Ritchie, and he looked at me with utter disdain. "Tell you what to do, Lieutenant," he said. "Dump your gear and go and find out who is firing at us, and where they're firing from!" I swallowed hard, saluted (again!), did an about-face, and marched out into the night, knowing that my end was near. "Hey you stupid ass, get back in here!" he roared. "What the hell do you think you are doing!" He didn't take me very seriously again, at least while we were in uniform.

Martin was from Chicago, a lawyer by training, educated in the U.S., in England, and at the Sorbonne. He was extraordinarily well read and extraordinarily articulate. He had been in a landing craft in the first wave of American troops to hit the beaches at Oran in

1942; and while the defending Pétain French and the Germans (as well as U.S. naval guns) were creating the usual racket, Martin was screaming into a public address system in his Sorbonne French, "*Ne tirez pas! Ne tirez pas! Nous sommes vos amis!*"—a message somehow lost in the prevailing din.

Several weeks later, after having been slightly wounded by an Italian sniper whom he had tried to capture by hand (considering Italians unfit for serious combat) and who probably mistook him for a raving maniac, Martin wrote a letter from a field hospital to a friendly editor at *The New York Times,* explaining that the Allied (and especially American) field commanders in North Africa were idiots or worse. The letter was intercepted by U.S. Army censors, and Martin, who was a lieutenant colonel at the time, was officially reprimanded, returned to the U.S., and reduced in rank to something fairly piddling. When I met him on that dark night in the German village, he was on his way back up in rank, having been promoted to major fairly recently and awarded various ribbons for bravery and sundry acts of lunacy.

This little would-be martinet, in tandem with two or three very junior graduates of Camp Ritchie, established a small editorial office in a corner of the undamaged I. G. Farben headquarters building, on the edge of what little was left of Frankfurt. There we produced our weekly intelligence analysis, a typically opinionated pamphlet pretending to "report" on what was happening in our world, but in fact concerned with telling the brass in Europe and back home at the Pentagon what we (i.e., Martin Philipsborn, Jr.) thought should be happening. I don't know who, if anyone, ever read our analysis; but I know we hugely enjoyed putting it together and imagining how many stuffed shirts would be outraged by our highly argumentative prose.

Once I had settled down in Frankfurt, I received a letter from Willo asking me to try to find Helmuth's widow, Freya, and their children. Many of the families of those whom Hitler had put to death for their part in the 20th of July attempt had been scattered by the Gestapo, as additional punishment—children separated from each other and their mothers, and so on.

Fortunately this had not been done in the case of the von Moltkes; in fact, by the time I received Willo's letter they had already been rescued from Kreisau, where they had found themselves at the end of the war. A very courageous ex-German, Gero von Schulz Gaevernitz, who had been an associate of Allen Dulles in the Office of Strategic Services (OSS) in Switzerland during the war, had driven all the way through the Russian-occupied zone of Germany and into Silesia, which was being turned over, rapidly, to the Poles. Although hundreds of thousands of German Silesians had been uprooted by the Poles and Russians and dispatched westward in cattle cars, the von Moltkes were able to hang on at Kreisau for a number of weeks; and Freya, a woman of sunny optimism and utterly without fear (and with a political past that commanded some respect from the Poles who were taking over Silesia), actually thought she might be able to continue at Kreisau forever. Von Gaevernitz, it seems, explained the grim realities of postwar East Germany to her, loaded her and her family and their essential belongings into his truck, and drove them to Berlin—which by then was under Four Power control and more or less undivided.

As soon as I heard that Freya had made it to Berlin, I took the Allied train through the Russian zone and met her and von Gaevernitz in West Berlin. She was remarkably composed, and determined to stay and help some of the survivors of the 20th of July who were in worse shape than she. This was incredibly difficult: there were no normal methods of communication, no postal services, no telephone or telegraph service, no trains, cars, or planes available to Germans; there were no banks (and no money, food, or clothing); in short, the only way of finding out where any of the survivors had ended up after the Nazi surrender was by word of mouth—and Freya felt that she had to remain in Berlin, where her friends and relatives might be able to locate her, and to serve as a kind of information center for those who were trying to reconstruct their shattered lives.

Unfortunately, the Soviet NKVD (later KGB) was highly suspicious of the 20th of July survivors, since most of them were left/liberal and pro-Western rather than Communist and pro-Soviet in orientation. It was quite common for former German resistance people to be kidnapped by the NKVD and taken to East Berlin or East Germany, where they might disappear without a trace. (Some who resurfaced after many months told horror stories of having been interrogated around the clock in NKVD prisons and threatened with permanent imprisonment in gulags, or worse, unless they were willing to work for the Soviets and against the Western Allies.) All of us were aware of this, and I was greatly concerned about Freya's safety in Berlin, since the NKVD seemed to be especially interested in pursuing 20th of July survivors.

Since there was no way for Freya and her children to take a train from West Berlin to Frankfurt without having her papers checked and being intercepted by NKVD officers as the train passed through the Russian Zone, we decided to get her to Frankfurt by plane. One of Freya's brothers lived near Frankfurt with his family, in a lovely little farmhouse, and he wanted Freya to join him. The only problem was that German nationals had no access to air transport, which was limited to Allied air force planes. The only way to fly Freya out of Berlin, I discovered, was for me to have her and her children arrested and taken under guard to U.S. Headquarters in Frankfurt "for interrogation." Which is what I did.

It turned out that this was a highly effective way of moving both friends and foes around Europe with relative ease. There was no regular transport available to civilians in occupied Germany until about the middle of 1946, and even then the available transport was extremely primitive. But as an intelligence officer, with all sorts of impressive documents authorizing me to do almost anything outrageous that I wanted to do—and no questions asked—I found it quite easy to move friendly as well as unfriendly civilians around Western Europe by simply placing them under arrest and then releasing them once they had arrived at their destination. On one occasion, when I moved the Norwegian wife and daughter of a very bright German anti-Nazi professor from Oslo to Frankfurt (they had been separated in the final chaotic weeks of the war), the U.S. military attaché in Oslo responded to my request for the mother's and daughter's arrest by wiring that he would indeed comply, and that "Interrogation of Rande Anete Hartner should prove highly illuminating since she is six months old. [Signed] Gerald Pierce, Colonel, U.S. Army."

Meanwhile, Gero von Gaevernitz and I had become very friendly. In the final days of the war, he had located and liberated a number of prominent anti-Nazi Europeans who were being marched by SS guards from one concentration camp to the next, always a few hours ahead of the Allied advance. After the Nazi surrender, Gero was assigned to serve as a kind of godfather to this remarkable group of people, and he commandeered a mansion near Frankfurt to house the former prisoners and whatever relatives and survivors of the anti-Nazi resistance he was able to round up.

It was about time for Gero to return to civilian life, and he suggested to my commanding officer that I should be assigned to helping take care of his wards, and to exploring ways of using their personal and political contacts with "reliable" Germans in Eastern Europe to our intelligence advantage. So I was loaned to the OSS and given some complex assignment that involved smuggling "reliable" Germans with good connections in East Germany across the border, and then picking them up, several weeks later, and "debriefing" them to find out what they had observed on the other side of the Iron Curtain. It was one of those cops-and-robbers enterprises that U.S. Intelligence loved to engage in and that, by and large, produced no information of any importance to anyone—and certainly no information that could not be obtained more easily from newspaper stories, radio intercepts, and other readily available sources.

It was, however, an interesting assignment; and since nobody seemed to be able to check whether the information gathered by me and my "agents" was accurate, the operation continued until I was finally sent back to the U.S. and to civilian life in the middle of 1947. The thirty months or so that I had spent in Western Europe had covered a range of human experience that most people would not expect to encounter in a lifetime: the brutality of war and of the final disintegration of the Nazi state; the misery of starving and homeless displaced persons and of German civilians; the hideousness of the Red Army's rape of defenseless Germans; the decency and resilience of the small band of survivors of the anti-Nazi German Resistance; the gradual revival of a shattered nation and its people; the ignorance of some of our military governors and their utter naïveté, especially in their dealings with the Soviets and their German fellow travelers; and, most of all, the basic decency of many very ordinary and not very sophisticated people, in and out of uniform, who seemed totally baffled by the chaotic aftermath of this terrible war, but responded by and large with much generosity and kindness.

The three of us—Van Eyck, Harnden, and myself, all forenamed Peter, and hence known to each other by our surnames—remained friends for many years.

Van Eyck married the beautiful Inge in Berlin, where he had been sent once the city had come under Four Power control. He had stayed on as a Military Government officer to rebuild the West

Berlin film industry, using cartons of Camel cigarettes (supplied by Hollywood friends and worth a fortune on the black market) to rebuild film studios, reequip the crews, and pay actors and actresses. (Military Government had no budget for such unimportant endeavors.) After 1947, he left the Army and he and his new wife went to live in Hollywood, where the demand for super-Aryan, German-accented actors was minimal. By the end of the decade, the Van Eycks returned to Europe and bought themselves that splendid *anständigen Herrensitz* on the Swiss side of Lake Constance. His acting career flourished—he was a huge success in roles that seemed precisely tailored to his looks, accent, manners, and bearing. He played leading parts in *Wages of Fear,* in *The Spy Who Came In from the Cold,* in *Five Graves to Cairo,* and in dozens of other films, speaking German, French, and English interchangeably and sounding roughly the same in all those languages. He died in Zurich in July of 1969, of too much fast living, barely fifty-six years old, much too young, a very dashing gent to the end.

Harnden joined Military Government in Munich and designed and built exhibitions for something called the Information Control Division. Shortly after the war, he had met a White Russian princess called Marie ("Missie") Vassiltchikov, who had somehow landed in Berlin at the beginning of the war and worked as a translator in the German Foreign Office, with such anti-Nazi activists as Adam von Trott zu Solz and Helmuth James von Moltke. Harnden and Missie got married and moved to Paris, where he became the leading designer of stationary and traveling exhibits for the Marshall Plan organization. In the early 1950s, Harnden asked me to join him in Paris to work with him in his design studio; I was sorely tempted, but in the end, for family reasons, found it impossible to leave New York.

Missie Vassiltchikov and Peter Harnden sunbathing near Munich, ca. 1947.

Peter and Missie, both of whom spoke flawless French, loved Paris, but found the French unbearably xenophobic; and, so, in the late 1950s they moved to Spain, establishing a highly successful architectural office in Barcelona and building a beautiful house for themselves in Cadaques, on the Costa Brava. They lived splendidly with their three children and many friends, and I saw much of them in Paris, New York, Barcelona, and Cadaques—spending one deliciously happy summer there with my own children. Peter died in Barcelona in 1971 of lung cancer, having been a heavy smoker most of his life. Missie then moved to London, where she died of leukemia in 1978. It is hard to write down these facts and figures:

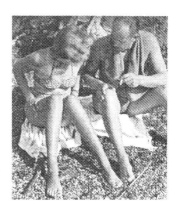

Missie and Peter transformed the lives of those who loved them, and whom they loved, in ways not many people can or do.

In 1985, Missie's brother, Prince George ("Georgie") Vassiltchikov published her diaries under the title of *Berlin Diaries, 1940–1945*. We had always known these diaries existed, and Peter often teased Missie about them, feeling, I suspect, that they were a part of Missie's *verboten* German past! When Georgie finally published them, they were a huge success, in the U.S. and wherever they appeared in print. I was not surprised—Missie was a person of enormous intelligence, education, charm, wit, and style. She spoke half a dozen languages fluently (as did Peter, whose father had been a U.S. Foreign Service officer), and her story dovetails in many ways with mine.

Two or three aspects of Missie's diaries have struck me as remarkable: first, the fact that there seems to have existed a sort of Aristocratic Underground, worldwide, whose members managed to keep in close touch with each other regardless of bombings, invasions, absence of normal communications, or of any other disruption or disasters that inconvenienced normal human beings. If Prince A. in London had the flu, Missie, in bombed-out Berlin, knew exactly what his temperature had been the previous night; if the Duchess of B., temporarily staying with Countess C. in New York, had a baby, Missie would know its name, sex, and weight at birth—within days. And so on. No Allied or Axis intelligence service was as well informed as the Aristocratic Underground, and none of us were as efficient.

Second, there was Missie's extraordinary, insouciant noblesse: this beautiful, sophisticated young princess, making do in a menial job and in constantly shifting, bombed-out quarters, had the world at her feet, at all times: when her Foreign Office section in Berlin was evacuated to escape the bombings, she traveled in hideously crowded cattle cars to her safe assigned destination in some rural retreat—with all her steamer trunks, of course, and her fur coats. (Young German officers could be relied upon to fall all over themselves to assist Missie with those steamer trunks.) I can see it all: her beauty, her charm, her seeming innocence, and her assumption that there was no reason to dispense with the niceties of life just because there was a silly war on. Less understandable, to me, is the fact that her diaries hardly mention the concentration camps and their Jewish victims at all; perhaps she assumed that everyone knew, or she recoiled from the subject—or perhaps, in those elegant circles in which she traveled, one tried to put those distasteful matters out of mind.

What does come across in her diaries is her enormous humanity. She may have been a congenital snob (although I doubt it); but, to Missie, every human being, however lowly by the standards of a century or two ago, was her brother or her sister—unless that person's own actions toward fellow humans were contemptible. She was a very worldly, very sophisticated saint; and Peter Harnden, that slick smoothie, only barely deserved her.

Willo von Moltke joined me briefly in Frankfurt, in U.S. Army Intelligence, after the war was over. I had managed to get him assigned to a slot in the G-2 Division of U.S. Headquarters, European Theater; but when he finally got to Germany, some airheads in Counterintelligence decided that a "von Moltke" (even in a U.S. Army officer's uniform) had to be a Nazi spy—and so he had to return to the U.S. after a few months in Frankfurt. Still, he had managed to see Freya and other friends and relatives, and I would see him again, shortly, upon my own return to the U.S.

Once he was out of the Army, Willo went back to architecture—first working for Eero Saarinen in Bloomfield Hills, Michigan; then taking a job with Edmund Bacon, in the Philadelphia City Planning Commission, probably the most effective and creative public agency of its kind in the U.S. In 1964 he returned to Harvard, where he had studied and where he continued to have many friends. While José Lluis Sert was the dean of the Graduate School of Design, Willo organized an Urban Design Program and headed it for many years, until his semiretirement in 1977. He died in 1987, in the middle of August. I was in Berlin at the time and heard of his death only upon my return at the end of the month. He was seventy-six years old. I wrote to his widow, the concert pianist Veronica Jochum, but there was nothing to say.

Except perhaps this: Willo was an extraordinarily talented designer, a draftsman with such a sensitivity and delicacy of line and touch that I always wondered why he insisted upon getting involved in administrative efforts—running a section of a planning commission, heading up an academic program, and so on. He was so sensitive to aesthetic as well as humanistic concerns that I simply could not understand why he wanted to waste his time on matters so far removed from architecture. One day, in the 1970s, Lou Kahn and I were talking about the work of a rather mediocre architect who had, however, done one very excellent Defense Housing Project in the early 1940s. Lou couldn't figure out how that little group of buildings had come out of that man's office. "Oh, you know, Willo was working in that office when that was done, and he was in charge," I said to Lou. "Well, that explains it," Lou said. "Why in God's name is Willo wasting his time being an academic? He is much too good for that!"

The answer, I think, was that Willo really loved teaching. To him this was easily as creative an effort as designing buildings—and he was so gentle and thoughtful and patient at it that no one ever subjected to his guidance was likely to forget it.

Martin Philipsborn went back to Chicago to work on projects having to do with his family's business and his various interests in law and in history. Somehow, he never became quite reconciled to civilian life. I saw him in New York, in Chicago, and elsewhere, and—out of uniform and into a Savile Row suit—he was mellow and happily married and a little unfocused: he was very wise, and full of good advice, and full of reminiscences. I grew fonder of him each time I saw him, and he became my son's godfather. And then, he decided in 1977 to join a proper law firm in Chicago, as if he had finally decided what he wanted to do, now that he was all grown up. And then he suddenly dropped dead, much too early and much too unfulfilled.

And so it went. Fabian von Schlabrendorff, that gentle soul who was one of the bravest of the German Resistance, and became my chief contact in the Establishment Underground when I was told to play "Cops and Robbers" for the OSS, ended up on the West German Supreme Court, and died in the 1970s. So did Gero von Gaevernitz and numerous others who were really much too young, and much too bright, to pass from the scene.

I sometimes think that we lived so intensely during those few years in the 1940s that many of us were worn out before our time. When we went home from the war, most of us were still in our twenties—and many of us actually went back to school and studied in classrooms we shared with mere children, and under professors younger than we were. Many of us had lived so passionately, so intensely, and, I suppose, so dangerously during our four or five years in uniform that we were more than a little worn out; and after a few years it began to show.

CHAPTER NINE

In the summer of 1947, I came back to New York from overseas, having spent some four years in the U.S. Army—most of them in Europe. Like many ex-GI's, I now faced two problems: first, how to find a job; and second, how to finish my education, interrupted when I was drafted in 1943.

The problem of finding a job turned out to be rather more difficult than I had expected. I called my friend Howard Myers, the *Architectural Forum*'s editor and publisher, as soon as I got off the boat and dropped by to see him the next day. He was full of enthusiasm—but there seemed to be something wrong. Finally, he came to the point: I had written several letters to him from Germany during my stint as an intelligence officer there, and some of these letters dealt with the sobering encounters I had had with our Soviet allies, both in the last weeks of the war, when my armored division was on the Elbe River, and in the months following the German surrender, when much of my work brought me in contact with various forms of Soviet oppression throughout Eastern Europe. "I showed your letters to some of the people on our editorial staff," Howard told me, "and I couldn't believe my ears—they told me that it would be 'disruptive' of staff morale if you came back, in the light of your political views!" Howard still seemed in a state of shock as he tried to explain. He was quite naïve politically and quite unaware of what many of us knew only too well, and from bitter personal experience: that the journalists' union, known as the Newspaper Guild, was—in New York, at least—under full control of Communist Party members and their fellow travelers; and that the Time Inc. chapter, in which several of the top *Forum* editors were extremely active, was notorious for its rigid adherence to the party line. Not until a couple of years later, after some bloody internal battles, did the membership of the Newspaper Guild overturn its Stalinist leadership.

For the present, however, I thought it would be unwise for Howard to insist that a returning veteran (i.e., myself) was morally or legally entitled to claim his earlier civilian job. To solve the problem, Howard came up with an extraordinarily generous suggestion: he believed it would be useful for the *Forum* to conduct a series of surveys of key American cities, and to find out what, if anything, the public and private sectors in those cities were planning to build for the bright new postwar world. It would be difficult, Howard thought, to spare a regular staff member to conduct these on-the-spot surveys, and he wondered if my wife and I would mind spending the next few months traveling around the country, meeting with the key urban activists in each city—architects, planners, developers, public officials, and so on—and reporting back to him on what we found.

Needless to say, we agreed that it was a splendid idea. I, for one, had never seen much of the U.S. outside the Northeast (and one or two depressing military training centers usually located in the midst of some improbable swamp). It never occurred to either one of us that Howard could have undertaken a much less costly and much more perceptive survey by simply writing a few dozen letters to his numerous friends around the country; and it never occurred to me that he was doing us an enormously generous favor. We accepted the assignment with enthusiasm and packed our bags.

The second problem of many returning veterans—how to continue and complete their interrupted education—was thus put aside for the present. It was difficult enough to find openings in any school of architecture—least of all, one that one respected. And so I decided to postpone my educational plans for the time being.

Our first stop was Chicago. Among the people I had got to know in postwar Germany were several old friends and acquaintances of

Ludwig Mies van der Rohe, who had left Germany in 1936 and settled in Chicago as head of the school of architecture at the Armour Institute. (It was later renamed the Illinois Institute of Technology, or IIT.) In his capacity as head of the school, Mies had been busy developing an extremely rigorous, highly disciplined program which trained a new generation of American architects in a clear language of steel, glass, brick, light, space, and refinement of proportion and detail. The buildings just beginning to emerge from this school, and from Mies's own architectural office, had a purity of space and form reminiscent of the polished sculptures of Constantin Brancusi; and they revealed an almost religious dedication to structural order and material perfection.

Mies's work at this time was known to most of us only from photographs of some of his early work in Europe—especially his 1928 Barcelona Pavilion and his 1930 Tugendhat House, in Brno, Czechoslovakia—and from the few exquisite pieces of furniture that had somehow made their way to the U.S., to be reproduced by the manufacturer Hans Knoll. We also knew several of his projects then on his drawing boards—the steel-and-glass Farnsworth House and the IIT campus buildings—but that was about all.

I met James Speyer and one or two of the other young men who worked for Mies in those days, and who treated him as if he were some sort of deity, to be shielded from the intrusive outside world. I asked if I might meet Mies, and after considerable consultation back and forth among the bodyguards, I was told that I might see him after dinner, at nine that evening. "But don't stay longer than an hour," the bodyguards said; "he gets tired very quickly!" We rang the bell of Mies's apartment, in an old building on East Pearson Street, at 9 P.M. sharp, and the door flew open—and there he was, jolly, massive, and beaming from ear to ear. Unlike some of his bodyguards, Mies was very fond of women, and clearly took an immediate liking to my wife, Martha, who looked rather like a Lehmbruck statue. He ushered us in, offered us drinks, and made us feel thoroughly at home. Since his command of the English language was rather tentative (and remained so for the rest of his life), the fact that I spoke German helped establish an almost instant rapport.

We talked about his German friends—I told him about Frau von Schnitzler, the wife of the former (and now imprisoned) head of I. G. Farben, who was living in a fairly modest but still elegant apartment in Frankfurt. "She was trying to prove to me how badly she and her husband had suffered under the Nazis," I told Mies.

Mies van der Rohe, ca. 1965, admiring a sculpture of himself by his friend Hugo Weber. (Courtesy, Hugo Weber)

"She told me that every time von Ribbentrop came for dinner, they had to hide their Picassos in the basement!" Mies roared. He took us on a tour of his apartment—an extraordinary collection of stately, high-ceilinged, and virtually empty rooms, with white walls punctuated by Mies's impressive collection of paintings—mostly by Paul Klee. "When that man Hitchcock came to see me," Mies said (referring to the historian Henry-Russell Hitchcock), "he was astounded that I had these Klees—he thought I'd have nothing but Mondrians! Some critics don't know how to use their eyes."

Mies was in absolutely spectacular form that night, and we didn't leave his apartment until 3 A.M.—he wouldn't let us go. But though we were quite close over the subsequent twenty years or so, until his death in 1968 (as close as our considerable age difference would permit), he was never again so voluble, not even in German. One reason, I think, was that we didn't talk about his own work at all that first night. I asked him what he was working on at the moment and he said: "Come to the office after lunch tomorrow. I'll show you." In all the years I knew him, Mies hardly ever talked about his own work; he seemed to feel that it would and should speak for itself. It did.

His office was as austere as his apartment. In one of the rooms, toward the rear of the large, white loft space, there was a beautiful scale model of one of his proposed buildings for IIT, set on a large table. Mies sat down in a chair of just the right height to bring his own eyes to the eye level of the scale model before him. The rest of us stood around watching him. He was puffing away at a big, black cigar, saying nothing. Every now and then, as he pointed and grunted in what appeared to be English, one of his assistants would move a wall, or a platform, or a piece of furniture in the scale model this way or that until he nodded, satisfied. It was very quiet. When he was done, he got up and said "Good" and grinned, and we left. The assistants would take over and translate Mies's changes into detailed working drawings and specifications.

In those years, the modern movement in design in Chicago had two centers: Mies's school, and the Institute of Design, a school patterned after the Weimar and Dessau Bauhaus, and established in 1937 by the ex–Bauhaus master Laszlo Moholy-Nagy. Moholy had attracted some of the best young European and American designers to teach at his institute and almost at once began to develop some extraordinary talent among his students. He had managed to get the support of such local patrons of the arts as Walter Paepcke, president of the Container Corporation of America, who saw the potential value of the visual arts to American business and industry. When Moholy died in 1946, my former teacher Serge Chermayeff was appointed to the directorship of the institute; and I went to see him shortly after arriving in Chicago.

The Institute of Design was located in a marvelous old Victorian armory on North Dearborn Street, on the near North Side. Among those who taught there were Konrad Wachsmann, the German-born technocrat who had joined Walter Gropius in 1941 to develop the General Panel prefab housing system in southern California; and Richard Buckminster Fuller, the developer of the Dymaxion House (and other futuristic gadgetry) in the 1920s and 1930s.

Bucky, who lectured at the institute sporadically, happened to be in town. "He is living in a trailer, on a parking lot in the Loop," Serge said. "He seems to be conducting some kind of experiment on himself." Since neither the trailer nor its parking lot had a telephone, Bucky was generally unreachable. "He usually turns up after lunch," Serge said. "Why don't you wait for him, if you want to meet him."

It was Saturday, and there were not many students or teachers in evidence. Bucky's studio was a drafting room located in the basement of the armory, and that is where I waited. After a while, Serge appeared, with Bucky in tow. I had never met Bucky in my life, but he started talking—bubbling over—as if he and I had been interrupted in the middle of a sentence about ten minutes earlier. "What I have just discovered is that bebop has the same beat as the new mathematical shorthand I have been working on," he said, and jumped on top of one of the drafting tables lined up in the studio. "It goes like this," he said, snapping his fingers and tapping his feet—while calling out an incomprehensible sequence of numbers, something like "five, nine, seventeen, twenty-nine, fifty-three. . . ." I was totally mystified and utterly charmed. It happened that I had taken some courses in pure and applied mathematics, and I thought I knew a little about numbers. "You see what I mean, don't you, dear boy," Bucky called out, over the drumbeat of his tapping toes. I just stood there, openmouthed, not believing my eyes or ears. He was obviously quite mad, and utterly disarming. I didn't know then that he called everyone "dear boy" or "dear girl" from Day One, and that I would be one of his tens of thousands of Dear Children for the rest of his life—some thirty years during which our paths would cross in many parts of the world, and under some circumstances even more bizarre than the ones I was experiencing that Saturday afternoon.

When Bucky finally jumped off that drafting table, I asked him what he was doing with his students currently. It turned out that he was asking them to look into the kinds of resources they absolutely needed for survival—what kinds of furniture, what kinds of equipment, what kinds of clothes, what kinds of tools to obtain food and shelter if they were suddenly forced to leave the city forever and establish a new life somewhere out in the middle of nowhere. "And I am asking them, first of all, to select all this equipment, to measure and weigh it, to find out how much it costs; and then I am asking them to figure out how they will be able to transport it to some new location—how big a truck they will need, how they will load and unload this truck, how they might redesign a typical truck to double as a shelter, how they might use the truck's engine to generate electricity for their new locations." We were talking at a time when people still thought that survival in a nuclear holocaust was a possibility; Bucky's theoretical project was not entirely farfetched. He had to get back to his trailer before I could ask him what he hoped to accomplish with that mathematical shorthand—or for that matter with his newly acquired skills as a bebopper.

Konrad Wachsmann was quite different—reserved (or, perhaps, courtly), short, Germanic, and intense. His thick accent was made even more incomprehensible by what seemed to be some sort of chronic adenoidal congestion. He was a single-minded technocrat—he had invented the most beautiful, most complex, and probably most impractical prefabrication system created in this century when he designed the prefab General Panel housing kit in collaboration with Walter Gropius during the early years of the war. It employed a steel connector that resembled an intricate Chinese puzzle, and probably made not the slightest sense to a typical American carpenter used to framing houses with two-by-fours and two-by-eights and tenpenny nails.

Wachsmann believed in his rarefied, advanced-technology systems with the fervor of a religious fanatic; and he was now involved in the design of a new structural system, which would consist of hollow tubes twisted into some sort of hairpin configuration, and attachable to each other to form dazzling space frames extended into infinity. I was immediately taken by the exquisite drawings produced by Konrad and his students, and he presented me with a lovely blowup of one of those diagrammatic projections into infinity. Although we became good friends (he was much wittier, much more relaxed upon closer acquaintance), I was never able to get him to explain what possible uses this structural system might possess, or to what purpose it might be applied.

These three—Mies, Bucky, and Konrad Wachsmann—could hardly have been more different in the way they related to the world: Mies, the somewhat enigmatic deity worshiped largely from afar by a coterie of admirers who did not really understand him, largely because his command of the English language was not up to establishing close personal friendships. Bucky, the extrovert, bubbling over with enthusiasms and selling his snake oil to growing hordes of believers totally mesmerized by his cosmic visions. And Konrad Wachsmann, the introverted technologist, a very private person, single-minded in his pursuit of narrow and highly disciplined objectives. What did they have in common?

For one thing, of course, all three of them took the world and its obvious problems very seriously indeed. Unlike the current crop of postmodern poseurs, whose false fronts seem to pass for architecture, these men felt that architecture in a chaotic, overpopulated, self-destructive world must in some way contribute to the survival of mankind. All three believed that advanced technologies offered some of the answers; in any case, all three were determined to find out. Mies was content to stretch existing technologies to their currently acceptable limits (he was after all, the only one of these three who actually built things—so he did not enjoy the luxury of fantasizing); Konrad believed that certain technologies—those that involved new structural systems and new methods of prefabrication—could be stretched beyond their current limits; and Bucky believed in a future so far distant that he could afford to dream about it, and no one (in his lifetime, anyway) could ever prove him wrong.

The second thing these three had in common was that they never talked about "art" when they spoke of their own work. Although Mies's buildings were breathtakingly beautiful, and established a standard for minimalist architecture that has rarely been matched to date, he spoke only of technology and of "economic considerations," "rationalization," and "standardization of construction"—on the few occasions when he said anything at all. Bucky designed and built some lovely structures: his Dymaxion House, and some of his later geodesic domes, were delicate, translucent, shimmering—like flowers imagined by a computer. But Bucky absolutely refused to discuss them as works of art. Only Konrad, who may have been the most romantic of these three, reveled in the beauty of his structures and in the incredible delicacy of the drawings that preceded them. Yet even he talked only of rational concepts and of technological breakthroughs—at least in public.

The third characteristic these men had in common was boundless optimism. Despite many disappointments—especially in the case of Bucky and Konrad Wachsmann—they seemed absolutely certain that the future was theirs and that it was, moreover, just around the corner. Obviously, the cold logic of the industrial age was about to produce technological breakthroughs that could occur only by way of modular standardization of building components (and of entire buildings); obviously, too, the cold logic of population pressures and attendant urbanization was about to produce radiant cities of gleaming towers, spaced far apart and linked by high-speed transportation systems. (Actually, it was Le Corbusier who had most clearly spelled out those visions in his various Villes Radieuses starting with sketches from 1922 on; but Mies had brought his old cronies Ludwig Hilberseimer, or "Hilbs," and Walter Peterhans to Chicago with him, and their visions of the City of the Future were even more glittering and more scary than those of Le Corbusier.) And obviously—at least to Buckminster Fuller—the natural resources of what he later called "Planet Earth" had to be reordered and redistributed to avoid the unthinkable—i.e., starvation, genocide, and mankind's final war.

All of these notions suggested, or at least implied, the establishment of a planned society. But while Mies had briefly flirted with socialism in the early 1920s, neither he nor Bucky nor Konrad Wachsmann seemed to have any special interest in radical politics when I met them in the years after the war. Still, it seemed clear to

Detail of Mies van der Rohe's Crown Hall, at the Illinois Institute of Technology, Chicago, ca. 1952. (Hedrich-Blessing)

me that they assumed, without ever bothering to pursue the notion, that some sort of planned society would have to be established to solve the monumental problems of population growth, urbanization, and redistribution of the earth's resources. The fact that there seemed not the slightest intention in America to establish a planned society in the traditional Marxist sense, didn't seem to have been noticed by any of them, or by any of the other avant-garde architects and planners demanding to be heard. Yet clearly the fact that American free enterprise, with its dedication to unfettered chaos, was in no immediate danger of overthrow would profoundly challenge many of the basic assumptions made by the avant-gardists.

For example, it would become clear that unplanned, chaotic free-enterprise competition was infinitely more productive than planned order of the sort implied or assumed by the avant-garde; that it would produce a kind of cityscape—colorful, varied, chaotic, without any semblance of order—that might be infinitely more stimulating than the deadly visions of Ideal Cities drawn up, painstakingly and humorlessly, by the bureaucratic Hilbs and his driven disciples; and that unfettered competition, in housing and in all other forms of construction, might well produce qualitative advances in areas that really mattered to ordinary people (for exam-

Ludwig Hilberseimer's proposal, ca. 1928, for an Ideal City project to be built in Berlin.

ple, efficient kitchens, sleek bathrooms, compact laundries), and that would outpace anything and everything produced by single-minded socialist planners.

And it would further become clear that a democratic, egalitarian society—as opposed to an elitist, authoritarian order—might produce a very different urban and suburban image of itself than that imagined and built by the kings of France and Prussia and the princes and dukes of Italy; that an ordered society—however rational, however logical, however seemingly productive of a more humane environment—was hardly expressive of the kind of chaotic, creative anarchy represented by American capitalism.

None of this, I suspect, ever occurred to the leaders of the postwar avant-garde—at least not until the 1960s, when such ideas began to surface in the writings of Jane Jacobs and Robert Venturi. It certainly did not occur to me until I had been exposed to their ideas.

Chandni-Chawk, Delhi's "Main Street." Lewis Mumford once observed that "Life is really more interesting than Utopia."

You cannot become an American architect without spending a great deal of time in Chicago. It is, after all, the city of Burnham,

Root, Louis Sullivan, Dankmar Adler, Frank Lloyd Wright, and many more. It is the city which, more than any other, invented the skyscraper. Mies was fortunate to have been invited to come to Chicago (rather than, let us say, Los Angeles or Philadelphia). Chicago was where the action had been in American architecture for more than half a century before Mies arrived, and it was quite clear that he instantly fell into step with Chicago's traditions and its energy and momentum.

I spent as much time as I could, during this first visit, looking at all those stunning monuments to American capitalism that I had known only from the books of Sigfried Giedion and of one or two others. It is almost impossible not to be shaken by the rugged massiveness of Burnham & Root's Monadnock Block, or by the brutality of Adler & Sullivan's Auditorium Building. These and many others—those gloomy monuments to unfettered free enterprise—were enough to send shivers down your spine. Wright's buildings, on the other hand, were entirely suburban: houses, almost exclusively, plus that extraordinarily "modern," articulated building, his 1906 Unity Temple in Oak Park—a building that antedates Mondrian and Rietveld by a dozen years or more and contains many of Mondrian's and Rietveld's decorative motifs in its skylights and its lighting fixtures; and that has a plan as clearly expressive of the function as any produced by later Constructivists or Functionalists when they built their so-called "binuclear" structures.

All this was enormously exciting. But, in addition, there were a number of younger people who were beginning to make their mark: Harry Weese, a tremendously talented young architect, whom I had met earlier when he was still in the Navy, and who had studied under Alvar Aalto at MIT; Bertrand Goldberg, who had been one of the few Americans at the Bauhaus in its final days before it was closed down under Nazi pressure; and James Prestini, a sculptor who was doing research for Mies in connection with the master plan for the new IIT campus.

Of these three, Pres was, in some respects, the most fascinating. He was more Miesian than Mies himself—just as laconic and inarticulate as Mies, and even more disciplined in his way of living and working.

During the week, Pres would make his rounds, interviewing the various faculty members at Armour Institute to find out exactly what they would need in terms of new research and teaching facilities in the building that Mies was designing for them. (After all the research was done, Mies simply gave the faculty and students great big "universal" loft spaces that could in theory be divided up in any way that the occupants found convenient. Since "function"—especially future function—was inherently unpredictable, "form" clearly couldn't be anything but amorphous. . . . So much for that!)

But on weekends, Pres did his own work. He lived alone in a small apartment, in which he had painted the walls, floors, and ceilings pure white. Each surface had been given successive coats of flat enamel, which Pres would then, after it had dried, sand down to the thinness of a hard film, ready to receive another coat of the same treatment.

After he had done his weekend's stint of painting—one wall would take up one Saturday morning, roughly—he would go to his favorite lumberyard to pick out a very special block of walnut or maple or African mahogany; and he would then withdraw to his workshop to transform those blocks of wood into paper-thin bowls of absolutely breathtaking beauty. They would be milled into something close to seashells in translucency, and into forms of the most delicate purity, their rims razor-sharp and their balance as tenuous as that of an eggshell. I confess that few things leave me colder than bowls—wooden, porcelain, or clay—but these simple works of Prestini's were on a par with Brancusi's *Birds in Space.* Like Mies, Pres pursued a single theme, single-mindedly, over and over, year in, year out. Only when he thought he had made *the* perfect bowl, and could not possibly make anything more beautiful, did he turn to something else. By that time, IIT was built and Pres was asked to teach at Berkeley. What did he teach? I could never find out, because he was about as communicative as Marlon Brando in one of his more loquacious roles. I suppose he taught Zen Buddhism or possibly mathematics.

At infrequent intervals, Pres would get married, or almost married, but nothing much ever came of it; I suspect he was impossible to live with.

After Chicago there was Boston, Detroit, St. Louis, San Francisco, Los Angeles, and Houston. I met Gropius, who had helped me get into Serge Chermayeff's London office as an apprentice when I started out after finishing school in England; I met Giedion, who was teaching at Harvard, and some of the people who taught at MIT. I met Yamasaki and Eero Saarinen in Detroit, William Wilson Wurster and Gardner Dailey and Robert Anshen and Harwell Harris in San Francisco; and I saw Houston when it was not much more than a single paved main street next to a Mexican ghetto, plus a gold-plated one known as River Oaks, where the superrich lived protected by their own private police force and their own private fire brigade. Finally, there was Los Angeles, with its cardboard architecture and synthetic weather, where Richard Neutra played king, and where Charles and Ray Eames, and John Entenza, and Raphael Soriano, and Rudolph Schindler, and one or two others were revving up to change the world.

What changes did they have in mind? The most interesting fact about the postwar situation in the U.S. and elsewhere was that there was a solid consensus about what architects and planners had to do.

Clearly, we had to rebuild our cities and our countrysides. In bombed-out Western Europe and parts of Japan, the need was desperate—and the only way to meet it (or so it seemed) was to mass-produce buildings, which meant, of course, developing certain standardized norms that would inevitably produce repetitive patterns of the sort that had long characterized other forms of mass production—for example, automobiles, trailers, even bricks and concrete blocks.

It seemed perfectly obvious to everyone concerned with designing and building for the postwar world—with its impending population explosions, and its desperate and predictable need for the larger urban centers—that the new architecture would have to be modular and machinelike in appearance; it also seemed obvious that this modular, repetitive look would be expressive of certain modular, repetitive structural and mechanical systems, as well as systems of cladding, fenestration, or other forms of enclosure; and so there was almost complete agreement that the eclectic styles of the previous hundred years or so were not merely out of fashion—they were also inappropriate to an architecture of a new, advanced industrial era. In short, the new look that began to appear in all industrialized nations, in every part of the globe, was no arbitrary, stylistic fad (as so many historians and academic critics, who may not understand the imperatives of building, tend to claim nowadays); it was the direct outcome of what all of us felt were the needs of our time and of our predictable future.

While the need for industrialization was at the center of our concerns, this led to a series of equally compelling, equally logical convictions. For example, industrialization of the sort we felt was central to all of our work implied a high degree of planning—which, in turn, meant some form of socialist order.

Very few of my friends—after the Berlin airlift, the takeover of Czechoslovakia, and the total subjugation of Eastern Europe—retained any illusions about the Soviet Union. But we did believe that a modified socialist system—a kind of social-democratic society patterned after that of Sweden, for example—was a prerequisite to the kind of planning that the postwar world seemed to demand.

And we believed in modern architecture—by which we meant something akin to the work done in the years between the World Wars in Germany, Switzerland, France, Holland, and elsewhere—as inherently democratic and certainly antifascist. It is often forgotten nowadays that the style of Hitler and of Stalin was a kind of souped-up neoclassicism—very similar to what is currently being touted by some exterior decorators around the world; and that even Mussolini's tolerance of modern architecture was brief: the final years of his empire were characterized by a stripped-down, slicked-up neoclassicism not unlike the facade-pastiche currently peddled by some postmodernists. To those of us who saw a direct connection between the flight of such people as Mies, Gropius, Marcel Breuer, Erich Mendelsohn, Laszlo Moholy-Nagy, and others, and the growth of the Modern Movement in the democratic world, there was simply no issue at all: modern architecture spoke the language of a free, social-democratic society deeply concerned with the real problems of the postwar years. Neoclassical architecture, on the other hand, spoke the language of elitism and totalitarianism.

CHAPTER TEN

■ That fall, after getting back from our scouting trip for Howard Myers, Martha and I spent a weekend in Easthampton and were asked to a cocktail party at Mary Callery's, a sculptress who had rented a house on eastern Long Island that year. She was a close friend of Mies van der Rohe, and though I didn't consider her work especially interesting, I gathered that she herself was. In any case, we went and there met Philip Johnson, who was then about forty years old but had only recently received his degree in architecture from the Harvard Graduate School of Design.

Although he had only built a couple of houses at the time—including a remarkable, very Miesian courthouse for himself, in Cambridge, Massachusetts, which turned out to be his thesis work, leading to his degree—Philip had already made something of a name for himself in several interesting areas.

He had, for one thing, been very deeply involved with people like Lawrence Dennis, who (according to Alan Brinkley) "hoped to begin the work of building an American fascist movement." In 1934, Philip, his friend Alan Blackburn (of the staff of the fledgling Museum of Modern Art), and Dennis went to visit Huey Long to "study" Long's methods. "Huey Long took one look at this bunch of ——," Dwight Macdonald told me many years later, "and had them escorted out of his presence, across state borders." However that may be, Philip and his friends didn't give up and next "surfaced as supporters of [Father] Coughlin's Union Party; and Johnson, at least, apparently played briefly a minor role on Coughlin's staff."

I had heard a good deal about Philip's "fascist past" from Bertrand Russell and his wife, who had met him in Cambridge in the early 1940s, and from their ex-Communist friend Freda Utley, who knew him well. The Russells, while repelled by his political views, found him quite fascinating—he was the only person of such convictions who seemed to be both enormously bright and very amusing.

Although many architects were aware of Philip's "fascist past," they knew him best as *the* American disciple of Mies van der Rohe. Philip had admired Mies's work from his very first encounters with it in Germany in the 1920s. He had been largely instrumental in getting Mies to come to the U.S. in the 1930s—helping him get a major commission to design a house for the Stanley Resors (which was never built, but was widely publicized and very influential in the development of modern American architecture); and helping him, too, to obtain the directorship of the school of architecture at Armour Institute in 1938. Philip had always gone out of his way to pay homage to Mies and to acknowledge his personal debt to him in the development of his own projects and early houses. And, finally, it was Philip Johnson, more than anyone else, who saw to it that the Museum of Modern Art gave Mies a stunning one-man show in 1947—a show which Mies himself designed, and for which Philip wrote an important catalogue. There was probably no other disciple of similarly single-minded devotion, in any of the visual arts, in America in those years before and after World War II; and there was something rather touching about the deference shown by Philip to his master—especially since Philip was not exactly given to modesty and deference then, or ever.

Philip Johnson, ca. 1985. (Tom Wolff)

And people knew Philip because of his part in the preparation of the most important exhibition on modern architecture held in the U.S. in the years before World War II. The exhibition was held in 1932, at the then newly established Museum of Modern Art, where it was seen for a very brief period—from February 10 to March 23. Subsequently, it traveled around the U.S. and was seen in Philadelphia, Los Angeles, Cleveland, Cincinnati, Harvard, and elsewhere—but, curiously enough, not in Chicago, where much of modern architecture was invented.

The exhibition was prepared by Henry-Russell Hitchcock and Philip Johnson (the latter being listed as "Director of the Exhibition," with Alan Blackburn as his "Secretary"). Hitchcock and Johnson wrote the catalogue for the show, and Lewis Mumford contributed a separate chapter on housing. The catalogue published for the exhibition had a photograph of Mies's Tugendhat House of 1930 on its cover, and the title of the exhibition was "Modern Architecture—International Exhibition." It was the foreword to the catalogue, by Alfred H. Barr, Jr., then director of the Museum of Modern Art, that first used the term "International Style" to describe the architecture of the Bauhaus and its allies in Europe since the end of World War I.

When this exhibition was shown in New York, Philip Johnson was all of twenty-five years old. He was a student (in philosophy) at Harvard and had had no training in architecture or architectural history whatsoever. Yet it was clear that his enthusiasm and perceptiveness had been crucial to the successful launching of this historic show.

I knew this and more about Philip when we met that afternoon at Mary Callery's. He was in terrific form—witty, charming, and, most of all, quick. To talk to him was to employ a kind of shorthand in which all issues were dealt with in a very few words and settled in no time at all. It was one of the many things that would make working with Philip in years to come a great pleasure.

That afternoon, he was full of some article by Lewis Mumford that had just appeared in *The New Yorker*—an article which I had not read but which (I gathered) attacked all that Philip and the Museum of Modern Art held most dear. According to Philip, Mumford had said that "modernism" as represented in the 1932 exhibit was old hat and that the new wave in architecture was not functionalism but humanism—especially humanism as represented by such regional movements as the redwood tradition of the San Francisco Bay Area and the shingle tradition of New England. What was needed, so Philip thought, was a symposium on "What Is Happening in Modern Architecture" at which Mumford would be confronted by some of those whom he had singled out in his attack. Would I be willing to speak as a "representative" of the "younger generation"?

Was he serious? He had known me for approximately half an hour, hardly long enough to find out where I stood in this contro-

What is Happening to Modern Architecture?

Mumford

Johnson

Barr

Hitchcock

Charmayoff

Blake

**A Symposium
At the Museum of Modern Art**

Tunnard

McAndrew

McQuade

versy. (I myself, not having read Mumford's piece, couldn't have enlightened him in that regard.) I explained that I had not even graduated from a school of architecture, that my credentials were therefore extremely tenuous. . . . No matter, he insisted that I was just the man to join the fray.

The following week I got a chance to read the Mumford article and thought it typically old-fashioned and sentimental. (I was just as wrong about Mumford as everybody else.) Philip called to confirm that I would be one of the speakers and mentioned some of the others: Alfred Barr, Hitchcock, Gropius, Marcel Breuer, Eero

Saarinen, and Mumford himself—plus several others who terrified me only slightly less. Over the next several weeks, I busied myself with drafting a statement that I would read at the symposium. The longer I worked on it, the shorter it became. In the end, it was a rather cryptic comment that took me less than a couple of minutes to read—luckily so, since my knees were shaking and my voice was rapidly turning to a whisper.

The gist of what I said was that "the Industrial Revolution in building has not yet occurred . . . and those who today are going in for a new romanticism . . . are delaying that Revolution. . . . In his attack on what he calls the 'mechanical rigorists,' Mr. Mumford assumes that . . . the battle for a new [industrialized] architecture has already been won. I don't think that is the case." Well, it wasn't a very profound statement, but it touched on an issue that was of interest to a few of the people in the audience.

Several of the statements made by others at the symposium, in February 1948, were vastly more profound and I will return to some of them shortly. But a few days after that evening's symposium, Philip and Alfred asked me for lunch. It seemed that Mary Barnes, the wife of the architect Edward Larrabee Barnes, was leaving her position as the Museum of Modern Art's curator of architecture to have a baby. Would I like the job?

I was stunned. I explained again that I was going to try to complete my education at some school of architecture and that I really had no credentials to hold down such a position. My arguments were ignored, and so I accepted. Despite the absurdity of the situation, I was tickled pink. I had no idea what a curator did—I knew I would have three or four assistants to help me do it—and Mary Barnes, whom I had known for a number of years, thought I'd have no trouble at all.

In fact, though not officially, Philip was the director of the department, and I worked under him. The reason this arrangement was unofficial (as he explained to me, with typical candor) was that "some of the trustees can't forget my Nazi past and would resign if I became the official director of the department." We maintained the fiction—I was the head of the Department of Architecture and Industrial Design, and Philip was a sort of unofficial consultant. Nobody, needless to say, was fooled.

MOMA was an interesting institution in those days: although its director was René d'Harnoncourt—a huge Austrian bear of a man, full of sweetness and diplomatic charm and considerably more brains than was apparent to most of us most of the time—the real head was Alfred Barr, whose title at this stage was director of the museum collection. Alfred's vast scholarship and integrity, and his unequaled judgment, made him the heart and intellect and conscience of MOMA. He was reserved, quiet, undemonstrative, and in total control. There was no decision made, on any level of MOMA's operations, that was not first cleared with Alfred—not because of some political jockeying for power on his part, but because everyone at MOMA knew that Alfred's judgment was vastly superior, in every respect, to that of everyone else at MOMA.

To document Alfred's extraordinary talents it is necessary only to look at the quality of MOMA's permanent collection—a collection that continues to be his monument. When MOMA devoted its entire space to an enormous Picasso exhibition in 1980, every single period, however brief and however experimental, in the artist's work was represented by several key paintings or drawings or sculptures or ceramics of that period. Most of those objects were on loan from other institutions; but in almost every case, in almost every period and in almost every medium, the very best object was one that already belonged to MOMA, that was part of the stunning collection assembled by Alfred over the years.

This infallible collection assembled by him gave him a standing at MOMA that no one could hope to challenge. And since he was a very decent man, sometimes almost approachable behind that massive wall of reserve, no one ever thought of challenging his authority—at least not in my time at MOMA.

That fall, in Easthampton, I also ran into Herbert Matter, the gifted Swiss photographer and graphic designer, and his wife, Mercedes. She was very beautiful, and her high-pitched voice, always on the verge of laughter or hysteria or both, made her totally captivating. Mercedes had been a student at Hans Hofmann's school in the early forties and helped support herself as a fashion model. My mother, who was a fashion illustrator, used her often, and I had been utterly smitten with her.

Through the Matters I met their closest friends: Jackson Pollock and Lee Krasner, his wife. Lee had been a student of Hans Hofmann's also, and modeled for my mother as well. Although Lee was as grotesquely ugly as Mercedes was beautiful, she had a certain grace and patience that made her an extraordinary model.

In those days, Jackson was barely known in the New York art world. Peggy Guggenheim had recognized his talent and was giving him $3,000 a year to stay alive. Clem Greenberg had written some flattering things about him, and Betty Parsons—that perceptive and courageous gallery owner—had taken him on.

But to the New York art establishment, Jackson was an enigma—possibly a fraud and, in any case, extremely difficult: he was a violent and often unmanageable alcoholic, and very few people except for Lee Krasner and Herbert Matter were able to cope with his monumental drinking bouts. He was probably suicidal— he seemed to seek out violence: Burgoyne Diller, the abstract painter, once told me of the days when he and Jackson were working together on the WPA "Federal Art Project," doing murals in Post Office buildings while these were under construction. According to Diller, Jackson would show up on those construction sites blind drunk and proceed to pick fights with the biggest, toughest construction workers in sight, who would then knock him down and leave him flat on his back, barely conscious.

Oddly enough, Jackson was never violent with me. The reason, I think, was that I was smaller than he, and he only picked fights with guys twice his size. Anyway, as his drinking became fiercer and fiercer, Lee would ask me to come out on weekends and stay with them in their house in The Springs because Jackson needed help to make it up the stairs to his bedroom whenever he returned from his drunken drives around the countryside in the early morning hours; and I was one of the few people whose touch he would tolerate as I helped drag him upstairs.

The day after I met him and Lee, however, he was on reasonably good behavior. I went over to look at his paintings, and he led me to his barnlike studio. He was very quiet, probably suffering from one of his daily hangovers. We walked into the studio, and it was like entering a palace: his canvases were pinned up all over the walls, and one huge one was still stretched out on the floor, where he had been working on it. (His technique, of course, was to drip Duco enamel and other paints with a brush onto the canvas—or onto panels of Masonite—while walking or virtually dancing around the periphery of the work.) The colors were dazzling—silver, shades of off-white, traceries of black, lavender, blue—the splashes all quite controlled, the finished canvas luminous, almost translucent, shimmering in the sunlight.

I was overwhelmed by the sheer beauty of his work. I don't

know what I expected, but it was clearly the work of someone who understood light and space, and the transparency of the wide, horizontal landscape of the inlets just beyond the little shack. I had never been so moved by any contemporary painting, and I guess Jackson knew it.

He didn't talk much, except when he was drunk and obscenely disorderly. Like Mies, he let his work speak for him. After he died, some eight years later, various critics published "conversations" with him, and quoted him at length on art and life and so on. Very odd. He hardly ever said a word to anyone who knew him reasonably well—and those he liked best (like Herbert Matter and the photographer/sculptor Wilfred Zogbaum) talked even less. Zog and Jackson and I would occasionally go fishing on some of the beautiful inlets behind the Pollocks' house in The Springs. We'd take off in Jackson's rowboat, sit there with our fishing rods, pull in a fish or two, and go back to the house. Nobody talked, and we had a lovely time.

I don't really know if we were friends—I guess we were, for four or five years. In 1949 he asked me to hang his show at Betty Parsons' Gallery, and for this exhibit I worked out something I had thought about ever since that first day in his studio: I designed a large, somewhat abstract "exhibit" of his work—a kind of "Ideal Museum" in which his paintings were suspended between the earth and the sky, and set between mirrored walls so as to extend into infinity.

Jackson Pollock (left) with me, inspecting my model of an "Ideal Exhibition" of his work. He made his only known sculptures (of wire dipped in plaster and painted) for this model. It was displayed in Betty Parsons' Gallery in 1949. (Ben Schultz)

Beyond these floating canvases would be the marshes and the inlets of The Springs—the relentlessly horizontal landscape of that end of Long Island. I built a large model of this "Ideal Museum," and Jackson made some small-scale sculptures to be placed into the model, using wire dipped into plaster and splashed with paint—a kind of three-dimensional interpretation of his drip paintings. My project was obviously influenced by Mies van der Rohe's *Ideal Museum for a Small City,* designed and published in 1942. (Jackson and Mies seemed to have a very similar attitude toward the nature of space.) The model of my "Ideal Museum" was exhibited in the Pollock show at Betty's gallery, and it disintegrated shortly thereafter.

Before it did, an article appeared in *Interiors* magazine, written by a young critic named Arthur Drexler, who would one day succeed me at MOMA. Drexler wrote, in part: "The paintings [in the Ideal Museum project] seem as though they might very well be extended indefinitely, and it is precisely this quality that has been emphasized in the central unit of the plan. Here a painting 17 feet long constitutes an entire wall. It is terminated on both ends not by a frame or a solid partition, but by mirrors. The painting is thus extended into miles of reflected space, and leaves no doubt in the observer's mind as to this particular aspect of Pollock's work. . . . In its treatment of paintings as walls, the design recalls an entirely different kind of pictorial art; that of the Renaissance fresco. The project suggests a reintegration of painting and architecture wherein painting *is* architecture, but this time without message or content. *Its sole purpose is to heighten our experience of space.*" (My italics.)

Except for this article, and one or two mentions in art magazines, there is no record of the project; but when the Centre Pompidou in Paris mounted its big Pollock retrospective in 1983, the management asked me to reproduce the structure, full size, in one of the galleries. Alas, there wasn't enough money to get it done.

Drexler understood not only what I had tried to do in that little project; he also understood what intrigued me in Jackson's work. The one, most obvious difference between European and American artists, in their visual experience, was and is that of space. In Europe, as Naum Gabo pointed out in that debate at the Architectural Association, one is constantly reminded that "just over the river is Peckham Rye." But in North America the seemingly endless "open road," the seemingly endless broad horizons, the vastness of everything—landscape, bridges, coastlines, big skies—was the one experience that set you apart from European artists. That experience, further intensified by the broad sweep of seascape that American artists seemed to be drawn to, gave their work a very special quality: even Picasso's images, though increasingly concerned with multiple vision and vision-in-motion, seemed somehow finite and spatially circumscribed when compared with the strangely radiant landscapes and seascapes of America's Luminist painters of the mid-nineteenth century; and Jackson's work, to me, seemed much more closely related to the work of those painters, and to the work of poets like Whitman and writers like Kerouac and architects like Wright, than it did to the painters whom he professed to admire—especially Joan Miró and Arshile Gorky. Jackson's passion—after painting and women—was the open road and the automobiles that traveled it. And those automobiles, of course, were the death of him.

In all the years of my friendship with Jackson, we rarely talked about art. But one day, out of the blue, he said to me: "The trouble is you think I am a decorator." I was taken aback—perhaps because he seemed so precisely on target. But the more I thought and think about it, and I still do, some forty years after the fact, the more I think Jackson was wrong: *of course* I thought his paintings might make terrific walls (after all, architects spend a lot of time thinking about walls). But what his paintings really meant to me, from the first day, was something I can only describe as the "Dream of Space"—a dream of endless, infinite space in motion. To look at some of his paintings, to me, was like sitting on a dune for hours on end and looking out to sea, at the endless horizon and the shifting waves and clouds and banks of fog. Was that the way Jackson saw his work? I haven't the remotest idea. We never talked about it.

There was a painting he finished in 1949 that seemed more beautiful to me than anything of his that I had seen before. I told him how much I liked it and asked if I could buy it and for how much. Jackson seemed delighted that I liked that particular painting. He smiled and said: "Just pay me $50 a month for the next two years and it's yours." Well, I was a student and a recent father and an underpaid curator at the Museum of Modern Art, and I didn't have $50 a month to spare. So the painting was bought, for a little more than $1,200, by our wealthy friend Alfonso Ossorio, a prolific artist and collector, who was living on the former Christian Herter Estate in Easthampton, and who had helped finance my Ideal Museum Project.

The painting I had fallen in love with was *Lavender Mist*, and thirty years later the National Gallery bought it from Alfonso for $1.5 million or thereabouts.

Although Jackson was probably the central figure in what became known as the New York School, he was not the only artist who had gravitated to the end of Long Island in the years after World War II. Bob Motherwell was out there, and he had commissioned Pierre Chareau to design a house for him. Chareau was a rather uneven French architect who had fled to New York when the Nazis captured Paris and was trying to make a living in a new and baffling land. Motherwell, who was rumored to be quite wealthy, found himself supporting several refugee French artists during those war years, and Chareau was one of them. The Motherwell House in Easthampton was a bit of a joke—Chareau, like other French visitors, was greatly impressed by American technology; and he decided that the U.S. Army's wartime Nissen huts—vaulted, corrugated iron shelters, rather like sheet-metal igloos, that were meant to protect soldiers stationed more or less temporarily in inhospitable climes—were just the thing to use in building a fairly luxurious summer house in the Hamptons. The Nissen hut was placed on the ground, above an excavated living room, so that Motherwell and his family were condemned to living in what amounted to a basement, at the end of a three-hour drive from Manhattan. Chareau had some fairly exotic notions about interior finishes, which turned out to be so expensive that Motherwell never quite finished the house. It was eventually sold to Barney Rosset the publisher and viewed as a landmark, especially by those not condemned to living in it. After Rosset sold the house, in 1985, it was demolished by its new owner.

Bill De Kooning was another early summer resident in the Hamptons, as were Franz Kline and number of other painters and sculptors. It always struck me as appropriate that American artists—at least those who seemed most alienated from the mainstream of their time—tended to gravitate toward the extremities of the North American continent: Provincetown, Carmel, Key West, and now the Hamptons. In any event, the Pollocks, who lived in The Springs year round, were the center of all this flight from the mainstream. And Jackson was, without the slightest doubt in my mind, the most important new artist of those years in America.

To realize what this meant one should remember that until World War II the art establishment in Europe and America thought that there was really no significant modern art being done by Americans. Even Alexander Calder, who had spent much of his time in France, was not really considered a "Serious Artist" (he and his work were too witty); Isamu Noguchi *couldn't* be American; and Man Ray, who had become almost completely assimilated to the French scene, was thought to be more of a graphic designer and photographer than a painter or a sculptor. New York's Museum of Modern Art showed very little new American art; I remember attending a meeting of the American Abstract Artists, sometime in the early forties, and listening to plans for throwing up picket lines around MOMA to protest the discriminatory, anti-American attitudes attributed to the MOMA management. And Curt Valentin, probably the most successful dealer in modern art in America in those years, would not have been caught dead showing anything but Picasso, Braque, Magritte, Miró, and other Europeans in his Buchholtz Gallery in the years during and after World War II. Only a very few dealers—primarily Betty Parsons, in fact—had the courage to show American artists like Pollock and Motherwell and De Kooning. Curt Valentin, who was a charming boulevardier, thought she was clearly a sweet and pitiable lunatic.

Yet, in the four short years between the end of World War II and the publication, in 1949 in *Life* magazine, of a major article on Jackson's work, the entire modern art scene in America and the rest of the world had changed dramatically: American painting, and some American sculpture, had not merely caught up—it was the most relevant, the most exciting work being done anywhere. It had broken away from easel painting and embraced all of space, all of motion, all of action; it was as violent and as passionate and as "engaged" as life itself. And because of its attitude toward space—because of that "experience of space" that Drexler had described so vividly—such painting could only have been done by a North American, an artist as responsive to our most visible inheritance as Whitman had been. It could not have been produced by an artist living on a tightly crowded continent.

And so, in four short years, Jackson and one or two others changed the direction of modern art and shifted the center of gravity of the Modern Movement from Paris to New York. It was absolutely staggering. To young architects like myself, who believed that a similar shift of emphasis was possible in *our* art, this accomplishment seemed enormously encouraging.

Jackson and I continued to interact in certain ways. I was designing my first house, a small summer cottage which would be built in Water Mill, near Southampton; and this house had a pinwheel plan and great sliding walls, eight feet high and eighteen feet long, which were designed to slide out on rails into the landscape and open the interior to the sun and the breezes, and close it up

Nineteen fifty-two design for a pinwheel beach house, whose walls could slide outward to open up spaces and views at will, or inward to close the interior. The house, my first, was built in Water Mill, Long Island, in 1954.

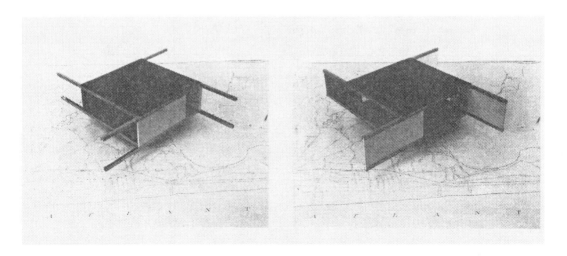

Pinwheel House with all four walls open. Various combinations of open and closed walls are possible, in response to changing views, breezes, sunlight, etc. (Hans Namuth)

Interior of Pinwheel House with walls wide open. Petty Nelson Blake is watching children at play outside. Two bedrooms and bath are located on a lower level, under the living area. (Hans Namuth)

tight in the event of hurricanes. These sliding walls, I thought, might be large paintings that would seem suspended in the land-scape, and Jackson was enthusiastic. (Since I was not rich enough even to pay for the physical cost of these large paintings, the pro-ject was never realized, though the house was, in fact, built—with bare sliding walls.)

On another occasion, Jackson and I discussed the possibility of painting on tempered glass so as to make the paint seem suspended in space, with views of the landscape through the painting's surface and beyond. This notion was realized several years later, on a rela-tively small scale, by the photographer Hans Namuth when he filmed Jackson in action through a sheet of glass and from below. (Jackson by this time painted only on floor surfaces, dripping his paint in characteristic—and virtually inimitable—calligraphic pat-terns.) Finally, in what turned out to be the only one of our joint fantasies to reach fruition, I introduced Marcel Breuer to Jackson and his work, and Breuer commissioned a mural for one wall of the dining room of his Geller House in Lawrence, Long Island. When the Gellers later sold the house, Jackson's painting turned out to be worth considerably more than the rest of the structure.

CHAPTER ELEVEN

■ It was a great time to be alive, and all of us sensed it. With the war over, the country—indeed, the world—seemed ready to accept new ideas, in all the arts, that had somehow failed to develop during the oppressive thirties. All the pent-up energy, all the determination to change the world, suddenly erupted and manifested itself in dozens of ways. What I and others saw in the new painting in New York and in the Hamptons was only the beginning; we were sure that a similar architectural energy would soon manifest itself all around us. And we felt we were ready.

It must be remembered that prior to World War II the fascists, the Soviets, as well as the New Deal and the establishments in many other Western democracies, had all opposed modern architecture; and that they had, all of them, promoted one or another sort of neoclassical eclecticism. In the Soviet Union and in Nazi Germany this had been an ideological commitment, and modern architecture was perceived as an enemy to be destroyed. In the U.S. and in most of the Western democracies there had been no such ideological commitment: modern architecture was simply treated as an aberration, to be ignored by most of those who counted in the public and private sectors. People like Le Corbusier, Mies, Gropius, Wright, and others were turned down again and again for any significant

Le Corbusier relaxing in Amagansett, ca. 1950. (Tino Nivola)

commissions; in fact, most of them designed little more than small villas or apartments for a few nonconformist families of wealth.

Now, however, things were about to change—and the break-through spearheaded by the New York School seemed to be an indicator of what all of us in related fields would soon experience. The evidence was everywhere: in New York an international group of architects appointed by the member governments of the United Nations met over several years to design the new UN Headquarters; and the French representative was none other than Le Corbusier, whose extraordinary project for the League of Nations Headquarters in 1927 had been laughed out of court. (The Swedish representative was Sven Markelius, the Brazilian representative was Oscar Niemeyer, and there were others of their caliber from other UN member nations.)

Le Corbusier, best known as a visionary architect, had been a painter ever since World War I, and (under his original name, Charles Jeanneret) he had been a leading member of the cubist or "Purist" movement in Paris. He continued to paint throughout his life, at a prolific rate; and while he was working on the UN project in New York, he stayed with Tino Nivola, both in Nivola's studio on 8th Street, in the Village, and on weekends in the Nivolas' country house at the end of Long Island.

Corbu, on those occasions out in the country, was very different from the aggressive, contentious, remote personality he presented to the official world of architecture and architectural politics. He was relaxed, dressed in sloppy overalls, happily playing with the Nivolas' children, friendly and warm. Nivola had developed a way of casting sculpture on the beach; and Corbu, who was fascinated by the process, began to do his own sand sculptures. They were extraordinarily surreal and very colorful. Moreover, as a thank-you gift to the Nivolas, he decided to paint two murals on the plaster walls of their living room, and was hard at work on those one morning before anyone else in the household had begun to stir.

Corbu met Pollock and saw his paintings. Diplomatically, he lapsed into French, telling Tino Nivola that painting was really more exacting than that. He had no feeling for Pollock's work at all—though, after receiving a lift back to Manhattan after a long weekend on the Island, he conceded that Jackson might not be a very interesting painter but was certainly a terrific driver! Corbu's judgment in other matters was, however, more dependable: although Jackson did know a great deal about cars and kept his old, decrepit Model A Ford in remarkably good running condition, he died in the summer of 1956 because a car he was driving careened off the road between The Springs and Easthampton, overturned, and killed him and another of its occupants, severely injuring a third. As so often in the past, Jackson had been blind drunk while tearing down Fireplace Road that day, a road he knew intimately.

Enough has been written about the final ten years or so of Jackson Pollock's life. To those of us who were his friends they were years of constant tension: when he and I first met, he was drinking the way he had been drinking for years, and would, again, after a two-year interval of total abstinence—that is, he was drinking constantly, taking time off occasionally to paint (or dance-paint around huge canvases or sheets of Masonite laid out on the floor of his studio); or to pass out on the nearest couch or floor; or to drive around the countryside in his ancient Model A; or to visit terrified friends and acquaintances, making a pest of himself wherever he went; or to pass out again. I had known a number of alcoholics but never one so desperately, tragically self-destructive.

For that period of almost two years, between 1948 and 1950, Jackson had managed to go on the wagon with the help of an Easthampton doctor who prescribed some newly developed tranquilizers. The change in him was dramatic: he grew thin, very shy and quiet, very polite and docile. He drank coffee constantly and dressed very "properly." He went to all the expected cocktail parties and usually stood in a corner, smiling when spoken to, and sipping coffee. Needless to say, those of us who had known him before he went on the wagon sensed the constant, almost unbearable tension underlying all of this: I remember the way Lee and I and some of the others—John Little, Franz Kline, Alfonso Ossorio, Jim Brooks—would look at one another for a fraction of a second across a room filled with the Easthampton art crowd; and we were terrified, all of us, that this violent force within Jackson might explode almost any moment, demolishing everything in sight.

That this period of abstinence lasted for two years was amazing. Then, on Thanksgiving Day in 1950, Lee invited me and a few other friends to come out for a great feast—an enormous Thanksgiving dinner which she had spent hours preparing in her large, open kitchen in the house in The Springs. It was a very bright, sunny, wintry day; the winds were howling across the flat Long Island landscape; and Hans Namuth, the photographer, had planned to film Jackson painting on a sheet of plate glass raised up on a scaffold so that the camera could focus on him from below, dripping and splashing paint on the transparent surface.

The scaffold was all set, and there was a kind of walkway constructed around the perimeter of the horizontal sheet of glass so that Jackson would be able to reach over the surface from all directions. Hans had set up his camera below, and both he and Jackson were all set to go. It was incredibly cold, and the rest of us decided to go inside the house, leaving the two of them outside to film the footage that Hans wanted.

I went to the kitchen, where Lee had set up the huge table weighted down with all sorts of Thanksgiving delicacies. The others went into the living area. After half an hour or so, Hans and Jackson came inside, having completed the footage. Both were frozen—almost blue. Jackson went to the kitchen sink, set up two tall glasses, and filled them to the rim with whiskey. He said to Hans: "This is the first drink I've had in two years—but, Christ, we need it after this." Hans, who had met Jackson after the latter had gone on the wagon and had never seen him drunk, sounded uncertain—obviously, he had heard stories about Jackson's drinking habits, but perhaps didn't take them all that seriously. I did, and I think my heart stopped. Lee came in from the living room and said something to Jackson, but it was too late—he had downed the whole tumbler of straight whiskey and was pouring himself a refill.

Things got out of control very rapidly after that. Jeffrey Potter, who was there, too, remembers that Jackson started to bait Hans, who responded rather angrily. In any event, there was a violent scene, in the course of which Lee's spectacular Thanksgiving dinner and the great oak table that supported it ended up halfway across the dining room, scattered all over the floor. Jackson, now at his most violent, headed for the back door. Jeff said something to him about being sorry he was so upset. "Shit, I wasn't upset!" Jackson said. "The table was." And he stormed out. He lived for another six years or so, and I never saw him sober again.

Jackson was not uniformly violent or abusive during those last years, but there was always that terrifying underlying tension that made being with him very difficult. I had remarried after my divorce from Martha, and my second wife, Petty Nelson, a very elegant fashion reporter at *Life* magazine, was pregnant. She had had some earlier problems with miscarriages, and so we didn't encourage too many visits by Jackson to our new sliding-wall house in Water Mill, although we were still hoping that we would, someday, be able to afford to get him to paint those huge murals. . . .

He did drop in now and then, and he was usually on his best behavior (that is, he was foulmouthed but not violent). He didn't lunge, or stagger about, or fall through panels of glass; he was sad, and depressed, and bloated, and black-bearded. His work, when he was working at all, was becoming more figurative: black-line traceries depicting people's faces and figures—"indoor" paintings, rather than "outdoor" murals. Yet, whenever we talked about the possibility of doing those sliding walls, his eyes would light up: he was clearly excited at the prospect, the possibility of having those large, abstract webs of line and color seemingly suspended in midair in the flat, dreamlike landscape of Water Mill and Mecox Bay, so much like the landscape behind his and Lee's house in The Springs. He didn't talk much about the project, but now and then he'd call me to double-check the exact dimensions of those walls, and to ask me what kind of paint I thought would stand up best on those surfaces. But, of course, there was never enough money to get the walls done, and so the project remained a dream.

How do you describe the final years in the life of a person close to you who was moving inexorably toward a terrible death? There were about a dozen of us out there, in the Hamptons, who were almost like a small family: we talked on the phone several times a week, met as often as we could, gossiped, chatted, dropped in, kept in close touch. At the center were Jackson and Lee. (Lee's own work as a painter was not taken seriously by any of us, or by anyone else, during those years; and though I was extremely fond of her and saw a good deal of her long after Jackson died, I never liked her work at all.) Next to Jackson and Lee were Alfonso Ossorio and his friend Ted Dragon; then there were Jim and Charlotte Brooks, Hans and Carmen Namuth; Wilfred and Betsy Zogbaum, Herbert and Mercedes Matter; Jeffrey and Penny Potter; and a few others. The constellations sometimes shifted; people were sometimes on speaking terms, sometimes not; sometimes married and then divorced; Lee was jealous of every attractive woman in sight—assuming, quite rightly, that Jackson could be counted on to lurch in the general direction of any such female. But, by and large, we all remained friends and more than friends; and one of the ties that bound us together was our terrible fear for Jackson.

Sometime in the 1950s, Martha Jackson, the owner of an interesting New York gallery, came to spend a summer in the Hamptons. She had an Oldsmobile 88, and Jackson leched after it the moment he saw it. It was a big car, and a fast one, and a convertible. It was exactly what he wanted. And when Martha Jackson offered to give it to him in exchange for two paintings that she wanted, Jackson agreed instantly.

Jackson's earlier car, out in The Springs, had been that decrepit Model A Ford, which could attain speeds of up to twenty-five miles an hour with a tail wind. Jackson, who liked to drive around the countryside at night while drunk, had managed to slam into assorted trees and telephone poles in his Model A at various times, but had never received more than a scratch or two.

When Martha Jackson traded him her convertible, we all knew, I think, that this was the beginning of the end. I remember hearing about the deal from Alfonso; we looked at each other, and he simply shrugged. He knew, and I knew, and all of us knew that Jackson would use the car to kill himself. He did, on August 11, 1956.

CHAPTER TWELVE

■ On my first day at the Museum of Modern Art, Alfred Barr came walking past my open door deep in thought. He was tall, thin, bespectacled, and slightly birdlike of mien—rather appropriately so, I discovered later, since his favorite hobby was bird watching. He saw me sitting at my desk, stopped short, and came in saying: "I just want you to know, I am very pleased that you are here." He was slightly embarrassed, as was I, cleared his throat, and added: "Well, anyway, it's very nice." With that he turned around and continued his walk down the corridor.

I was touched, of course. And I was even more touched when, a couple of weeks later, precisely the same scene was reenacted: Alfred came to my door, stopped short, came in saying, "I just want you to know . . . ," cleared his throat, and continued his walk down the corridor, deep in thought. He was the personification of the proverbial absentminded professor: scholarly, profound, thoughtful, and usually operating on several wavelengths simultaneously. He was a person of vast integrity and conviction, a lovable but utterly remote father figure to most people at MOMA—and quite unaware, I suspect, of the vast affection and admiration that he inspired. There were many people at MOMA who were admired both within and without the organization; but no one commanded the utter devotion and respect that Alfred, in his oddly remote and distracted way, seemed to inspire in everyone who knew him.

We all realized, of course, that the name of Alfred Barr, in the U.S. at least, was virtually synonymous with the recognition and acceptance of the Modern Movement in all the visual arts. But if he had developed any arrogance from the knowledge of his remarkable reputation, he showed no evidence of that: he seemed, at times, almost painfully modest in expressing his critical views, listening to others—including patent idiots—long before expressing his own opinions. Like most people at MOMA, I never got to know him very well; but when he died in August 1981, after a long battle with Alzheimer's disease, I felt incredibly sad. For one thing, I had never told him how very pleased *I* was to be working in *his* museum.

For it was Alfred's museum, despite the fact that he had been "demoted" a few years earlier by a cabal of trustees, from the directorship of MOMA to the directorship of the Museum Collections. And even today, with all the crass physical alterations that have turned the original MOMA into a vast Cultural Shopping Mall, with wall-to-wall escalators and souvenir bargain basements throughout, all that is beautiful and moving and sublime in those galleries is the work of artists discovered and supported and collected by Alfred Barr. It was Alfred who saw their work; it was Alfred who persuaded museum trustees—many of them barely literate in any area, and especially in the visual arts—to contribute the sums needed to buy the works; and it was Alfred who wrote about those works—in brilliant, concise, explanatory wall labels, and in equally brilliant and concise catalogues and monographs—and whose writings, to this day, form the heart of all modern art-historical teaching in the U.S. and beyond.

When Alfred died, I was head of the Department of Architecture at Catholic University, in Washington, D.C., and I introduced and taught a course on the visual arts tangential to architecture, the arts that I thought my students should be aware of, vaguely at least, before they entered their chosen profession. For a series of lectures covering the history of "Modern Art Since Cézanne," I assembled several hundred slides that seemed relevant; and when I reviewed them I found, to no great surprise, that almost every one of them showed a work from MOMA's Permanent Collection—a work initially chosen by Alfred.

. . .

The Museum of Modern Art, in the late 1940s, was probably the most lively center for the visual arts to be found anywhere in the U.S.—and, possibly, anywhere in the world. Admittedly, MOMA did not generate works of art, except indirectly, but the museum exhibited the works of artists from all over the world who were beginning to emerge in the postwar years to take the place of the School of Paris. And under Alfred's direction, the museum acquired works that were being produced by artists of the New York School and by others not very widely recognized by most of the critics of those days. Needless to say, the imprimatur of a MOMA exhibit or acquisition was usually enough to launch careers that would have been stymied had it not been for Alfred Barr's extraordinary judgment.

He did not arrive at his judgments casually. Betty Parsons once told me that Alfred and his remarkable assistant, Dorothy Miller, called one day to make an appointment for a private viewing of the latest work by that strange artist—Jackson Pollock—whom Clement Greenberg had called "the greatest living painter in the U.S." MOMA had bought one of Jackson's earlier paintings, *The She-Wolf*, in 1944 for all of $600; but that painting was still very much in the tradition of Miró, Gorky, and, of course, Picasso; and Alfred had been rather lukewarm about acquiring *it*. He simply didn't seem to know what to make of Jackson's drip paintings; and he and Dorothy Miller went over to Betty Parsons' Gallery to see for themselves.

According to Betty, Alfred just sat there and looked, as one painting after the other was brought out and propped up for him to study. (I am certain that Betty said nothing; she was quite possibly the worst salesperson in the New York art world, and much too shy and well-mannered to engage in any overt or covert huckstering.) "After what seemed like hours," Betty told me later, "Barr perked up." Apparently, he had found a "slot" in that remarkable "family tree" of the Modern Movement which he had first published in 1936, on the inside cover of the catalogue to his seminal exhibition entitled "Cubism and Abstract Art." This "family tree" was a chart that traced the development of modern art from Japanese prints (revealed to the West in the mid-nineteenth century) to what Alfred, in those years, referred to as "nongeometrical" and "geometrical" abstract art. It was the sort of chart that only an art historian (in fact, only a German art historian, it seemed to me) could love—and that only an art historian with Alfred's unfailing eye and taste and intelligence could possibly use effectively and creatively. In any event, according to Betty, it seemed as if he had suddenly found a slot in this "family tree" for Jackson's drip paintings—possibly somewhere halfway between Redon and Masson; and, after that, Pollock was "in," so far as MOMA was concerned. In fact, several years later, Alfred persuaded Andrew Ritchie, then the curator of painting and sculpture at MOMA, to postpone a De Kooning show and to prepare a one-man Pollock exhibit instead.

Although MOMA's activities in the areas of painting and sculpture were by far the most important of all its efforts in the visual arts, they were not the only ones by any means. Long before any other museum, anywhere, considered film, photography, graphic design, industrial design, or architecture worthy of documentation, exhibition, or collection, MOMA, under Alfred Barr's direction, accorded those arts and disciplines almost equal billing with the traditional arts that other museums collected and exhibited exclusively.

The people who were selected to direct those programs in the less conventional modern arts were chosen with as much care as those who were selected to direct the museum's more traditional programs: Beaumont Newhall and Edward Steichen, for example, established and directed the Department of Photography; Iris Barry, a British film critic, directed the Film Department; Eliot Noyes, Edgar Kaufman, Jr., Elizabeth Mock, John McAndrew, Mary Barnes, and, of course, Philip Johnson directed efforts in Architecture or Design; and innumerable others of comparable caliber were invited to design and direct special exhibitions dealing with significant areas in the visual and applied arts in which they were considered outstanding and innovative. And even though Alfred's prime expertise was clearly in painting, sculpture, and other visual arts closely related to these, his judgment in all areas was eagerly sought, and highly respected.

One area in which it was not was in the selection of an architect for the new building which the trustees decided to construct, on West 53rd Street, in the late 1930s. Alfred was anxious to get Mies van der Rohe to design MOMA's new structure and campaigned energetically for his candidate. But the trustees selected a fellow trustee, Philip Goodwin, instead. Goodwin, who had never designed a "modern" building in his rather undistinguished career, chose Edward Durrell Stone—a young architect who had, among other things, worked on the design of the slick Radio City Music Hall—to be his associate. The result was a building of limited distinction whose flat, bland, glass-and-marble facades expressed neither structure, nor function, nor any significant form. It was, however, superficially "modern"—an art box which satisfied the museum's more philistine trustees, but not Alfred: he had resigned from the Building Committee in protest; and while he later had a few qualms about Mies's devotion to functionalism, he never ceased to deplore the low level of sophistication displayed by the new building.

When the building was completed, in 1938, it was necessary to design and print new stationery as well. Monroe Wheeler, a charming and civilized snob, who was the director of publications for MOMA, commissioned the design of a new letterhead and asked Norman Ives, the abstract painter and graphic designer, to take a stab at it. Ives's design was carefully reviewed by all concerned and finally approved. It was a beautiful work of graphic art, using a sans serif type in italics that conveyed the spirit of modernism in every one of its strokes. It had only one flaw: the address on millions of letterheads and envelopes printed according to Ives's specifications read 11 *East* 53rd Street—which happened to be incorrect, since the new building was most visibly located *west* of Fifth Avenue. But neither Monroe nor anyone else in the upper echelons of MOMA had ever known anyone with a West Side address, and so this little mistake slipped by undetected. When I joined the staff some ten years later, people in the various curatorial departments were still using notepads made up of scrap from recycled East 53rd Street letterheads. . . .

Shortly after I took over the curatorship of the Department of Architecture at MOMA, René d'Harnoncourt, MOMA's director (and Alfred's successor in that post) came to talk to me. He seemed a trifle ill at ease as he explained that MOMA had decided to combine the departments of Architecture and Industrial Design into a single unit; and he asked if I would be willing to serve as curator of the combined departments. I was a bit confused—Edgar Kaufman, Jr., whom I had never met, was the renowned curator of the Department of Industrial Design, and I asked René what Edgar's role would be. (Edgar was in Europe for the summer.) René was a bit evasive but explained that things would be straightened out upon Edgar's return—some new position would be established for him, though René didn't explain what that position would be. So I accepted, assuming that all of this had been cleared with and agreed to by Edgar prior to his departure for Europe.

That, it turned out, was not the case. René—a huge, bearlike Austrian aristocrat who had worked with Nelson Rockefeller in an earlier incarnation and was assigned by Rockefeller to bring some sort of administrative order into the seemingly chaotic MOMA bureaucracy—was really a terrible administrator, and for a charming reason: he saw himself as a sort of latter-day Metternich and loved the art of diplomacy. He understood, instinctively, I think, that decisions are the end of diplomacy. And since he loved playing Metternich, he hated to make decisions—including this one. Neither he, nor anyone else, had ever bothered to clarify the matter of the joint departments with Edgar Kaufman—or the fact that I would curate both.

In any event, when Edgar returned from Europe at the end of the summer, he found me—a total stranger—installed at his desk. Since he was, even under the best of circumstances, a rather volatile individual, there was a small cataclysm; and he did not speak to me for a number of years. (I think he assumed that the entire business had been a plot contrived by his archenemy, Philip Johnson, and that I was a party to this, Philip's latest intrigue. He may possibly have been right on the first count, but he certainly wasn't on the second.)

The Department of Architecture and Design consisted of about half a dozen people, each of whom was an expert in one or several of our areas of concern: Ada Louise Huxtable, who would later become the country's first full-time architecture critic employed by a daily newspaper, was an architectural historian by training; Greta Daniel, a refugee from Nazi Germany, was our expert in all areas of interior design and in arts and crafts; Mildred Constantine was in charge of all exhibitions having to do with graphic design; and there were others whose expertise was primarily in areas of architecture or architectural history.

During the two years of my curatorship of the department we mounted numerous small exhibitions—including one on the remarkable glass designed for the Austrian firm of J. & L. Lobmeyr in the first two decades of the century; and another on the work of Hector Guimard, the Art Nouveau architect and designer who was best known for his design of the Paris Metro stations at the beginning of the century, and whose widow had donated some of her late husband's fantastic furniture to the MOMA collection. These small exhibits were, I suspect, Philip's idea; he probably knew more about the history of architecture and design than almost anyone else in the U.S., and it would give him great pleasure to unearth and display esoteric pioneering work of the sort represented in the small Lobmeyr and Guimard shows. While the work associated with those two names is fairly widely known as this is written—though very rarely taught in American schools of architecture or design— it was hardly known at all in the 1940s; and such offbeat themes and subjects would amuse and intrigue Philip. In any event, these and other small exhibits were his idea, and I simply carried them out in the galleries available to us.

In addition to exhibits of this rather esoteric sort, we prepared two or three MOMA traveling exhibitions on modern postwar architecture; we ran two or three competitions on poster design, on the design of lamps, and on the design of a building for a park site in a hypothetical American town—a contest open only to unknown, young architects and labeled "Hidden Talent Competition"; and we maintained an informal information service to anyone interested in matters involving recent architecture and design.

But most of our energies went into two major exhibitions held in the original Museum Garden, between the Goodwin and Stone building on West 53rd Street, and West 54th Street to the north. These exhibitions were of full-sized, specially designed one-family houses—the first by the Hungarian-born ex-Bauhaus architect Marcel Breuer; the second by the Californian Gregory Ain. Those two exhibition houses engaged most of our energies, and attracted hundreds of thousands of visitors. They will be discussed in some detail in the next chapter.

The most intriguing aspects, to a young beginner in architecture like myself, was that these activities introduced me to dozens of men and women who either participated in them or visited our department to make use of whatever resources we could provide. In the course of any one month we might be visited by the Dutch architect Gerrit Rietveld, who happened to be in New York (and who, to me, represented one of the noblest and most radical of all modern movements: the de Stijl, founded by Rietveld's friend Theo van Doesburg, and joined by Piet Mondrian, Hans Arp, J. J. P. Oud, Georges Vantongerloo, and others). On another day, the American expatriate architect Paul Nelson, whose amazing experimental house of the 1930s was in the MOMA collection, might drop in from France. On still another, Frank Lloyd Wright would walk in to sneer at some exhibit of pre-Columbian art just being assembled by René d'Harnoncourt. (Mr. Wright, I think, claimed that he had invented pre-Columbia.) Mies would come by to serve on the "Hidden Talent" jury—as would Eero Saarinen and several others. Amédée Ozenfant, who had once worked with Le Corbusier in the early 1920s, came to visit from his house on Gramercy Park. Frederick Kiesler, that nimble Austrian-born self-promoter, would come by to promote himself—as would another ex-Viennese, Richard Neutra, now vastly influential in southern California. Walter Gropius might stop in, though he (a rival of Mies van der Rohe) felt, quite rightly, that Philip despised him. (Philip had been one of Gropius's students at Harvard while a total devotee of Mies van der Rohe's work.) And Le Corbusier, living in New York some of the time, in Tino Nivola's studio, would drop in, on very rare occasions, to snarl at MOMA—a plaything of the Rockefellers, in his view. And there would be many, many others, including the charming Nellie van Doesburg, Theo's widow, and J. J. P. Oud himself.

Most of them, needless to say, came to see Philip and Alfred Barr, who had collaborated on the 1932 "International Architecture" exhibition that Philip, Henry-Russell Hitchcock, Lewis Mumford, and Alfred Barr had put together—an exhibition that introduced the work of most of these people to the U.S., and had introduced its organizers to them. But since Philip was busy building his own glass house in New Canaan and launching his own career as a practicing architect, it became my responsibility to greet, assist, inform, entertain, and be helpful to this remarkable stream of architects and designers; and, in the course of this, many of them became personal friends.

Like every other organization, MOMA had its internal politics—and the feud that seemed to exist between Philip and Edgar Kaufman, Jr., was one of those absurdities that enliven scholarly institutions, especially in the U.S. At MOMA, many political battles seemed to involve jealousies and intrigues among homosexuals on the staff: at least half the top people at MOMA were gay; and some of the male homosexuals, I suspected, were secretly in love with Alfred Barr and tormented by jealousy whenever Alfred seemed to show some sort of favoritism toward one of their rivals.

Alfred, who struck me as anything but gay, may have been quite unaware of these jealousies; but I suspect that Philip, Edgar, and several other staff members were deeply in love with him and felt themselves in competition with everyone else who might be seeking and finding Alfred's approval. Edgar's patent dislike of Philip may have been due in part to that real or imagined rivalry—and partly, perhaps, also to what Philip used to refer to, quite openly to me, as his own "Nazi past." In any event, without quite realizing what passions had been inflamed and why and how, I found myself in the midst of a feud that took some time to die down.

There were other, invisible currents and passions that seemed to govern policies and procedures at MOMA. There was a perfectly clear and uncomplicated "table of organization" according to which the museum pursued its various functions. But there also seemed to be a secret, invisible network—slightly conspiratorial in nature—which frequently influenced the selection of staff, the scheduling of exhibits and publications, and the points of view that would shade or determine all of these. This network was made up of homosexuals and their friends both within and without the administration, and it was not unlike the kind of Stalinist conspiracy that one might find in those years in the worlds of publishing and of entertainment. And while I never came across a situation in which a "straight" person was prevented from working at MOMA, or from exhibiting his or her work (assuming that it met MOMA's aesthetic standards), it clearly helped, in MOMA's world, to be one of the boys or one of the girls.

In almost any area of scholarly endeavor, the sexual preferences of a scholar are a matter of total inconsequence. In the *applied* arts—as, for example, architecture—those preferences can matter a great deal. Arthur Drexler, a highly intelligent writer on architecture who succeeded me at MOMA when I left in 1950 to rejoin the *Architectural Forum,* liked to say that, to him, architecture was an art—and would say it with eyes cast heavenward, as if reciting the principal catechism of his particular faith. Arthur was gay; and while this may have helped endow him with an exceptional sensitivity to aesthetic issues, it tended also to make him rather insensitive to the simple fact that, to most of humanity and especially in an egalitarian democracy, *architecture is not primarily an art at all,* but a discipline that is expected to provide housing, workshops, places to teach and learn and heal in, and one or two other things that most of our fellow men, women, and children have a right to demand from the designers and makers of shelter.

Such concerns, to many gays, were not always of primary significance—and that fact, together with one or two others, placed architecture at MOMA in a highly incongruous position. And the longer I stayed at MOMA—enjoying myself hugely, and learning a great deal from those with whom I worked—the clearer it became that there was a profound conflict between those who had fought for modern architecture in its formative years and were fighting for it still, and those who considered it to be another "art" exclusively, to be judged solely by the most esoteric, aesthetic standards, indeed by personal taste—those who did not appreciate the social and political issues raised by the new architecture, either because they were too rich or because they lived outside the concerns of most of the human community.

As time passed, it became increasingly obvious that while value judgments in the areas of the "pure" arts could be exclusively aesthetic—except if a museum or its director decided that a given work, while not especially beautiful, was of historic significance and hence worth exhibiting and collecting—value judgments in the "applied" arts simply could not be: it is clearly ridiculous to judge a building solely in terms of form (and not of function), just as it is ridiculous to describe a 60-cent cheese slicer as an object "of rough but noble beauty," as MOMA did in a memorable exhibition of "100 Useful Objects" displayed under Edgar's direction at Christmastime in 1947.

And not only ridiculous, but clearly elitist in a slightly irritating way. For the truth of the matter was that MOMA had always been a lovely plaything of the rich—the civilized, educated, cultured rich, admittedly, at least until a new generation of nouveaux riches trustees began to take over; but, still, a plaything of and for people to whom a building could always be made to work if one hired a sufficient number of servants to make it work—or to whom a cheese slicer did not, necessarily, have to slice cheese, just so long as it possessed that "rough but noble beauty."

I suppose I became aware of MOMA's elitist orientation quite early on, at least so far as architecture and design were concerned: for one thing, Philip was always outrageously honest about these and other matters. He liked being rich, and used his inherited wealth in a most civilized way—buying some of the best, farthest-out, avant-garde art; building himself and maintaining one of the most elegant houses of the century; helping to finance exhibitions, publications, schools; and performing, in general, as an enlightened patron of the arts.

All of which seemed quite admirable. But in the process, the very nature of modern architecture, as understood by those who fought for its principles in Europe and elsewhere in the 1920s and since, seemed to have become essentially corrupted. Some of those at MOMA who had at least a nodding acquaintance with those basic social and political tenets of the Modern Movement clearly realized that there was an inherent conflict in having a discipline that was governed by political, social, technological, and, most importantly, by humanistic considerations judged almost exclusively by aesthetic standards. Alfred, I think, was one of those who felt uneasy about this inherent conflict. On one occasion, long after I had left MOMA, I sent him a note about an article I was writing on the subject and asked him to respond. "It is not true," he wrote back, rather defensively, I thought, "that the Department of Architecture and Design can consider or has considered only one aspect of architecture, that is, its aspect as art. Our history of a dozen or more housing shows and various shows focusing on technology belies this. Make haste with your article so it can be debated publicly by people who know something about the subject rather than privately by me, who doesn't!" The last two words were added in his own handwriting.

CHAPTER THIRTEEN

■ Despite Alfred Barr's protestations, most of MOMA's trustees and officers had very little interest in architecture as anything other than walk-in sculpture—the more abstract, the better. Still, in 1948, when I began to work at MOMA, architecture in the U.S. and elsewhere had become inextricably mixed up with certain mundane but crucial economic, social, and political problems: hundreds of towns and cities in Europe, Africa, and Asia had been severely damaged and in many instances totally destroyed during World War II; millions of people in those same war-ravaged areas were in desperate need of housing and of other facilities; and even in the U.S., which had managed to survive the war largely unscathed, there were millions of ex-GI's and their families who were in fairly desperate need of affordable, mass-produced housing. Abstract, walk-in sculpture didn't seem to address these problems.

Although most of those involved with MOMA did not count homelessness as one of their own pressing personal concerns, they had probably seen newspaper photos of people who were homeless—both in the war-ravaged nations and closer to home. And so MOMA's trustees felt that the museum had to do *something* to confront what seemed to be a burning issue.

I suspect it was Philip's idea that MOMA should commission a first-rate modern architect to design a prototypical suburban house, for a prototypical young American family of four; and that this house should then be constructed, full-scale, in MOMA's garden off West 54th Street. In any event, the trustees thought it was a splendid idea, and the money was raised to retain such an architect and to build the house he would design.

The architect selected was Marcel Breuer, a prominent member of the pre-Hitler Bauhaus in Weimar and, later, in Dessau. Breuer had left Germany, practiced briefly in England, then joined his former Bauhaus mentor, Walter Gropius, to teach at the Graduate School of Design at Harvard. For several years, Gropius and Breuer had worked in partnership in Cambridge, Massachusetts, primarily designing and building houses that managed quite elegantly to translate the hard-edged industrial forms of the Bauhaus into white-painted wood structures somewhat (but not very) reminiscent of traditional New England clapboard houses.

The two had split up during the war years, and Breuer had moved to New York, where he was busy, after 1945, designing houses for adventurous younger clients. His houses were a felicitous blend of modern aesthetics and the sort of practical livability that young American families were thought to be seeking.

So Breuer was a good choice, though a curious one under the circumstances: Philip had been one of his students at Harvard, and while Breuer rarely bad-mouthed anyone, I had the distinct feeling that little love was lost between the former student and his former teacher. Conceivably, Breuer bore some sort of grudge against Philip from the days when the latter had been openly pro-Nazi; and it is conceivable that Philip selected Breuer to design this exhibition house because the latter (who came from a Hungarian Jewish family) offered him a perfect opportunity to atone for some of his past sins.

However that may be, the choice of Marcel Breuer by Philip Johnson seemed a trifle bizarre at the time: although Philip never ceased praising Breuer as the best studio teacher at Harvard, there was no doubt in anyone's mind that Philip Johnson was Mies van der Rohe's prime acolyte in the U.S.—and Breuer and Mies had had their disagreements in years past. Breuer felt that Mies had walked off with the mechanical patents for the famous tubular steel "cantilever chairs," a radically innovative 1928 design usually attributed to Breuer, but apparently a contested innovation, at the very least.

Philip's stance as an ardent partisan of Mies had made him one of the most controversial students in his class at Harvard's Graduate School of Design: Mies had been Harvard's first choice for the chairmanship of the Department of Architecture, and had turned down the job in a fit of pique—after which Harvard invited Gropius to take the position. To make his own position quite clear, Philip had firmly resisted the Gropius/Breuer line, which, to him, seemed to reduce architecture to a rather pedestrian social science; and he had disdainfully selected for his final thesis project an uncompromisingly Miesian townhouse of chromium-plated steel, plate glass, marble, and other luxurious, nonpedestrian materials and fittings. And not only had Philip designed this calculated insult to Gropius/Breuer in the uncompromising, minimalist manner of their severest critic, but, being both rich and sassy, he had then actually *built* the house for himself, thus upstaging his teachers (and his more docile fellow students) and establishing himself as a major creative force on the American architectural scene. Gropius, in one of his rare witticisms, called it a Sunday House.

Breuer and I, in the course of this exhibition house project and in the years that followed, became good friends. All of us—friends, relatives, former students—knew him as "Lajko," a Hungarian nickname for Lajos, his actual middle name. Lajko and I never talked about Philip, or about Philip's years at Harvard, or about Philip's decision to ask him, Breuer, to design MOMA's first exhibition house; but I suspect that Lajko was as baffled by the decision as I was—even though his selection, at that time and in that place, was probably as sensible a move as the museum could have made: had MOMA commissioned Buckminster Fuller, say, to design such a house, critics would have accused it of being (as usual) out of touch with reality; had MOMA commissioned Mies van der Rohe, Philip would have been accused of favoritism; and if it had commissioned Le Corbusier or Frank Lloyd Wright, all of us would have suffered a nervous breakdown in the course of getting the house designed and built, and the project might well have bankrupted the institution—or come close to doing so. Lajko could be depended upon to do a nice, modern job, livable, buildable, and within the budget. And that is exactly what he did.

The House in the Museum Garden was, indeed, a pleasant place, and it attracted hundreds of thousands of visitors. It was hardly one of Lajko's best houses. He once explained to me, several years later, that he was never at his best when trying to solve theoretical problems—he much preferred to respond to "real problems" and programs, presented to him by "real people" and "real sites." Still, the MOMA house, while not especially challenging, was a nice piece of work: it had a V-shaped, so-called "butterfly roof," a multilevel living area, sliding glass walls, and natural materials (stone, wood, and brick) as well as synthetic modern extrusions and finishes.

But what made it an unintentionally revealing piece of work was its scale: while in the "real world" American ex-GI's and their families were making do with compact little Levitt Houses (at $7,900 apiece, including land), this house was clearly designed for a considerably more affluent segment of American society: it was about four or five times the size of a typical GI-mortgage bungalow, and would have cost six or eight times the price of the Levitt Houses being constructed and sold by the tens of thousands in those same years. It was, in short, a "starter house" for the sons and daughters of MOMA's exceedingly affluent trustees—newly married just out of uniform or out of Ivy League college and living in Darien or in Westport. It had almost nothing to do with the housing problems of the "real world"—not even of the real affluent U.S. society that had survived the war unscathed and, in fact, considerably enriched.

I confess that my friends and I became aware only gradually of this elitist cast to MOMA's efforts in architecture. In all fairness, I should confess that we were pleased that a demonstration project would be built of what a *modern* house (as opposed to a cut-rate Colonial bungalow) could offer to a "typical" American family. And all of us who knew Lajko were pleased that he was given the opportunity to show the world what a bona fide modern architect could do when given a more or less free hand. (It is difficult to recall, today, that mortgage banks, building code enforcers, and others in charge of determining architectural taste in the United States were generally opposed to anything "modern," and that it was enormously difficult to translate any unconventional glass-walled house from blueprints into reality, given the horrendous obstacles constructed by public and private agencies. So the MOMA house, with its attendant publicity and wide public acclaim, clearly made life easier for young architects wanting to experiment with ideas they had absorbed at Harvard and elsewhere.)

But many of us were pleased, primarily, because Lajko was the architect selected. There was an entire mini-generation of architects who had gone to Harvard in the late 1930s and early 1940s and had been students of Gropius and of Breuer; and their names read like a roster of the leaders of the new architecture in post–World

War II America, and, in some cases, abroad: not only Philip Johnson, but also John Johansen, Ulrich Franzen, Paul Rudolph, I. M. Pei, Harry Cobb, Harry Seidler, Landis Gores, William Breger, Willo von Moltke, Bruno Zevi, Fumihiko Maki, and innumerable others came out of Gropius's and Breuer's studios at Harvard—and virtually all of them agreed that it was Lajko who taught them how to design buildings while Gropius provided the theoretical and philosophical underpinnings. They were utterly devoted to Lajko: he was a sweet, simple, generous friend, not the most sophisticated intellectual any of us had ever met, but a man of great warmth and kindness, and a designer of taste, sensitivity, and occasionally of genius. He did not have the flawless touch I found in Le Corbusier's work, which I had seen in Europe and was to see in India, Japan, and elsewhere; he did not have the rigorous discipline and spare elegance of Mies or the responsive humanity of Aalto. But he had some of those qualities, most of the time, in much of his work. And when he did the MOMA house, he had not done anything larger than a house—and it wasn't until his practice flourished and he had to tackle large and very complex projects like the UNESCO Headquarters in Paris, that Lajko slipped more than a little, here and there.

He had been born in 1902, in the university town of Pécs (Fünfkirchen), in southern Hungary—a little medieval town, almost on the outer reaches of the Austro-Hungarian Empire. Many years later, when I happened to visit Pécs, I realized what a courageous move it had been for Lajko to leave this little town at the age of eighteen and to move to Vienna to study furniture design and architecture—and thence to the Bauhaus, in Weimar, the center of avant-gardism in Europe in those years. When he got there, after a brief apprenticeship in Vienna, he was appointed head of the Furniture Workshop; and four or five years later he developed his first chromium-plated, tubular-steel chair—the one now known as the "Wassily chair," named after Lajko's friend Kandinsky. That was, in effect, the beginning of modern furniture as we know it today (virtually all other designs, in the nineteenth and twentieth centuries, had used traditional materials); and Lajko was just twenty-three years old. Not bad for a designer whom later critics, whose knowledge of the Modern Movement was perhaps just a little fragmentary, termed a "minor talent."

In fact, *all* basic notions of modern furniture design were developed by Lajko over a period of about three or four years, starting in 1925 or thereabouts: modular storage units and walls, steel supporting structure and softer, friendlier, more touchable contact surfaces, and much else. In later years some of these notions were further explored by Lajko (and manufactured in Switzerland and Britain), using aluminum, bent and molded plywood, and plastics. Charles Eames, the only major furniture designer in this century who developed a comparable range of innovative designs, once told me that he couldn't possibly have done what he did without Lajko's remarkable pioneering designs. But critics and home furnishing editors, from the 1960s on, with little of real interest to write about, forgot his work and began to tout shoddy imitations of the dozens of designs developed by Lajko in the 1920s, either for Thonet (the manufacturer of many of them) or for his own amusement.

When the MOMA house was being designed by Lajko, we decided to produce a book on his work. No such book had ever been done, in part, I suspect, because Lajko was too modest to promote himself; and I went through hundreds of photographs and drawings of his work, scattered around in various files, crates, and drawers in his office, and wrote the lengthy and, I suppose, definitive text. MOMA published the book when the house opened; and while I found it difficult to include more than a fraction of Lajko's early furniture designs, and his several projected and completed buildings, there were enough of these to amaze most readers who were unfamiliar with the radical work done by him in the 1920s and 1930s. (Some thirty years later, MOMA commissioned another, very handsome book on Lajko's work in furniture and interiors alone. That book was almost twice as long as my initial effort and much more comprehensive. It served as a catalogue to a major MOMA exhibit held in 1981, the year Lajko died.)

When I was working on my book, I once asked him how he came to the notion of using bent tubular steel to frame his furniture. "Well, I was living in a room at the Bauhaus, in Weimar," Lajko said, "and early every morning a milkman arrived to deliver his bottles. He arrived on a bicycle, and I kept admiring the elegance of those chromium-plated tubular-steel handlebars. So that's how it began." Lajko, who was very much a "hands-on" designer, knew how to bend tubular steel, and so he experimented with the material endlessly, developing different kinds of frames for chairs and stools, always trying to make his tubing act as a continuous, "organic" structure—resilient, but also very stable and strong. After he had constructed several prototypes, he approached the German steel manufacturer Mannesmann and proposed that they might want to manufacture the furniture. "They thought I was crazy," Lajko told me. "They were just as stupid as manufacturers are today." So he went to Thonet, the German/Austrian/American firm that had made some of the more interesting new furniture of the time, and Thonet agreed to manufacture several of Lajko's designs, as well as later pieces by others that were based on Lajko's innovations.

One of the latecomers was Mart Stam, the Dutch architect who had made a name for himself as a member of the de Stijl group. "Stam came to see me one day," Lajko told me, "and asked to see my furniture. I showed him the tubular-steel pieces, and picked up a small, U-shaped stool that I had just finished." Lajko set the stool on its side, creating the beginning of a "cantilever profile," and told Stam: "That will be my next chair. It'll be resilient, you see." Stam was impressed—so much so that he went home and tried to copy Lajko's "next chair"—the "cantilever chair" manufactured to this day and sold everywhere as a "Breuer" or "Brewer" or "Brauer" or "Breier" chair. Unfortunately for him, Stam—unlike Lajko—didn't know how to *bend* tubular steel (you have to pack the tubing with sand, and only then heat and bend it to avoid having it snap instead of curve); and so Mart Stam's chair was made with clumsy L-shaped plumber's connections and turned out to be something of a joke. Later critics, who didn't know much about the technology of modern furniture either, credited Stam for having produced what was clearly a derivative and unworkable nondesign.

The House in the Museum Garden was a popular success, and Breuer was asked to design and build several adaptations of it for various clients who had seen the MOMA version. After the exhibition in the Museum Garden closed at the end of the summer of 1949, Nelson Rockefeller bought the MOMA house and it was cut into two or three sections and moved on flatbed trucks to the Rockefeller estate in Tarrytown, where it was reassembled to serve as a residence for Rockefeller guests. It stands there still.

Philip and I were convinced that MOMA should construct another exhibition house in the Museum Garden, to be opened the next summer; and while we were pleased with the success of Lajko's house, we felt that something a little more closely attuned to the needs of young American families seeking a place in a typical suburban development would be more appropriate. The West Coast architect Gregory Ain had done two or three rather handsome suburban houses for developers around Los Angeles, and we thought he should be asked to do something similar for MOMA. He was and did. It was a very neat job, much more realistic in terms of size and amenities than Lajko's elegant residence; but, perhaps predictably, it attracted fewer visitors and less enthusiasm than its predecessor. It did, however, counter some of the accusations of elitism leveled at the earlier house. I wrote a small catalogue for that exhibition as well, but other exhibits, impending as well as projected for the more distant future, took up more and more of my time; and Philip, with his spectacular Glass House in New Canaan completed, was devoting more and more of *his* time to his own practice.

CHAPTER FOURTEEN

■ In the late 1940s, most of the architects who would later gain prominence on the American scene were just out of the armed services, or out of school, or both. There were not very many of them, and most were friends or acquaintances. Many of these young people had come out of Harvard's Graduate School of Design, and had been Lajko's students. A few had graduated from schools of architecture at MIT, Yale, Princeton, Penn, or Cornell. Pratt Institute, in Brooklyn, N.Y., was graduating a few bright young people—and we were aware of the fact that schools in the Middle West (like Cranbrook under Eliel Saarinen, and Illinois Institute of Technology under Mies) were also producing some promising talent. But most of the young people in American architecture had been trained at schools that still subscribed, more or less, to the Beaux-Arts system or its American equivalent; and while they often acquired admirable skills, they seemed to have none of the commitment or sophistication that those who had come out of Harvard, MIT, and Yale claimed for themselves.

I suppose that I was part of this little coterie, although I had not come out of Harvard. Still, I seemed to be generally accepted.

We were a very small group, and we all knew one another: some of us, like Ed Barnes, had taken the plunge and opened their own offices, doing small houses for adventurous friends; others, like John Johansen and Ulrich Franzen, had gone to work in larger, established firms, waiting for the opportunity to start on their own. One or two others, like Paul Rudolph, had formed associations with older firms, in other parts of the country, hoping to practice what they had been taught at Harvard and elsewhere under the umbrellas of established firms. There were so few of us that we saw one another constantly—at parties, in New York, or in New Canaan, Connecticut, where the Breuers had built a very handsome house for themselves and where Philip was building his glass house, and where half of our friends seemed to be in the process of building houses for themselves before very long: Eliot Noyes, who had been a student of Lajko's (and a curator of industrial design at MOMA before he went into the Army); John Johansen, another former student of Lajko's; Landis Gores, still another Harvard graduate; and numerous others had either built modern houses in New Canaan or were spending weekends out there visiting friends and looking for land on which to build.

We were all very clannish, just as the New York School painters were, and just as the radical writers around Dwight Macdonald were—hanging out in the same bars and restaurants; going to the same parties; swapping wives, husbands, girlfriends, boyfriends; and sharing some of the same political interests.

There were, in fact, several political clans of distinct colorations, ranging from Stalinists (whom most of us considered to be crashing bores) to fellow travelers (who supported Henry Wallace's presidential candidacy and seemed to me to be charmingly and sometimes irritatingly naïve), to people without specific political interests (like Paul Rudolph and Harry Cobb). And there were a few people, like Philip, who were known to have had a rather dubious political past and no discernible political present. But all of us, regardless of momentary allegiance, had a conviction that as modern architects we belonged to a totally dedicated avant-garde—the heirs of Le Corbusier and Mies and the Bauhaus, and, in a few cases, of Frank Lloyd Wright. We *knew* that the only valid architecture of the century was modern, and we *knew* that the world's problems called for the transformation of the larger human habitat, especially in cities. We also *knew* that this transformation implied a degree of planning that was possible only under a form of socialism; and while most of us had our doubts about the kind of planning that had been going on in the Soviet Union, we were convinced that a free enterprise system of the sort that had shaped the United States—especially in the 1920s—could not begin to solve the problems created by population explosion and dwindling natural resources that we recognized in every part of the world.

The reason our kind of architecture—modern architecture—had to look different from that of the past was fairly obvious to us: mass-produced, industrial, modular building technology would necessarily produce minimalist forms, repetitive patterns, "machine art" details. We felt that everything that had happened in the visual arts since the early 1900s supported and reinforced our kind of "modern" aesthetic: the cubists had laid the groundwork, as had the pioneers of Russian Constructivism and Italian Futurism. We felt that everything that was happening in advanced technologies—in the mass production of automobiles and of other consumer products, and the manufacture of aircraft, ships, rockets, and all the rest—seemed to lead to similar aesthetic conclusions: unadorned surfaces, precise assemblies, and articulated functional components. Everything we saw about us seemed to confirm our belief in a kind of architecture that was as neat and clean as a jet, as expressively articulated as a suspension bridge or a jeep or a stripped-down sports car, and as logically modular as a computer grid.

Moreover, everything that we saw about us in the modern world also seemed to fit in, neatly and often uncannily, with the cubist visions of Picasso and Braque, with the spatial definitions created by Rietveld and Oud, with the exciting structures dreamed up by El Lissitzky and Leonidov. We had absolutely no doubt that we were on the right track; and we thought that people like Lewis Mumford (who challenged much of our dogma in the name of humanism) and a few surviving classicists were sweet and sentimental holdovers from an earlier time—and obviously out of touch. We were the avant-garde—we would be described today as being at the "cutting edge" of things—and I am sure we were more than a little arrogant in parading our convictions.

For this architectural avant-garde in the U.S. and elsewhere, the Museum of Modern Art (and, especially, its Department of Architecture and Industrial Design) was quite clearly one of the established outposts. Whatever MOMA did in the way of exhibitions, symposia, or other public manifestations would attract everyone in our circle of accomplices. For young modern architects, MOMA was what "The Club" on East 8th Street in Manhattan was for the members of the New York School of painting and sculpture.

And yet there was that one false note in MOMA's view of modern architecture—and it was a note that came to trouble my friends and me the more we thought about it.

Because most of us believed that the Modern Movement was not merely—or even primarily—a new "International Style," as MOMA had described it in 1932, the museum's attitude toward architecture bore very little relationship to our conception of what we (and our movement) were all about. The Modern Movement, in our view, was a politically radical commitment to enhancing the human condition—a way of dealing with predictably desperate problems of excessive urbanization and universal overpopulation. Admittedly, we thought we could help create a more beautiful man-made world as well; but as Breuer liked to put it, architecture is shaped by a great many things—function, technology, economics, sociology, politics, and so on. "And then there is that one percent which is art." Most of us (including, I suspect, Lajko Breuer) thought that art accounted for a little more than that—perhaps twenty-five percent; but all of us were convinced that the new architecture was shaped by ideas and forces that were primarily political in nature, and radical at that.

To the wealthy trustees of the Museum of Modern Art, this vision of the Modern Movement was undoubtedly troublesome, to say the least. I became convinced, the longer I stayed at MOMA, that Alfred Barr's invention of the term "International Style" in 1932 was an unconscious attempt on his part to assuage the fears of the Rockefellers and of the other MOMA trustees who were clearly not prepared to endorse a new movement that was essentially anticapitalist in nature. When MOMA published its important catalogue to the 1932 exhibition, entitled *The International Style: Architecture Since 1922,* the foreword was written by Alfred—and it was in his foreword that he coined that term; the bulk of the rest of the catalogue was written by the brilliant architectural historian Henry-Russell Hitchcock (a close friend of Johnson's) and by Philip himself. Their text—cool, precise, and logical as far as it went—described the International Style as a new art form and related it knowledgeably to other "styles" and to parallel developments in painting and sculpture. After getting to know Johnson and Hitchcock, and their irreverent ways of dealing with self-important do-gooders and other bores, I could imagine that at some point while working on that catalogue, Philip must have thrown up his hands and said: "Heavens, we forgot all about housing!"—and Russell or Alfred (or Philip himself) would, in all likelihood, have come up with the perfect solution: "Let's ask Lewis to take care of it!" Lewis Mumford had all the right credentials: he was leftish, concerned with the human condition, knowledgeable about such things as "housing" (which I suspect bored Philip and Russell to tears), and admirably serious. He was ideally positioned to protect MOMA's left flank in the controversies that were sure to arise.

To people like Mies, Gropius, Le Corbusier, Oud, and others represented in the exhibition, the idea that the new movement was just another "style" was anathema. Mies had written in the early 1920s that "form is not the aim of our work, but only the result. . . . form as an aim is formalism, and that we reject." And the others agreed. Interestingly enough, a number of latter-day architecture critics, especially in the U.S., insisted on labeling the work of architects committed to Mies's and Le Corbusier's principles as "modernist" (as in "classicist" or "naturalist" or "fetishist") instead of "modern," and referring to their buildings as examples of the International Style—thus trying to dispose of what was a politically radical and technologically sound body of work as just another fashion, like such nouveaux riches vulgarities as Art Deco and postmodernism. Architecture critics, by and large, have little training and no experience in designing or building buildings, and their judgments are almost exclusively shaped by visual or historical criteria, or by what is stylish this month or, at most, this year.

I don't think that many of us were clear in our own minds what it was about MOMA's stance on architecture that made us feel uneasy. We all realized, I think, that the Goodwin & Stone glass box was not a very distinguished building—though vastly better than most of what was going up in Manhattan in those years. And we all sensed that architecture, in the eyes of MOMA's trustees, was an expensive (and hence luxurious) plaything of the rich. Still, MOMA was a great meeting place for like-minded young architects and designers, and its galleries were one of the few spaces in Manhattan where works of modern architecture and design could be displayed well and unfettered by commercialism.

But most of all we were drawn to MOMA because Philip was there. His quick wit, irreverence, scholarship, and wide-ranging interests in all the arts and in the work of artists in many fields and disciplines made him by far the most interesting and knowledgeable commentator on our segment of the contemporary scene. He could be infuriating, and he often was. He could be arrogant, insulting, cutting, bitchy, devastatingly nasty—and he often was all of those things. But he was never boring. Where almost every other commentator on architecture and related arts in the decades after World War II was likely to put you to sleep almost instantly with his or her predictable pomposities, Philip was totally unpredictable and therefore never dull.

Nor was he above poking fun at himself: I used to spend Saturdays and sometimes weekends at his glass house in New Canaan to discuss various plans for exhibitions and publications, and he would meet my train at the New Canaan station and we'd drive over to Ponus Ridge, where his house was located. One Saturday around noon, he met me at the station as usual and looked rather disgruntled. "What's up?" I asked him. "Oh, Iris Barry came by to see me this morning," he said, grumpily. "That's nice," I said noncommittally. (Iris was the director of MOMA's film program, and a lively and sexy Englishwoman whom all of us liked.) "She wants to marry me," Philip said, now steeped in gloom. "Oh, come on, you can't be serious!" I probably sounded unflatteringly surprised. "What do you mean?" Philip responded, quite huffily. "A rich fag—I'd be a perfect catch for her!" In those days (the late 1940s), no "fags" of my acquaintance, other than Philip, had emerged from their closets, and many of my homosexual friends were going through hell because their "affliction" was considered almost a crime by most Americans. Only Philip among my acquaintances was totally insouciant in the matter: he couldn't care less who knew that he was a "fag"; and while he was reluctant to parade his rather effeminate companion of those years before the likes of Rockefellers and Whitneys, his own mannerisms—his high-pitched voice, his mincing steps, his theatrical gesturing—left little doubt. I confess that after that morning's conversation, I would (and did) forgive him anything. I was totally charmed, and I still am.

The glass house was and is a wonderful place—not really a house, but a carpet of brick seemingly afloat in a lovely and ever changing landscape. To anyone who has not been fortunate enough to experience such a house it is difficult to explain: it is as if you were living in a wall-less garden in a clearing in the woods and the nonexistent walls around you were being transformed, almost every moment of the day and night, by changing light, by changing seasons, by changes in the weather. The house might seem like a glass-and-steel shelter at one moment, from which all the beauty of a

rain-swept landscape might be revealed; on another occasion, at night, the house would be lit only from lights reflected off the undersides of branches and leaves all around—a wonderfully poetic arrangement worked out by Philip and his friend Dick Kelly, a brilliant and often inebriated lighting genius who worked with Philip for many years. At other times the sun would come streaming in through the trees; or, in the winter months, it would be reflected off the snow that blanketed the countryside. It was never the same, not from one moment to the next, and in the first year or two after the house was completed, Philip would zip around the place adjusting dimmers, screens, replacing light bulbs, rearranging this and that, and driving most of us crazy.

He had as much fun with his new house as a toddler with a wonderful new toy—and his joy was infectious. One day, a group of very serious architects from North Carolina arrived to inspect the glass house—its fame had spread across the country and the world, thanks in part to Philip's uninhibited publicizing—and the visitors stood around him in a circle thinking of profound things to say and searching questions to ask. "What is the heat loss in your house on a typical December day?" one of the North Carolinians finally asked, trying to sound professionally concerned. Philip, who I am certain had never given the matter a moment's thought, threw up his arms in utter delight. "The heat loss," he said, "is absolutely tremendous!" And he beamed from ear to ear. Philip loved being naughty, and I confess that I found his naughtiness much more entertaining than the seriousness of many of my more solemn friends. Some of the latter thought he was positively evil. Perhaps they were not aware of the enormous generosity of which he was capable—in part, I suspect, because he made very sure that nobody knew. His generosity to me was a frequent delight: when Petty and I got married, in 1952, he was not only a witness to the proceedings, but insisted upon having a delightful champagne dinner afterwards for bride and groom at the glass house on Ponus Ridge. The house, the landscape, and the host were at their most splendid on that day.

To be invited to visit the glass house might seem like a sign that one had been admitted to a fairly exclusive club. Actually, the club had a very wide membership: sooner or later, everyone of any standing in the arts, in the U.S. or abroad, would show up at the house if he or she happened to be within a hundred miles or so of New Canaan. One weekend, when Philip and some of his guests returned from a nearby cocktail party, we found an amazing sight: someone had dropped in while we were gone and had written a long letter to Philip on the glass, using a cake of soap, with the sentences winding around the house in continuous, descending lines. What made this inscription even stranger was that it had been written in reverse, from right to left, and was therefore legible only from *inside* the glass house.

The only person any of us knew who was capable of writing backwards (as well as forwards and ambidextrously) was Eero Saarinen, and it had indeed been Eero who had dropped in to pay his respects, and to leave a note for Philip to express his delight and admiration. Philip was vastly amused—though somewhat less so after it had taken us several hours to hose down the glass and restore the house to its pristine beauty.

The glass house has been described at great length in books and magazines and newspapers. It has been photographed and filmed and televised. In short, most people have a pretty good idea of what it is like—though the magic of the constantly changing reflections, and the changes in light and shade, are hard to convey, even in photographs and on film. It is not really a single house at all, but two houses, separated by about 125 feet: One of them is the glass house framed in steel, containing a living-dining space, an open kitchen, a brick cylinder housing a bathroom with a fireplace notched out

Glass house, New Canaan, Conn. The long facade of Philip Johnson's own house measures about sixty feet. Like the other facades, this one has a centrally located door, hinged on the right. Unfortunately, when the door is open, the symmetry of the facade is violated. (Courtesy, Philip Johnson)

of one of the cylinder's sides, and a sleeping area screened off from the rest by a freestanding storage wall. The other house is a guest house containing bedrooms and bathrooms, and it is all brick: one entrance door, precisely in the center of an all-brick exterior, faces the glass house; and, facing uphill and away from the glass house, there are three large porthole windows set into the brickwork. ("The locals say that the brick box is where Mr. Johnson keeps his three-headed brother," Philip explained to me.)

What makes this composition rather curious is that both the brick house and the glass house have precisely symmetrical facades. Yet the two houses are offset from each other so that the centrally placed entrance doors don't face each other and are joined by a diagonal path that bisects a manicured lawn. This dichotomy between symmetry and asymmetry is evident throughout, and curiously revealing of Philip's own internal conflicts as an architect—and possibly beyond. For example, the glass house has four symmetrical facades, each of them with a tall glass entrance door in its center. Yet the interior, which is almost always visible through the glass walls, is quite asymmetrical in composition, and seemingly in conflict with the external composition.

Symmetry in architecture has frequently been equated with au-

Johnson glass house. The short facades are also symmetrically composed. Since the house is transparent, the asymmetry of the interior conflicts visibly with the symmetrical facades. Mies van der Rohe's Farnsworth House is deliberately asymmetrical, in plan and elevations. (Courtesy, Philip Johnson)

Mies van der Rohe's Farnsworth House, in Plano, Illinois, designed prior to Johnson's glass house, but not built until about 1950. Unlike Johnson's house, the Farnsworth House is asymmetrical and raised off the ground. (George H. Steuer)

thoritarianism; and most symbolic buildings of most great periods in Western architecture were symmetrical in elevation, and often in their relationship to nearby structures and gardens. The concept of symmetry seemed to imply the central, instantly recognizable reference point, the place to look for the symbol of authority. And so one of the articles of faith of modern architecture (the architecture of popular democracy, among other things) was a commitment to asymmetry: it is very difficult to think of a single significant building of the formative years of the Modern Movement that was symmetrical in elevation: Wright's Robie House of 1909, Mies's Barcelona Pavilion of 1928, Le Corbusier's Villa Stein at Garches of 1927, Alvar Aalto's Sanitorium at Paimio of 1928 were not merely asymmetrical—they were determinedly *anti*symmetrical!

But Philip's glass house and its companion piece, the all-brick guesthouse, seemed to contain this curious, internal conflict: both were symmetrical in their elevations but asymmetrically related to each other; and the glass house, while symmetrical in all its elevations, was quite visibly asymmetrical in its interior spaces—thus seemingly in conflict with itself.

Philip was always generous to a fault in giving credit to Mies for having designed the first all-glass-and-steel house—the house for Dr. Edith Farnsworth, designed in 1946 but not completed until a couple of years after Philip had completed his house. But while Philip's house clearly owed a good deal to Mies's initial idea, the two completed buildings were totally different: Philip's house sat sturdily, monumentally, on the ground, like a small classical palazzo—whereas Mies's Farnsworth House was elevated three or four feet above the ground, like a plane about to take off into space. Whereas Philip's house had massive steel columns (much heavier than structurally necessary) at its corners, Mies's Farnsworth House was cantilevered out from its recessed steel columns—and much more expressive of modern structural reality. And while Philip's house was symmetrical in its elevations, Mies's house was asymmetrical in composition—and its interior spaces were harmoniously asymmetrical as well.

In short, and rather oddly, Philip's house was classically European, and authoritarian at that; whereas Mies's house was free, "American," light, airy, and much closer to the Robie House in composition than to Karl Friedrich Schinkel's neoclassicism—the alleged inspiration of Mies's work, according to American theorists and critics who tried to classify Mies's work in ways that continued to surprise him.

I don't think that Philip was aware of these internal conflicts—or, if he was, that they bothered him at all. On one occasion, though, he was momentarily unhinged by a friend's critical observation: Jean Paul Carlhian, the Beaux-Arts–trained French-born architect whom Philip and I had met several years earlier, came to visit the glass house and to admire it. "But it's too bad about the entrance doors, of course," Jean Paul said as he was getting ready to leave. Philip, who respected Jean Paul's critical judgment, was startled. "What's wrong with them?" he asked. "Well, it's obvious, I should think," Jean Paul said in his heavily French-accented English. "Here you have placed your doors in the exact centers of your glass walls—but when you open them up it completely throws off the symmetry!" The doors, one in each of the four walls, were single doors, hinged on one side, so that the facades became instantly asymmetrical when the doors were propped open—which was, in fact, most of the time during the summer, to let the breezes sweep through the house. What Philip should have done, of course, according to Jean Paul and his Beaux-Arts deities, was to make each of the four doors a *pair* of double doors, to be opened in unison so as to preserve the symmetrical composition. Jean Paul had scored, and Philip was crushed. "Dammit," he said, slapping his forehead with the palm of his hand. "How could I have been so blind!" It was the only time I ever saw him shaken by a critical comment on his work.

Was he a good architect? Of course. Was he a great architect? Probably not. Philip's problem was that he simply knew too much. He was almost certainly the finest scholar, the finest historian among all the architects who practiced in the second half of this century. Each commission, to him, was an opportunity to try out an idea that had intrigued him for years—an idea, very often, that had first surfaced in the built or theoretical work of another architect, in another time—and to translate that idea into a modern idiom. Sometimes the translation hit a snag somewhere along the way; at other times it came off well: Philip had been fascinated by the projects of Claude-Nicolas Ledoux (1736–1806) long before many others had so much as heard of the *Architecte du Roi;* and I was certain that he would "do" a Ledoux building at the first opportunity. He did, when the University of Houston, in the 1980s, asked him to design a new School of Architecture; and so Ledoux's Maison d'Éducation now stands in Texas, some 200 years after it was originally designed. Philip tried his hand on several Schinkel interpretations, with less success; and on Pugin's and Sir Charles Barry's neo-Gothic fantasies, when doing the reflective glass headquarters for PPG, in Pittsburgh.

In many instances, I am sure, Philip was poking fun at the American scene—especially at the sort of nouveaux riches pretensions that would faintly amuse any well-born and well-educated, aristocratic Western European. For although Philip was, in fact, born in Cleveland, Ohio, of American-born parents, he was essentially European: his suits were unmistakably tailored on Savile Row, his German was virtually flawless, and I think his French was almost as good. He was totally at home almost anywhere in Western Europe, and I had the distinct impression that Americans—especially self-made and self-educated Americans—secretly amused him. In some of his later buildings, especially those he did for superrich clients in places like Fort Worth and Houston, I thought his approach was distinctly tongue-in-cheek.

But, most of the time, he was trying very hard to do buildings of great sophistication and quality; and there are enough of these to ensure him a secure place in twentieth-century American architecture: his twin-towered "Pennzoil Place" in Houston, his Crystal Cathedral in Garden Grove, California, and his Kline Laboratories at Yale—to mention only a few—are first- or almost first-rate, and characteristically grounded in historic scholarship as well as architectural talent.

Philip had been totally obsessed with Mies van der Rohe and his work—so much so that I felt he considered Mies his substitute father and loved him with a passion. (That love was not exactly returned by the old man, who once described Philip to me as a *Windhund*—German for whippet, with overtones of jittery slickness.) Philip broke with Mies, philosophically and personally, after the completion of the Seagram Building in Manhattan, for which Philip did the interiors of the Four Seasons Restaurant. After the break, Philip seemed architecturally adrift, designing and building several fairly absurd structures reminiscent of stripped-down neoclassicism of the sort practiced by some of Mussolini's architects in the years before World War II. In a sense, these neoclassical Texas palazzi were the beginning of postmodernism in America, and more will be said about that in a later chapter.

Meanwhile, from 1949 on, Philip's glass house in New Canaan was the place where he and I would get together on weekends to plan whatever next moves the Department of Architecture and Industrial Design should make, and to settle on some of the details of exhibitions and other events that we wanted to undertake. Although Philip was quite mercurial in arriving at decisions and might change his mind half a dozen times before settling on a proposal, he was a sheer delight to argue with. We discovered very quickly that we could communicate in a sort of rapid shorthand, that he would grasp instantly what I was trying to say long before I had finished saying it, and vice versa. There was a complete rapport between us in most respects, and we were able to settle most problems in our department at MOMA in a matter of seconds or minutes because we understood one another without any difficulty. After which we could concentrate on matters that took a little longer to decide.

Those weekends contributed enormously to my own education. I was still, theoretically, enrolled at the School of Architecture at

A multilevel house was my "thesis project"—an attempt in 1949 to create a spacious cube with virtually no interior walls, and privacy achieved by creating "rooms" on different levels.

Pratt Institute and was busy completing my thesis project—a very "Miesian" asymmetrical, multilevel house of glass and steel that would later be published in the *Architectural Record;* but my real schoolroom was the glass house on Ponus Ridge. Here I met that talented young Polish architect Matthew Nowicki, who had come to the U.S. after the end of World War II and was working with the American architect Albert Mayer on the plans for the new capital of the Punjab, to be known as Chandigarh—plans which were turned over to Le Corbusier after Nowicki died in an airplane crash in Egypt, on his way to India. And here I also met Lodovico Belgioioso and his partner Enrico Peressutti, who would become friends of mine in later years, in Milan. And there were many, many more: it was as if the glass house, for a few moments in time, had become the center of everything that was exciting in architecture in the U.S., in Europe, in Latin America, and in Asia. And not only in architecture: on a typical weekend, the most interesting new painters and sculptors would drop in, and there would be critics, museum curators, writers, composers, filmmakers, photographers, poets, and assorted academics. The glass house was a beautiful salon, and here the worlds of the new architecture and the new arts met on weekends and mapped out the future. Or so it seemed.

By the beginning of 1950, Philip and I had decided to mount a major exhibition on automobile design, and I began to spend most of my time looking at collections of great classic cars in the East, as well as in Chicago, Detroit, and Los Angeles. I spent some time with a man named Cameron Peck, in Chicago, who had built himself a huge warehouse near Evanston to house about 200 great automobiles which he had collected over the years—almost everything from the earliest electric car to the latest custom jobs by Pinin Farina. And I spent some time at the Henry Ford Museum in Dearborn, outside Detroit, to determine which cars from that remarkable collection should be shown in MOMA's planned exhibition.

By the summer of 1950, with the automobile exhibition well under way, I decided to accept an offer from the *Architectural Forum,* which was now being run by Douglas Haskell, a former editor on the *Architectural Record*. I had done one or two free-lance articles for the *Record* while I was at MOMA—in particular, one on the Soviet Architecture Purge, Stalin's destruction of the adventurous Russian Constructivist Movement, and his installation of neoclassicist commissars to direct the new architecture of the USSR—and I had got to know Haskell while doing these articles. Now that he was the editor in chief of the magazine I had once worked for, briefly, he asked me to come back to the *Forum* as an associate editor, at more than twice my salary at MOMA.

Although I had vastly enjoyed my time at MOMA and especially with Philip Johnson, I really couldn't afford to turn down Haskell's offer. Martha and I had a new baby daughter, and we needed the money. Moreover, I had a great sentimental attachment to the *Forum*, and to editorial work. And so I accepted. Philip asked me if I could think of someone to take my place, and I told him of a young writer for *Interiors* magazine, Arthur Drexler, who had done an interesting piece about my museum project for Jackson Pollock. Philip hadn't heard of Drexler, but they met and liked each other, and Arthur replaced me at MOMA. I am not certain that he ever knew I had recommended him; in any case, he took over from me and stayed on for more than thirty-five years, until he died in 1987, having accomplished infinitely more than I could ever have hoped to.

CHAPTER FIFTEEN

■ Many things had changed at the *Architectural Forum* since Howard
Myers's death in 1949, few of them for the better: My friend
George Nelson had left to concentrate on his practice as a designer,
architect, critic and gadfly; Henry Wright, an excruciatingly serious pioneer in the then rather esoteric area of energy conservation,
had left also. (The two of them had been joint managing editors
under Howard's inspired and diplomatic direction, but seemed to
have little in common other than their shared title.) And one or two
friends of mine had left to practice what they had preached, and so
had some of the rather notorious fellow travelers who had poisoned
the political atmosphere at the magazine for at least some of their
co-workers.

More important, Howard Myers had been replaced by a man
called Pierrepont Isham "Perry" Prentice, a wealthy former class-
mate (at Yale) of Henry Luce, and a reject from various key positions at Time Inc. Prentice had curious qualifications for his new
position: He knew absolutely nothing about architecture, and he
had been a spectacular failure as a publisher, business manager, circulation manager, and generator of advertising revenues. His principal claim to fame at Time Inc. was that he had almost succeeded
in single-handedly strangling *Life* magazine at birth, by vastly

underestimating its probable circulation. Advertising page rates had been determined by Perry's flawed estimates, and the magazine signed long-term contracts with advertisers based on those estimates. As a result, *Life*—which, thanks to its editors and photographers, was extremely successful and enjoyed a huge circulation almost from the start—had to print millions of advertising pages at a disproportionately low rate and at enormous cost; and this situation lasted until the advertising contracts could finally be renegotiated and renewed to reflect the magazine's circulation more accurately. Perry had not done much better in other important positions he had held: as publisher of *Time* he managed to antagonize a significant portion of the editorial staff, and similarly as business manager of *Fortune*.

Like his mentor, Luce, Perry had a dreadful stammer (as did several other close associates of the godfather); and, like Luce, he was vastly opinionated in virtually all matters. But, unlike Luce, he was also grotesquely wrong in almost all the opinions he inflicted upon the rest of us in that terrible stammer, in interminable nonstop lectures—and wrong, most particularly, in just those areas, like publishing, circulation, and advertising, on which he was in theory an expert. His political views were also noteworthy: Like Luce, he was an arch-Republican, but unlike Luce, who was open to almost any ideas so long as they were challenging, Perry seemed to have a mind that was hermetically sealed. He was about as far to the right politically as anyone I have ever met and showed signs of harboring any number of prejudices that his Yalie manners alone prevented him from expressing.

We had no way of knowing it at the time, but Perry would prove to be only the first in a succession of rejects whom the managers at Time Inc. chose to unload on our small and defenseless publication. His arrival at the helm of the *Architectural Forum* as "Editor and Publisher" should have been a warning to those of us who had carried the torch for Howard Myers and for modern architecture—a respectable cause then, as it is occasionally now. During Perry's tenure, we had to be ready, around the clock, to keep him from plunging the magazine into some mad economic or intellectual abyss—and we were on notice, almost around the clock, for a summons to his corner office and to sit still and silent, literally for hours on end, to listen to the Editor and Publisher's latest insights, and to prevent him from transforming our stories into shrill advertising copy seemingly phrased to sell the latest hooch or the latest Edsel.

In the end, he would turn out to be an almost unmitigated disaster, single-handedly destroying the *Forum's* economic viability.

And yet, all this said, it should in fairness be added that Perry was personally rather likable, possessed of a certain charm and, in his own way, not uninteresting. Like Luce and many other stammerers, he had that terrible uninterruptibility; but if you did succeed in stopping his interminable stream of drivel, you might occasionally engage him in something close to a discourse, and actually benefit from some of his amazing insights, or misconceptions. I remember one day trying to explain to him what Mies van der Rohe meant by "universality" in his buildings—the notion that the ultimate functions of a building were quite unpredictable nowadays, and that we ought to create open spaces that were infinitely flexible, that could in fact be converted without much trouble from their initial function (as a city hall, for example) into something totally different (for example, an automobile showroom). Perry listened to me with his mouth open, but not in its normal speaking mode. After I had finished explaining Mies's point, Perry could contain himself no longer. "That's a terrible idea!" he sputtered. "It would instantly destroy the American building economy! Don't you realize that we depend on replacing obsolete buildings with new ones, again and again? We'd be bankrupt overnight. What Mies is saying is practically a communist notion!"

It was my turn to be amazed. Without realizing it, Perry had put his finger on the significance of a key concept of modern architecture. To Perry, who had met Mies only briefly on some formal occasion, the idea that so elegantly dressed a gentleman might be a dangerous radical was clearly unsettling. But despite the fact that Mies loved his splendidly custom-tailored Knize suits, and lived a life of quiet opulence, he was *of course* a dangerous radical! And I hadn't realized just how dangerous until Perry had made his point—and, unlike Perry, I was delighted! I told the story to Mies the next time I saw him in Chicago. He was vastly amused.

There were, then, these unexpected and sometimes perceptive sides to Perry's infuriating personality. For example, he probably realized that even on this little magazine, Time Inc.'s smallest publication, with a circulation of around 70,000, he was far beyond his depth. And so he decided to hire a bona fide architecture critic, a person highly respected in the U.S. and abroad for his understanding of design and his ability to communicate with others similarly equipped—Douglas Haskell, then a senior editor on the staff of the

Architectural Record. The *Record* was then a mid-cult publication of little distinction and, perhaps for that reason, a favorite with advertisers: it made no waves. And for that same reason, Doug was not especially happy on its staff—he was an old-fashioned American radical; and it was to Perry's considerable credit that he hired someone so totally different from himself to become the *Forum's* "architectural editor." A year later, Doug hired me; and while Perry probably didn't have the remotest idea of who I was or what I thought, he went along with Doug's choice.

So now there was this relatively small kernel of people who believed in the magazine's "mission" and in a degree of editorial sophistication and quality—all headed by a person of monumental energy and an equal amount of ignorance. Among those who had been brought into the magazine by Howard Myers in the 1940s was Walter McQuade, a bright, witty, rather sardonic writer who had been trained as an architect at Cornell; and Louise Cooper, an extremely knowledgeable economist who supplied an expertise to the magazine that the rest of us lacked—and whose left-wing convictions never surfaced, so that Perry trusted her judgment implicitly.

But above all of us stood an extraordinary person really too good to be true. Paul Grotz had been trained as a landscape architect in his native Germany, left that country for the U.S. just before Hitler came to power, married an American artist and radical, and become, somehow, art director of the *Architectural Forum* in the early 1930s. He was not especially well equipped to be an art director; nor was his English ever quite good enough to qualify him as a communicator in that language. And yet Paul emerged as the heart and soul of this strange little group of idealists who had been assembled by Howard Myers; and after Howard's death the magazine became, and remained, the place that really belonged to Paul— where he spent most of his life.

It is hard for me, even after having been his friend and collaborator for several decades, to explain just what it was that enabled Paul to play so central a role among us. Perhaps it was his incredible integrity, his patience, his kindness, his good humor, his willingness to assume any and all burdens—including those dumped upon his shoulders by people (like myself, I am sure) who simply used him to evade some of their own more troublesome responsibilities. He was extremely good-looking (and all women I knew fell in love with him); he was kind, generous, thoughtful, angelic—in short, if he hadn't been Paul Grotz, he would have been a royal pain

in the neck. He was not unlike my friend Willo von Moltke—and there was something about those two that has always seemed very special to me about a small minority of Germans: both Paul and Willo had a decency about them that would be difficult to match anywhere. In Germany, a country where so many people demonstrate an insufferable arrogance, this very rare and special quality stood out as it would not in any other country. And, predictably, both of them had left Germany not under duress, but because they felt themselves to be strangers in their native land.

Every architect whose work we published came to know Paul Grotz, because Paul would design the pages of the magazine devoted to the architect's work. And since architects are largely illiterate, and care only about the way things *look* in print, Paul's layouts of those stories were really more important to them than the words supplied by the likes of Doug Haskell or Walter McQuade or myself. What set the *Forum* far apart from all other U.S. architectural magazines was the understanding supplied by Paul and one or two others that those who read our magazine were, above all, visually oriented people. We understood that the magazine had to communicate not only verbally but visually as well—words and images being composed in tandem, and mutually supportive.

When I returned to the *Forum* in the summer of 1950, there were only half a dozen people left on the staff who understood what Paul was trying to do, or what Howard Myers had been trying to do. Perry Prentice was blind as a bat so far as visual imagery was concerned; Doug Haskell, though he made valiant efforts to become visually literate, really didn't have an eye for color, form, typography, proportion, or anything else that could not be easily rationalized in words. Only Walter McQuade and one or two younger people on the editorial staff saw the magazine as a potential work of graphic art, as Paul did. And yet, despite our small number and the relative lack of support from above, we made the *Architectural Forum* into something very different from the ungainly design publications being produced by others in the U.S. in those years. We kept it to the standard first established by Paul and Howard in the late 1930s, in such exquisite inserts as *PLUS* and such special issues as the one on Frank Lloyd Wright.

Almost from the day on which I came back to the magazine, I was assigned to stories that lent themselves to that sort of visual and verbal integration. My first assignment was a story on the remarkable Case Study House done by Charles Eames for himself and his wife, Ray—a house sponsored by John Entenza's California magazine *Arts & Architecture* and built using standardized modern, industrial building components of steel and glass in ways that no one had quite managed to do before, and no one has done in the same way since. I went out to Los Angeles to see the house and to talk to Charles and Ray and to the *Arts & Architecture* editor, Entenza—a slightly misanthropic version of Sacha Guitry, invariably dressed in a black suit, white shirt, and dark tie, who ran his delightful little magazine almost single-handedly with intelligence, taste, and the least possible investment of effort. John had asked Eero Saarinen to build a second steel-and-glass house next door to the Eames House, for John's own use, and Eero did. Both houses, very different, very rational, very beautiful and very "honest" in their structural clarity and planning logic, represented an effort to create a new housing type that could be mass-produced on assembly lines, using industrialized components of great flexibility. They were enormously successful in an intellectual sort of way, and turned out to have absolutely no significant influence on the future of American housing as determined by mortgage bankers and government housing bureaucrats.

Still, my stories on these and other buildings, some of them designed by old friends like Lou Kahn and Philip Johnson, were attempts to accomplish what Paul had always tried to do—to integrate visual images and words, preferably of one syllable. Having learned to speak English primarily at a British public school, I was not burdened by that curse which afflicts some American writers who believe that ideas need to be framed in multisyllabic and incomprehensible words to be taken seriously. I had read somewhere that H. G. Wells once said: "I write as straight as I can, just as I walk as straight as I can, because that is the best way to get there." This seemed to me a wonderful prescription for a writer and for an architect as well; and it has come in handy on many occasions.

Perry Prentice, who knew even less about writing than he did about architecture, attempted to reshape each of our stories into his own sort of verbiage. In looking at some of those early articles that were mangled by Perry's editorial pen, I came across some wonderful examples of the sort of hucksterism that he liked to introduce into our magazine, presumably to wake up our readers. A story on a project by Bruce Goff for a crystal chapel, never built, starts off as follows: "Here at last is a rocket-flight use of techniques and materials never before available to realize a form of beauty and religious experience never before possible." A few pages farther on, a story starts with: "Here is fresh evidence that the Swedes have not lost their special gift for crisp, fresh design." A few pages farther on: "Here is an example of what a competent architect . . . etc." And, next: "Here is a true ranch house . . . etc., etc." Then: "Here is an exciting example of how imaginative handling of industrial materials and low-cost building techniques can produce richness . . ." and so on, ad infinitum and nauseam. Each of these lead sentences was designed to grab the reader by his or her lapels and ram his or her nose into the story at hand. Each and every one of these lead sentences was composed, with heavy hand, by the editor and publisher and swallowed (with heavy heart) by some intimidated writer. Each of these exercises in hucksterism represented a dreadful embarrassment to the people who had to accept this peerless leader assigned by the *Forum*'s owners to direct a magazine and a staff of some sophistication and quality.

What did we consider the *Forum*'s "mission" to be? I suspect we never tried to spell it out, in part because we all felt that the answer was obvious. Most of us, in one way or another, had been shaped by the experiences of World War II; and while we had our doubts about its outcome—especially in Eastern Europe and in China— we felt that our generation had the right and the obligation to help shape this new world for which we had fought.

We felt, I think, that much of this new world needed rebuilding, that many of its people needed rehousing, that new schools and other community facilities had to be created on a scale previously unknown to mankind, that new kinds of workplaces had to be designed and built, that, in short, new cities and new suburban and rural communities needed to be created, almost overnight and on an unprecedented scale. And we felt that this new world could and should be beautiful, and that modern architects knew how to make it so.

We knew that those of us who were born around 1920, when the earth's population stood at about two and a half billion—more people, altogether, than had inhabited the globe over its entire previous existence—would probably live to see an earth's population of around six billion; and that *everything* about architecture had to change in response to this one staggering fact: the way we designed, the way we planned, the way we built.

All this seemed so obvious to us that we hardly ever discussed it. We thought that any architects or designers who ignored these obvious and terrifying statistics were clearly out of touch with reality and that their work was irrelevant and probably elitist.

We felt, also, that this new world that we would help to design and build must differ in one other aspect from earlier societies: egalitarian, participatory democracy was apparently taking the place of authoritarian societies; and the sort of architecture that we should build had to reflect that fact, in its forms, in its contents, in every respect. We felt that monuments belonged to the times of Albert Speer and of Stalin's pet architects, and we thought those who insisted on pursuing such pomposities were not worth anybody's attention.

We felt, I know, that the *Architectural Forum* should be the voice for a new generation of young architects like ourselves, people who had recently graduated from innovative schools of architecture and were beginning to make their marks in daring and beautiful new structures across the U.S. Most of those structures were little houses, often built for the young architect's immediate family, and many of these young architects made their living, precariously, in large, established firms whose design direction they often changed dramatically. But regardless of how and where they worked, and what they built, we tried to be their voice.

That was not always easy. Unlike some European architectural magazines that appeared in the 1950s and later, the *Forum* did not feel that it should pursue or promote a single design direction—the direction of Mies, or of Le Corbusier, or of Wright. It should, instead, be a real *forum* for all serious efforts to address architectural problems of our time, from the fantasies of a Buckminster Fuller to the eminently realistic solutions of a Marcel Breuer. We would supply a platform for all such ideas and all such solutions, and we would encourage debate and controversy whenever we could.

So this was our unspoken mission—to address the problems of the real world through public discussion of imaginative, creative, daring architecture. Who was to decide whether an effort was "serious" and hence worth publishing? *We* were, of course! After all, that's what editors were for.

CHAPTER SIXTEEN

■ Because most of us on the editorial staff felt that the *Architectural Forum* was the voice of a new generation of architects, in the U.S. and elsewhere, we tended to publish work that was daring, experimental, controversial, and anything but routine. And because I had become quite familiar with that generation while I was at the Museum of Modern Art, Doug Haskell liked to assign stories to me that dealt with the work of this new generation, and with some of the issues that seemed significant to its members.

Some of these members were relatively young—though even they, by today's standards, were hardly juvenile: most of them had spent several years in uniform, and so their professional careers had not really taken off until they were in their late twenties or early thirties. But some of the architects now coming to the fore had been around for some time, without receiving much recognition until they were well into middle age: I was assigned to write not only about the work of Charles Eames and Lou Kahn—both of whom had been in architectural practice in the 1930s—but also about some of Philip Johnson's first houses, and about the new Graduate Center at Harvard, a complex of dormitories designed by Walter Gropius and his recently established firm known as The Architects Collaborative (TAC). Most of the partners in TAC were friends of mine from earlier days in New York, when they occupied a small townhouse in Greenwich Village and spent their time arguing over various shades of radicalism that they and I shared, more or less; and Gropius was an acquaintance from the days when he had (almost) succeeded in securing a Harvard scholarship for me while I was still in London, working for Serge Chermayeff. The Harvard Graduate Center was Gropius's first commission of a larger-than-domestic scale since he had arrived in the U.S., in 1937; and though some of us were to grow rather critical of the complex in later years, it represented a distinct departure in campus design in 1950, when it was completed. (It was then, and almost remains, the only significant modern architectural effort on the Harvard campus that employed the work of major modern painters and sculptors: there were murals by Herbert Bayer, by Joan Miró, by Gyorgy Kepes, and by Jean Arp; there was a relief by Josef Albers; and a freestanding sculpture by Richard Lippold. Although none of these works was the best ever done by the artist responsible, the fact of their existence gave considerable impetus to later efforts in this direction.)

But most of the young architects who were beginning to emerge in the early 1950s were still quite unknown: some of them had found jobs in large architectural firms like Skidmore, Owings & Merrill, where they found security as well as anonymity; and others were struggling in one-man (and, occasionally, one-woman) offices that consisted, more often than not, of a drafting table in a one-room apartment. There were not many clients for *modern* architects—especially for modern architects who had built very little beyond a remodeled kitchen or a small house for their parents.

Still, I was convinced there was an impressive body of new and as yet undiscovered talent, and so I persuaded Doug Haskell to let me put together a special issue of the *Forum* devoted entirely to this new generation of American architects—their work, as well as their ideas. Many of the people I chose have since become widely admired—or, at least, quite controversial; but in June of 1951, most of them were unknown, and their work had rarely, if ever, been published. They included Paolo Soleri, Paul Rudolph, Ulrich Franzen, Edward Larrabee Barnes, Harry Weese, John Carl Warnecke, and many others. There was even a house by the then Yale instructor Vincent J. Scully, Jr.—the only one he ever designed and built—who was to become the most charismatic and influential teacher of architectural history and theory in the U.S. and possibly the most effective promoter, in later years, of the careers of architects like Robert Venturi and other postmodernists. Scully's one and only house, however, was clearly influenced by Philip Johnson's own glass house—a very modern, Miesian pavilion—and in some details by Marcel Breuer's own house in New Canaan, another uncompromising exercise in the Bauhaus/Harvard idiom. It was a very nice house, I thought, and very different from the sort of "populist" architecture Scully would later espouse.

In retrospect, what made those years so remarkable were two facts: first, there were so few of us who were passionately committed to modern architecture and to modern design and modern art; and second, we all knew one another, and we were all fairly good friends. There were no significant feuds. Certain frictions did exist between Stalinists, Stalinoids (Dwight Macdonald's term), and socialists—but these began to evaporate when all of us found ourselves suddenly under attack from Joe McCarthy and his pals. There were frictions between International Style loyalists, Wrightian America Firsters, and Old Shoe, shingle-style-and-wood-siding regionalists, and social realists (who were designing and building very practical and sober no-nonsense boxes)—but nobody took these little feuds very seriously. And there were a few people who never forgave Philip for his prewar fascist flirtations—but most of them, after a while, succumbed to his outrageous charm.

With whatever minor differences, then, we all held certain beliefs: we believed that modern architecture was not a "style," but a language that could be used to speak prose as well as poetry, a language that could address some of the obvious problems caused by overpopulation and massive urbanization; and we believed that it was our responsibility as modern architects to set the highest possible standards of excellence and, I suppose, of social and political responsibility in whatever we did. If that meant firing a client who wanted to use us to make vast profits by building shoddy housing, so be it. If it meant fighting for an impoverished civic group that might oppose your client, so be it. If it meant designing, pro bono, a proposal that stood no chance of realization but that would elevate standards of architecture and urban design to their peak—well, then, you could always make a living by teaching on the side and support your practice that way. There were very few good modern architects, in those days, who seemed to think very much about making money; most of us felt that this was not in the cards, ever— and of limited interest in any case. We thought we had something fairly useful to contribute to the human race, and it would have been unthinkable for us to engage in the sort of frivolous self-promotion that today characterizes so much of postmodernism and its practitioners.

We all knew each other, and formed friendships that were unusually close—and some of them lasted for many decades. One of my closest friends in those days was a young German named Hans Knoll, a maker of modern furniture. It all started in 1943, when I first went to work for the *Architectural Forum* as its most junior writer.

It was my first assignment, and Howard Myers told me to take a look at some chairs that were about to be produced by H. G. Knoll Associates. The firm, it seemed, was an offshoot of a company that had made early modern furniture in Germany and England in the 1920s and 1930s; and these new easy chairs were about to be made and distributed by Hans, the original Knoll's son, who had come to the U.S. in 1937. The chairs had a form-fitting wood frame and a continuous seat-and-back made out of surplus parachute webbing—one of the few materials still available in the civilian sector in 1943. "You'll like Hans Knoll, I think," Howard said.

As a matter of fact, I wasn't sure I did. I went up to that little showroom at 601 Madison and met Hans, and together we looked at the chairs. The trouble was that Hans was just too beautiful, too charming, too elegant, too blond, his voice (that Swabian accent, overlaid on European English) just a bit too mellifluous. He was just too much.

Well, of course, we became (just about) each other's closest friend. He and Florence Shust (who later became his wife) and I became almost inseparable. Hans and Shu worked like maniacs, day and night, trying to find ways of designing and manufacturing this or that, squeezing materials out of the war economy, discovering and then supporting young and relatively unknown designers. And whenever Hans and Shu were ready to call it a day—usually around 10 P.M.—I'd drop by and we would go out for a late dinner, or to some nightclub conveniently located on the way back to their apartment in one of those charming, black-and-white-striped houses that used to inhabit Sutton Place.

The nightclub we liked best was a place called Cafe Society Uptown, and we had a regular table there on the balcony level. There was a delightful little clown called Jimmy Savo who performed at Cafe Society Uptown, and he sometimes joined us after he'd finished his act. There was also Hazel Scott, and a nonstop drummer whose name I have forgotten.

Shu was even more elegant than Hans, even more beautiful, even more charming—and also very cool and very sophisticated. Hans was probably the smoothest salesman I had ever met, but while he was totally dedicated to what we used to call "Good Design" (capital G, capital D), Shu was the one with flawless taste.

Even their dog was ravishingly beautiful. His name was Cartree, and he was an enormous, enthusiastic, fluffy, and playful English sheep dog. I don't know who laundered him, but he, too, was impeccably groomed all of the time—quite an accomplishment in itself in view of the fact that Cartree spent most of the day asleep on a fire escape overlooking Sutton Place. When Hans and Shu and Cartree went out for a walk, they caused traffic jams.

Hans and Shu, in the 1940s, were really at the center of everything that was happening in modern furniture design in America. They attracted everyone in those fields who had anything to contribute—including some people who had little to show other than promise.

It wasn't the beginning of modern furniture design by any means, of course. There had been all those remarkable Breuer and Mies and Le Corbusier pieces in Europe in the 1920s and 1930s, and we knew all about them. But in the U.S. there was only imported Aalto furniture, and the so-called Butterfly Chair, and an occasional piece imported from Sweden or Denmark. There really was no one else in the U.S., with the possible exception of Herman Miller Inc., who was trying to manufacture well-designed modern furniture in a consistent way. Hans and Shu led the way.

The event that triggered much of this was the so-called organic design competition organized in 1940 by the Museum of Modern Art's Eliot Noyes. The most interesting winning designs were some proposals for molded plywood chairs by Eero Saarinen and Charles Eames. These were extraordinarily innovative; unlike Aalto's earlier plywood chairs, which bent laminated sheets of wood veneer in one direction only—the way one might bend a flat sheet of paper—the Saarinen and Eames designs consisted of three-dimensionally formed (i.e., molded) shells of plywood, manufactured in a process that was being developed during the war years for the U.S. Navy.

None of the MOMA competition designs could be manufactured until the war was over and industry had been permitted to revert to civilian production. When that happened, the Saarinen and Eames entries to the organic design competition were divided between Knoll and Miller: Eero Saarinen's pieces were manufactured by Knoll, and Charles Eames developed a whole series of molded chairs for Miller. (Saarinen and Eames, incidentally, remained close friends and frequent collaborators until Eero died in 1961. They went their separate ways only in this particular effort because neither Knoll nor Miller was in a position to develop all the MOMA designs.)

It was the spring of 1945, and I was serving with the U.S. 5th Armored Division, which had just reached the River Elbe. It was very late at night, and the war was nearly over. A ragtag army of Germans, Hungarians, Rumanians, Ukrainians, and God-only-knows-who-else—something like 250,000 troops in all—was fleeing across the river from the east, pursued by the Red Army, and surrendering to us. Among this tidal wave of sick and hungry and wounded humanity I saw an unbelievable character: a kind of comic-opera Rumanian field marshal wearing a green-and-red-and-gold-braid shako, carrying a long silver sword, and lugging, over one shoulder, an enormous sheepskin coat. In exchange for a carton of Camels (worth a small fortune on the black market), I acquired the sheepskin coat. It was filthy, but I knew it would fit Hans to perfection.

Hans and Florence Knoll ca. 1950. (Courtesy, Knoll)

It took me another two years to get myself and that Rumanian field marshal's coat back to the U.S., but when I did, and delivered it to its only rightful owner, Hans and Cartree created a sensation on their walks along Sutton Place. By this time, things on the New York design scene had changed quite a bit: Hans and Shu were well on their way to making Knoll Associates the most prestigious firm of its kind in the U.S. Many new designers had been discovered and added to the Knoll stable. There was Harry Bertoia, who had worked with Charles Eames and contributed significantly to the design of the original Eames Chair, and whom Hans (typically) established as a sculptor, in a studio next to the Knoll plant in Pennsylvania, in the hope that Bertoia would be producing innovative furniture as a by-product of his sculpture. (Bertoia did, in his plastic-coated wire chairs.) And there was Eero, of course: his huge, molded and upholstered easy chair was finally in production in 1948. At the press party for the chair, my wife, Martha, who was enormously pregnant, sat in it happily and comfortably. So Shu named it the "Womb Chair," and the name has stuck. Our daughter was born a few days later.

Before long, almost all the leading U.S. and European furniture designers, with the exception of Charles Eames and George Nelson, were working for Knoll. There were pieces by Franco Albini, by Pierre Jeanneret, by Ralph Rapson, and by many others—in addition to the Jens Risom designs that I had seen the day I met Hans. Moreover, Hans and Shu had noted a growing interest in early modern classics, like Marcel Breuer's tubular steel furniture of the 1920s and Mies van der Rohe's Barcelona chairs, stools, and tables. And so they signed up Breuer and Mies and began to make those "modern antiques" in factories in Italy, Germany, and the U.S.

Although we saw less of one another than we had before I had gone into the Army, we continued to be close friends. But Hans was spending more and more time traveling to the many different showrooms that Knoll had opened in the U.S. and abroad. I would run into him in the Middle West, in France, in Italy. He was not only establishing new showrooms all over the place, but arranging to have Knoll furniture made in various other countries as well. I would run into him in Paris, where he was setting up a Knoll showroom on the Left Bank, with Yves Vidal in charge, and we'd promise each other that we'd have dinner as soon as we both got back to New York. Occasionally I would see him in East Hampton during the summer months. But, most of the time, it was "work, work, work" for all of us—and for Hans that meant, more often than not, travel.

So there was less and less time to meet—but we were young, and there would be plenty of time to catch up next year or the one after that. But, of course, we were wrong. All of a sudden, time had run out for the three of us.

When the news came in 1955 that Hans had been killed in an automobile accident in Havana on one of his business trips, it was in a way the end of our youth. I looked at Shu at the funeral, and she was shattered; and so was I; and so were many of us there. It was the end of our youth, and our hearts were broken.

I saw Shu, on and off, for a number of years after that day, after we had pulled ourselves together. The Los Angeles architect Craig Ellwood and I designed a house in East Hampton for her and Hood Bassett, whom she married several years after Hans's death, but it never got built because she and Hood decided to buy a farm in Vermont instead. I sometimes think of Hans and what it would have been like if he had lived beyond his forty-first year. And I realize now that it would have been impossible—he was always young and beautiful and charming and more than a little silly, and I am glad that he never grew old.

There were other friendships, both with architects and designers, and with photographers, filmmakers, graphic artists, painters, and sculptors. I was beginning to spend several weeks each year in Europe, and so there was soon a network of friends extending all across Western Europe. When I look back at those days, and at the closely knit family of modern artists and designers of which I became a part, it almost seems unreal: surely, there must have been feuds and jealousies and character assassinations—all those charming ingredients that characterize social intercourse among intellectuals and artists nowadays.

But except for an occasional exercise in McCarthyite character assassination, there was very little of this. One of the exceptions was a lengthy editorial campaign launched and run by the editor of the Hearst publication *House Beautiful,* a combative lady named Elizabeth Gordon, in which she attacked everyone from Mies to Gropius to Breuer and Le Corbusier as some sort of subversive—a sleazy maneuver evidently intended to build circulation. She was joined in her campaign by Frank Lloyd Wright, who had clearly begun to lose his marbles, and by the equally combative wife of the talented California architect Harwell Hamilton Harris. Mrs. Harris, better known as Jean Murray Bangs, seemed to believe that the International Style was a fascist/Communist plot to overthrow the American way of life. (Her husband, a decent and quiet gentleman, did not join in his wife's and Miss Gordon's campaign.)

There were one or two such unpleasant diversions, and in the paranoid atmosphere created by Senator McCarthy and some of his pals, they could not be laughed out of court. I had met McCarthy and a slew of his maniacal cronies, because the Russells' dear and sad ex-Communist friend, Freda Utley, had become a friend of mine; and Freda, like many disillusioned ex-Communists, had joined the lunatic fringe on the other end of the spectrum. After attending one of Freda's birthday parties in Washington, which was graced by the presence of the inebriated Joe McCarthy and a couple of dozen other prominent members of the fringe, I was in no mood to underestimate the viciousness of this bunch of fanatics. Still, they served only to cement the friendship of those of us who found ourselves under attack for whatever un-Americanism the Hearst press was pillorying that year; and so we happy few became a network of friends that would soon extend over a large portion of the free world.

Many years later, an acquaintance of mine asked me what it was that made the *Architectural Forum* such a splendid magazine in those years and in the years that followed. And I suddenly knew the answer: we were writing not for some audience, demographically analyzed and averaged out to whatever common denominator an advertiser might want to reach; we were writing for that small band of perhaps not more than a hundred or two hundred friends, all of them at least as bright as we were (or thought we were); and we were talking to them, and they to us, through their work. It was as simple as that.

CHAPTER SEVENTEEN

■ What, exactly, did our magazine stand for? I don't think that any of us who wrote for the *Architectural Forum,* or any of our readers, had the slightest doubt: we stood, first, for modern architecture—in all of its many manifestations. We stood for something popularly known as "urban renewal"—a determined effort to rebuild and revitalize our cities. And we believed that modern architecture and modern urban design implied the development of new technologies, and we attempted to explore and promote those.

We also believed that the new architecture reflected certain social and political attitudes very different from those that had formed architecture in the past. All of us realized that architecture, certainly prior to the industrial revolution, had been an elitist pursuit—a game to be played by kings, princes, popes, and others primarily interested in using buildings and other monuments to promote their own images and those of the forces they represented. The new architecture, in our view, was dedicated to the service of a very different kind of society—an egalitarian democracy largely centered in enormous urban areas, requiring living, working, healing, teaching, and other facilities of a scale and a nature totally unfamiliar to mankind prior to the twentieth century. And we believed that the solutions that seemed to us so desperately urgent had to be tackled by architects with a degree of idealism, dedication, imagination, and talent that added up to a motivation very different from the sort that had governed architecture and its practitioners in the past. And so we looked for such people, and their work, and gave them and it as broad a platform as we could.

In short, the *Forum,* as I have suggested earlier, stood for four things: a new architecture, a new kind of urbanism, a new building technology, and a new set of social and political priorities that would govern the work of this new generation of architects.

I don't think we ever spelled all this out in just those words. We didn't have to. People after World War II became architects because they were fired by an almost religious idealism and by a profound conviction that the ideals they were trying to pursue could be guar-antors of a new kind of world. The new architecture was inevitable because the facts of life on our planet were terrifyingly clear. To ig-

Le Corbusier's Unité d'Habitation in Marseilles was finished around 1952. It seemed to many of us the most splendid proto-type of a new world. (G. E. Kidder-Smith)

nore the state of the earth and the predictable state of mankind, and their implication for architecture seemed to us worse than frivolous. The only issues worth discussing had to do with the nature and quality of the solutions that were being proposed by those who took the world and the future of its inhabitants seriously: people like Le Corbusier and Mies and Aalto and Wright, all of whose work was directly related to such broader concerns.

There were other reasons we felt at ease with the new architecture: not only did we feel that its forms and spaces reflected the needs and aspirations of an egalitarian democracy; its forms and spaces and the details that generated them seemed to grow, quite naturally, out of the kind of mass production technology without which the needs of our century and of the next simply could not be met. Mies van der Rohe, whose work was typically misunderstood and misinterpreted by certain academics and other critics, liked to say that he wanted his buildings *to be easy to copy*, since the facts of our time obviously made it impossible for architecture to be reinvented every Monday morning. (A perfectly terrible idea in the eyes of those who continued to regard architecture as an elitist art for the amusement of the rich: after all, what would happen to copyright lawyers? how would you secure royalties? how could a "name architect" protect his own private "image"?)

Above all, we believed that the new architecture was really part and parcel of the philosophical and artistic spirit of our age; that there was a profound kinship between what was being designed and built by Le Corbusier and Mies and others and what was being painted by Picasso and Braque and Klee and Mondrian and sculpted by Brancusi and Calder and Gabo and Henry Moore. We felt that the writings of James Joyce or of Robert Musil and of others of their generation spoke to us as clearly as the flowing and reflective spaces of the Barcelona Pavilion, and that the experimental music and poetry and dance of the years between the World Wars were part and parcel of a modern culture that was at the heart of our architecture. In short, we felt that there was a profound unity in all the creative work that moved us and spoke to us, and that we were an integral part of a major artistic revolution that was sweeping the world.

Its manifestations were all around us: our architecture spoke to people like Jackson Pollock and Bill de Kooning and Bob Motherwell and Franz Kline. And all around us, especially in New York, there were artists of absolutely staggering talent—quite unmatched before and since: in the graphic arts, in stage design, in photography and all the rest. They spoke our language of vision, as Gyorgy Kepes put it, and we spoke theirs.

Our editorial concern at the *Architectural Forum* with something then known as "Urban Renewal" was a great deal more questionable. Most of us, myself included, believed that the only solution to urban decay—and the only way to reconstruct cities bombed out in World War II—was to raze large portions of what was left and replace it with something akin to the diagrams drawn up, in the 1920s, by Le Corbusier and others, in projects like Corbu's Ville Radieuse.

These projects seemed entirely rational in the 1920s, and seemed almost as rational to many of us in the 1950s: because there was likely to be an increasing concentration of people in cities, the way to house and otherwise accommodate them was in high-rise buildings; and because these concentrations of people should not be deprived of sun and air and greenery, it seemed reasonable to house them in tall buildings spaced far apart and interspersed with parks and other outdoor amenities. This, it further seemed, would mean abolishing traditional streets (which Le Corbusier had called "sewers" in one of his more intemperate urban manifestos), because traditional streets suggested traffic and other congestion; and all of this, in turn, seemed to lead quite logically to a vertical garden city in which zones of different usage would be separated by parks, linked by elevated (or underground) expressways, and interspersed with schools, shopping centers, and so on.

Most of us accepted all this as a sort of modern urban catechism and rarely questioned it. Only a very few among us were ready to challenge Le Corbusier's diagrams—and the brightest of these critics, by far, was Jane Jacobs, one of the *Architectural Forum*'s associate editors. While the rest of us continued to promote urban renewal diagrams of the sort originally proposed by Le Corbusier—and later adapted by people like Ed Bacon, the "master planner" of Philadelphia—Jane raised more and more questions until, in 1960, she spoke out passionately at an urban design conference at Harvard and challenged virtually all the notions up till then accepted, without question, by the rest of us. Her challenge then, and her subsequent book *The Death and Life of Great American Cities*, completely altered the discourse on the nature and the future of cities.

While our convictions in matters of urban design were soon to be challenged by Jane Jacobs and one or two others, our dedication to the principles of modern building technology as we saw it—mass production and, hence, standardization of building parts, etc.—seemed to remain unshaken. Because such industrialization of building parts suggested some sort of modular design—that is, the assemblage of identical, modular components—the aesthetic that emerged from this kind of industrialization had its own, unmistakable characteristics: repetitive patterns made up of identical units, very much in the manner of Donald Judd's and Sol Lewitt's sculpture of twenty or thirty years later. The forms and spaces that came out of this rational analysis of a new kind of building technology seemed to us totally in keeping with the principles of our time, and with the patterns that were appearing in other forms of human endeavor—music, poetry, painting, and all the rest.

There was another aspect to this dedication to rational technology, and a rather mundane one: those of us who were designing and building, as well as talking and writing about doing it, knew that the cost of building was one of those facts of life that you had to confront in the real world. And we also knew that buildings that were designed and constructed rationally—often using modular, repetitive, and identical components—generally cost less to build than structures that did not follow that sort of discipline. This was and is the sort of thing that seems to escape the notice of many critics: in recent years, a famous New York commentator on architecture pointed out that the houses I designed and built in the Hamptons in the 1950s, while rather interesting, suffered from my apparent allegiance to structural discipline. I was pleased with the writer's grudging compliments and amused that he missed what was my proudest achievement in getting those little houses built: the fact that their cost was ridiculously low—a fact that could be directly attributed to the designer's self-imposed structural discipline! In the real world, as every practicing architect knows, nothing can ever get built without a client—and most clients are loath to spend more money than they absolutely must. So, unless you want to be a nonbuilding theoretician (i.e., a critic), you have to learn how to build well and economically. Which means that you have to learn a great deal about structure. (No such constraints apply to any of the other arts.)

There is one exception, of course: if the architect is his or her own client, and the architect also happens to be enormously rich, there is no need to worry about such boring things as cost. My charming friend Philip Johnson was born very rich, and became

Russell House, Bridge-hampton, Long Island. This summer cottage was designed (by me, in partnership with Julian Neski) and built in 1956. It was raised off the ground to permit spectacular views from the upstairs living areas. (Hans Namuth)

richer as time went on; and he was probably born naughty, and surely became naughtier with age. And because he was so charmingly articulate, he liked to make fun of pedestrian arguments involving cost, practicality, and so on: if he built himself an all-glass pavilion that cost a small fortune to heat or cool, so be it—he had that small fortune and enjoyed spending it. And if he built himself a "Sunday House," that was no problem either: all you needed to keep it in impeccably pristine condition was a small squad of well-trained servants who could be housed in a nearby cottage purchased for that purpose. And you didn't have to invite the Gropiuses over for dinner—according to Philip, they were bores anyway. Philip hugely enjoyed being naughty, and because he also enjoyed surrounding himself with fawning academics and other critics, they liked to emulate his naughtiness. So it became very chic to profess a certain insouciance about the real world and about such issues as cost, practicality, or most other functional concerns.

It was all great fun, and I confess I enjoyed it as much as anyone. Philip thought that serious young architects (like me and my friends) were a bunch of hypocrites or worse, pretending to pursue our profession for the noblest of reasons—pretending to be selfless, idealistic, solely dedicated to the welfare of mankind. Whereas he

Russell House. The structure of steel and wooden planks was pared down to an absolute minimum, and the house was thus constructed for an unbelievable $8 per square foot—or $13,000. (Hans Namuth)

was convinced we were, in fact, as ambitious, as totally preoccupied with self-interest and self-perpetuation as any prima ballerina (Philip's idea of the lowest of the low). Architecture, in his view, was clearly one of the few professions guaranteed to permit its practitioner to beat the actuarial tables, to leave his more or less permanent mark on the face of the earth. He was refreshingly outrageous, and while I thought he was cynical beyond belief, and largely wrong, I found his cynicism a wonderful antidote to the stuffiness that marked many younger architects of my generation.

Perhaps one reason the *Architectural Forum* was so much fun to read and so much fun to write for was that it was rarely pompous and therefore rarely boring. Admittedly, we held our beliefs about architecture and its probable future course firmly and with conviction; but we spoke about this in a rather low-key, rather civilized way. Moreover, the graphic quality of our presentations was of the highest standards of its time: people like Paul Grotz saw to this, as did his extraordinary assistants—artists like Ray Komai, Adrien Taylor, Madeleine Thatcher, Charlotte Winter, and many others. Several of them later worked for much larger and wealthier publications and left their marks on graphic design in New York and around the world, but they had all started with Paul and the *Archi-*

tectural Forum, and helped shape our magazine and win all sorts of awards for it.

One result of this fact—and of the general overall editorial excellence of the *Forum* in those years—was that we were able to publish the very best work being designed and built just about anywhere in the world. Every architect in the U.S., and many architects in Europe, Asia, Latin America, and elsewhere, tried to have his or her work published exclusively in our magazine; and the other publications then produced in the U.S. and abroad had to make do with whatever stories we rejected. On occasion, when it

Tobey Barn, Amagansett, Long Island, ca. 1962. An old barn was moved to this site and transformed into a spacious house in which old beams and posts were stained black to articulate the interiors. I designed it with Julian Neski. (Hans Namuth)

Hagen House, Sagaponack, Long Island, ca. 1960, designed with Julian Neski. As in most of my Long Island houses, the spectacular views were much more important than the facades. (Hans Namuth)

proved impossible for one reason or another to obtain exclusive publication rights to a building or a story, we would simply go ahead and publish the work in question so splendidly, so intelligently, that the parallel stories in the other magazines in our field looked as if they had been assembled by a crew of dispirited plumbers.

I am sure that much of the credit for maintaining this standard of editorial excellence belonged to Douglas Haskell, the editor hired by the uninterruptible Perry Prentice—and thus, indirectly, to Prentice himself. Although the latter had been handed down to us by the business geniuses on the top floor of the Time-Life Building, he served us well in a rather surprising way: any story that would render Perry apoplectic was almost certain to be precisely the kind of story we should be publishing. And thanks to Doug Haskell's vast reservoir of "counterplexy," as it were, we usually did.

We had another ally in the upper reaches of Time-Lifedom, and a rather surprising one: Henry Luce, Time-Life's founding buddha, was a remote deity to most of us in those days. We knew that his politics were, as the saying goes, several degrees to the right of Genghis Khan; and we also knew that he had strong views on every single subject, and that most of those views were, to put it mildly,

Eckstein House, Kings Point, Long Island. Another house planned to face some beautiful views—rather than advertise its architect. It was designed ca. 1965 with Dorothy Alexander. (Gil Amiaga)

bizarre: Henry Luce, in describing his own country, once announced that "no nation in history, except Israel, was so obviously designed for some special phase of God's eternal purpose!" Admittedly, he arrived at this conclusion some years prior to the time when God moved His servants Reagan, Bush, et al. to display His eternal purpose by bombing the living daylights out of such strongholds of the devil as Grenada, Panama, Nicaragua, and Iraq; even so, it was more than a little worrisome to have a powerful friend and fan who was clearly out of his mind. Still, we could use all the help in high places that seemed available, and the very fact that Harry Luce was said to hold our magazine in great esteem protected us, in many situations, from the inspired leaders who had originally visited Perry Prentice upon us, and who tried on other occasions to send us helpers of similar caliber.

So we managed throughout the 1950s to produce the finest magazine on architecture and design then being published anywhere in the U.S. Every major architect and designer, from Frank Lloyd

Temple Emanu-El, Livingston, New Jersey, designed with Julian Neski around 1960. An extremely low-cost structure that dramatized its functions—as a place of worship, and a religious school—and helped attract a large congregation. (Gil Amiaga)

Allen-Stevens Offices and Warehouse, Astoria (Queens), New York. It was designed around 1960, with Julian Neski. Its rough brickwork has retained its rich colors and textures.

*Blake House, Bridge-
hampton, Long Island. I
designed and built this
house in 1960, after selling
the Pinwheel House. The
Bridgehampton House was
shaped entirely to face the
views from its beautiful
site. Here, on the deck
overlooking Mecox Bay,
are (left to right) my
daughter Christina, my
son Casey, and his cousin
Elizabeth. (Esto)*

*Casey Blake and his
cousin Elizabeth engaged
in intense discourse. The
Bridgehampton House was
divided by a twelve-foot-
wide slot that framed the
view.*

Martinez House, Pound Ridge, N.Y.: a modular structure whose shell was literally prefabricated on the site and built for a very low budget around 1960. (Hans Namuth)

Wright to Mies van der Rohe, wanted his best work to be published in our pages. Every young (and still unknown) architect, from Paul Rudolph to John Johansen to Craig Ellwood and Paolo Soleri, was "discovered" by us and introduced by us to our readers. Only the splendid little California publication *Arts & Architecture,* produced by my brilliantly lazy friend John Entenza, came even close to the *Forum* in quality; all the other "professional" publications lagged far behind.

Yet, in spite of our remarkable editorial success, in spite of our enthusiastic following among readers around the globe, and in spite of an endless array of annual awards and other honors, the *Architectural Forum* failed to make much money. The reasons were twofold: First, there was the preoccupation at Time-Life with bigness—and our staff was one reflection of this. We had about two or three times the number of people a magazine of this sort needed to function properly. The second reason was our circulation/readership. Time-Life saw enormous circulation as the only index of success—a misconception that would kill off the weekly *Life* magazine a few years later, and severely damaged the *Forum,* whose readership was at least twice that of its competitors. But many of our readers, like CBS president Frank Stanton, who wrote us enthusiastic mash notes once a month, were not people likely to order any steel gird-ers or bathtubs anytime soon, and such nonprofessional readership was of no interest at all to our advertisers.

So our staff was too big, and our circulation was not only too big, but also too unfocused in the view of our advertisers. On top of that, our publisher, Perry Prentice, had come up with a spectacu-larly misguided notion and put it into effect with typically mis-guided bravado: he had argued that there were actually *two* building industries in the U.S.—one using wooden studs and shingles, the other steel and concrete and elevators—and so, he further argued, the *Architectural Forum* should be split into two magazines, one to be known as *House & Home,* the other to continue as *Architectural Forum.* Superficially, the notion seemed harmless to us from an ed-itorial point of view, although rather simplistic, since some of Mies's and Corbu's most interesting *houses* were built of steel and concrete, while some of the more intriguing nonresidential structures (in the San Francisco Bay region, for example) were built of wood. Still, we had more important editorial matters to think about—or so we

South Bay Bank, Man-hattan Beach, California, 1957. The first commercial building designed by Craig Ellwood, and typical of the elegance of detail and clarity of structure that marked all his work. We published much of it. (Marvin Rand)

believed; and so we let Perry become the publisher of not one but two publications, since this seemed to be what his heart desired.

Unhappily, the result was a major disaster; two publications of course required an even larger staff and a larger promotional budget. Moreover, while the undivided *Architectural Forum* had managed to earn a modest profit year after year, the two separate publications succeeded from day one in losing money. Despite vast promotional efforts, and the infusion of much "business talent" from the upper reaches of the Time-Life Building, the twin publications almost instantly went into a steep economic decline. Only the presence of Harry Luce, who continued to admire our efforts, kept Time Inc. from selling us off to the first bidder. We on the editorial staff sensed all this, but we assumed that those self-assured business types in the Time Inc. management surely knew what they were doing. The fact was that they hadn't the foggiest idea.

CHAPTER EIGHTEEN

■ Those of us who had spent most of the 1940s either at school or in uniform really began to grow up and into our world in the 1950s. What a marvelous time it was, especially if you were involved in architecture and all the related visual arts. Just how great a decade we entered and populated became evident only in later years, when the artists who had been our friends and teachers in those postwar years were long gone and had been replaced by self-styled "name artists" of a shallowness and arrogance unmatched in any field except, possibly, snake oil marketing and Washington think-tanking. Our mentors and teachers were people like Corbu and Mies: the former in and out of New York and environs in connection with his work on the new UN Headquarters in Manhattan; the latter always available in Chicago, and frequently in New York, where he had remodeled a townhouse in the East Sixties for his charming friend the sculptress Mary Callery, and on Long Island, where he had remodeled an old barn for Mary into a studio next to Wally Harrison's country house.

Frank Lloyd Wright was in and out of Manhattan working on early schemes for the Guggenheim and insulting all his peers with equal abandon. Lou Kahn, my former employer, came up regularly from Philadelphia—partly because he was working on his first really important building, the Yale Art Gallery, which he completed in 1954, when he was well into his fifties; and partly because he had started teaching at Yale as well. Architects like Richard Neutra, Raphael Soriano, Charles Eames, Harwell Hamilton Harris, and others from the West Coast stopped off in Manhattan at regular intervals (and visited our editorial offices whenever they came to town). Alvar Aalto was still occasionally teaching at MIT and elsewhere and liked to visit such former students and friends as the architects Harry Weese and Ralph Rapson. Walter Gropius frequently came down from Cambridge, Massachusetts, to grace us with his Germanic platitudes. Fritz Kiesler, a man who had succeeded in building a vast reputation on a foundation of one or two art galleries, one or two stage sets, and one or two highly derivative "visionary" projects—plus several thousand incomprehensible words published in the *Partisan Review*—graced us with much of the same. And such great historic figures as Auguste Perret, Hans Scharoun, Paul Nelson, Sven Markelius, Erich Neuffert, Alfred Roth, Ernesto Rogers, Wells Coates, Oscar Niemeyer, Kenzo Tange, F. R. S. Yorke, and all the rest kept drifting in and out of Manhattan, and in and out of our editorial offices. What seems most interesting about these encounters, in retrospect, is the fact that very few of these architects tended to talk about their own work; they seemed much more interested in what was happening in the U.S. and specifically in New York—and in what young people like ourselves were thinking and doing.

My memories of some of these encounters are detailed and quite vivid, and they may convey some of the excitement of those days. There was an occasion, in the early 1950s, when I met the vice president of a New York insurance company, which was building enormous housing projects in Manhattan and elsewhere. He told me that he had recently seen Le Corbusier's Unité d'Habitation in Marseilles, and was greatly impressed. He had heard that Corbu was in New York, and he wondered if I could arrange an introduction.

I called Corbu at Tino Nivola's studio, where he was staying, and explained to him that this man was a potential client, apparently very enthusiastic, and that it might be a good idea for Corbu to meet him for a drink. The response was typically grumpy—some words about "American gangsters who are always trying to steal my ideas"—but he finally agreed. A couple of days later, I picked him up at the studio to take him over to a bar down the block, at Number One Fifth Avenue. The Master was in blue jeans and a checkered lumberjack's flannel shirt—no tie. His boots, as I discovered as we marched down 8th Street, were hobnailed. He looked ready for combat. It was not a propitious beginning.

Things did not improve when the maître d'hôtel stopped us at the entrance to the bar announcing that Corbu would have to wear a tie and a jacket. Since the maître d' pretended to speak French, Corbu responded in that language, starting with *merde,* after which it was all downhill. Fortunately, the vice president had arrived earlier and intervened when he observed the contretemps, and the crisis was temporarily averted. We sat down, Corbu refusing to speak English (which he actually spoke quite well), and I attempting to act as an interpreter. The conversation was brief and unproductive. We adjourned after one drink, as I recall. On our walk back to Tino's studio, the Master told me—having suddenly regained his command of the English language—that things had gone just as he had anticipated: the "American gangster" wanted to copy the Unité—probably without paying a fee, needless to say.

Corbu had a fairly clear and not entirely paranoid conception of the American business world. While I was at MOMA, he told me that this "nest of the Rockefellers" had "stolen" models of some of his early buildings for MOMA's collection; moreover, he liked to point out, the scheme for the United Nations Headquarters, which clearly owed a great deal to Corbu's sketches and models of the 1930s, had been "stolen" from him also, and was now going to be built by the Rockefellers' favorite architect, Wallace K. Harrison, on land donated by the Rockefellers.

A few years later, when the UNESCO Headquarters were being planned in Paris, Corbu told me that the committee which had been set up to select an architect had been cleverly rigged by "the Americans" so that this commission—which in Corbu's view and in that of many others "belonged" to him—was given instead to Marcel Breuer.

Le Corbusier felt that he had spent some twenty years between the World Wars fighting for a new architecture and a new urbanism, developing great numbers of inspired and beautifully detailed schemes for a whole range of new cities and new city centers and their buildings, and that he should now be commissioned to realize some of the projects he had originally drawn up. He felt, quite rightly in the view of many of us, that his time had now come; yet, instead of gaining some of the great commissions for which he had prepared himself during those decades, he saw others benefiting from his pioneering work, and often designing and building large structures and complexes—and whole cities—that were little more than poor copies of Corbu's earlier visionary schemes. This was true especially in the U.S., where a great deal of building was being done by people who had learned the lessons of Le Corbusier fairly well, but were very reluctant to give him credit for the inspiration he had so generously provided. He was very bitter when the UNESCO commission, in Paris of all places, went to an American architect; and he privately approached Breuer with the suggestion that the two might collaborate.

A few years after Corbu had permanently returned to France from his work in New York, a very interesting man by the name of Eddie Swayduck called me to ask who was the greatest living architect, in my view, to design and build a "City of the Future" on the West Side of Manhattan. Swayduck was not trying to be funny: he was the president of the New York branch of the Lithographers' Union, and his union had managed to gain control of a large expanse of above-the-tracks real estate on Manhattan's West Side. This was the same expanse that has, in recent years, tempted real estate operators to propose vast and profitable developments of luxury housing and luxury offices to be built on so-called "air rights" above the West Side tracks; and Swayduck, who was the first to grasp the potential of this large expanse of real estate, wanted to build a "Litho City" on a platform above these tracks. He wanted to know whom he should hire to do the job.

I had no doubts at all, and told him that he simply had to go and talk to Le Corbusier—that it would be quite wonderful, Jane Jacobs notwithstanding, to realize something like Corbu's Ville Radieuse in New York City. Swayduck agreed; and without a moment's delay, he and his staff (most of them bodyguards, I suspected) took off for Paris to meet the Master. Shadrach Woods, an American architect who had been working for Le Corbusier ever since the end of World War II and had become one of his closest friends, was still living in Paris and practicing there with two other Corbu disciples, and so I called him to see if he could arrange a meeting. Shad told me that Corbu was spending much of his time now in semi-retirement, painting at Cap Martin in the South of France and cursing Americans; but that he, Shad, would try to get the old man to meet Swayduck nonetheless.

Alas, it was really too late: Corbu refused to see the American delegation, assuming once again that the Americans were solely interested in "stealing" his ideas and transplanting them to New York. So the plans came to naught; Swayduck and his bodyguards returned to New York; and a rather wonderful opportunity was missed. Many years later the air rights over those West Side tracks were acquired by a yuppie prince, and his architect came up with an appropriate monument—or, rather, with a proposal for one. Although Corbu's Litho City might not have met the standards newly established by Jane Jacobs, it might have been a superb prototype— if only one against which to rebel.

The trouble with Corbu's paranoid anti-Americanism was that it seemed at least partly justified. Because he was so hopelessly difficult, nobody in any position of authority in the U.S., or anywhere else, for that matter, looked forward to working with him. The selection process for the UNESCO commission had, indeed, been set up in such a way as to eliminate Corbu from consideration automatically: by inviting him to serve on the selection committee, a U.S. State Department official told me, UNESCO in effect disqualified Corbu from consideration. (The U.S., being the principal financial supporter of UNESCO in those days, was in a good position to manipulate selections of this sort, and did.)

Still, there was another reason, I suspect, why architects like Le Corbusier felt distinctly uneasy about working for the kinds of private developers who were building more and more in the capitalist world. They felt, and many of us agreed, that the kinds of cities they dreamed of building could not be realized if private profit was to be the prime criterion of success. Corbu and others probably sensed long before their American admirers did that free enterprise would never build truly humane and civilized communities—that the only motivation for building communities in a capitalist society was greed.

Admittedly, some housing and even some "mixed use communities" were being built in the U.S. and in other capitalist nations with some public funds; but even when the financing came from local, state, or federal agencies, and even when some of the financing came from labor unions, the basic philosophic attitudes long bred into the process in a capitalist society were the attitudes of mortgage bankers, and of private developers who worked hand in glove with mortgage bankers much of the time. The sort of idealism that motivated the likes of Le Corbusier was, quite simply, in-

Le Corbusier, in front of his Unité at Marseilles, ca. 1952. He was convinced that "American gangsters" would steal the ideas contained in this block, and nothing I could say would change his mind. (Fenno Jacobs)

comprehensible to people whose sole criterion of performance was maximum profit; and Corbu, I believe, could smell a rat from as far away as Cap Martin.

Many American critics, in later years, would point an accusing finger at Corbu and others for allegedly having created the original image of the sort of "urban renewal" horror that would soon be visited upon most American cities—the image, supposedly, being that of Corbu's Ville Radieuse, a city of tall towers set into spacious parks, and originally sketched out by him in the early 1920s. This allegation seems largely unfair to me: The entire point of Corbu's Radiant City was its spaciousness, its greenery, its sunlight, its rich mix of many different facilities and many kinds of housing scaled to many different kinds of families; and this generous, spacious, rather lively image was rarely, if ever, attempted by private capitalist developers. Their principal motivation was to make as much money for themselves as possible, and the only way to do that was to cram as many income-producing buildings into each acre of land as the law would permit—or as politicians could be bribed to grant through special "variances." Corbu's Radiant City may have had its social problems; but it was intended to be a model of generosity and humanity. If some of today's urban renewal projects, in American cities, bear a faint resemblance to Le Corbusier's sketches of the early 1920s, that resemblance is superficial indeed and bears little relationship to the ideals and principles that motivated their designer.

I met Alvar Aalto only briefly in the late 1940s and in later years, when he visited the U.S. He had spent much of his time before and after World War II in Cambridge, where his students at MIT, I gather, worshiped him. What I had seen of his work, until I visited Finland in the late 1950s, was limited to a few structures built in Western Europe and in the U.S., and to the somewhat fragmentary photographic record that had been published over the years. Although his buildings and his furniture were clearly the work of a completely self-assured artist, they reflected a certain sentimentality that was foreign to those of us who were under the spell of Mies's and Corbu's Machine Art rationalism: like Lewis Mumford, Aalto seemed a bit old-fashioned in his concerns, motivated by certain formal and philosophical principles found in nature—rather than by the rational logic of twentieth-century industrialism.

That, at least, was the view of many of us who had absorbed the hard-edged notions of the new, industrialized architecture. Aalto's world was clearly amiable and benign, and just a trifle old-fashioned. Whenever I met him, especially in later years, when he had remarried after Aino Aalto's death, I thought he was an extraordinarily likable person but not a very profound innovator.

But then I came across several examples of his work that made me change my view quite drastically.

The first of these was Baker House, a student dormitory building in Cambridge, Massachusetts, which Aalto designed and built for MIT shortly after the end of World War II. Its plan was unusual, to say the least: its configuration was that of a zigzag curve, a kind of flattened-out letter W; and virtually all the 300-odd student rooms faced the Charles River and the Boston skyline beyond. The building was largely clad in rough brick and looked not at all "modern" in the conventional, hard-edged way. I didn't know what to make of it: Aalto's earlier work had been generally white, cubist, minimalist (with only an occasional vernacular touch of wood or brick); had he suddenly gone soft, become sentimental and hopelessly "folklorique"? I asked him, as politely as I could: "Somehow, you'd expect this sort of building to be a flat slab, with its broad sides parallel to the river's edge. Why did you build it in a sort of whiplash curve?" Aalto realized, I am sure, that he had confused all of us young "modernists" by this apparent relapse to Art Nouveau or worse. "Well, I'm not sure that a flat slab would have been right," he said with a smile. "You know, it is much more interesting to look up and down a river than to look straight across. I'm sure you noticed that." I hadn't noticed anything of the sort, needless to say, but I was suitably chastened. He was absolutely correct, of course; and by curving his building as he did, he made sure that each student room had a different sort of view—and that almost all of the rooms faced up or down the Charles River, rather than blindly across, toward identical vistas.

There was something else to the student rooms in Baker House that became evident as I went through the building: each of the rooms was slightly different in configuration from every other room—as well as in its view, as Aalto had pointed out. While Aalto was working on the drawings for Baker House, Walter Gropius and his young associates in The Architects Collaborative (TAC) had been busy with the plans for a new complex of student dormitories for Harvard University, just a mile or so away. The Harvard complex turned out to be one of Gropius's more sensitive projects—a pleasant complex of connected buildings and spaces, all framed in the conventional, geometric, modern idiom: modular dormitory units, all more or less identical, all eminently rational and diagrammatic.

But while Baker House reflected a sensitive, humanistic understanding of how students lived and how they like to be perceived (as individuals, for example), Gropius's complex implied that all students were more or less alike and had more or less identical needs. Some twenty years later, when both Harvard and MIT (and most other American universities) were shaken by radical uprisings,

Baker House, Cambridge, Massachusetts, is a student dormitory designed by Alvar Aalto for MIT and built in 1948. The double-curved facade faces the Charles River and the Boston skyline.

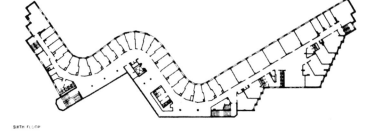

SIXTH FLOOR

Plans of Baker House show that student rooms vary in size and shape, and look up and down the Charles River. Most of the rooms that face north are devoted to circulation and other services. (Courtesy Architecture Plus)

GROUND FLOOR

students at Harvard openly revolted against the sort of life implied by Gropius's dormitories and refused to live in them; while Baker House continued to enjoy long waiting lists of students anxious to move into Aalto's sensitively designed residential quarters.

To most people outside the architectural profession Aalto's concern with the *users* of his buildings—rather than with the "image" those buildings might project—may seem quite unsurprising. After all, aren't buildings, especially buildings in and for an egalitarian democracy, meant to be designed and built for those who live and work in them? Quite so; but to anyone familiar with the recent history of architecture, and with the ego trips performed daily by "name architects" interested primarily in promoting themselves, Aalto's gentle and selfless modesty is and was enormously refreshing. Like everyone else involved in writing about and publishing architecture, I was preoccupied with imagery—with the way buildings looked in photographs, most of them taken from the outside; and Aalto's total concern with the way buildings felt to those who actually lived in them was a true revelation.

After the experience of Baker House, I began to look at Aalto's work in a very different way: I noticed that he would place his windows so that views from inside out would be most convenient and most pleasant, even if you were bedridden in a sanitarium, for example; that he would cover his interior surfaces with "warm" mate-

Harvard dormitories by Walter Gropius and his associates were designed at the same time Aalto designed Baker House. But the Harvard buildings are modular, geometric, and repetitive. Students, generally speaking, are not.

rials like wood or brick in areas likely to be touched by human hands, and with cool and flush materials on surfaces that were out of reach; that he thought of the way light entered a space in daytime, and the way it could be made to enter at night—and of ways in which furniture might be placed in response to both conditions; and I noticed how thoughtfully he responded to the ways in which people lived alone, as well as in groups, and how carefully he reexamined preconceived notions about this, and about almost everything else.

In 1957, when I spent a fair amount of time in West Berlin on the design of a large exhibition on American architecture, I saw the buildings going up in the Tiergarten as part of the Interbau (International Building) Exposition then being held in the city. West Berlin had decided to commission leading architects from all over the world, including Gropius, Le Corbusier, Niemeyer, Aalto, and many others, to design and construct major structures that would reflect the then state of the art at its most advanced; and most of the architects invited did predictably interesting apartments and other structures.

Aalto's apartment block was deceptively "ordinary" in appearance—neat, clean, plain, stone-faced, and modestly fenestrated. It was unexceptional, and not at all startling.

That is, until you walked into a typical apartment and found that each unit plan was in a surprising way a reexamination of the manner in which people really liked to live. Unlike the typical "modern" apartment plan, which might be "zoned" into daytime and nighttime areas, with the main entrance at the center, Aalto's plans turned the living room into a kind of large indoor piazza—a place in which family members could get together and talk and play and enjoy each other's company; and this indoor piazza was surrounded on three sides with private rooms into which each family member could retire if and when he or she wanted to be alone. (The fourth side would be a large balcony, an outdoor extension of the indoor piazza.)

It was a very simple plan, really, but quite startling to any of us who had been brought up on the rational diagrams that characterized modern housing. Here was an architect who had really thought creatively and originally about the ways in which families functioned (or failed to), and who had attempted to develop new ways of creating spaces that would serve those families and their ways of living and working together. The very last thing Aalto considered, I am absolutely sure, was the "image" of himself that his building projected. Unlike today's "name architects," whose main concern seems to be with advertising their own monumental egos, Aalto concerned himself with the ways in which people might best live in the spaces he was able to build for them.

Admittedly, I felt (and still feel) that Aalto's aesthetic sensibilities were sometimes flawed—that Le Corbusier and Mies and some of the later Italian architects, especially Terragni and Gregotti, had a more finely honed sense of modernity than Aalto did. But I don't believe, in retrospect, that any of those architects had a more gentle sense of humanity. I saw many more of Aalto's buildings in Germany and in Finland in later years, long after I last met him in Miami Beach, of all places; and my admiration for his humanity has never diminished.

The other Finn who dominated the scene, in architectural terms, throughout the 1950s was Eero Saarinen, the phenomenally successful son of Eliel. The latter was in all our history books for having designed the late–Art Nouveau Main Station in Helsinki in the first decade of the century, and for having almost won the 1922 Chicago Tribune Tower Competition (and having dramatically transformed the direction of American skyscraper design with his unbuilt second-prize entry—while nobody even remembered who had won the first prize, which did get built). We knew Eliel, too, for having founded, built, and run the remarkable Cranbrook Academy of Art in Bloomfield Hills, Michigan—and, of course, for having fathered Eero, with whom he later went into partnership and who became, without question, the most visible modern American architect in the years after World War II.

Eero was an extraordinarily talented designer: together with his friend and fellow Cranbrook graduate Charles Eames, he had won the Museum of Modern Art's Organic Design Competition in 1940, and had developed his own contributions to that competition entry in numerous remarkable chairs and tables for Knoll Associates in the fifteen years or so after World War II. He had won numerous architectural competitions, most notably the Jefferson Memorial Competition for a site on the bank of the Mississippi, in downtown St. Louis—a 600-foot-tall parabolic arch clad in stainless steel; and he had designed and built some of the most important modern projects of the postwar years. They are discussed in some detail in Chapter Twenty-one.

Dulles Airport Terminal, Chantilly, Virginia, was designed by Eero Saarinen but not completed until a year after his death. It forms an impressive gateway to the nation's capital.

Eero was clearly obsessed and vastly ambitious, and he died very suddenly of a brain tumor when he was barely fifty years old. In retrospect, it seems as if he had always known that his life would be cut short and that he would have to work at full speed, night and day, and explore all kinds of alternatives before it was too late. And he was quite aware of all sorts of alternatives—stylistic, aesthetic, structural, and political. He was a frequent visitor to New York and New Canaan, very conscious of the fact that ideas were being bounced around, fast and furiously, in those centers of sophistication—or, anyway, of talk. Eero didn't want to miss a thing, and rarely did. He wanted to be the first architect to design a major shell concrete building—and he was, at MIT. He wanted to be the first one to apply Mies van der Rohe's glass-and-steel aesthetic to a large-scale American industrial complex—and he was, at the General Motors Technical Center. He wanted to be the first one to explore "contextualism" and build modern buildings that seemed to relate in scale, finish, form, and detail to buildings of an earlier period nearby—and he was, at Yale and in the new U.S. Embassy in London. He wanted to be the first to build a major tensile structure—and he was, in the construction of the Dulles Airport Terminal with its suspension roof. He wanted to be the first one to translate Le Corbusier's sculptural architecture into modern, American idiom—and he tried to be, in his TWA Terminal at Kennedy

Airport. And when he was asked to design a new headquarters tower for CBS in Manhattan, he wanted it to be the best skyscraper since Mies's Seagram Building, and preferably better than Mies's bronze shaft if at all possible—and it wasn't a bad try.

When Aline Loucheim, the art and architecture critic of *The New York Times,* called me one day and said: "I have to go and interview this odd character, Eero Saarinen, in Michigan. What is he like?" I thought for a moment, and said: "Well, he looks and sounds like a gentle and modest little country doctor from Finland, or from the backwoods of Minnesota. And he puffs on a pipe. But don't be fooled." A few years later, after Aline had married Eero, she reminded me and said: "You know, I almost was. But not for long."

Eero was frighteningly sharp. I think that Philip Johnson worried only about two potential competitors in the years when he and I saw a great deal of each other: one was Matthew Nowicki, the charming and brilliant young Polish architect who had come to New York after the end of World War II and had been the original planner and designer for Chandigarh, the new capital of the Punjab, which would later become Le Corbusier's most impressive work; and the other was Eero. Nowicki was killed in a plane crash in Egypt, when he was on his way back from India. He was all of thirty-nine years old. But Eero was overtaking Philip (and everyone else) at a phenomenal pace. Quite clearly, he would have been a new Stanford White had he lived long enough. His death, though it saddened the rest of us, may have come as something of a relief to Philip.

In a curious way, Eero was a very good teacher. He was interested in nothing, really, except design, and he was perceptive about all of its aspects. I remember once having lunch with him and Willo von Moltke (who was then working for Eero in Bloomfield Hills) and listening to Eero discuss, in great detail, the pros and cons of the latest Ford sedan—why a certain piece of chromium trim was not quite in the right place, why the rear bumpers were too bulky. There was nothing that seemed to escape his attention, and he liked to say that a really successful work of architecture had to be "all of one thing"—by which he meant that every detail had to be in the same idiom, the same family of form and texture and color as every other aspect of the building. He worried endlessly about certain details of his buildings, and their resolution: for example, his chief concern in the design of the Dulles Terminal, much of the time, seemed to be the exact form and location of the downspout that would drain the suspension roof of the terminal—a detail that very, very few visitors to the building would ever notice.

But Eero did have his weaknesses. Not only was his ambition sometimes overweening to the point where he seemed determined to beat all potential competitors to the draw, even if he really wasn't ready to take on the task at hand: there was also a tendency for his ambitious projects to misfire in matters of taste. Eero's most remarkable projects tended to be flawed in certain details. I thought the boldly sculptural TWA Terminal really wasn't very good as sculpture; that the three-pointed concrete shell for his MIT Kresge Auditorium was too fat and too crowded inside; that the Yale Ice Hockey Rink looked like a "Scandivegian" soup tureen, complete with artsy lid; and that his U.S. Embassy in London was klutzy in detail and curiously deficient in the way it failed to meet the corners of Grosvenor Square. Unlike the buildings of Le Corbusier and to some degree Mies van der Rohe, which had always seemed to me totally flawless in form and detail, I found Eero's buildings, almost invariably, somewhat deficient in aesthetic terms. He never seemed quite sure of himself.

Lou Kahn was nowhere near as prolific as Eero. Many potential clients, I am sure, thought he was a bit of a screwball, especially when he began to talk about his work. As a former apprentice in his Philadelphia office, I had grown extremely fond of him, and I was not particularly disturbed by the typical academic gobbledygook that had engulfed him (and that he had a tendency to spout forth) as he and his work became better known. But potential clients must have been slightly befuddled by the sort of double-talk he would utter when he began to teach at places of learning such as Yale, delivering discourses in which theory seemed to have taken leave of art, science, practice, and all other forms of intelligence.

In spite of all the double-talk, Lou was a wonderful teacher, and for two very simple reasons: first, because he had something important to teach; and, second, because his work spoke for him in utterly convincing ways.

What he had to teach was this: the first generation of modern architects had been preoccupied with structure as a basic discipline, and with ways of expressing that structure. Admittedly, there were other concerns—function, and the expression thereof, as well as more traditional concerns with space and form and materials. But structure was the overriding concern, in part because in the nineteenth century the development of new structural materials such as reinforced concrete and high-strength metals profoundly reshaped the kinds of forms and spaces architects were able to build.

Lou thought that structural expression alone should not be the dominant concern of architecture. He realized, more clearly than others, that the kinds of things that *served* buildings—ducts, pipes, cables, elevators, and all the rest—were becoming increasingly important and seemed to call for expressive forms of their own. I once asked Mies about that—he was probably the most prominent advocate of structural expression in architecture—and he said, "Well, I don't think you can make architecture out of plumbing." But I suspect that he wasn't quite sure. Lou wouldn't have put it quite that way—he wasn't especially interested in plumbing—but he did think that you could make architecture out of *services* as well as structure. And that, to many of us, was an intriguing notion. Ulrich Franzen, one of the very best architects of my generation, was one of those influenced by Lou's ideas; and he applied them very elegantly to a major building (the Agronomy Tower) on the Cornell University campus several years later. Others, like I. M. Pei, with whom Franzen had worked immediately after World War II, were similarly influenced by the idea of buildings consisting of service elements (often towers or interstitial service floors), and of significant spaces served by them.

Lou was not insensitive to structure and to ways of expressing different kinds of structures. Far from it. But he balanced his concerns for structural expression with other concerns as well, and his buildings tended to be an amalgam of different priorities. In his Richards Medical Research Buildings on the University of Pennsylvania campus, the primary concern was expressed in the almost medieval service towers containing ducts and other mechanical equipment; whereas in his various museums the primary concern was the manipulation of natural and artificial light. In some of his buildings and projects, structural expression would be a paramount concern; in others, it might be the wall or the roof or the window or the pattern of prefabricated concrete panels.

Lou's buildings invariably had a kind of texture that showed the imprint of a builder's or an artist's hand; they spoke *of* him and *to* the rest of us. Eero's buildings, on the other hand, tended to have very little of that texture; in fact, they tended to be quite imper-

LEFT: *The Richards Medical Research Buildings at the University of Pennsylvania were designed by Louis Kahn and constructed between 1957 and 1961. The towers contain various vertical services.*

RIGHT: *The silhouette of Kahn's Richards Medical Research Buildings fits in well with the neo-Gothic skyline of the older Penn campus.*

sonal. Lou once said: "I dreamed I lived in a city called Le Corbusier"—a typically poetic dictum reflecting his responsiveness to Corbu's unfailing touch. I think Lou had that same touch—in his buildings, in his drawings, even in his words. He died of a heart attack in New York's Pennsylvania Station at the age of seventy-three, while returning from an exhausting trip to India and Bangladesh, where he was busy with several large commissions. I can't think of many artists who meant so much to my generation, and whose death we felt so crushingly.

I suppose that the "First" or "Second Generation" modern architect I knew best in the decades after World War II was Marcel ("Lajko") Breuer. I had met Lajko when I was at the Museum of Modern Art, and had written a book on his work as a catalogue to the exhibition of his "Model House" in the museum garden. He and I had become friends in the process of getting all this done.

I have written earlier about Lajko's career—his revolutionary work in the development of modern furniture, his work in architecture in pre-Hitler Germany, in Britain, and in New England, in partnership with Walter Gropius. And I have also written about his work as a teacher at Harvard, about the remarkable group of students he inspired in his studios in the late 1930s and early 1940s—students who later came to be the most influential modern architects in the U.S.

One day, some years after I had left MOMA, Lajko told me that a publisher, Dodd, Mead & Company, had asked him to produce another, updated book on his work. He was reluctant to do so, since he wasn't sure his English was quite up to the task. (He was almost equally unintelligible in English, German, French, and, I assumed, Hungarian—a fact which made his tremendous success as a teacher all the more remarkable.) Would I be willing to work with him on the new book? It was his idea that he and I would engage in conversation about various aspects of his work, that we would tape the conversation, and that I would then rewrite the text and make it more or less comprehensible.

I was a little dubious about the project, but it was hard to turn Lajko down in any matter—he had a sweetness and warmth that was difficult to refuse. And so I agreed, and we went to work.

Since the book was bound to be full of illustrations of every kind, it was almost as critical to pick a graphic artist to design the book as it was to find a translator/editor. Lajko had long been friendly with Herbert Bayer (who had taught at the Bauhaus when Lajko himself was there), and I had known Bayer almost as long, since my mother worked with him briefly in prewar Berlin. But Herbert was living in Aspen, and we felt we needed someone closer by, preferably in New York. I suggested Alexey Brodovitch, the art director of *Harper's Bazaar,* whom I had met several years earlier when I was at the Museum of Modern Art. Lajko didn't know Alexey, but I assured him that there was simply no one with a finer hand. Lajko agreed, and we began to work together.

The resulting book, *Sun and Shadow—Sol y Sombra,* was not the best publication Alexey ever designed; for one thing, he had to make do with old photographs that could not be duplicated thirty years or so after the fact. But to work with him was one of the most exciting experiences of my career as an editor, and I think it was a great experience for Lajko as well.

Brodovitch had a fearsome reputation as an art director. My mother had faced him on many occasions and seen him go through her drawings wordlessly and without a moment's hesitation, tossing aside most of them as being obviously (in his view) not up to snuff, but picking out one or two with his unfailing eye. After which he would look up from his work table, crack a small, pained smile, and allow that these were "quite nice." I remember that an audience with Brodovitch left her limp for hours afterwards, and though I had got to know him quite well, I was terrified by the prospect of working with him.

He turned out to be not at all frightening. He was tremendously shy, seemingly frail, and quite small, barely articulate in English, but with a perceptiveness that placed him far ahead of all art directors of his time. He had worked as a photographer at one point and published a magnificent book of photographs on the ballet, the book having been beautifully designed by him. He was teaching photography at the New School and elsewhere, and his students became the finest photographers in America. He had an eye for typography, for layout, for color, for every aspect of printing, for paper, for communicating tenderly, wittily, and boldly that I had never encountered before—and have never encountered since.

Lajko and I thought at first that Alexey was so formidable an artist that it would be difficult to work with him, but we soon discovered that this was not so at all. We would meet in the evenings at Alexey's small apartment or at Lajko's office, and Alexey would roll out a stack of photostatic layouts showing page after page of photographs, drawings, and typography, arranged in perfect compositions. There would be old photographs and drawings that were quite familiar to Lajko and me from their use in earlier publications, but Alexey had cropped them and rearranged them in ways that transformed them into entirely new and often startling images. He would lay them all out on the floor without a word and wait for our reaction. At first, Lajko and I were far too scared to question or challenge any of Alexey's layouts, but we soon discovered that he really enjoyed our critical responses. And if either one of us raised any questions about an illustration or a page, Alexey would return a couple of days later with half a dozen alternative layouts, all of them dazzling.

When the book was finished, the result was an extraordinary piece of design in itself—much the best aspect of the completed work. And although I was to work with numerous other art directors in later years, not one of them ever proved so easy to work with as Alexey Brodovitch, or so inspiring.

Alexey and I began to see more and more of each other, not because we had much to work on together, alas, but because we en-

joyed each other's company. We would have dinner at one of his favorite places, a steak-and-martini joint on Second Avenue called
Billy's, and he would gradually tell me a little about his past—his
time as a cavalry officer in the Tsarist Guards (he sometimes wore
a single earring as a memento of those years), the way in which he
met his wife, Nina, as they were fleeing the Bolshevik Revolution,
their days in Paris, his fondness for horses. We sometimes met with
Carmel Snow, the remarkable editor of *Harper's Bazaar,* who adored
Alexey—a seemingly frail lady, flawlessly and fashionably dressed to
the hilt from morning to night, usually energized by a martini or
two or three (as were the rest of us), her hair tinted blue, her drill
sergeant's voice summoning BRODOVITCH! to her side at regular intervals to obtain his reaction to this dress design or that illustration. We sometimes met with Frank Zachary, the editor with
whom Alexey produced three issues of an extraordinary (and com-
mercially unsuccessful) magazine called *Portfolio,* the most beautiful
journal ever produced in the U.S. (Alexey and Frank put together
Portfolio's pages on the floor of some office building's corridor after
the regular staffers and the cleaning ladies had gone home.)

But most of the time we would meet at his apartment or at
Billy's. His life was almost a caricature of a dark Russian tragedy:
the Brodovitches' son, Nicky, was a sick man and was suspected of
setting fire to his parents' various houses. Nina and Alexey both
drank like sailors—or Cossacks—and she died when their second
country house, in Sagaponack, Long Island, near my own place,
burned to the ground. Alexey was constantly in treatment for alco-
holism, and Nicky for all sorts of other dreadful illnesses. Alexey finally quit *Harper's Bazaar* and free-lanced for a while in New York
(he designed, among many other things, a beautiful jacket for one
of my books). He kept on teaching and was supported in numerous ways by such former students as Richard Avedon and Irving
Penn. And then, one day, he went back to Europe to die, in Le
Thor, near Avignon, at seventy-three, almost destitute.

There had never been an art director in the U.S. like Alexey
Brodovitch—or anywhere else, I should imagine. For decades after
his death, dozens of imitators lived off his innumerable, published
visions. Not many of those who, to this day, owe almost everything
to his extraordinary talents, give him credit. Some years after
Alexey left New York, I tried to have the *Architectural Forum* redesigned by the people with whom I worked—talented designers
like Paul Grotz and Charlotte Winter. Although we rarely talked

about Brodovitch, all of us knew what we were trying to accomplish: we were trying, in some way, to make over our magazine in the sort of image that Alexey would have given it. In 1972, when all of us on the *Forum's* staff left to start a new magazine, *Architecture Plus,* Paul and Charlotte and I finally had the opportunity to design a magazine that might meet Alexey's superb standards. Alas, he had died a few months earlier; but virtually every magazine of any quality produced to this day owes its appearance in almost every detail to the genius of this strange and lovely and lonely artist.

There were many, many others in New York and environs in the first dozen years or so after the end of World War II who taught us, indeed inspired us—whose talents in every aspect of design continue to enrich and replenish our lives. They differed from today's "name architects" and "name artists" in two significant respects: first, they had remarkable resources of talent; and, second, they taught us by the example of their work, not by massive outpourings of gobbledygook. I find it extraordinary, in retrospect, that Mies spoke almost not at all, that Breuer was quite inarticulate, that Corbu and Aalto spoke very little English, that Jackson Pollock, when sober, was quite silent, and that Alexey Brodovitch, the greatest teacher in our time of photography and graphic arts, rarely opened his mouth between puffs on his cigarette. Yet, all of them left indelible marks on my generation of designers; and what remains of their work continues to have the power to inspire us beyond anything that has been produced by designers and architects since.

CHAPTER NINETEEN

■ There was a little Italian restaurant at 33 West 47th Street, a couple of blocks from the old Time-Life Building, where Tino Nivola had established an informal "Round Table"—a place where he and the rest of us would meet every Wednesday for lunch. The place was called Del Pezzo's, and it was located on the bottom two floors of a rather gloomy old townhouse that belonged to a man named Antonio Santiccioli. The Santicciolis occupied the top two floors of the building. The food was indifferent, and the waiters were middle-aged and rather disgruntled Neapolitans; but Tino, with his dazzling smile, had managed to melt their grumpiness so that they became almost friendly to us on occasion.

As for the Santicciolis, they remained a total mystery to most of us throughout the years during which we met at Del Pezzo's every Wednesday: at first they were totally invisible, and I assumed that the top floors of the townhouse were occupied by squads of mafiosi; then, as one or two women would occasionally peek around the corners of the stairwell, I came to believe that the upper floors contained a fairly exclusive bordello; only much, much later, when I met a delightful lady called Valerie Ceriano who, it turned out, had grown up on those mysterious upper floors, did I discover the prosaic truth—that the Santicciolis were a very proper family of

Italian immigrants who were just as baffled by Tino and by his companions as we were by them.

Tino's Wednesday lunches at Del Pezzo's occupied a large, circular table in the center of the second-floor dining room, and the weekly get-together was easily as entertaining a *Stammtisch* as the widely advertised Round Table that operated at the Algonquin, some three blocks to the south. In fact, some of *The New Yorker's* most distinguished contributors much preferred Tino's Wednesday lunches to whatever was supposed to be going on down the street: Saul Steinberg, the artist whose Klee-like cartoons dominated *The New Yorker's* pages and covers for several decades, was a close friend of Tino's and became a friend to the rest of us as well. Niccolo Tucci, the eccentric *New Yorker* writer and mimic, came every week, and ate exactly one orange for lunch. (He was very vain, and seemed to be on a permanent diet.) Dwight Macdonald, who wrote for *The New Yorker* also, came as often as we could drag him there. And there were numerous other *New Yorker* types who came occasionally: Geoffrey Hellman, Charles Addams, and assorted hangers-on.

Most of us were artists, writers, or architects: I brought Hans Namuth, the photographer, and he stayed; there was Stamos Papadaki, the Greek architect and art director of the magazine *Progressive Architecture,* who preferred, for some reason, to eat at a separate table next to ours, in quiet solitude; there was Leo Lionni, the charming Dutch-Italian artist who was then the art director of *Fortune* magazine; there was Joel Carmichael, a free-lance genius whose precise field of expertise escaped definition, but who was brilliantly eloquent in virtually all areas of human knowledge; and there were too many others to mention, or to remember. We brought different guests, week after week—assorted intellectuals and artists from Europe, Latin America, Asia, and elsewhere. And we were joined by favorite collaborators: I often brought colleagues from the *Architectural Forum,* especially Paul Grotz, the art director and my closest friend on the magazine's staff; and Aline Loucheim, the art and architecture critic of *The New York Times* before she married Eero Saarinen.

In fact, it seems in retrospect that no one in any of our areas of interest set foot in Manhattan for any length of time without showing up, sooner or later, at Tino's Round Table at Del Pezzo's. And as it became more and more common for some of us to take off on brief trips to Europe, we could depend upon running into assorted alumni of the Del Pezzo's gang in Milan, Paris, London, Barcelona, or Berlin.

One of the curious aspects, in retrospect, of life in the avant-garde and on its fringes during the late 1940s and the 1950s was that there were so few of us: most architects in the U.S. and elsewhere were barely literate in the new language of modern architecture and were, at best, designing boxes that, from a very great distance, looked as if they might hold some promise. Most American artists were similarly awkward in their idioms—vaguely aware of the radical new work being shown in a few galleries like Betty Parsons', and trying to emulate some of the new images without really understanding what they were doing. The men and women who worked with real conviction were very few and far between, and they stood out: there was no need, at our Round Table, to argue with Sandy Calder or Bucky Fuller or Franz Kline or Bob Motherwell about their work—we knew that they operated on a level of sophistication and conviction that spoke for itself. So we talked about other things—politics, sex, movies, love, Picasso, how to bake bread, and where we wanted to live when we left the U.S.—or, anyway, New York—which would probably be very soon.

While all these interesting things were going on on the periphery of my life as an architect and architecture critic, the *Architectural Forum* was doing well editorially, and indifferently in financial terms. It was doing well editorially in spite of the leadership of the Time Inc. rejects who had been put in charge of us by the corporate management, and in spite of the bulky superstructure imposed upon us from above—two or three times the number of people on the editorial and business staffs justified by a relatively small publication.

The reason we were doing well was quite simple: we had some very, very good people on our editorial staff, and their work somehow survived the onslaught of Perry Prentice's illiteracy. Douglas Haskell, that curiously old-fashioned idealist hired by Prentice to edit the magazine, was an odd duck—Frank Lloyd Wright liked to call him a "synthetic Yankee," which was neither fair nor accurate, nor especially perceptive: Doug Haskell was born the son of an American missionary family while his father, who had been from Ohio, was stationed in some obscure Balkan backwater; and Doug made up for his foreign birth by becoming exaggeratedly American—speaking in a searing Midwestern whine and vehemently defending all things

American, irrespective of merit. Moreover, his mind seemed to operate on wavelengths that most of us found difficult to tune in on, much of the time: he seemed possessed by a number of private demons, specifically "furriners," capitalists, journalistic competitors, and, I think, Lewis Mumford. Doug, in short, was an amiable nut, and all of us liked him, especially at a slight distance.

To his enormous credit, he had assembled a staff of rather remarkable people, among them Jane Jacobs, a wonderfully likable, contentious, opinionated woman from Erie, Pennsylvania. After spending half a dozen years on the *Forum*'s staff observing the magazine's commitment to such mixed utopian blessings as urban renewal, Jane stunned everyone by questioning virtually all the basic premises by which modern planners had functioned since the end of World War II and before. To conventional "modernists" like myself, her devastating attacks on Ideal Cities and other modern fantasies and her advocacy of a form of creative chaos were unsettling, to put it mildly. It took me several years to come to terms with her extraordinary vision of a truly free, egalitarian society, and when I did, I suddenly remembered what Bertrand Russell had once told me: that to keep one's thinking fresh and creative, one should periodically question one's own most sacred convictions—and assume, for the sake of argument, that the precise opposite of those convictions might be true.

Doug's hiring of Jane Jacobs, in retrospect, was probably his most courageous move. I suspect that it was made possible in part because Perry Prentice believed that Jane's libertarian notions were closer to his own right-wing devotion to free enterprise than those of utopian, Radiant City ideologues (like myself and others of similar ilk). But I am not really sure that Perry had the insights or instincts that I occasionally gave him credit for.

In retrospect, it is not very clear to me just why the *Architectural Forum*, in those years, had become the leading magazine of its kind in the U.S. Admittedly, the *Forum* published all the most interesting work being done at the time: Doug published Frederick Kiesler's egg-shaped "Endless House"—a rather mindless and derivative effort that never went beyond its author's sketches and clay models, but was presumably considered to stand, or teeter, on the "cutting edge" of its day; he published the brilliant little constructions being designed and built in Florida by Paul Rudolph, clearly the most talented architect of the new, postwar generation; he published the best work being done by Lou Kahn, by Philip Johnson, by Ulrich Franzen, by Edward L. Barnes, by John Johansen, by Mies van der Rohe, by Gropius, by Harry Weese, by Ieoh Ming Pei, and by some of the new West Coast designers like Craig Ellwood; he published the most intriguing projects by that science fiction guru Bruce Goff; and he published everything that Mr. Wright designed and built, in splendid photographs by Ezra Stoller, and in dazzling color. (Paul Grotz saw to it that Wright's work was given its due editorially.)

And there were other articles that went beyond the mediocrity of professional or "trade" magazines: a debate, amongst the leading architects involved, over the new UN Secretariat building; and regular and sophisticated coverage of the work of pioneering technologists such as Paul Weidlinger, Bucky Fuller, Pier Luigi Nervi, Frei Otto, and many more.

But most of the magazine was filled with deadly discussions of the sort that Perry Prentice found fascinating: mortgage rates, zoning policy, home-building trends, and the economics of parking lots. When Perry finally split off the suburban home-building "component" of the magazine as a separate publication named *House & Home,* some of the interminable articles dealing with dreary suburban tracts and other blessings of the free market were syphoned off from the *Forum* and the latter improved perceptibly. But even then it really wasn't as good a publication as it could have been, or as good as, for example, the British *Architectural Review,* or the Milanese magazine *Domus.* It stood out only because the other U.S. magazines—*Architectural Record, Progressive Architecture,* and one or two others—were so mindless.

The trouble was that Perry was visually illiterate, and Doug was, in this respect at least, little better. And Paul Grotz, who was the art director throughout those years, seemed to find the daily battles with the management over simple matters of typography and composition so exhausting that he concentrated his considerable talents on one or two stories a month and abandoned the rest of the magazine to the vulgarians. For a publication addressed to an audience of more or less sophisticated designers to settle for such compromises—in an age of graphic artists like Brodovitch and Leo Lionni and Herbert Bayer and Herbert Matter—was depressing indeed. We excelled only because our writers, in matters of architecture, were so knowledgeable, and because the competition did not really exist.

In part because of the frustrations that dogged all of us, I began to spend more and more time in my tiny architectural practice. I had been very lucky: my first house, a small vacation cottage I designed for my family and myself, turned out to be quite a success, and was published in magazines all over the U.S., Europe and Japan. This meant that everybody thought I was pretty good at designing small vacation cottages with sliding walls; and that is what I did, for young couples who had settled in the Hamptons because they had heard that was where the avant-garde hung out. (This was many years before the Hamptons became the playground of rich yuppies and others whose tastes, in architecture, tended toward the nouveau-riche pretentious.) My houses were simple, austere, minimalist, inexpensive to build, and rather self-effacing. Today, most of them are virtually invisible, because I would surround them with hedges and trees so as to make them blend into the beautiful landscape. Meanwhile the lovely fields and marshes that characterized the Hamptons when the first artists moved out there to escape the American marketplace have been savaged by "name architects" whose "architectural statements" seem to announce little more than the designer's name, as loudly and arrogantly as possible.

One day, in early 1957, I received a call from a man called Jack Masey, who was then in charge of cultural exhibits that were being put up all over the world by the U.S. Information Agency. Masey had worked briefly in the *Forum*'s Art Department in the years after World War II, and I had formed an instant dislike for him—which it turned out was mutual. He had struck me as loud, vulgar, imperious, and generally unattractive, and I was rather relieved when he departed for government service in 1950. He had been sent to Delhi to supervise USIA exhibit efforts in India and nearby countries, and nobody had heard any more of him for several years.

When he called me from Washington, I was surprised and on guard; and he was rather cool. Would I be available, he asked, to design an exhibition on U.S. architecture to be mounted in West Berlin? My first inclination was to say "No, thanks," or "Why me?" He seemed to anticipate my reaction and said that USIA was committed to having such an exhibit, and that I seemed to be the only person available who had a fairly complete knowledge of the current state of the art in the U.S., who spoke German, who could, presumably, work with German contractors in putting up the exhibit, and who was also a practicing architect and could therefore design the installation.

I had not spent much time in Berlin in the years after I left the Army, and the idea of taking several months off from the magazine and spending them in my former hometown sounded attractive enough. Masey, I assumed, would be in Washington—probably something of an irritant, but far enough away to cause few problems. "Well, I guess I am interested," I told him. He didn't sound especially enthusiastic: "OK, can you meet me in Berlin on Monday?" I said I could and would.

The plane landed on Monday evening at the old Tempelhof airport, and there was Masey, fairly scruffy as always, and otherwise unchanged also. He was with a couple of Berlin-based USIA bureaucrats in Brooks Brothers suits, and all of us drove directly to the exhibition site—a large, ungainly postwar building named the Marshall Haus (in honor of General George C. Marshall, whose Plan had saved Western Europe from economic and political collapse)—and made our way into its cavernous interior. It looked roughly like a huge, abandoned automobile showroom, and it became clear to me that the only way to tackle the job was to use the exhibition to transform its interiors into a series of very different spaces. I said so to Masey, and he said fine. The Brooks Brothers said something about the "budget," and Masey said "we'll manage." I was slightly under the weather from jet lag and went to my hotel—a villa in Dahlem that the U.S. Army had converted into a kind of hostel for visiting consultants—to get some sleep.

I stayed in Berlin for several days, meeting local contractors and other potential collaborators, and visiting old friends and making new ones—especially among young architects and artists. But most of the time I spent with Jack Masey, who spoke no German and yet managed to dominate all conversations by decibel count and similar means. He was as much of a pest as ever—but, for some reason which remains a total mystery to me as well as to him, he and I became fast and utterly devoted friends, and remain so, with interruptions, to this day.

It became obvious from the moment Jack and I met at Tempelhof, in Berlin, that he was the most improbable Foreign Service officer I or anyone else was ever likely to meet. It wasn't just his appearance, which was not exactly suave, or his speech, which, while extremely articulate, would not pass muster in a girl's finishing school—or at a Foreign Service seminary. It was the fact that he had first-rate judgment in all matters of art and design, and the raw courage to make decisions and to put them into effect. My exhibition in Berlin was a relatively minor effort initiated by him; but in later years, when he became increasingly involved in major U.S. exhibitions in the Soviet Union, and when he became the principal government official in charge of the stunning U.S. World's Fair pavilions at Expo '67, in Montreal, and at Expo '70, in Osaka, Japan, Jack showed a degree of imagination and perseverance that I had never before met among organization men or organization women, and have never met among such types since.

While all his superiors and other associates in government sat back on their behinds in government offices twiddling their thumbs and waiting for Jack to fall flat on his face in the pursuit of one of his outrageous efforts, he went out on limbs, daily, hiring Bucky Fuller to design and build the huge plastic bubble that housed the U.S. Pavilion at the Montreal World's Fair, hiring David Geiger—a young, brilliant, and virtually unknown experimental engineer—to design the air-supported structure that housed the U.S. Pavilion at the Osaka Fair, hiring artists like Andy Warhol and Bob Rauschenberg and Roy Lichtenstein and Helen Frankenthaler and many, many others to work on those U.S. Pavilions, and hiring Charles and Ray Eames to make a multiple-projection, seven-screen film for the American National Exhibition in Moscow's Sokolniki Park in 1959—a film, the first of its kind ever made, that virtually reduced Khrushchev to tears.

With all the great risks he took, I don't know if Jack ever failed; I know that LBJ hated the U.S. Pavilion in Montreal, and that some Neanderthal Republicans in the U.S. Senate tried to bully the USIA into *not* assigning one Foreign Service officer Jack Masey to the Osaka World's Fair project. But aside from such predictable reactions, there was virtually nothing but unstinted praise from people who saw those two U.S. pavilions. Françoise Choay, the French architectural historian and critic, told me that she and some French friends had been in Montreal for Expo '67. "And you know, we were prepared to hate the U.S. exhibit—the Vietnam War, and all that—and we simply couldn't believe how civilized an effort this was, how witty, how sophisticated, how avant-garde."

All this, of course, was Jack's doing. I had mentioned Ivan Chermayeff and Tom Geismar to him and suggested he should get them to design the exhibits inside Bucky's bubble. He had barely heard

of them, but he followed my advice and gave them a free hand to do the best job they had ever done. As for hiring R. Buckminster Fuller to design the building—an absolutely harebrained notion, in the eyes of the bureaucrats—that had been Jack's own idea. He had first met Bucky in Kabul, Afghanistan, where one of Fuller's little geodesic domes housed an official U.S. exhibit, and he had hired Bucky to design a large geodesic dome of aluminum to house a part of the U.S. exhibit in Moscow, in 1959. But the Expo '67 Pavilion for the Montreal World's Fair was much larger, and a much more elaborate affair, and the USIA bureaucrats were licking their lips in anticipation: this time, surely, Masey was bound to fail!

As a matter of fact, he almost did: the manufacturer of the plastic hexagons and other geodesic elements had guaranteed that the acrylic used to make them was fireproof, and Bucky Fuller, who knew roughly as much about advanced technology as did Jack Masey, believed the manufacturer implicitly. Unfortunately for all concerned, the 200-foot-diameter dome caught fire about half a dozen years after Expo '67 had closed, and burned to ashes in a matter of minutes. Fortunately for all concerned, there was no loss of human life. On a typical Expo day, the dome might have had at least 2,000 visitors inside it at any given moment. . . .

During our initial meeting in Berlin, Jack and I spent every day interviewing contractors and others who would contribute to my exhibit, and we spent every night exploring Berlin's unbelievable nightlife. I think, in retrospect, that we behaved like a couple of wild, besotted kids night after night—and we had the time of our lives. No city that he or I knew, in those years, could compare with Berlin in sheer, unbridled madness; and we loved every moment of it.

My Berlin exhibit was reasonably successful, in part because of the splendid graphics done for me by Robert Brownjohn. BJ, as all of us knew him, was a partner of Ivan Chermayeff's and Tom Geismar's, and I thought of him as a genius on a par with some of the finest graphic designers around. Unfortunately, he was a terribly troubled young man, a heroin addict from the age of fourteen, when he and his family lived in a Chicago slum, and an alcoholic as well. Still, he functioned incredibly well on and off the sauce, and on and off dope: I can think of little that he designed in those early years that has not survived the test of time, and much that has never been improved upon. I was very lucky to have BJ working with me, and to have him as a friend. I last saw him in London, where he had gone to live, abandoning his family and his partners and his many pals in the U.S., hoping to be able to take advantage of Britain's liberal narcotics laws. He was in terrible shape, both physically and emotionally, but just as creative as ever. I asked him to design the jacket of a new book, but the publisher was too dim-witted to accept BJ's brilliant creation. He had done a stunning package for a new brand of British cigarettes, and also the titles for the first James Bond movie. But this enormous creativity was all in vain—he killed himself a few months after I saw him. His loss is still felt by those of us who cared about him and care about the quality of graphic art.

My exhibition was timed to celebrate the opening of a very impressive exposition of modern architecture—an event known as "Interbau," for which some two dozen architects from all over the world had designed and built major structures near the center of West Berlin, in a configuration not unlike that originally proposed by Le Corbusier in his Ville Radieuse drawings of 1925. Interbau was a remarkable effort, a powerful demonstration of the will of this beleaguered city to set an example to the rest of the world—and especially to Eastern Europe—of what an Ideal City might look like. Some excellent architects were represented: Le Corbusier (who insisted on putting his building on a site on the edge of West Berlin, rather than next to the others); Brazil's Oscar Niemeyer, Walter Gropius, Sweden's Sven Markelius, Finland's Alvar Aalto, and many others. There were some young German architects as well, in particular one Werner Düttmann, who became a close friend, and who designed the new building for the Academy of Art. And there

LEFT: The exhibition (entitled "Amerika Baut"—"America Builds") consisted in part of full-scale mock-ups of modern U.S. building facades. Here is a close-up of the Union Carbide Building wall, with mirrors creating the illusion of great skyscraper height.
RIGHT: The facade at right is that of Mies van der Rohe's Seagram Building. The exhibition was designed in collaboration with Julian Neski.

was another building, the so-called Congress Hall, designed by the American Hugh Stubbins, and funded by an American foundation.

The Congress Hall was an interesting structure of concrete arches holding a suspended roof—a structure which was, however, flawed in its concept: some twenty-five years after the hall's completion, one of the huge arches of the building collapsed, as did the roof, killing or injuring several people in the building at the time. The Berlin administration, determined that the symbolic building should stand again, rebuilt the structure (with much additional reinforcing), and it is back in service. The brilliant German structural engineer and architect Frei Otto, who was becoming known as the inventor of an entirely new family of tensile structures, had predicted the hall's failure in an article published in the *Forum* by Doug Haskell—but no one had paid any attention to him. "The unsolved question remains," Frei Otto had said. "Does each part of the building serve the organism as a whole?" He clearly thought that in the Congress Hall each part did not. He was proven right when that

The Congress Hall, built in West Berlin in 1957, collapsed in May 1980. Frei Otto, a brilliant German engineer/architect, had predicted its structural failure in an article in Architectural Forum *more than twenty years earlier. (Mrotzkowski)*

224

300-foot-long concrete arch came crashing to the ground. It was supposed to serve as a part of the supporting structure; instead, it turned out that the arch was, in fact, being held up in place by a few thin tension cables quite inadequate to the task. The Congress Hall was perhaps the first in a series of faux structures that would later become the playthings of so-called Deconstructivists, whose knowledge of *real* structures was, to put it mildly, limited.

During the early summer of 1957, while Interbau was under construction, Le Corbusier arrived in Berlin to inspect his apartment block. Unbeknownst to Corbu, the German contractor for the building had made significant changes in the design; and Hans Scharoun, one of the surviving patriarchs of modern German architecture, was asked to take him to the site—all the while making amends or trying to explain to the Master what had happened and why. Scharoun, in turn, asked me to come along, because he knew that I had been friendly with Corbu in New York and Long Island, and might be able to soften the impact of the contractor's "improvements." Scharoun, who looked a little like Winston Churchill (with half a dozen hairs added to his bald head), was rather shy and inarticulate: he had a small cigar butt permanently attached to his lower lip, which further reduced his already limited articulation. He did not look forward to the encounter.

We met Corbu at Tempelhof Airport and took him to the site not far from the old Olympic Stadium built by Hitler in the 1930s. What the German contractor had done, among several other things, to "improve" Corbu's tall apartment house, was to replace the intended asymmetrical and offbeat pattern of the windows with typical ribbon windows of the sort found in speculative office buildings—much more practical, of course, but hardly in Corbu's spirit. They looked, in fact, awful.

Corbu took one look at the completed floors—six stories raised on top of rows of tall "pilotis"—spat out something like "*Merde!*" or "*Scheisse!,*" and started to sketch furiously on a little pad he carried with him. After a few minutes, during which we watched apprehensively, he showed us what he had done: he had drawn a kind of abstract pattern of colorful "camouflage" that would be painted to cover the so-called spandrels—the horizontal bands of concrete between horizontal bands of glass—and this pattern, he thought, would instantly break up the monotony of the contractor's ribbon windows. "As for the rest of the building," he said, "that will be built exactly as designed!" He would brook no further compromise.

Corbu spoke excellent German, and Scharoun's French and English were limited. I was suitably impressed, both by Corbu's command of the language and by his command of his temper. He had, in fact, become rather sad and gentle. His wife of many years—a wonderfully earthy peasant woman who loved to poke fun at him and his highbrow friends, and whom he adored in spite of, or perhaps because of, her seeming crudity—had died a few months earlier, and he never quite recovered from the blow.

Today the Berlin apartment slab—a soberly Germanic version of the wonderfully exuberant Unité d'Habitation built outside Marseilles some five years earlier—stands in splendid isolation in a suburb of West Berlin, its bottom half a "practical" German block brilliantly camouflaged by Corbu's colorful patterns; its top floors built as originally intended, with bright color accents between windows from the same palette Corbu used to camouflage the lower floors. Few people who visit the building notice the underlying contradictions.

The opening of Interbau and, incidentally, of my exhibition attracted the usual artists, politicians, and architectural eminences, and we all hobnobbed happily for a few days. Thornton Wilder presented his play *Our Town* in the Congress Hall and, in the evenings, treated various assorted young Germans whom I had assembled to drinks and marvelous conversation (in precise though somewhat old-fashioned German). Werner Düttmann, who could drink most of us under the table in the course of a typical evening, found Wilder totally invincible, as did several other young Germans whom Wilder cross-examined on their convictions with unflagging interest until the early hours of each morning.

We were a motley crew: myself, Jack (when he was not back in Washington slugging it out with the bureaucrats), a lovely young black actress called Billy Allen, Hans Scharoun (and his companion, Margit von Plato, the former coeditor of the *Gebrauchsgraphik* and an old friend of my mother's), half a dozen young German artists and architects, an occasional politician like Willy Brandt—plus Thornton Wilder, the latter utterly articulate, charmingly inquisitive and, I think, always behatted, indoors as well as out. It was a great time to be in Berlin—four years before the wall went up and some time before the Germans became as rich and as *insupportable* again as they are today.

I have been back to Berlin many times since those months in 1957—at least once a year, and recently much more often. And, on one or two occasions, Jack and I managed to meet in Berlin and re-visit the scenes of our earlier excesses. I went back again and again after the Berlin Wall went up, and I was there when it came down, almost thirty years later. The city has never lost its excitement for me, or its special brand of wonderful decadence. But those days in 1957, when I served as Jack Masey's guide to this giant madhouse, had a special quality all their own.

CHAPTER TWENTY

.

■ A year after the Interbau exhibition in West Berlin, Jack Masey was appointed by the U.S. Information Agency to be the director of design for a large exhibition to be held in Moscow's Sokolniki Park. The exhibition would be the first presentation of American cultural and other achievements in the Soviet Union, and was part of an exchange program negotiated by the Eisenhower administration with that of Nikita Khrushchev. (The Soviets would be presenting an exhibition of their own in New York.)

Jack picked George Nelson to be the overall designer for the Moscow exhibition, and George, in turn, selected a number of people to work in specific areas: he chose Bucky Fuller to design a large geodesic dome of aluminum, Robert Zion to design the considerable landscaping required, fashion experts to put on an American fashion show, and art curators to assemble an exhibit of the most advanced work being done in the U.S. in the visual arts; and he asked me to design an exhibition on modern American architecture.

The understanding with the Soviets was that while each country would design its own exhibits and send its own experts to supervise the installation, most of the actual construction work would be done with native labor—Soviet in Moscow, American in New York.

The U.S. exhibit in Moscow would be housed in several structures—not only in Bucky's aluminum dome and under a forest of large, reinforced plastic umbrellas designed by Albert Dietz of MIT, but also inside a banal glass-walled pavilion designed by a singularly untalented firm of California architects which, apparently, had the right political connections to land the job. (Jack had not picked them.) There would also be a typical American suburban house (in whose kitchen the then vice president, Richard Nixon, would engage in his famous "Kitchen Debate" with Nikita Khrushchev), and a series of other structures that would contain radio and television studios, movie theaters, administrative offices, and other facilities.

The whole complex, while not uniformly impressive in terms of design, was big enough to qualify as a mini–World's Fair. And the setting, in Sokolniki Park, was reminiscent of Manhattan's Central Park—if Central Park were ever to lend itself to the construction of a World's Fair. (The Soviets, in New York, were relegated to the old Coliseum, on Columbus Circle, for their typically boring exhibit of machine tools and hydroelectric power stations manned by battalions of Stakhanovite laborers.)

All of us went to work in New York and elsewhere preparing the necessary drawings and models and all the rest. Considering the fact that those in charge—Jack, George, and an ever present company of Washington apparatchiks—were not exactly known for their seamless efficiency, the entire operation went almost like clockwork. Jack was on the verge of a permanent nervous breakdown, as usual, and for various uninteresting reasons; George was between marriages, and hence, for some reason, permanently becalmed; Bucky was happily designing his 30,000-square-foot dome; and the Washington apparatchiks were being helpful by writing memos, sending out forms, and holding meetings at which nothing was decided. The situation, in short, was normal. Our work progressed.

Although assembling all the vast amounts of miscellaneous "stuff"—George Nelson's favorite term—and shipping it all to Moscow on time was a major problem, there was another and more serious one: how to fill Bucky's 30,000-square-foot dome; no one had figured out what, if anything, this vast structure might house.

Jack's suggestion was to get Charles and Ray Eames to fill the space with a multimedia event of some sort—to project films onto the interior surfaces of the dome so that visitors to the show, who would be entering the exhibition grounds through the vast aluminum dome, could be given a kind of introduction to "Life in America" as they passed through the space.

Charles, who had made a considerable reputation for himself as a designer of molded plywood and plastic furniture, had recently concentrated on making highly experimental documentary films. He and his wife, Ray, had transformed their workshop in Venice, California, into a kind of mini–film studio; and the documentaries they had made were remarkable for their inventiveness—some very abstract, some quite surreal, some very realistic, and all of them full of imagination and wit. But, like most of the artists and designers sought out by Jack during his checkered career, Charles and Ray were hardly in the mainstream of American culture. They were very much "on the cutting edge"; and for a staid U.S. government agency to commission two such unpredictable experimenters to produce what was to be the theme song of our exhibition was mind-boggling. Only Jack's determination, or pigheadedness, especially in times of crisis, made their selection possible.

Nobody had a very clear idea of what Charles and Ray were going to produce. Charles had an incoherent semistammer that communicated little except his own boundless enthusiasm, and his incoherent "explanations" of whatever it was that excited him most at any given moment were punctuated by Ray's shrill giggles, designed to second her husband's enthusiastic double-talk. It was not very reassuring, especially if you had to translate and convey the Eameses' plans to the apparatchiks in Washington. On one occasion, Jack invited Charles to attend one of the interminable meetings that, in Washington, take the place of thought and action. Charles appeared, in California garb with Leicas dangling from around his neck, and proceeded to jump on the conference room table to snap pictures of the proceedings and their participants— right, left, and center—while the bureaucrats sat aghast around the table observing this circus act. No "minutes" of this meeting were kept, and no agenda was observed. It was not your typical bureaucratic briefing session.

While Jack and George commuted feverishly between Washington and Moscow, the rest of us were completing our drawings and making preparations to take them to the Soviet capital. Finally, early in the summer of 1959, the time came for me to take off for Moscow too. George Nelson happened to be taking the same flight as far as

Helsinki, where both of us stopped off for a couple of days to steel ourselves for what we expected would be a monstrous final push to meet the August deadline: there were icy Finnish lakes of unimaginable beauty, purple-eyed Finnish women (whose beauty rivaled the lakes'), and much aquavit to make it all bearable.

I don't know what I expected Moscow to be like. I had lived in totalitarian countries as a child and assumed it would be like that, only worse. Like most Americans in the 1950s—especially anti-Communists, like myself—I was utterly paranoid about the USSR and expected it to be an enormous concentration camp inhabited by prisoners in chains, and their snarling guards armed to the teeth with submachine guns and instruments of torture.

Our arrival late in the evening at Moscow's airport did little to allay those fears: the first thing that happened was that our U.S. passports were confiscated, to be returned to us (we were told) upon our departure several weeks hence, and after we had received an exit visa. Not very reassuring. Next, our baggage was searched for books, films, magazines, and other subversive material; and, finally, we were permitted to depart in a U.S. Embassy car (which, we were told by Embassy officials sent out to meet us, was certainly bugged) and driven through miles of seemingly deserted Russian landscape—dark, quiet, and barely inhabited.

Our hotel, the Ukraina, was a huge, Stalin-style wedding cake of singular gloom, policed on each floor by a uniformed KGB guard (usually female) at a desk, who handed us our room keys and would collect them each time we went out. The rooms were barren and equipped with a radio that was permanently preset to two or three Soviet wavelengths. According to Jack Masey, who had met us at the airport, there were see-through mirrors in the bedrooms and bathrooms, so that KGB agents could observe guests from some sort of passageway concealed within the walls. (To retaliate, Jack, who had brought exactly one set of drip-dry clothes with him to Moscow, would take a shower every night while fully dressed—and leave his wet clothes on hangers to dry by the morning. He was convinced that this drove the KGB agents behind the see-through mirrors out of their minds, since no one had ever heard of, much less seen, such miracle vestments in the USSR.) The walls of our hotel rooms also contained bugs that would pick up any conversations within the rooms—and the telephones were bugged also. Twice a week the maids who cleaned our rooms would search our baggage and repack our suitcases neatly.

All of this was probably or possibly true, and there was much evidence in the weeks to come that we were being followed and otherwise surveilled by teams of singularly inept agents. None of this was especially pleasant, but we soon got used to it and discovered that the KGB agents were so obviously incompetent at sleuthing that we began to enjoy playing games with them.

As things turned out, there was very little time for games: every morning, around 7 A.M., we would be picked up at the Ukraina in taxis and taken to the site in Sokolniki Park, in the northeastern sector of the capital. The site was a sea of mud, punctuated by the principal U.S. pavilions that were going up fairly rapidly. Bucky's dome had been assigned to an Italian contractor from Turin, whose expert team of metalworkers managed to assemble the prefabricated aluminum elements in record time. The California-designed pavilion was well under way, being put up largely with Soviet labor. But few of the other structures, and even fewer of the exhibits, had been constructed or put in place. We had about six weeks to go, and it looked highly unlikely that we would be able to get it all done by Opening Day.

There were several problems: aside from the Italian metalworkers, a few West German technicians, and a handful of Finnish painters, we had only Soviet workers—men and women—to complete the job. There were some among them who were exceptionally competent—I remember, especially, the foreman of all the truck drivers, a tall, white-haired Russian who looked like Boris Pasternak and had the most beautiful smile I had ever seen—and there were a few who were obviously KGB, including one slick, Italian-suited playboy who kept trying to invite us to come to his pad to listen to his Louis Armstrong records, and who was known, by all Westerners living in Moscow, as the KGB's expert at getting his foreign guests into compromising situations in his audiovisually wired bedroom, and with equally expert KGB ladies.

But most of the workers were bona fide Soviets of varying competence. I discovered, some years later, that it was highly advantageous in those years for a Soviet to put in time in a construction trade: after two years of pouring concrete or hammering nails, a Soviet man or woman was entitled to receive a brand-new apartment. And so I realized, in retrospect, that the thirty-odd men and women I had working for me on my portion of the exhibition were probably dentists or ballerinas or professors of philosophy in real life; they were certainly not construction workers.

Moreover, they had virtually no tools, and those that the U.S. government kept importing from Western Europe—hammers, saws, shovels, screwdrivers, and so on—would disappear at the end of every day; so that, in desperation, we would spend much of our time trying to purchase tools from any number of sources—even from the wonderful Moscow store Detskii Mir (Children's World), which did occasionally have toy hammers and screwdrivers in stock.

Each morning, the foreman of my bedraggled little construction gang—the "brigadier"—would assemble his men and women and deliver an impassioned address, summoning them, I gathered from my American translator, to superhuman efforts to demonstrate to the capitalist guests the superiority of the Soviet system. After which the brigadier would sit down on a log for the remainder of the day, to smoke innumerable cigarettes and to watch over the labors of his crew. For close to six weeks he never lifted a finger except to light another cigarette.

The problems mounted almost daily. My exhibit consisted in part of very large photographic blowups of American buildings that were to be mounted on walls the way posters are mounted on billboards. It turned out that the paste used by my helpers was watersoluble; and since there seemed to be torrential tropical rainfalls at 6 P.M. sharp every day—accompanied by deafening claps of thunder and blinding flashes of lightning—the photographs mounted each day would peel off their walls by nightfall. There were other problems: Bobby Zion, the talented landscape designer recruited by Jack to transform the sea of mud that was left after the cloudbursts into something resembling a park, found that there were no waterproof cables or outdoor lighting fixtures—so that, at cloudburst time, any light bulbs being tested at that moment would explode all over the site like firecrackers.

But by far the most disastrous mishap had to do with the acres of concrete that needed to be poured to provide floor slabs in our pavilions and walkways between them.

The Soviets, determined to demonstrate that they were as "modern" as the rest of us, insisted on premixing all the concrete for our site in a factory on the edges of Moscow. Every morning, then, a small truckload of premixed concrete would arrive on the site, to be poured in place by our workers; and every morning, the amounts of scientifically premixed concrete that arrived on the site proved woefully inadequate.

So the Soviet workmen tried to stretch the amount of concrete

George Nelson, chief designer of the U.S. Exhibition in Moscow, in 1959, was an avid photographer. He thought this photo I took of him in action was semipornographic—and distinctly flattering—and asked me to send him a dozen prints.

One part of our Moscow Exhibit was a display of huge blowups of significant, modern American buildings, and small-scale models of others. The plan of our exhibition (designed with Julian Neski) shows two areas—one, geometric in layout, devoted to urban structures; the other, organic in layout, devoted to rural buildings.

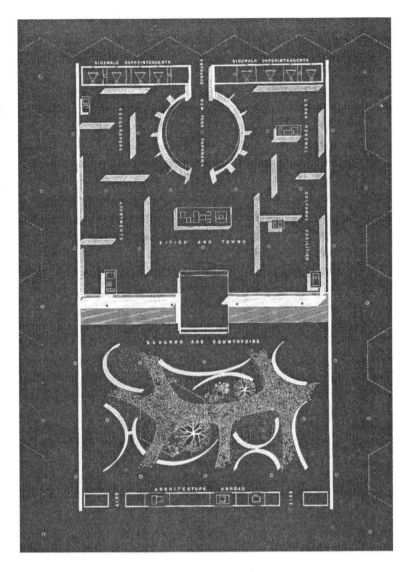

to cover the day's quota of floor area. And they stretched it by adding great quantities of sand from the surfaces of Sokolniki Park.

What happens when you "stretch" concrete in this fashion is that it becomes more and more sandlike and less and less cementlike as it dries and hardens—so that, when the "concrete" floors had finally settled in place and people began to walk on them, the concrete turned into enormous clouds of dust. As a result, the exhibits contained within the enclosed pavilions would soon be caked in sand; the Russian-speaking American guides who were being imported by the U.S. Information Agency to explain the exhibits to the expected Soviet visitors, would surely suffocate while trying to hold down their posts in the various pavilions; and the pulverized sandstone—it never even remotely resembled concrete—would get into everyone's eyes, clog up cameras and lights, and in effect turn the entire exhibit into a torture chamber.

But while all of this became increasingly predictable as our work progressed, the sand clouds were still almost bearable so long as there were no hordes of Soviet visitors. There were only a dozen or so Americans on the site, plus a couple of hundred workers, and while we expected the worst, we could still function much of the time. The sole exception, perhaps, was the period of the 6 P.M. cloudbursts: they transformed the entire site into a watery swamp of such fluidity that we often sank into the mud way above our knees; in fact, I once had to jump out of my sneakers to keep from drowning in mud after a particularly fierce cloudburst—and I always wondered what some latter-day archaeologist might conclude upon discovering a pair of petrified tennis shoes from Abercrombie and Fitch, carbon-dated to 1959, among the ante- or postdiluvian remains in a site that used to be known as Mockba.

These were some of the daily and hourly problems. There were many more: the heat and humidity in Moscow that summer became at times intolerable, and the only air-conditioned room in the city, to the best of my knowledge, was Lenin's Tomb, which in those days contained the bodies of both Lenin and Stalin. Whenever the heat became completely unbearable, I would call Jack on one of our field telephones (which were, of course, monitored by our attractive KGB-supplied telephone operators) and suggest to him that we go "visit the cold cuts"—my code name for the departed rulers of the USSR. Whereupon we would commandeer a taxi, take off for Red Square, and make a beeline for the entrance to the tomb. There were always long lines of Soviets waiting to inspect the bodies (and often to cross themselves in their presence), but they recognized us as Americans even in our mud-caked clothes and insisted that we go to the head of the line. "You are our guests," they would say in Russian (which Jack had learned to speak), or in German, or in English, or in French. When was the last time a New Yorker addressed a foreigner in his native tongue, or insisted that he or she go to the head of a queue?

· · ·

I think it was on my second or third day in Moscow that I began to fall in love, quite hopelessly, with the people of Moscow. It wasn't only their generosity, their hospitality, their almost childlike determination to show us how good and bold and modern they were; it wasn't only the sweet ways in which they treated their children; and it wasn't their invariable pleasantness—not at all: you have not experienced boorishness until you have been exposed to surly waiters in Moscow restaurants. Nor was it their uniform beauty: while there are few people more beautiful than the towering, bearded monks and priests of Zagorsk, there are plenty of Soviet men and women in the streets of Moscow who look like Nikita Khrushchev's and Nina Khrushchev's doubles.

It was, I think, their incredible warmth, and the sadness of their lives. In Nazi Germany, more than ninety percent of the population was passionately supportive of its murderous leaders—regardless of what "good Germans" will tell you today. But in Moscow that summer, there were only vast numbers of people desperately cowed and frightened and oppressed—and a government of heavily armed oppressors. To see the young mother who tried to pour concrete in my exhibit so she could feed her daughter, and to hear of the long hours she had to queue up to buy milk, or—God forbid!—to find a little birthday gift for her child, would break your heart. And to remember the night after the exhibition finally opened, when some of us planned a dinner in honor of our wonderful friend the Boris Pasternak of the truck drivers, and to have him tell us almost tearfully at the last moment that it was too dangerous for him and his wife to be seen socializing with Americans—that, too, was enough to break your heart.

We had many opportunities to make friends among the Soviets who worked with us, and the most surprising fact, to me, was the detailed knowledge of the United States possessed by many of the Soviets whom we met.

Some of them—not necessarily KGB types—were remarkably willing to engage us in political discussion. (The Khrushchev years, of course, showed the first signs of a "thaw" in the USSR after Stalin's death.) And they were not especially defensive about their own system. Instead, they would challenge us to say how many women there were in the U.S. Congress, how many of our congressmen were workers and farmers rather than lawyers and businessmen and millionaires. (We didn't have the answers, but they did—and embarrassingly so!) In 1959 many people in the USSR and, for that matter, in the U.S., believed that the next presidential election might pit Nelson Rockefeller against John F. Kennedy; and one young Soviet, an artist, asked me: "One millionaire against another—what kind of choice is that?" Some of the Soviet intellectuals we met would ask what I thought of Arthur Koestler and did Americans know about Eugene Debs. And all of them knew a great deal more about European and, for that matter, American politics than many equally well-educated Americans knew about either. Some were quite critical of Stalin's policies; others were even more critical of Khrushchev's, and often for the "wrong" reasons—they said that Nikita Khrushchev wasn't tough enough! Very few of the young Soviets whom we tried to engage in political conversations begged off for obvious reasons. On the whole, they were at least as interesting and as "engaged" as Americans of their vintage—and usually much more so.

I am sure there were and are savages among Russians. After all, there were some who happily and profitably served the oppressors and murdered their opponents, real or imagined. But that summer in the capital of what a famous American paranoid would later call the "Evil Empire" served to clear the air and the minds of many of us who had, until that time, viewed the world in absurdly simplistic terms.

One of the revelations came not from the many Soviets with whom we talked and worked every day, but from the Americans at the U.S. Embassy whom we would encounter frequently. They were living a life of almost complete isolation in the Soviet capital—no Russians, except for obvious KGB agents and other government officials, dared to talk to them in private or in public. "What do these people talk about?" the Embassy types would ask us, sounding desperate. "What do they think? What are their attitudes?" I suddenly realized that American intelligence regarding the USSR was based to a large degree on fantasy—on fantasies often advanced by ex-Communists whose own genuinely horrifying experiences within the Communist world had left them severely disoriented. I had been aware of the fact that most of the more sophisticated and perceptive people whom I had met in Army Intelligence and in the OSS during World War II had left the service as soon as they could, honorably, return to their civilian careers—and that most of those who remained in the OSS and later formed the nucleus of the CIA were among the less competent and less intelligent I had encountered—men who really had nothing in civilian life to which to return. But I did not realize, until my weeks in Moscow, that most of our national paranoia regarding the alleged Soviet threat to mankind was based on almost total ignorance of what was really happening in this sad and backward nation.

Anyone from the West visiting the USSR in those days could plainly see that virtually *nothing* worked: not the manufacture of goods, not the distribution of food, not the building of buildings or highways, not the making of anything much more complex than tasseled lamp shades. (In fact, that particular sector of the Soviet economy seemed to be functioning splendidly: one day I walked into a store off Red Square and found it stocked, literally from floor to ceiling, with the kinds of tasseled lamp shades that my great-grandmother used to love! No one, it seems, was buying them in 1959, however.) In Finland, a trade agreement forced upon that small country by Stalin included a requirement that the Finnish government import thousands of Soviet-made automobiles each year; because no consumers in Finland would, in turn, buy those lemons, the Finnish government was forced to establish a Public Taxi Company which used up all the Soviet imports, rather rapidly.

There were one or two areas in which the Soviets would, inexplicably, excel: they made first-rate fountains of stainless steel, and these adorned many parks and public squares; and, of course, they produced some excellent spacecraft—though possibly not as uniformly successful as they, and the CIA, claimed.

In fact, it became fairly evident to all of us—Americans and West Europeans alike—who had a chance to work in the Soviet Union that the country was decades behind most of the industrialized nations, and especially far behind the U.S. in material terms. For the USSR to represent a serious threat to those nations was a ridiculous idea—and one that would make sense only to those interested in milking popular paranoia for all it was worth. Clearly, the CIA would have had its mysterious budgets severely slashed if the truth about the USSR had been widely known; and the Pentagon would have had its budgets cut even more drastically. All those military advocates with a vested interest in the "Red Menace," to whom it meant generous promotions and much expensive military hardware with which to parade and play, were inclined to invent and exaggerate all those frightful threats posed by the "Evil Empire." And so, needless to say, were the manufacturers of all those expensive weapons that American taxpayers were persuaded, by salesmen of fear, to purchase at enormous financial and social costs.

Many years later, one of the few U.S. senators with both the brains and the integrity to speak the truth had this to say: "If ten or fifteen years ago we had had any understanding of just how *weak* the Soviet system was," wrote Daniel Patrick Moynihan of New York, "we would have been far more husbanding of our own resources, basically waiting the Soviets out. How did we miss this? . . . The [U.S.] national security state developed a vast secrecy system which hid us from our own miscalculations. The mistakes, you see, were secret, so they were not open to correction. . . . We will be paying for those mistakes for a long while."

That was written in 1990. Many of us could have written much the same thing thirty years earlier. When we returned from our stint in Moscow, we were visited by CIA types who came to "debrief" us with regard to our experiences in the USSR. I told my CIA visitors what I thought of the Soviets' capabilities, pointing out that I was not unfamiliar with the business of arriving at "estimates and appreciations" of potential opponents. My visitors did not want to hear about Soviet weaknesses—they were looking for more grist for the national paranoia, to help boost budgets for themselves. Needless to say, they excused themselves after a few minutes and I never heard from them again.

It was the last week of July, and Opening Day would be July 25. All of us were working around the clock to get our exhibits in place on time. The pavilions were beginning to fill with clouds of dust generated by the adulterated concrete. We hosed down the floors periodically, and this helped a bit. Some seventy or eighty Russian-speaking American guides, selected from various Russian-language programs at American universities, had arrived in Moscow, and they pitched in enthusiastically.

Meanwhile, the Soviets sent over a team of censors from the KGB to make sure our exhibits contained nothing subversive. (They objected to a couple of references in one or two books— mostly *World Almanacs* and similar radical tracts—but they left other printed material alone.) Curiously enough, they paid little attention to what turned out to be one of the most successful exhibits assembled by George Nelson and his crew. It was a table, perhaps 100 feet long, on which were mounted dozens of typical telephone directories from American cities from New York to Dubuque and beyond: directories that listed names, addresses, and phone numbers in the way they are routinely listed in any free and open society—but in a way totally unfamiliar to the Soviets, to whom such routine information had become highly confidential and frequently quite unobtainable. That long table, with its rows upon rows of American telephone directories, became the number-one attraction—and political lesson—in the American Exhibition.

As were the hundreds of American books on display elsewhere. While the telephone directories were bolted down (since they were difficult to replace), the examples of contemporary American literature were loosely placed on shelves and tables, to encourage Soviet visitors to walk off with anything they found interesting. (The U.S. Information Agency had shipped duplicates and triplicates in great quantities to Moscow, and we planned to have stolen books replaced every morning, before the next wave of visitors came rushing through the gates.)

Everything was beginning to fall into place, and it looked as if we might, just possibly, meet our deadline. Bucky's huge dome was up, ready to receive the multimedia production that was supposedly on its way from Venice, California. Seven giant screens had been mounted in a cluster on the inside surface of the dome, and in two rows—four screens on top, three below—and seven movie projec-

Entrance to the Architecture section of the U.S. Exhibition in Moscow. The photographic blowups were sheltered by large, reinforced plastic umbrellas. (Robert Lautman)

tors had been mounted on precisely angled concrete wedges, each projector aimed at one of the seven screens. Even Bucky had arrived in Moscow, with a small entourage of fans.

There was only one problem: Charles and Ray were nowhere in sight, and neither were their seven films. Jack, George Nelson, and the rest of us were beginning to have a collective nervous breakdown. How could there be an "opening" to this exhibition if there was no overture? There would be thousands of visitors, all lined up for hours to admire all these visions of the American Paradise—and their first experience, upon entering the exhibition grounds, would be the inside of a huge and empty aluminum can! We had grievous intimations of doom. Then one evening, with about forty-eight hours to go, we were informed that Charles and Ray had just landed in a plane from Helsinki. As we all stood around inside Bucky's dome, the two of them walked out of the dark of Sokolniki Park and straight into Bucky's dome. They were dressed in typical California garb—wrinkled camping togs and over-the-shoulder bags—and the bags contained seven reels of film, in cans. The Eameses were beaming from ear to ear—and if we hadn't been so relieved, we probably would have wrung their necks. Charles went up to the projectors, checked them out, inserted the reels, and flicked the various switches. And on the seven screens, projected precisely and in total synch, appeared a multimedia show that was, quite simply, flawless.

The story told in film was simple: two typical days in the life of America—a typical weekday and a Sunday. The images, always in tandem, were of ordinary things: people waking up, having breakfast, going off to school or to work, having lunch, coming home, and so on. There were scenes of play, of worship, of art shows, of sports, of traffic jams (and interminable highway intersections), of travel—trains, buses, planes—of innumerable details that added up to a rather routine travelogue of the USA.

But to the Soviets, none of this was in the least bit routine—and the thousands of images chosen by Charles and Ray each told a direct story and a subliminal one, the latter being what it was like to live in a free, capitalist society. Some of the images were still photographs—for example, seven images of little kids rolling on the floor of a kindergarten, each flashed on for a fraction of a second; other images were films, and some of the latter would suddenly extend, again in synch, across all seven screens, to show a single horse race on a track extending the full width of the dome. The voice-over narration, in Russian, was straightforward, descriptive, not polemical. And, at the very end, there was a great and colorful offering of beautiful flowers—the implication being that this was a gift from two young American artists to the people of Russia. And then, a close-up of a single flower, a forget-me-not. "I discovered that its name has the same meaning in Russian," Charles said. There wasn't a dry eye in the house.

Well, it was a spectacular piece of highly sophisticated propaganda. Sweet, innocent, possibly naïve, obviously one-sided. There were no images of crime, of poverty, of racial tension, or of the kind of inequity that would characterize America in the yuppie decade of the 1980s. It was a multimedia vision of a latter-day Norman Rockwellian America—and it worked.

Just as impressive was the fact that Charles and Ray had produced a technically perfect work in a medium that was still quite untested and that they had invented for themselves. They had put together these seven simultaneous films—each about fifteen minutes long—with little projectors aimed at little screens tacked up in their Venice studio. And from this small-scale mock-up, they produced seven final, finished footages that were flawless in every detail. Not many artists or designers, before or since, have matched their extraordinary professionalism.

Somehow, the entire U.S. National Exposition was ready on Opening Day. I don't think that any of us quite understood why or how this was accomplished: almost everything had gone wrong, somewhere or at some point along the way. In retrospect, I think we got it all in place in large part because of the demented energy poured into the endeavor by George Nelson's principal sidekick, a designer by the name of Phil George, who generated a seemingly tireless momentum around the clock, shifting workers and resources from this job to that, managing to be everywhere simultaneously and making himself thoroughly unpopular in the process with all concerned. Without his ferocious energy the exhibition would have never opened on time—especially once the apparatchiks began to trickle into Moscow from Washington to take a bow for whatever had been accomplished by Jack Masey and others, and to attempt to screw up the works before it was too late. Fortunately, most of them busied themselves with sightseeing trips of the city and the region, when they were not holding meetings with each other or fir-

ing off memos. Jack, who knew how to handle this crowd, kept them out of our hair—and so we opened on schedule, on July 25.

Portion of the Architecture Exhibition showing photographic blowups of urban structures.

On that morning, everything was ready: we had been told that Vice President Richard Nixon would officially open the show and tour the exhibition grounds with Nikita Khrushchev and other Soviet bigwigs, and presumably explain the exhibits to them. We had been almost completely cut off from the outside world for several weeks: only the Soviet-produced English-language *Moscow News* and the British *Daily Worker* had been available to us, plus an occasional news summary prepared by the U.S. Embassy for its personnel. We had no idea that our exhibition was attracting as much attention in the outer world as it seemed to be doing that morning: not only

Another part of the Architecture Exhibition, showing rural buildings displayed on curved walls. The entire U.S. Exhibition was mounted in Sokolniki Park, and most of the existing landscaping was retained.

did we get the vice president and his retinue of Secret Service men, but also dozens of journalists and photographers from the U.S. and elsewhere who had been sent to cover the occasion.

I stood near the entrance when Richard Nixon arrived, and my first experience of the event was to see a harmless little French news photographer who had been crouching with his camera in Nixon's path, picked up by two U.S. Secret Service types and tossed unceremoniously into the bushes! It was the first police state–type action I had actually observed since arriving in Moscow. . . . I spent most of the next two or three hours in close proximity to Nixon and Khrushchev, photographing both at various times; and while Nixon's entourage tended to play it tough most of the day, my snapshots proved that Khrushchev was accompanied by no more than one apparent bodyguard, who kept himself discreetly and politely in the background. . . .

As the two bigwigs and their entourages made their way into Bucky's dome, the seven-screen production came on and Khrushchev stood absolutely mesmerized. And when the films ended, on the "forget-me-not" note, we all—Khrushchev included—wiped away the obligatory tear.

Outside the dome, I ran into a *Life* photographer I knew from New York. He asked me about the best locations on the exhibition grounds to get good photos of the proceedings. I suddenly remembered that we had often climbed up on the outside of Bucky's aluminum dome, where there were numerous struts that you could hang on to. "You can get terrific views of everything from up there, especially with your telephoto lens," I told him. He didn't seem much interested. "I've been told there would be something special happening in that model house, in the kitchen," he said. I thought he was crazy. "That's the most boring place in the entire exhibition," I told him. "You can't be serious." Still, someone had tipped him off—and so, he, and other photographers who had been similarly alerted, were ideally placed to photograph what would go down in history as the famous Nixon-Khrushchev Kitchen Debate.

For some reason, I did not make it to the kitchen. Instead, I photographed Nixon, Khrushchev, Voroshilov, Kozlov, Mikoyan, and others in a rather amiable conversation in the TV studio we had constructed on the exhibition grounds. The Kitchen Debate, of course, was anything but amiable: the vice president of the United States, a visitor to a foreign land that he knew only from hearsay, took it upon himself to deliver an arrogant lecture to his host—a

A few minutes before the notorious (and possibly staged) Kitchen Debate took place at the American Exhibition, I took this picture of then vice president Nixon in a very friendly mood. His equally friendly companions are (from top down) high-level Soviet officials Kozlov, Mikoyan, Voroshilov, and, of course, Nikita Khrushchev, hat in hand, behind his back. The others present are assorted interpreters. The location was a TV studio erected on the Exhibition grounds.

man who was totally mystified as to what had so suddenly made his guest so ill-mannered. Khrushchev, of course, did not know about the manipulation of the media in a free society. He didn't know that the public relations man for the little model house was one William Safire, who would turn up again, ten years later, as a speech writer in the Nixon White House (and later as a *New York Times* pundit on international affairs). Nor did Khrushchev realize, I suspect, that a few photographs of his rude guest shaking his fist in his host's face were worth millions of votes in 1960 and in 1968. And neither did any of us innocents, who had worked hard to make this day an occasion of better understanding (and so on), realize that a couple of political operators would grasp the opportunity to practice their sleaze.

In any event, it was not quite the happy day all of us had hoped for. "Forget-me-not" became a rather ironic footnote to the intended festivities.

We stayed on in Moscow for another few days. I had been so busy trying to finish work on our exhibition that there had been little time to see the sights. Now we were able to drive to Zagorsk, a lovely little walled city—really a monastery town—inhabited by tall Russian Orthodox priests and monks and visited daily by peasants from the neighboring villages, who brought empty metal canisters to fill at the shrine of Saint Sergei, where a spring supplied what was thought to be holy water with powers of healing the sick. Despite much official anti-Church propaganda designed to debunk the alleged healing qualities of the water, the locals kept coming back, standing in line for hours to refill their canisters. We took Bucky and his crew to Red Square, and he kept telling me that he was recognized everywhere he went. "You see, dear boy, these people know all about my work," Bucky said, as Muscovites kept circling him and staring at him in amazement. I did not have it in my heart to disillusion him by telling him that nobody in the USSR had ever seen a man in glasses of the sort Bucky was wearing—a pair of enormous, thick lenses held in place by a wide, black rubber band that circled his shiny bald head! We went to the incredible GUM Department Store and bought beautiful fur hats and wooden replicas of the Kremlin's colorful Spassky Tower. And we walked the streets of Moscow gawking at Le Corbusier's 1928 Tsentrosoyuz Office Building on Miasnitskaia Street—now the headquarters of the Ministry of Light Industry and hence barred to foreigners—and at the lovely old wooden churches, largely in disrepair. We found the early Picassos and French Impressionists in a basement of the Pushkin Museum, and we saw the incredible Moscow Circus and the wonderful puppet shows. And we kept going back to see the "cold cuts," and to watch the sweet and pious and frightened men and women and children from all over the USSR who had come to visit this tomb of the Saints of Communism.

Mary Lou and Jack Masey, who met in Moscow, are shown here several years later at the Aspen Design Conference.

And, of course, we mingled with the visitors to our exhibition and listened to the amazed comments of people from all over the Soviet Union, many of whom had come hundreds of miles to see what was to them an extraordinary display—and listened also to the tirades delivered by trained agitators who had been sent in to debunk the explanations of the American guides stationed in the exhibits, and to intimidate some of the Soviet visitors. (The Soviet government had attempted to distribute tickets only to people whom it considered politically dependable—but this did not seem to work very well: there were plenty of budding dissidents in the huge crowds that jammed our exhibition.) And we tried to help

246 |

our enthusiastic guides, who were having a very hard time handling the thousands upon thousands of curious visitors—while inhaling clouds of dust generated by the rapidly disintegrating concrete floors, hour after hour, day after day.

But it was clearly time to leave. We received our "exit visas" and passports miraculously, and exactly as promised, and our bags were inspected one last time in our hotel rooms by the KGB's meticu-

My last view of Moscow: the changing of the guard at Lenin's and Stalin's Tomb.

lous chambermaids. Only Jack stayed behind: he had met one of the Russian-speaking American guides—a beautiful and brilliant linguist named Mary Lou Leach—and after the exhibition closed in mid-September, he and Mary Lou took off for India and Southeast Asia, got married, and returned to New York. As for George Nelson, he returned to New York and married Jacqueline Griffith, who had been Jack's assistant in the U.S. Information Agency.

Nothing quite so romantic happened to any of the rest of us. I went over to Red Square on the last night of my stay to watch the marvelously theatrical changing of the guard at Lenin's (and Stalin's) Tomb, at midnight. At the stroke of the clock, the bells in the Kremlin's churches began to ring, spotlights illuminated a fluttering red flag over the Kremlin's walls and Spassky Gate, and there came, across the vast emptiness of Red Square, the sounds of three Red Army guards goose-stepping out through the gate, along the massive walls of the Kremlin, and toward the tomb—where they would relieve the guardsmen who had stood there, immobile and at attention, for the previous hour. Somehow the guards parading back and forth between the Spassky Gate and the tomb seemed more like performers in an extraordinary precision ballet than the menacing cops they undoubtedly were. The dramatic lighting at midnight, and the ringing bells, made this a theatrical production unlike any I had ever seen in the West.

I left Moscow the next morning, sad but also relieved to be free from the oppressiveness of a closed society. After a few weeks in Denmark and in Italy doing absolutely nothing, I returned to New York and my job at the *Architectural Forum*. It had been an instructive interlude.

CHAPTER TWENTY-ONE

■ During the fifteen years or so after the end of World War II, architecture and all the other visual arts underwent an explosion of energy that seems, in retrospect, nothing short of miraculous.

In this very brief period of time, Le Corbusier designed and built
his stunning Unité d'Habitation on the outskirts of Marseilles—a
185-foot-tall, 450-foot-long block of reinforced concrete containing some 340 apartments, plus offices, stores, and a roof garden endowed with playgrounds, restaurants, gymnasiums, pools, and
innumerable other amenities. It was, in short, a slice of a prototypical Ville Radieuse, first sketched out by him some thirty years earlier. Shortly thereafter, he built his chapel at Ronchamp, his
monastery of La Tourette, his city center at Chandigarh, in India,
consisting of a Parliament Building, a Palace of Justice, a Secretariat,
and a great deal more. In addition, he designed major structures in
France, West Germany, India, Japan, Latin America, and the U.S.
During this brief period, all the promise of his previous decades
seemed to come to fruition. But, to the astonishment of his innumerable admirers, he greatly expanded his own architectural vo-
cabulary and virtually invented a new idiom or series of idioms:
departing from the machine-art purism of his earlier work, he developed a new, rough-hewn language of "brutalism"—exposed

Detail of the Brazilian Pavilion in the University City, in Paris. Designed by Le Corbusier and Lucio Costa in 1957, it shows Corbu's concrete detailing at its best.

concrete that carried the imprint of the boards that formed it, and of the hands that assembled those boards. It was as if he had embarked upon an entirely new poetic vision, and immersed himself in images of nature, of organic forms, of humanism, even of romantic arts and crafts—a language far different from the cool Cartesian rationalism of his earlier work. Like his friend Pablo Picasso, Le Corbusier had explored entirely new directions in his art in response to new problems and situations as he saw them.

Meanwhile, in Chicago, Mies van der Rohe was developing another, very different language—a rational, universal language of steel and glass—in tall towers along the edges of Lake Michigan, and in low-slung prisms on the campus of the Illinois Institute of

Corner of Mies van der Rohe's New National Gallery in West Berlin, completed in 1968. It is a lovely, infinitely flexible space framed in steel and modulated with huge walls of glass.

Technology. He built his Farnsworth House, a glass-and-steel pavilion designed a couple of years before Philip Johnson built his glass house in New Canaan. He designed the Seagram Building in Manhattan, which, some thirty-five years after its completion, continued to outshine all other towers built in any major city since. He designed a lovely pavilion for the Bacardi rum people that was to have been built in Cuba of posttensioned, reinforced concrete—a delicate, minimalist structure on eight cruciform columns forming a vast, glass-walled space for offices and exhibits. The pavilion was never built because the advent of Fidel Castro's regime forced Bacardi to change its plans, but a very similar structure of steel and glass would be constructed as the New National Gallery in West Berlin, some eight years later—and it stands there to this day, by far the best Berlin building of the postwar years.

And Frank Lloyd Wright, during the final decade of his life, designed and built the laboratory for Johnson Wax in Racine, Wisconsin; he designed and built several polygonal structures for Florida Southern College and the Price Tower (a combination of offices and apartments) in Bartlesville, Oklahoma, and he projected structures for Baghdad, for Chicago, for Pittsburgh, for Madison, Wisconsin, and, most importantly, for Manhattan—the Guggenheim Museum, completed a few months after his death in 1959.

Many other architects in the U.S., in Europe, and elsewhere, who had made their names in one way or another in the years between the two World Wars, began to design and build on a significant scale after 1945: Marcel Breuer, who had designed much of the most radical new furniture produced in the 1920s and 1930s, suddenly managed to attract several stellar commissions: he was

Frank Lloyd Wright's Guggenheim Museum, completed shortly after his death in 1959. It borrowed from the language of organic structures like seashells and snails. (George Cserna)

chosen to be the architect for the new headquarters for UNESCO, to be constructed in Paris; he was chosen by several colleges and universities to design and build significant structures on their campuses; he was picked by a Benedictine Monastery to design its new Monastery and Abbey Church in Collegeville, Minnesota; and he was commissioned to do IBM buildings in France, a ski resort in Flaine, in the French Alps, and much more. While most of his work continued to reflect a preoccupation with articulated forms and contrasting details and materials, some of his larger buildings lacked the sure clarity of his earlier work. Still, all of his work continued to be extraordinarily well built: his Whitney Museum of American Art, on Madison Avenue—which became the center of much controversy later on when a widely publicized "name architect" was chosen by the Whitney's overseers to add to Breuer's granite-clad building—seemed to defeat all the attacks upon its integrity by the power of its form, and by the lasting quality of its detail.

Louis Kahn, another one of my early teachers, had been virtually unknown outside Philadelphia, where he had practiced prior to World War II. Once the war was over, Lou got his chance: his one-time partner George Howe had been appointed head of the architecture school at Yale; and Howe persuaded Yale to commission Kahn to design a new Art Gallery for the university. It was Lou's first building of any size or significance, and he was fifty years old when he was commissioned to do it.

As I have indicated elsewhere, Lou was the first architect of his generation of "modernists" to make a truly innovative contribution to the theory and practice of the new architecture. While Mies and, to a lesser degree, Le Corbusier, believed that structure was the fundamental discipline of the new architecture, Lou found that there was something other than structure that deserved "expression," and that was what he liked to call "services." Many kinds of modern buildings, he would point out, consist of elaborate and costly service systems—ducts, plumbing stacks, cables, and all the rest—and these service systems deserve just as much attention as do columns and beams. And so he began to make his buildings out of a framework of structure, interlaced with a network of "services"—shafts, usually vertical, containing everything from air-supply ducts and plumbing stacks, to cables, elevators, and stairs. These shafts were usually "expressed" or dramatized in architectural form, so that

Lou's buildings began to look a little like the early skyline of San Gimignano, with clusters of service shafts in place of San Gimignano's fortified towers.

Although Lou's form-making theory—the creation of two kinds of interlocking networks of columns and beams, and ducts and shafts—was entirely rational, he (being a lovely poet and dreamer at heart) soon translated his perfectly rational theories into the kind of double-talk that was becoming fashionable at schools of architecture everywhere. Lou was a spellbinder, and the more incomprehensible he got, the deeper the swoons that greeted him in academia. One night in New York, an Italian friend of mine, the architect Gino Valle, came with me to a party being given at the flashy home of a then renowned "name architect." When we arrived, late, we found Lou sitting on the floor, surrounded by a couple of dozen swoonies and holding forth about some incomprehensible theories that had recently been formulated to describe his latest work. We listened for some minutes, respectfully, and then Gino couldn't take any more of it. "Lou, cut it out, and tell us about Salk!" Lou looked up, astounded, and then beamed and came to embrace us. When he smiled, his scarred face became radiant. There was no more talk about "the wall wanting to be a wall," or about a "house inside a house." There was only talk about how a building like the Salk Institute—raw concrete, poured-in-place, neat but not too neat—could be finished to look right in the light of southern California, in the sun as well as the rain. The difference between the way Lou would talk to someone like Gino Valle (who knew a great deal about making art out of concrete), and the way Lou might talk to the swoonies (or they to him) was this: he and those whom he respected most knew how to build, and the swoonies and their academic cheerleaders knew only how to talk.

Lou did talk beautifully, and convincingly (despite all those walls wanting to be walls), because he built beautifully, too. He was an artist, not only a builder—a poet, not only a writer of specifications. He had a clear and rational grasp of the way buildings were assembled, and he knew a great deal about the nature of certain materials and the ways they are best detailed. But, beyond that, he had a sense of what could be created with these materials: what kinds of spaces, in what sort of progression, and how to make them come alive through light. If Le Corbusier hadn't said it first, it might have been Lou who said that "*L'architecture est le jeu savant, correct et magnifique des volumes assemblés sous la lumière.*" He was the American architect closest in spirit and in action to Le Corbusier, and his poetic vision of architecture went beyond Corbu's somewhat diagrammatic solutions.

Still, although I was almost invariably impressed by Lou and his buildings, I must confess that—unlike Le Corbusier—he did not seem to have that certain, unfailing touch: some of his later buildings were not as good as they were cracked up to be—his building near Harrisburg, Pennsylvania, for Olivetti, was less than flawless, as were the very sleek dormitories for Bryn Mawr College. His Kimbell Art Museum, in Fort Worth, Texas, which would later become the subject of passionate controversy over plans to expand it, was and is a splendid design for a railroad station, with an ingenious lighting arrangement that does, indeed, bring life and mystery and poetry and movement into the vaulted spaces; but as a museum, the parallel, tunnel-like galleries simply do not work very well for most art exhibits, especially exhibits of very large works that might occupy more than one vaulted gallery. (Most critics, who have grown orgasmic over the quality of Kimbell's spaces, have never designed a museum exhibit.) And I am glad that Lou's bridgelike project for a Palace of Congresses, to be built on the edge of Venice, never saw the light of day. When Lou presented it, one winter day in a spectacular room in the Palazzo Ducale, I had the feeling that he wasn't convinced by his design either—not an infrequent occurrence in his professional life. He liked to change his designs until the very last minute, until he was totally satisfied; and I remember his talking with me one day, at great length, about a small but significant piece of metal trim at the Mellon Center for British Art, at Yale, when I thought the construction drawings for the truly spectacular building had long been finalized.

But Lou left behind him some buildings that have not been equaled since his death in 1974, and were not equaled by many others in Lou's lifetime: the Library at Exeter is an incredible form and space—a wonderful marriage of exterior restraint and interior structural drama. And I hope someday to see his buildings at Dacca, in Bangladesh, and in Ahmedabad, in India—his only major works that I have not been able to visit.

Lou Kahn was probably one of the most influential *new* architects of the years after World War II, but this fact did not really become clear until well into the 1960s. The architect who seemed to win a large share of the most interesting commissions, and whose work was most widely published in the 1950s, was Eero Saarinen, the son of Eliel Saarinen, Finland's somewhat overrated contemporary of Peter Behrens and others of that generation.

Eero had been born in 1910, in Finland, and came to the U.S. when his family moved to Michigan after Eliel had won second prize (and huge acclaim) in the 1922 competition for the Tribune Tower in Chicago. Eliel, although he lost the competition, influenced a generation of admiring neo-neoclassicists through his design, and was invited by an American patron to help establish the Cranbrook Academy of Art in Bloomfield Hills, Michigan, and to design and build its buildings. So Eliel moved his family from Finland and began to practice and teach in the U.S.

Eero was a little younger than Philip Johnson, and a little older than the new, young postwar architects who were beginning to make their marks. Unlike most of the latter, who had graduated from Gropius's and Breuer's school at Harvard, Eero had gone to Yale, then still a fairly conventional school of architecture. But at Cranbrook, Eero had come into contact with Charles Eames, with Harry Weese, with Florence Shust (later Knoll, who once told me that she spent a lot of time in Finland with the Saarinens, and that it was always assumed that she would eventually marry Eero). So Eero had been exposed to as much avant-garde experimentation as one was likely to find in U.S. schools in the late thirties and early forties. He did not lack sophistication.

Nor did he lack ambition. From the early 1940s onward, Eero was an associate in his father's and Robert Swanson's architectural firm in Ann Arbor; and so, although he was merely in his thirties, Eero was able from the start to work on projects of very considerable size: his father's firm, which increasingly became Eero's firm, won several major competitions, including that for the Jefferson Memorial in St. Louis, and was commissioned to design the huge General Motors Technical Center in Warren, Michigan, just outside Detroit.

Eero was extremely good at winning. After he had come in first in the Jefferson Memorial competition in St. Louis, I asked him how he managed to win so many competitions. "Well," he said in his slow, slightly Scandinavian drawl, "first you have to analyze the jury that is going to judge the entries. Who is going to be the dominant member of the jury, the one who is going to steer the others toward his preferred scheme." In the case of the Jefferson Memorial competition, Eero decided, the strongest member of the jury was sure to be George Howe. "George had been trained in the Beaux-Arts tradition," he said, "and so I decided that our drawings should be done in the most perfect traditional manner—rendered in Chinese ink, shades and shadows, and all the rest. That was sure to stop George and get him to take a second look." In addition, needless to say, Eero's proposal for a vast parabolic arch clad in stainless steel and framing a grand view across the Mississippi was a very powerful solution and might have won on its own merits. A few weeks later, when I happened to see George Howe, I told him the story. He was vastly amused: "That son of a bitch—he was absolutely right. Those renderings stopped me cold. I hadn't seen anything quite like it since my school days. But it was a very good scheme—you'll have to admit that."

Eero was not always quite so sure about his competition entries. On one occasion, when he was in competition with half a dozen other architects for the design of the new U.S. Embassy in London,

LEFT: *Eero Saarinen's Jefferson Memorial Arch, in St. Louis, was completed some five years after his death.*
RIGHT: *Detail of stainless-steel arch in St. Louis. Unlike some of Saarinen's somewhat heavy-handed structures, this one is extremely elegant and subtle in detail.*

his friend and neighbor Minoru Yamasaki came over to Eero's house a couple of hours after each had handed in his proposal and they compared notes. "Eero was absolutely crushed," Yama told me some years later. "He was sure I had won, that my design was better than his." And perhaps it was. But the jury decided otherwise, and Eero—as usual—won first prize. He had done a building that somehow caught the klutziness of certain neoclassical Portland stone structures in Mayfair—and that, apparently, proved persuasive. Eero's building now stands on Grosvenor Square—and it looks exactly like the sort of thing America would build during the stodgy years of the Eisenhower administration.

Although Eero probably didn't think of that building in those terms, he was extremely shrewd in analyzing the people and the forces that might successfully shape his buildings. He had no recognizable "style" of his own—each building was designed in response to its program, site, client's preferences, and in response to some intangible thing like the "spirit of its time" or the "appropriate imagery." Eero had his fingers on every pulse; he knew what was going on at the cutting edge of architecture, and what was going on in the marketplace. He wanted to be the first to do a shell-concrete structure (when that was clearly in the air); he wanted to be the first to translate Mies's austere purity into a sleeker, more "American" package. He could smell when historicism was about to raise its head and built a neomedieval stage set of dormitories fit for a production of *Hamlet* on the Yale campus. And his sixth or seventh sense told him when it was time to try a pop image and design an air terminal in the shape of a giant bird. That might be in the same year or week in which he also designed a sleek, minimalist, steel-and-glass complex of laboratories, or a Corbusian structure on pilotis on the edge of Lake Michigan. Eero knew everything that was going on in architecture at any given moment and sensed everything that was about to happen. And he was determined to be the first to try.

Perhaps because he was in such a hurry—or perhaps because he had a somewhat limited talent—almost all his buildings had a small but clearly noticeable flaw: they seemed to be slightly lacking in "taste," for want of a better term. I can think of absolutely nothing ever designed by Le Corbusier that was not flawless as a work of art, in every detail and in overall form—except for those buildings that were corrupted by some outside "collaborators," like the apartment block in Berlin, which bears the imprint of some very heavy German hands, or the Carpenter Center at Harvard, which was somewhat compromised by American building codes and American overdetailing. One needs only to compare Corbu's stunningly clear combination of glass and concrete at his Brazilian Pavilion in the Cité Universitaire, in Paris, with the heavy-handed aluminum sash at Harvard's Carpenter Center to get the point. And I can think of almost nothing ever designed and built by Mies or by Lou Kahn that did not reveal a sure touch, the absolutely flawless imprint of an artist's hand.

But Eero's buildings rarely seemed to make it, quite. The overall forms of his TWA Terminal in New York and his Ingalls ice hockey rink at Yale look disconcertingly like enlarged Danish Modern salad bowls; his detailing at the General Motors Technical Center is not quite right in the handling of windows—in either their scale or their frames—except in one or two instances. And some of his lesser-known buildings, like the women's dormitory at the University of Pennsylvania and some other university structures in Chicago and at Vassar, are best forgotten. They are not only banal in overall concept but insensitive in detail as well. They have a curious inconsistency—curious for the work of someone so knowledgeable and so intelligent. For Eero was probably the best-informed architect of his generation, except for Philip Johnson (who was the best-informed architect of several generations, both preceding and succeeding him). In some of his most successful works, Eero borrowed liberally (and sometimes shamelessly) from others: the Jefferson Memorial Arch was "borrowed" straight from Le Corbusier's and Pierre Jeanneret's 1931 project for a Palace of the Soviets—and, perhaps even more directly, from the 1942 proposal by Adalberto Libera for a fascist "Universal Exposition" to be held near Rome, under Mussolini's aegis. And other completed projects designed and constructed in Eero's name were quite clearly based on earlier projects by more inventive designers.

There were two reasons why this did not seem to matter—why even a project like the Jefferson Memorial Arch (with its fascist antecedent) was never exposed as a fairly patent example of plagiarism: the first reason was that few contemporary critics in those days knew much about the history of modern architecture. (And not many more of them know much about it today.) And the second was that Eero, while not especially innovative, deserved enormous credit in every one of these cases for one all-important fact—unlike most of the original innovators, Eero got his projects built! And that is, most of the time, no mean achievement.

Moreover, Eero's built designs usually worked very well indeed—which is more than could be said of some of the original models by such brilliant innovators as Mies, Corbu, or Louis Kahn. The latter's enormously important Richards Laboratory complex at the University of Pennsylvania, which profoundly influenced everyone from I. M. Pei and Ulrich Franzen, to Kisho Kurokawa in Japan, simply did not work very well at all; and while the General Motors Technical Center owed almost everything in its form and detail to Mies van der Rohe's Illinois Tech campus, Eero made his buildings work, whereas Mies left a thing or two to be desired, in functional terms.

In short, Eero was the ultimate modern pragmatist. He borrowed liberally from everyone, and he had the good judgment to borrow from some very fine precursors. He was an innovator primarily in the area of getting things done—of deciding what to borrow to solve what problem and for which client; of knowing how to persuade his clients to go along; and of getting his projects built, and usually well built.

Eero had another talent, not often recognized: although his office was relatively small, consisting of a mere two or three dozen people during its most productive years in the 1950s, he was able to select some truly extraordinary assistants: my close friend Willo von Moltke worked there, as did Kevin Roche, Gunnar Birkerts, Tony Lumsden, Cesar Pelli, John Dinkeloo, and—surprisingly enough, in the light of later developments—Robert Venturi, who spent a great deal of time on the very Miesian General Motors Technical Center and was, according to Kevin Roche, a first-rate job captain! Eero's favorite collaborators, on the outside, were people like the landscape architect Dan Kiley—a wonderfully sensitive Irish sprite whose landscapes seemed perfectly to blend nature and architecture, and to enhance both; there was Charles Eames, whom Eero had met at Cranbrook, and who managed to dramatize Eero's ideas in persuasive documentary films that explained complex notions to the densest of clients; and there were many others, like Shu Knoll, to whom Eero entrusted many of his interiors, and the talented architect Harry Weese, from whom he learned more than either may have realized. Even though Eero was strangely reluctant to credit his many first-rate collaborators, all of them continue to credit him with a guiding vision—and with exceptional judgment. Not many of us recall the names of more than one or two people who worked with Mies or Corbu or with Wright. But Eero's extraordinary collaborators built some of the most significant structures of the decades since their mentor died. And his influence, sometimes a trifle distorted, continued to enliven the American architectural scene for thirty years and more after his death.

There were dozens of other bright young architects who were coming up in the ten or fifteen years after the end of World War II. We all knew Ieoh Ming Pei's work, mostly on paper in those years; he was the in-house architect of William Zeckendorf—an adventurous developer whose proposals for high-rise buildings in various places, including the East River in New York, were drawn up by I. M., but often seemed intended as gambits in the real estate game rather than as actual buildings meant for three-dimensional realization. And we knew of the talents of Pei's principal collaborators, especially of Harry Cobb, Jim Freed, and Ulrich Franzen. (I. M. and his closest associates established their own, independent firm in 1955.) We knew and admired the work of architects like Eliot Noyes (who became the first major American architect/industrial designer in the U.S., working primarily for IBM and one or two other industrial giants); and we knew and admired the delicate structures designed by Edward Larrabee Barnes, of John Johansen, of Craig Ellwood in southern California—a young American whose training was almost entirely in real building rather than in academic theory, and who translated the Miesian glass-and-steel aesthetic into something more minimalist, more economical, more practical and, quite often, more elegant. We were aware of many others all over the U.S.—some of them working in large offices like Skidmore Owings & Merrill—and we were beginning to become aware of some of the new people coming up in Europe, like Egon Eiermann in West Germany, Kenzo Tange in Japan, Harry Seidler in Australia, and innumerable impressive disciples of Le Corbusier in South America. And we met many of them on their visits to the U.S., and on our increasingly frequent trips to Europe and Asia.

But among the new architects beginning to make their marks in the years after World War II, the one whose work I found most impressive was Paul Rudolph, a person of absolutely staggering and incorruptible talent. Paul was born in Kentucky, went to architecture school in Alabama, and ended up at Harvard, in Gropius's and Breuer's school, roughly in the same shift with Philip Johnson, Ulrich Franzen, Harry Seidler, Joe Passonneau, Ed Barnes, John Johansen, Landis Groes, I. M. Pei, and all the rest. Some friends of his and of mine told me how they got to know Paul when he first arrived in Cambridge straight from a small-town upbringing in the South, in a family so conventionally conservative that Paul felt very ill at ease among the Harvard sophisticates. My friends claimed that he had never been to see a movie and that his social life was non-existent.

But his talent as a draftsman and designer soon became evident; and after some time in the U.S. Navy in World War II, he went directly into partnership with an older, established architect in Sarasota, Florida.

Like the rest of his generation and mine, Paul started out by designing and building small houses—in his case, vacation houses and other somewhat playful structures for a benign and very special climate. From the very start, those little houses were breathtaking in their purity and daring: to Paul, it seemed, certain principles of modern architecture—maximum economy of means, simplicity and clarity of structural expression, and so on—were the basic articles of his faith as an artist. Unlike later, so-called Deconstructivists, whose knowledge of structure was largely nonexistent and whose "expressions" of structure were largely decorative and often tasteless, Paul never seemed to have the slightest doubts about the place of structure and of detail and of the quality of materials in the making of his buildings. From his very first buildings he revealed so sure a hand, so flawless and original a command of detail, and so sure a sense of quality that one felt these little buildings in Florida must be the work of an accomplished and fully experienced architect. Yet they were merely the first, experimental works of a very young designer—a designer, moreover, who was enormously self-critical and not at all sure of his own talent.

Paul was as demanding of his friends as he was of himself. We met at some chaotic party in the vast loft of the painter Arshile Gorky, just off Union Square in Manhattan, and Paul claims that he came up to me saying something like "I think we have a lot to talk about"—to which, according to him, I answered "I doubt it" and turned my back. The story sounds highly unlikely to me, since I had admired Paul's work long before I met him (and since I am never rude to strangers); however that may be, it was all uphill from

*Art and Architecture
Building at Yale Univer-
sity, designed by Paul
Rudolph in the 1960s.
The architect had learned a
great deal from the work of
Wright and Le Corbusier,
and translated those
lessons into his own
distinctive language.
(Ezra Stoller)*

then on, but we became friends, with reservations: I resented many
of the things he said about his own work, which I found virtually
flawless, and I think he resented my uncritical admiration. In any
event, the friendship has lasted, more or less.

Paul left his partnership, became chairman of the Department of
Architecture at Yale, moved to New Haven and, later, to New
York, and managed to get an increasing number of larger com-
missions.

He seemed to learn from every building he designed and built,
mostly because he worked so incredibly hard on every project and
was so mercilessly self-critical of every building once he had completed it. Unlike the growing number of "name architects" who
were beginning to promote themselves in the professional and
popular publications, Paul had no talent for self-promotion and
seemed to find the whole business slightly obscene. His work did
receive increasing notice—not because Paul promoted it or himself, but because his work was so good. The forms of his buildings,
and their materials and details, continued to change in response to
the fact that he was building for a more severe climate and for more

demanding programs; he developed a type of striated concrete, formed with slats nailed to plywood sheets and forcefully removed from the building surface once the concrete had hardened; and this rough, striated concrete gave that normal dull and drab material a texture as lively as that of wood or brick or stone.

But, more importantly, Paul expanded his range of forms from those created by structural and mechanical systems to those created and animated by light and shade. He learned from everything he saw and read: one day, after he had returned from his first extended trip to Europe, he told me, almost as if he was in a state of shock, that he had had to relearn everything after seeing the towns and cities of Italy and France.

But he talked not only about those experiences, but also about the experience of seeing some of Wright's early buildings transformed by light in the course of a day, and of seeing Le Corbusier's later buildings and their plastic strength. And when he saw Mies van der Rohe's 1929 Pavilion, reconstructed in Barcelona sixty years later, he spent a week making drawings of every aspect of this seminal structure which he thought was the best building Mies had ever done.

Unlike any other architect of his generation, Paul managed to reinterpret all the important lessons learned from the likes of Mies and Wright and Corbu and recast them into his own molds. Although few of his buildings directly resembled any one or two buildings by Wright or Corbu—in the manner in which, for example, certain buildings by Richard Meier derived from specific antecedents by Le Corbusier—Paul's work owed something, in spirit, to all the architecture of all the periods he had studied and experienced. He was, I think, the one direct descendant of, the one heir to, the work of what Alison and Peter Smithson like to call the "Heroic Period" of modern architecture.

To me, and to others who experienced his work, he was the most important architect of the years immediately following the end of World War II—in the U.S. and probably in the industrialized world. He sometimes, in his fierce determination, pursued concepts—modern, twentieth-century concepts—that did not work out in practice, such as the notion of building megastructures with what he called "Twentieth-Century Brick": huge, modular, prefabricated boxes, like mobile homes, plugged into a structural frame and piled up roughly in the manner of Moshe Safdie's "Habitat," at Montreal's Expo '67; and he sometimes pursued slightly frightening notions, like his beautifully rendered megastructure that was to have cut through Manhattan's SoHo and was his proposal for a Lower Manhattan Expressway—a megastructure that would have destroyed that part of town and much to the north and south of it.

But Paul pursued these mad schemes with a degree of talent, and with a passion and dedication, far beyond that displayed by any of his contemporaries. Moreover, everything he did was a determined effort to address a problem of the twentieth century and the next. Everything he did was totally responsible, and even when he made mistakes he was the first one to point this out.

As this is written, Paul is doing much of his work in faraway places like Hong Kong and Singapore and Jakarta. Many young architecture students, mesmerized by self-promoting name architects and their verbal calisthenics, have never heard of Paul Rudolph. But I suspect they will, one day, hear of him, and visit the vast amount of his beautiful work—the finest work produced by his generation.

The *Architectural Forum* published virtually all of the most important work built in the fifteen years after the end of World War II in the U.S. and elsewhere; and for various reasons I was assigned to write many of the stories. As a result, most of the leading architects whose work appeared in our pages became acquaintances and friends—some of them very close friends. My own work as an architect was hardly ever published in professional magazines in the U.S.: I could not very well have it published in the *Forum,* and it would have looked just as strange if it had been published in the pages of one of our would-be competitors. My friend John Entenza, who produced that delightful California magazine, *Arts & Architecture,* published some of my buildings of those years, as did magazines like *Holiday, Life, Vogue,* and a few professional publications in Italy, Germany, Japan, and elsewhere. But not very many people in the U.S. were aware of the fact that I was not "merely" a critic, but a rather actively practicing architect as well. In retrospect, I think I should have made more of an effort to have my built projects more widely published, if only to enhance my credibility.

I suppose that there was some nonmodern architecture being designed and built somewhere in the late 1950s; but what we saw of it looked to most of us like a bad joke: neoclassical pomp of the sort that Europeans frequently associated with Yankee vulgarity and pretentiousness. There were a few critics known for their early years in various Stalinist camps who were now promoting a sort of "Stalinist Revival" in architecture; but no one took them very seriously, even when they launched various tirades against the Modern Movement, denouncing some of its practitioners as "fascists" or worse. They were taken even less seriously than the purveyors of what I called "neoklutz," which was beginning to go up around Capitol Hill, in Washington. For all intents and purposes, the Modern Movement had won out, at least in its imagery; and modern architects, like Gordon Bunshaft, were routinely commissioned to design headquarters for America's most conservative corporations. The International Style, at least in the U.S., seemed to have made common cause with the capitalist establishment.

A few months after I returned from Moscow, the *Architectural Forum*'s newly appointed publisher, Ralph Delahaye Paine, Jr., asked me if I wanted to be the managing editor of the *Forum*. I was a bit stunned, since there were several writers on the *Forum*'s staff—especially Walter McQuade—who seemed to be better qualified and, in any case, more thoroughly committed to journalism than I. I brought this up, but Del, a charming giant bear of a man, who had been the editor of *Fortune* during its finest years, insisted. "You'll have to give up your architectural practice, of course, and make this a full-time job," he told me. I swallowed hard, thought about it for a couple of days, discussed it with my talented partner, Julian Neski, and told Del I would do it. Joe Neski would take over our joint office—he had been one of Lajko Breuer's best assistants, and I was very sorry to have to divorce. In retrospect, I am not at all sure I made the right choice.

Still, there did not seem to be very many architecture critics around who actually knew how to design and build buildings, and who had done so fairly successfully. And there are virtually no critics around today, in the U.S. or anywhere else, who know how to build. Which probably accounts for the fact that there is a vast amount of incomprehensible double-talk about architecture nowadays—in the presses as well as in academia—and very little clear and convincing building of the sort that was done so beautifully by those who inspired my generation when we embarked upon our careers.

CHAPTER TWENTY-TWO

■ So much has been written and said about the political and social explosions which rocked the 1960s that it seems unnecessary to add to the record, except perhaps in one respect: the millions, in the U.S. and elsewhere, who had served in World War II and had hoped that the postwar world would bring with it a new era of decency and of justice, had instead seen a return of the same old gang, in the 1950s, and the same old ideas: Adenauer, John Foster Dulles, Stalin & Co., and others with similarly myopic vision. The advent of John F. Kennedy—someone who had served in World War II like most of us (and not at any Supreme Headquarters)—was an extraordinarily exhilarating event. We could relate to him, we believed, and he to us; and he brought to Washington all sorts of people who would not, in previous years, have wanted to associate with the pompous asses who, till then, inhabited the nation's capital and still do. He was one of us, though perhaps a little richer, and everyone we knew was willing to drop everything and come to work for his administration if asked. Many were, and all accepted.

In retrospect, we were probably more than a little naïve: things hadn't changed all that greatly, and were unlikely to change so long as much of the country was run by people in the pay of special interests and their lobbyists. Too much money was being made by manufacturing and selling things with which to kill, and too much money was being made by exploiting the many to enrich the few.

Still, there was a real sense of euphoria among those of us, now about forty years old, who had been waiting for the past fifteen years for the advent of a more civilized postwar world. This seemed to be it, we thought. Or a reasonable facsimile thereof.

The three years or so of euphoria, as we all know, came to an absolutely terrible end—the killing not only of a president, but the killing of a euphoric dream, and the final cheating of an entire generation. But while the euphoria lasted, there was an energy and an enthusiasm, in almost all the arts and sciences and other civilized pursuits, that seemed to infect all of us—though we were not really aware of it until it was suddenly all over.

Nothing that my friends and I were able to do in architecture and the other arts and disciplines seemed at the time to be very much affected by the political changes taking place in the U.S. But I think, in retrospect, that there was a visible change in attitude, in the way we lived and worked, and in the enthusiasms we brought to all pursuits; and this change manifested itself in numerous ways: a new generation of relatively young architects was now very much in evidence, both through their work and through their teaching in schools of architecture across the country. People like Pei, Rudolph, Ellwood, Weese, Johansen, Franzen, and many, many others began, increasingly, to be commissioned to do buildings of a scale much larger than the houses they had designed when they first started out. And they worked with the conviction that whatever they were doing would help, in some small way, to change the world for the better.

We didn't talk about this very much, and we would have felt deeply embarrassed if someone had accused us of trying to save the world. Or, more probably, we would have laughed it all off as a pretentious joke. But, in fact, we did take ourselves seriously in private—or, if not ourselves, then certainly our work. Only Philip Johnson, for whom some of us were willing to make excuses since he was obviously rich and spoiled and hence underprivileged, was permitted to be frivolous. He had finally shaken off his father fixation vis-à-vis Mies van der Rohe and was designing and building rather flashy temples for nouveaux riches clients. I, for one, thought it was perfectly all right for Philip to be playing amusing architectural games, and his clients were vulgar enough to deserve being the butts of his private jokes.

Still, most of us on the staff of the *Forum* took our work very seriously indeed. I don't think we ever sat down, after I took over, and asked ourselves what we should do with the magazine, or do differently; we agreed in most respects or, when we didn't we found each other very stimulating. Jane Jacobs, one of our senior editors, had just published her extraordinary book, *The Death and Life of Great American Cities,* which challenged virtually all the basic beliefs on urban design held by the Modern Movement. In *Death and Life,* Jane pointed out that the one quality that made certain cities so good to live in was their chaotic variety—the fact that uses were mixed and that this mixture of uses and the resulting round-the-clock liveliness of streets and squares created a sense of community and a degree of safety, as well as a certain organic texture in streets and other public spaces, that can hardly be created by orderly notions of planning and zoning.

About the time I became editor of the *Forum,* Jane decided to leave and start another book—a move that I and all of her colleagues deeply regretted. We remained friends, although she and her family left New York and moved to Toronto when the Vietnam War made life in the U.S. increasingly difficult. In any event, she had dramatically changed all our thinking about "Ideal Cities" and similar fantasies—especially, I know, my own.

And not only in the U.S. Several years after Jane had left the magazine, but when she was still living in Greenwich Village, my friend Werner Düttmann came to New York on a short visit. Düttmann, an extremely energetic and bright young architect whom I had originally met in West Berlin when doing an exhibition there in 1957, was now the chief architect for the West Berlin Senate, and in effect responsible for much of the new building and development of that lively place. He phoned me as soon as he had checked into his hotel on Central Park and said that although he would like to see me, he really wanted, above everything else, to meet Jane Jacobs, whose book had totally discombobulated him and everyone else he knew professionally in Europe. Could I arrange it?

I called Jane, and she immediately asked us over to her house for dinner. We spent a long and marvelously exciting evening with

Jane and her husband, Robert, an architect who specialized in the design of highly innovative medical facilities. Werner was euphoric when we left—Jane's enthusiasms were enormously infectious.

Some twenty years later, when the city of West Berlin undertook a major infill renewal effort and asked architects from all over the world to design and build structures on bombed-out sites still left untouched since 1945, Jane's notions of how cities might grow were a major factor in determining West Berlin's imaginative effort, known as IBA (for Internationale Bauausstellung). My pal Werner Düttmann, alas, did not live to see it happen—he had died from too much energetic living before IBA got under way; but others whom he and Jane had inspired directed this effort and tried their best to create a more organic, less "utopian" city. I became intimately familiar with IBA, since I was one of the architects who designed and built a building as part of this undertaking; and I know that all of us who worked in Berlin during those later years were conscious of the fact that it was Jane Jacobs's ideas, as much as any one thing, that shaped this effort.

There were others on the *Forum* staff who held fairly unorthodox views at variance with my own, and taught me a great deal thereby:

Doug Haskell stayed on for a while as a kind of "editor emeritus," and he amused and often baffled the rest of us with his curious, early populist notions. We humored him, although some of us found him increasingly incomprehensible, especially in his curious pet hatreds for certain ideas he considered at odds with American populist values. In retrospect, some of his notions that seemed baffling at the time turned out later to be intriguing and, occasionally, almost prescient: he liked to write, in editorials published before I took over, that there was a certain energy in the wildly chaotic townscapes of the sort created by American free enterprise—as, for example, in Times Square—that expressed a new kind of vigor and might develop into a new kind of urban art. (This was at least half a dozen years before the emergence of Pop Art on the American scene!) And Doug's occasional outbursts against the excesses of market forces in the shaping of our environment were much more perceptive than we realized at the time. . . .

Walter McQuade, a senior editor, had joined the *Forum*'s staff about the time I had returned to it after the end of World War II. Walter had graduated from Cornell in architecture and was an extremely bright, witty, sophisticated writer on that subject, and on numerous others. I had always assumed that he would end up as Doug Haskell's successor—he struck me as perfectly qualified, with just the right combination of knowledge, talent, and taste to make a first-rate editor. I had told Del Paine as much when the latter first asked me to take over, but Del, who agreed that Walter was a first-rate writer, for some reason thought he would not necessarily be as effective as an editor. However that might have been, Walter and I remained friends—interested in much the same sort of things and in the same sort of people. But I realized that he would probably leave before long, now that I had been chosen to run the magazine; and before long he did: he joined *Fortune* magazine (possibly Del had wanted him in that slot all along), but he continued to write for us month after month, and to amuse and alert us with his charm and wit.

Paul Grotz, our art director and my closest associate on the magazine's staff, had been on the *Forum* longer than anyone else. He and I did not talk about politics, because many of his friends were far to the left of me and I didn't want to discuss them or their ideas with him; we did not talk about Frank Lloyd Wright or Taliesin, because Paul venerated Mr. Wright and I venerated only his buildings; and we didn't ever speak in any language other than English (although both his and my native tongue was German) because we shared a fairly strong dislike for a good many things German. There were one or two other matters we didn't discuss, such as our personal lives, all of which were too complicated to untangle; but aside from all of that, we were extraordinarily close, and I found it an enormous pleasure to work with him. Paul was a person of such decency and tact that all problems that arose in the course of our lives together—personal as well as professional—seemed to evaporate in the light of his wisdom and kindness.

One of my concerns, when I took over the *Forum,* was to reshape its graphics, literally from cover to cover. My predecessors had not been very literate, visually speaking—in fact, the only reason the magazine looked considerably better than its competitors was that the latter were simply pathetic. But by comparison with certain European magazines, like the British *Architectural Review,* the Swiss *Graphis,* or the Italian *Domus,* our magazine looked pedestrian. I was determined to change this dramatically, in part because I felt that our most interesting readers were visually literate, and in part because I thought I was, too.

Paul had produced some impressive issues of the *Architectural Forum* over the years—in particular some special issues devoted to the work of Frank Lloyd Wright. But most of the issues done under his direction tended to be compromises between the demands of writers and editors, who had very little sense of graphic design, and those of Paul himself, who was a gentle soul, too willing to compromise in matters in which he should have held firm.

Now he had an editor totally dedicated to graphic excellence, and I think he was pleased. And he had two or three very excellent assistants with unusual graphic skills: Charlotte Winter, Ray Komai, and my former wife, Martha Blake. Together, Paul and his crew redesigned the magazine from cover to cover, from its logo to the basic page formats, headline type, and so on. Starting with the January 1962 issue, the magazine looked fresh, exciting, and roughly what I wanted it to be: the best-looking design magazine then published in the U.S.

Alexey Brodovitch, as I have mentioned earlier, used to have one admonition for the students in his Design Laboratory at the New School for Social Research: he would say to them, "Astonish me!" When Paul and I decided to redesign the magazine, we wanted each issue to "astonish" our readers and, as a matter of fact, ourselves. We were determined that we would never bore anyone who hadn't bored us first.

In looking back at those issues of the magazine I am amazed how well we succeeded. While all the other architectural publications in the U.S. devoted their pages to typically mid-cult buildings of the sort likely to satisfy advertisers of American building products, the *Forum* devoted at least half its pages to the work of new architects and radical engineers emerging in Europe, Asia, South America, and elsewhere—people still quite unknown to most of our readers and destined to shape the direction of modern architecture in decades to come. Since the work of someone like Egon Eiermann in Germany, Jim Stirling in Leicester, Hector Moreno in Mexico City, Le Corbusier in India, Riccardo Morandi in Turin, or Kenzo Tange in Tokyo was not very likely to incorporate such heavily advertised U.S.-made materials as asphalt tile or imitation walnut paneling, the manufacturers of such products much preferred to advertise in magazines like the *Architectural Record* and *Progressive Architecture,* which could be depended upon to play the advertisers' games editorially. In fact, I would frequently receive slick packages of photographs and drawings (all ready for instant editorial use) from potential advertisers, documenting the latest mid-cult box assembled from the advertiser's products, with a letter suggesting that this was exactly what we might be looking for, editorially speaking. The slick offering, routinely returned to sender with the editor's tongue-in-cheek regrets, would then—just as routinely—appear in the pages of other magazines, often using the text thoughtfully supplied by the advertising agency verbatim.

Since the *Forum* displayed a degree of editorial integrity, and had done so long before I became its editor, our editorial judgments had a fair degree of credibility among our readers. But we had to pay a high price for this: unlike other magazines in our field, we began to report on some of the spectacular failures of certain building products that had been widely and inaccurately publicized by their manufacturers—asbestos in its many forms (which turned out to be dangerous to everybody's health), self-oxidizing steel (which turned out to continue rusting long after it was guaranteed to stop, and discolored its environment beyond recall), miracle plastics (which invariably turned a bilious green), and other blessings of building research and development. Our reports, while interesting to practicing architects and other users of buildings, did not amuse our potential advertisers—with predictable results.

But while I was proud of our editorial exposés of frauds and semifrauds, I was just as proud of some of our other editorial efforts: we would commission some of the finest photographers Paul and I could find to produce absolutely spectacular stories for us: Walker Evans, one of Paul's oldest friends, let us publish a "gallery" of his photographs of American warehouses of the past, and wrote the text as well; and George Cserna, a Hungarian photographer discovered by Paul, photographed Jefferson's central complex at the University of Virginia for us—and documented this splendid work of our past better than it had ever been documented before, or has been documented since. This particular story was written by a young Yale graduate named Warren Cox, whom I had managed to entice to come to work for us after he got out of school. Warren wrote that "this is the first time in over thirty years that a major article on Thomas Jefferson's buildings at the University of Virginia has appeared in a magazine connected with architecture." (Warren is, as of this writing, one of the few outstanding architects practicing in his native Washington, D.C.) And Paul persuaded Clemens Kalischer, another great photographer then hardly known, to photograph Beacon Hill in Boston for us with rare—indeed, unequaled—sensitivity.

But the most important innovation we brought to our magazine, and to the notion of architectural journalism in the U.S. and else-where, was to devote entire issues of the magazine to significant cities and their past, present, and potential future. There was a sense in Washington, now, that the future of American cities was a sub-ject of interest to our government, and that architecture was no longer thought to be a matter of isolated buildings, but of urban complexes of considerable size. This was not exactly a novel idea to anyone familiar with the history of the Modern Movement since about 1850, but it was a new concept to people on the fringes of the design professions, whose ideas about America's future had been shaped largely by free enterprise notions of uncontrolled and haphazard growth.

The first city we decided to tackle was Chicago, the place where, in the minds of many of us, modern architecture had been born. We put together a crew of half a dozen editors and sent them off to Chicago to examine various aspects of the city—its history, its eco-nomics, its potentials. We put together a beautiful collection of photographs of great landmarks from Sullivan's and Adler's Audito-rium to Mies van der Rohe's Crown Hall at the Illinois Institute of Technology; and we discussed some of the more outlandish poten-tials of the city, such as the possibility of expanding the Loop onto artificial islands to be created in Lake Michigan. It was the first time that the *Forum* (or any other architectural magazine in the U.S.) had ever devoted an entire issue to a whole city, and we were decidedly pleased with the results. Ray Komai designed a spectacular cover for this issue, consisting of typographic patterns constructed to form a city skyline.

It was not the last issue of the magazine that we devoted to an entire city, or the last one Ray helped design: nine months later we did an entire issue on Washington, D.C.—its past, its serious social and racial problems (this was almost thirty years before those be-came evident to the entire country, including even its Republican administration), and some of the possible solutions. George Cserna took some beautiful photographs for us of the Renwick Building, the Walsh Mansion, the Pension Building, Union Station and the Executive Office Building, among others, long before these be-came the objects of massive restoration and the guideposts for his-toric preservation across the country. And Warren Cox and others who knew Washington extremely well provided much of the text.

I thought Ray should do the cover, and Paul agreed. Ray there-upon disappeared for a week or two, very mysterious in his elegantly Asian way, and made everyone extremely nervous: was he going to meet our printer's deadlines? And what on earth was he going to produce? With a few minutes to spare before the printer threatened to shut down his presses, Ray Komai walked into our offices and unwrapped what looked like an odd sort of pillow: he had sewn together a wonderfully zany fake "souvenir"—a kind of pillow case of the sort that souvenir peddlers might (but never did) sell to Washington's millions of tourists, a fabric collage of blue velvet, gold thread, red-white-and-blue thread, golden tassels, stars, eagles, images of the Capitol and the Washington Monument (disguised as a barometer), plus innumerable other pieces of tourist junk—all neatly assembled by sewing machine and with infinite patience to form the very best embroidered "faux" souvenir pillow case ever produced by anyone. I suspect that Ray was hoping we would have every cover done in velvet and gold thread and tassels, but since our circulation was well over 50,000 copies a month, this proved to be infeasible, and a color photograph had to do.

About a year after we put out the special issue on Washington, we produced another one on a single city—this time, Boston. The city had just the right mix of great historic interest, first-rate modern architecture, farsighted planning and rebuilding of its center—plus, needless to say, a vast number of social and economic problems. And I think we had the right people to deal with each of these. It was an impressive piece of work involving the talents of many on the staff; and the cover, this time, was done by Ivan Chermayeff and Tom Geismar, using a calligraphic notion—an assemblage of "ancient" pen-and-ink strokes spelling out the significant names in Boston's history.

But the finest special "city issue" I decided to do was one that never saw the light of day: about ten years after our issue on Boston appeared, I prepared one on the city of Paris. And so I asked a young graphic designer called Annegret Beier to do the cover for us. Annegret, who was German by birth, had lived in New York for some time and had worked with the extraordinary graphic designer Herb Lubalin. She was now living in Paris, and I gave her a call. She seemed pleased by the idea and promised to think about it.

I hadn't the remotest idea of what Annegret might produce. All I knew was that she was far and away the most talented young graphic designer I knew in Europe and could be depended upon to "astonish me" without fail.

Cover designed for a special issue to be devoted to the city of Paris. The designer was Annegret Beier, a resident of the French capital, and she literally baked it and covered it with sugar candy of various slightly nauseating colors. The silver sprinkles at top right spell out "Paris." It would have made the finest cover we ever printed, but our magazine folded before we could go to press with this issue.

She did. She decided that the most "astonishing" image of Paris was that of Sacré-Coeur in Montmartre; and that the only way to replicate this kitschiest of all kitschy works of architecture, and to convey its full flavor, was to *bake* it, and then to cover the baked cake with a pink sugar glaze! This is precisely what she did. And having baked the basilica (and before, presumably, eating it), Annegret photographed the assemblage in color, having first encrusted the cake with golden angels, clouds, stars, and one or two other mad embellishments. The entire work—a fairly hefty package by the time it had been fully collated and assembled—arrived heavily wrapped and laboriously inspected by suspicious customs officials; and the memory of this "astonishment" brightens my life to this day. Alas, my magazine had just bitten the dust, and so the special issue on Paris and its incomparable cover never saw the light of day.

More and more of our covers were being designed by Ray Komai and others of his talent: on one occasion, when we put together an issue on new airports, Ray made a squadron of folded paper airplanes, using airline schedules of different colors, and we photographed those in a scrambled pattern. On another occasion, when we needed a cover for an "international issue" dealing exclusively with new architecture abroad, Ivan Chermayeff and Tom Geismar constructed a kind of skyline out of pieces of world maps. In November 1962, when we decided to publish an elementary school designed by Gropius's firm, The Architects Collaborative (TAC), I felt the photographs taken for us were rather boring and asked the school's art teachers to get the kids to make paintings of their new school as it looked to them. The results were spectacular—much better than the actual building—and gave us many pages of dazzling color, and a magnificent cover by a ten-year-old artist named Deborah Winchester. On still another occasion, when we published a major story on new architecture in Canada, the cover was a lovely collage of translucent green maple leaves, photographed by Len Gittleman and Deborah Sussman. And a few months later, for an issue devoted entirely to questions of urban transportation, Ray Komai did a painting of a typical yellow, diamond-shaped traffic sign (actually square and on edge), with a huge black question mark in its center—where a regular sign might have had a YIELD admonition—all on a bright-orange background.

We not only kept astonishing each other and our readers—we also had an enormous amount of fun. No other magazine in any field, in those years, could boast so remarkable and consistent a gallery of first-rate graphic art. And people outside the design professions (and who rarely saw our magazine in the flesh, as it were) kept seeing those remarkable covers reproduced in various publications all over the world.

We also poked fun at the architectural establishment at regular intervals. When the American Institute of Architects, a rather solemn club, was having one of its annual conventions in Manhattan, the routine architectural magazines threw predictably awful and expensive receptions for all the attendees at awful and expensive hotels. I decided to have an exclusive garden party instead—the best available garden being, of course, Central Park. After pulling a string or two, we were able to reserve the area around Calvert Vaux's 1870 Bethesda Fountain—an appropriate venue, I thought. We pitched some garden-party tents, rented some chairs and tables, and used whatever influence I had to retain the services of an exclusive band known as the "Fourgone Conclusions," which consisted of four ten-year-old classmates of my ten-year-old son, Casey Nelson Blake. He was their manager and would later become even better known as one of America's more prominent cultural historians.

Everybody who was anybody that year came, and everyone else tried to crash the party. It was an enormous success—one of the great garden parties of our time. Among those present were several spectacular fashion models, including the former model Josephine Franzen, a lovely friend who was married to the architect Ulrich Franzen. Jo, who is brilliant and talented in several disciplines, did not, alas, wear her most famous dress—a form-fitting body stocking made up, in its entirety, of about 200 colorful metal and plastic zippers sewn together side by side and clinging to her in vertical stripes. She had designed and made the zipper dress for a MOMA opening the night before, and it was promptly confiscated by the management, probably to be included in the Museum's permanent collection.

But, however much fun we might have on the side, as it were, our primary mission was, of course, to publish and evaluate significant buildings around the world, and significant technological and social developments that might shape our buildings. And it does seem to me in retrospect that we did all of that, while not neglecting our principal task of reporting on important works of architecture in the U.S. and elsewhere. The work of the most talented architects around the globe regularly appeared in our pages, and we published everything they designed and built if we thought it was good. We had it photographed by the world's best photographers—not only first-rate architectural photographers like Ezra Stoller or Robert Damora, but also photographers of a different sensibility, like Evelyn Hofer and Walker Evans; and we had the work evaluated by first-rate critics whom we sent to inspect the buildings and to talk to their architects, users, and neighbors.

Most magazines in our field, in those days, tended to publish stories based entirely on what could be gleaned from photographs, and on selected facts supplied by the designers. That is a good way of holding down your editorial budget and of keeping your advertisers happy. We established a new standard of journalism in our field: not only did we produce a magazine that was literate and graphically exciting; we also produced one written by people who knew what they were talking about. While most of the critics of architecture in the U.S. had little, if any, training in that discipline, our critics and their editors had usually been trained as architects and had worked as architects, and were thus familiar with all the infinite complexities of building, and all the factors that tend to shape buildings.

Some of the most interesting new buildings seemed to be going up abroad, especially in Western Europe and in Asia—but also in such unlikely places as Eastern Europe and Fidel Castro's Cuba. To keep abreast of what was happening in those areas, I spent a great deal of time attending conferences, delivering lectures, and finding other excuses for visiting West Berlin, Paris, London, Prague, Rome, Teheran, Delhi, Tokyo, and other places where new ideas seemed to be percolating. As a result, I made friends in many parts of the world, and most of those friends tended to be architects, designers, planners, artists, and critics. There developed a kind of network which continues to this day—a network that gave our magazine access to the most significant new work being done anywhere, and to people qualified to write about it. Although I did not really plan it that way, I was laying the foundations for a magazine I would be producing in later years, a magazine devoted to the international scene, rather than one limited to what was being done in the U.S.

In deciding what to publish and what to pass up, did we develop any sort of party line? I really think not. I myself was obviously influenced, in my own buildings, by the work of Mies van der Rohe, though probably modified by many other things I had seen—especially buildings done by Le Corbusier and Aalto and one or two others. But, as editor, I felt we should publish everything that was a serious effort to advance the art or technology or humanistic values of architecture. Although I did not understand the work of my friend Paolo Soleri, I thought it was serious and significant and worthy of wide publication—and so we published it. Although I was not wild about Giovanni Michelucci's Church of the Autostrada, near Florence, which I knew quite well, I thought we had to publish it as a significant expressionist effort—and so we asked Jimmy Fitch to write about it. And although much of the Bay Region architecture on the West Coast left me lukewarm, I felt we should publish the best work of that "school" since its practitioners clearly belonged to a serious humanist tradition.

And we published things I actively disliked as well: when Henry

Hope Reed, the revisionist critic and historian, told me on a radio program that there was a conspiracy not to publish buildings done in historic styles, I told him I would publish anything he wanted to write about and illustrate—and as soon as he could get it to us. He did, and we did. I don't think he made a very good case for *faux* history, but we gave him his chance.

And we published Philip Johnson's post-Miesian work—not because I was fond of Philip, but because he designed and built his strange buildings so well, and claimed to take them so seriously, that I thought he deserved a hearing. I still don't like many of his historicist concoctions, but I would still publish them—even though I am no longer sure that even he took them all that seriously.

We did not publish schlock or kitsch or junk—and I realize that those are value judgments and hence subjective. So be it: we did not publish things that *I thought* were schlock or kitsch or junk. Or, rather, we did not publish such things unless someone on our anything-but-monolithic staff made a compelling case for publishing the stuff. This happened not infrequently—largely because we all respected one another, even if we did not always agree.

Although ours was the smallest of the Time Inc. publications—not counting Rosalind Constable's weekly newsletter on the avant-garde—we had numerous admirers on the other mammoth publications: editors at *Life, Fortune, Time* and elsewhere frequently picked up stories that we had run for our professional readers and passed them on to their own faithful millions. And several of us were frequently asked to write special articles for *Life* and *Fortune,* and we enjoyed doing that. Despite the fact that Del Paine had returned to *Fortune* as its publisher full-time and handed over his duties at the *Forum* to our longtime colleague and friend Joe Hazen, Del and others on *Fortune* continued to support our efforts in various ways, and often contributed to our stories—especially in areas such as economics where they might be more knowledgeable than we.

There was another side to this interaction, however, and it was less helpful: increasingly, the *Forum* became a place where Time Inc. would dump those who had, for some reason, failed to perform very well elsewhere in the company. Perry Prentice, as reported earlier, had been donated to us after proving spectacularly unsuccessful on both *Time* and *Life.* He proceeded to transform a fairly successful magazine—the *Architectural Forum*—into two publications: one, *House & Home,* to be devoted to the home-building industry; and the other to continue as the *Architectural Forum,* and this would devote itself exclusively to buildings of a larger scale. It was an artificial division of a profession that Perry never understood, into two enterprises that he understood even less.

Not content with having unloaded Perry Prentice on us, the great minds at Time Inc. began to send us people who felt that what we needed most was more circulation. While that formula may have worked for a mass-circulation magazine like *Life*—although it failed there also, ultimately—it was a disastrous formula for us: the *Architectural Forum* had a "natural" audience of about 50,000 or 60,000 professionals and others devoted to design and building—and those professionals were the same people that our advertisers wanted to reach. So far, so good; but when the experts from Time Inc. tried to increase our circulation, they were attracting readers whom our potential advertisers were not interested in reaching.

So, as our circulation increased, and our page rates for advertising increased correspondingly, potential advertisers abandoned us in droves, and went instead to magazines that could demonstrate that *their* readers—unlike our mixed bag of followers—concentrated exclusively on the excellence, say, of rustproofing. Although we kept winning awards for editorial excellence, the advertising agencies that determined where to place their customers' ads for rustproofing decided that the magazines to support were those read exclusively by rustproofing fanatics.

Before long, we began to sense that Time Inc. was worried about our losses and was trying to unload both the *Forum* and *House & Home* on anyone willing to pay a small price. I never really believed we were going to be unloaded—our losses were so minimal, by Time Inc.'s standards (never more than $250,000 a year, if that), and the cures were so obvious. Moreover, we had a great and loyal champion at the very top of the company: Henry Luce, a brilliant editor with political views so bizarre that few of us took them very seriously, but with a degree of integrity and basic decency I found impressive. I would be summoned occasionally to have lunch with him in one of the private Time dining rooms, and his secretary invariably warned me to keep in mind that he was "slightly hard of hearing." In truth he was stone-deaf and too vain to wear a hearing aid; so our "conversations" either took the form of two-way shouting matches or one-way (his way) lectures delivered by Harry

Luce to this very minor editor of a very minor publication, who was invariably seated at the opposite end of a very long and intimidating table.

Although these shouting sessions were not especially productive as exchanges of ideas, they were illuminating to me in several ways. There was no doubt in my mind that the basic editorial integrity of Time Inc. publications was established by Luce, and that while he was in charge there were no two ways about this: the business types on any of his publications—advertising salesmen and so on—were not permitted to speak to editorial types. There would be no pressures of this sort, ever. Period. (It occurred to me, in later years, that this was not an unmixed blessing: most of the business types who determined everything on our magazine *except* editorial content could have vastly benefited from advice from the editorial sector. . . . But by that time, it was too late.)

Aside from laying down the law in all matters of editorial ethics, Luce cared enormously about such things as architecture and the quality of the environment. He was very proud of our little publication, which he had acquired in 1932—when it was even littler, and made virtually no sense as a very tiny cog in the expanding Time Inc. empire. I remember Luce once telling me that it was strange for him to have no "hometown" in his own country. (He had been born in China, where his father was a missionary and, by chance, a friend of my first father-in-law.) Perhaps, in some strange way, Harry Luce was trying to build himself a "hometown" in America.

Whatever his reasons, he followed our editorial progress avidly, though I don't recall ever receiving any editorial suggestions from him. I think he might have considered such suggestions a form of interference—which they would indeed have been. So far as I was concerned, Harry Luce was as crazy as a loon, politically speaking (and in one or two other ways as well), and utterly supportive of me, and I was delighted he was there to watch over us.

When, in the spring of 1964, he stepped down as editor in chief for Time Inc., I began to feel uneasy. And, sure enough, one evening in the early summer I received a call from Joe Hazen telling me that there would be a meeting of the staff the next morning to announce the closing down of the *Forum*. Press releases had already gone out. Apparently Luce's successors—most of them from the business side of Time Inc.—had thought it unnecessary to keep the editor of the *Forum* informed of what was going on.

On the following morning, the official announcement came: McGraw-Hill would buy *House & Home* and continue to publish it, and Time Inc. would cease publication of the *Architectural Forum* in the fall. I was outraged when I got the news and decided to take the matter up directly with Henry Luce. He was very friendly and deafer than ever: I explained to him what had happened, and I got the distinct impression that he was almost as surprised as I had been the night before. Apparently, people either hadn't told him, knowing of his affection for our magazine, or they had told him in whispers and the words had not registered. McGraw-Hill published *Architectural Record* (our strongest competitor). The story was that in exchange for their buying *House & Home*, a rather pathetic publication that barely broke even, Time Inc. had agreed not only to close down the *Architectural Forum* but *not to sell it to anyone*. Since I was shouting, Luce got my message loud and clear.

"You're sure they promised McGraw-Hill that we would not sell the *Forum* to anyone?" he asked me. "That's what I heard." Luce grinned at me and said, "I guess they didn't put that in writing. In any case, we didn't promise not to *give away* the *Forum* to someone else, did we?" Now it was my turn to grin. I could have hugged the old bastard. "Do you think you could find someone to carry on with the magazine if we gave it to him?" he asked. There obviously hadn't been time to give the matter any thought, but I said "Of course" without a moment's hesitation. "I'll tell you what," Luce said. "I'll pay your editorial salaries for at least six months, to give you a chance to find a new sponsor and keep your staff together. How does that sound?" It sounded terrific to me, and I left to tell my associates.

Whether the story about the McGraw-Hill arrangement was true or not I couldn't—and can't—prove, but it sounded plausible to me. I gather that some questions were raised about the whole transaction; I heard that people from the Justice Department showed up in the Time Inc. offices and tried to find out more. But no suits were filed. In any case, McGraw-Hill disposed of *House & Home* not long thereafter, and it shortly sank without trace.

It has always seemed to me, in retrospect, that this episode was the first clue to the kind of ethical decay that set in at Time Inc. the

moment the old man stepped down—the kind of decay that cul-
minated, some twenty-five years later, in the Time/Warner merger
in which Luce's successors vastly enriched themselves, and in the
process came close to destroying the company Harry Luce had
founded, and its very real integrity.

CHAPTER TWENTY-THREE

■ It took me about six months to find someone willing and able to resuscitate our magazine: Augie Heckscher, a very civilized gentlemen whom I had met briefly a year or two earlier, told me one day that some friends of his seemed interested in investing in a significant effort to help America's cities, which were clearly in a state of disintegration. Augie thought that one way might be to establish a foundation that would attempt to do something to halt this decline; and publishing a very outspoken magazine devoted to excellence in architecture and all other areas of design could be one of the efforts the foundation might want to undertake.

The people who, according to Heckscher, might be willing to undertake all this were a young couple named Stephen and Audrey Currier—two heirs to a great deal of money, whose politics, I gathered, were liberal and whose interests were in the arts and in social issues.

All this sounded exactly right to me and my associates at the *Architectural Forum,* and so we decided to pursue it. After brief negotiations, the Curriers agreed to establish a foundation to be known as Urban America, and this foundation would, among other things, publish the *Architectural Forum* under our direction. I could hardly believe our good fortune—especially after meeting the Curriers and finding them delightful. And I think they were rather pleased with the prospect of becoming energetically involved in our efforts and beyond.

Some six months had elapsed since we were set free by Harry Luce, and we had spent the time revving up for a fairly spectacular comeback. Several of our associates, who had lost faith in our ability to resuscitate, had accepted offers from other publications; but most of our key people had stuck it out and spent the enforced interlude preparing for a considerably improved magazine. We decided that our coverage should be much broader than before—both geographically and in content. And so I put together a team of "stringers" who would contribute regularly to future issues, covering the most significant developments in Europe, Asia, Latin America, and elsewhere—and, also, in such fields as urban design, industrial design, historic preservation, economics, and the visual arts. Most of these stringers were friends with whom I had established contact over the years in various ways, and they would become an invaluable resource, contributing to our magazine regularly and knowledgeably.

Paul and I, meanwhile, completed the redesign of the magazine that we had started when I first became its editor, some five years earlier. But now we were freed from the problems that invariably arise when too many people need to justify their existence: we had an editorial staff of fewer than half the editors, writers, and graphic designers whom Time Inc. had employed to produce the *Forum*. And so we were able to make intelligent decisions quickly and well—and it showed in everything we did.

The format of the magazine became clean, intelligible, effective, and distinctive. (It has been copied by dozens of design magazines since, in the U.S. as well as abroad.) The content became much more interesting, covering, in our first issue, everything from serious articles examining (and dramatizing) America's urban crisis to something called "Le Hot Drug," a surreal drugstore designed and built in Montreal by one of my more outrageous cronies, François Dallegret. In addition, our first resurrected issue contained a beautiful story on a complex of student dormitories designed and built by another friend, Giancarlo de Carlo, on a hilltop near the ancient walled city of Urbino, in northern Italy—a city which de Carlo, incidentally, was in the process of reconstructing and replanning to save it from the automobile and other modern blessings. (De Carlo's dormitories were uncompromisingly modern, yet clearly

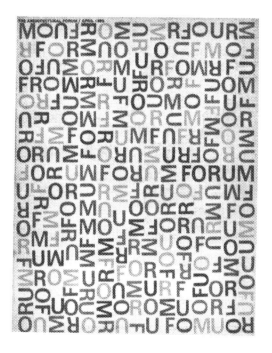

simpatico with Federico da Montefeltro's Urbino next door.) And there were stories on historic preservation in Chicago, high-tech prefabricated schools in California, a giant thin-shell concrete brontosaurus in Weeki Wachee Springs, Florida, a City of the Future proposal by Norman Mailer, and futuristic notions of how to heat buildings with light. The issue was graced with a cover designed by Ivan Chermayeff and Tom Geismar, which subsequently won awards, showed up in exhibits in the USSR, and meanwhile pleased us and our readers immensely.

It would be hard to explain how my associates and I assembled a typical issue of the *Architectural Forum*. I vividly remembered that the geniuses at Time Inc. would, not infrequently, subject a typical issue of our magazine to the analysis of some expensive consulting firm whose experts would inform us that this page or that spread had a readership of forty-seven percent, say, but that another page or spread had a readership of ninety-three percent or twelve percent respectively. They spoke with voices of authority, and their authoritative insights were accepted as gospel truth by the business types at Time Inc. The implication of all this was, of course, that our publication would be vastly more successful if we edited it to

LEFT: *April 1965 issue of the new* Architectural Forum: *the cover—a wonderful mosaic of typography in half a dozen colors—was designed by Ivan Chermayeff and Tom Geismar.*
RIGHT: *Our May 1972 cover, designed by Charlotte Winter, used a delicate engraving of the Usine Menier, a chocolate mill outside Paris. The building was designed in 1877 by Jules Saulnier.*

attract a higher percentage of readers—by whatever means the consulting firm might be able to suggest. Needless to say, we paid no attention.

But we did, of course, address *someone* in our stories. We addressed perhaps a hundred of our brightest and most critical readers—people whose opinions and whose knowledge we respected, and whose responses we sought. I know I often wondered what Philip might say to this article or that—whether he would be amused or infuriated; or what my friend Patwant Singh, in Delhi, might think (he was the editor and publisher of a magazine called *Design*), or what the reaction would be among friends in Europe or in Japan or in Eastern Europe, for that matter. And their reactions were never slow in coming, and often not especially flattering. But regardless of how my friends reacted, they held us to a standard considerably higher than that maintained by other publications geared to some common denominator of its readership, whatever that may mean.

In a sense, we maintained a dialogue with those hundred or so of our brightest readers—and we discovered that there were many others who wanted to join in. Evidently, a publication that assumed its readers were people of intelligence could expect a rather enthusiastic response.

LEFT: *The June 1966 cover, designed by Peter Bradford. The* Forum's *special issue that month was devoted to transportation, and the brilliant yellow and red streaks against a black nighttime sky suggested a play of head- and taillights along a superhighway.*
RIGHT: *Our May 1967 issue was devoted to New York, and we constructed a Lower Manhattan "skyline" out of assorted souvenirs. (Clara Aich and George Senty)*

What were our principal concerns? I think all of us thought that something rather dramatic was happening in the 1960s—a political and philosophical realignment that challenged a great many of our beliefs as architects. The political murders that rocked the U.S. and its institutions, the violent opposition to the Vietnam War that played havoc with university communities and quickly spread to communities of every kind, and the way in which these violent up- heavals put into question most aspects of the social and political compacts that had kept American society in balance for close to a hundred years—these matters obviously affected all of us, and es- pecially those of us committed to helping create a better world. It was probably an accident that the first explosion to rock American university campuses occurred at the School of Architecture at Columbia University. Or perhaps not: Columbia, like other insti- tutions of privilege in an allegedly egalitarian society, had long been notorious for the way it exploited and dominated its neighbor- hood—much of it poor and black. And the architecture students, more than any others, became aware of the manner in which their university was imposing its will upon these neighbors. In any event, that's where it all began, and all of us were aware of it. Some of us were indeed rather proud of those scruffy students.

LEFT: *The December 1965 issue was a photo- graph, by Balthazar, of a detail of a resurrected nineteenth-century facade in Columbus, Indiana. The colors were dazzling.* RIGHT: *Our August 1969 cover showed a close- up of an apartment building in Sitges, Spain, by Ricardo Bofill. The photograph was by Deidi von Schaewen, and the colors were pink, blue, and black.*

Aside from the violence that erupted all over the U.S. in the sixties—much of it random, much of it irrational—there were two or
three intellectual and philosophical upheavals that would profoundly change the direction of architecture and urban design all
over the world, and not necessarily for the better: the first of these
was the publication, in 1963, of Jane Jacobs's first book, *The Death
and Life of Great American Cities;* the second was the publication, in
1965, of Robert Venturi's book *Complexity and Contradiction in Architecture;* and the third was the emergence of postmodernism on
the American scene. These three events were not necessarily of
equal significance, but they were clearly related in the way they addressed the physical world as it existed then, and the way architecture might be directed to deal with it.

I have referred to Jane Jacobs's book in earlier chapters. She did
what Bertrand Russell had once suggested everyone should do at
frequent intervals—pretend that his or her firmly held beliefs might
conceivably be wrong, and that their very opposite might be closer
to the truth. Jane had said, in effect, that virtually all modern dogma
regarding the planning and design of cities was seriously flawed:
that chaos was often preferable to order, that variety was preferable
to neat uniformity, that small was better than big, and that the ways
in which communities developed and grew, naturally, was much
more in keeping with the way a free and egalitarian society wanted
to function than the sort of predetermined orderliness suggested by
such heroes of mine and of my generation as Le Corbusier and
Ludwig Hilberseimer. As Lewis Mumford had put it earlier, "Life
is really more interesting than utopia."

I have compressed Jane Jacobs's message and possibly oversimpli-
fied it; in any case, it was literally shattering to those of us brought
up on various neat and seductive dogmas and diagrams of the Modern Movement. Yet it became increasingly persuasive, the more we
thought about it: the fact was that Le Corbusier, who had designed
his ideal Ville Radieuse in 1922 (and redesigned it again and again
over the subsequent forty years), much preferred the chaotic, picturesque parts of Paris in which he lived to the kind of "ideal city"
he kept drawing up so beautifully. My guess is that he would have
gone mad in such "ideal cities" as Brasilia—which, admittedly, was
designed by people somewhat less talented than he. But the fact remained that the architects who gave us those utopian images almost

invariably lived in picturesque settings very different from those they had proposed for the rest of humanity.

Jane Jacobs was criticized by Lewis Mumford for holding a rather simplistic view of the probable future of urbanized humanity. Jane and her family lived in a very nice old townhouse in New York's West Village, in a neighborhood of a scale established in the nineteenth century and rapidly being wiped out in the twentieth. With the earth's population exploding at the terrifying rate projected by everyone, the kind of small-scale, comfortable neighborhood that Jane held up as ideal did not seem a realistic solution for the predictable future. Still, neither did Mumford's idyllic notion of residential garden cities divorced from centers of industry and administration, or somehow integrated with such dispersed settlements. In any event, Jane's book, more than any other manifesto published since the early 1920s, forced me and my friends to reexamine virtually everything we had ever learned or believed about ideal cities.

Unlike Jane, who was educated as an economist and absorbed most of her wide knowledge of modern urban and architectural theory and practice while seething as a senior editor at the *Architectural Forum,* Bob Venturi was a very sophisticated architect, educated and experienced in the modern tradition. He had worked for Eero Saarinen when Willo von Moltke was there, and I met him on one of the occasions when I visited Willo in Bloomfield Hills.

Venturi, who would challenge architectural form and content as dramatically as Jane had challenged urban form and content, had spent much time supervising the work on Eero Saarinen's very "Miesian" General Motors Technical Center outside Detroit— about as neat and minimalist a work of high-tech modern architecture as was built by Saarinen or just about anyone else in the 1950s.

Yet, in spite of his experience with pure modern dogma, or perhaps because of it, Venturi began to reexamine many of its tenets. His two most important books—*Complexity and Contradiction in Architecture,* published in 1965, and *Learning from Las Vegas,* published ten years later (and written in collaboration with Denise Scott Brown and Steven Izenour)—suggested that there was another way of looking at architecture that had somehow escaped most of the modern pioneers: for the architecture of an egalitarian democracy to be meaningful to the majority, much of the elitist imagery that, in Venturi's view, had clung to architecture from an earlier time needed to be discarded; and new images that were acceptable and understandable to a majority had to be given a chance. He pointed out that much of the architecture of the past that moves us today was really a collage of many periods and many people—a collage formed of the imprints of many hands and uses. He went on to suggest that there were popular images today that might be meaningful sources of architectural form. These images could be found in many places on the American scene: false fronts that spelled out, in clearly understandable language, what the building behind them housed—or billboards that spelled out the same sort of thing even more specifically. Venturi believed that this kind of imagery had always been part of architecture; and that the anonymous facades that were favored by people like Mies and Corbu communicated nothing and hence failed to elicit any sort of response from the man, woman, or child in the street.

Venturi was clearly a serious and thoughtful critic of the Modern Movement. He was also a witty one: I had recently published a book entitled *God's Own Junkyard* in which I attacked the sort of commercial vandalism that was destroying the American landscape and townscape. Most of the book consisted of photographs of what to me seemed exceptionally vulgar examples of this sort of vandalism—and these were contrasted with examples of natural and manmade environments that struck me as idyllic and increasingly threatened by vulgarians. One of the "vulgar" examples I showed was the Big Duck near Riverhead in Eastern Long Island, an area which I had come to know very well and to cherish before it was yuppified by rich summer people; and the Big Duck was a store for the sale of dead ducks and their premortem by-products.

Venturi argued that the Big Duck was a perfectly valid architectural statement—a building that announced, very clearly, what its contents and purposes were: i.e., to sell dead ducks. And he further argued that every building that expressed its purpose with clarity and effective imagery was doing precisely what the Parthenon (for example) had done in its own time and place. "The Parthenon," Venturi wrote, "is a Duck!" And this became one of the slogans of the Postmodern Movement—at least of the faction led by Bob Venturi.

I must confess that I laughed out loud the first time I read this definition of the Parthenon. Within a year or two of the appearance of *God's Own Junkyard* (in 1963), to the applause of thousands of do-gooders, I had begun to realize that my view in writing the book had been more than a little narrow and obvious, and that I had shown almost no interest in popular imagery or, for that matter, in the increasingly visible images of Pop Art. Still, I felt a bit squeamish about Bob Venturi's "ironies." He said, for example, that Main Street (with all its billboards and other eyesores) was "almost all right"; he said that Mies's minimalism, expressed in "Less is more," was boring, and coined another phrase—"Less is a bore"—which was intended to demolish Mies's ascetics once and for all. (Venturi withdrew the phrase some twenty years later, admitting that he regretted ever having coined it.) And he suggested, in effect, that the architectural imagery of a free society might well end up being rather chaotic, but that the pieces of the resulting kaleidoscope should be understandable to all—commercial images as well as images of a free and varied community.

All of this seemed to make superficial sense, if you believed that architecture should *mirror* its time rather than inspire it and give it some aesthetic and social direction and form. Because Bob Venturi, unlike some of those who rallied to his postmodern banner, was a serious and responsible architect, I did not think that he was being condescending; but, clearly, his kind of populism was open to such interpretations, and many of Venturi's sycophants adopted "irony" as one of the major guideposts in their elitist pursuits.

It was open to other interpretations as well. The Modern Movement in architecture was, above all else, fueled by *optimism*. Le Corbusier, Mies, Gropius, Wright, and all the others were convinced that they had a chance to make a better world—to create a more beautiful, a healthier, a more egalitarian environment in which free people could live and work and learn and enjoy themselves. But Venturi's vision, it seemed to many of us, was fueled by profound pessimism: the American scene was pretty grim (unless, of course, you were one of the very rich who could always take off for a vacation in the South of France, and who seemed, increasingly, to run things in the U.S.); and there appeared to be very little that the average person could do to improve that situation. What Bob Venturi seemed to suggest was that the best to hope for was compromise, to make the best of a fairly hopeless situation. If I hadn't known better, I would have thought that his prescription for the future—vulgarity, dumbness, ugliness, and boredom being "almost all right"—was just what Nixon's mid-cult America was all about. It seemed to me a profoundly depressing prescription—very far removed in spirit from the optimistic visions advanced by the modern pioneers whom Venturi and his elitist followers now sneered at from their Olympian heights.

What made Venturi's theories even less convincing was the fact that the buildings he proceeded to design and build were almost uniformly distressing. A small house for his mother—heralded by his sycophants as a work of earthshaking significance on a par, possibly, with Wright's Falling Water—turned out to be a rather sad little "Levitt House" with some pointless trim applied to its street facade. (This "ironic" exercise promptly triggered innumerable, incomprehensible dissertations in Little Magazines spawned by academia.) Another structure of similarly distressing presence rose at about the same time on Spring Garden Street, in Philadelphia. This was an apartment house for the elderly, sponsored by the Society of Friends; and it was apparently intended to look indistinguishable from apartment houses of this sort routinely found in places like Flushing, Queens, N.Y.—that is, banal (Venturi's term). The building was crowned, if that is the appropriate term, with an anodized gold TV antenna. Venturi suggested that this could be "interpreted in two ways: abstractly, as sculpture in the manner of Lippold; and as a symbol of the aged, who spend so much time looking at TV." The "aged" were not amused—they found the ironic TV antenna condescending and hence offensive.

Finally, after *Learning from Las Vegas* appeared in 1972, Venturi and his partners designed an addition to a lovely École des Beaux-Arts museum at Oberlin College, in Ohio. The existing Allen Art Museum, designed by Cass Gilbert in 1917, had an extraordinary and civilized presence; what was added to it was a mid-cult, Los Angeles–modern box (vintage approximately 1938), faced with a checkerboard of pink granite and rose sandstone—to which was then added another box (vintage approximately 1946-L.A.) faced with "ordinary" commercial ribbon windows and buff brick spandrels. The entire ensemble—a work of almost mind-boggling mediocrity with deliberate touches of schlock—required thousands of words of gobbledygook to make itself "understood" to Yalies and other profound shapers of architectural theory. A friend of mine, an architect (trained at Yale, by the way) who was teaching at Oberlin at the time, suggested that visitors to this baffling ensemble should be handed audio devices with tape-recorded descriptions of what it was they were looking at—the sort of audio devices popular in museums to explain to the visually illiterate what it is the work on view is attempting to communicate. Her constructive idea was not accepted by the college. If it had been, it might have spared us some of the interminable verbiage invariably unleashed each time Bob Venturi, Denise Scott Brown, John Rauch (and other associates) produced another work of condescending irony, banality, and ordinariness.

The *Architectural Forum* published everything designed and built by Venturi and his various partners—not because I thought the work was convincing as architecture, but because it was so serious, so desperately serious, in fact. I had no doubt that he was right in trying to find a way of relating architectural idiom to some aspects of popular preference and taste; I had no doubt that he and his associates were right when they adopted Jane Jacobs's insights into the characteristics of street life in all its forms; and I therefore thought that Venturi & Co. deserved a hearing, and we gave him and his associates as much space as we could.

Actually, I always thought that he was at his best as a graphic designer of exhibition images. His various projects for billboardlike facades, for pop monuments, and for similar enhancements of the urban scene always struck me as witty and charming. He and I, in fact, occasionally pursued some remarkably similar ideas in later years: sometime in the 1980s there was a competition to replace the badly vandalized Times Square Tower, in Manhattan, with something else—and my entry to the competition was a large building, up in the air, in the form of a "Big Apple." Bob Venturi, by coincidence and quite independently, was designing a Big Apple Monument at the same time for Philip Johnson. His was much smaller than mine, and mine was much better than his—both in scale and in its placement in the very heart of New York. . . . Still, I had obviously learned a great deal from him in the years since I published *God's Own Junkyard!*

Although Venturi & Co. were and are very serious about their revisionist views of the Modern Movement, there were others whose motivations I found highly suspect.

I don't know if there is an exact date or a specific building or project that signals the advent of postmodernism in the U.S. Our magazine published the neoclassical Getty Museum by the previously little-known firm of Langdon & Wilson, in 1974, with a

A grain silo somewhere in Kansas. It suddenly appeared on a prairie skyline as I was driving west, and I stopped to snap this picture with the last frame of film in my camera. It is one of the truly great works of anonymous American architecture.

glowing article endorsing this extraordinary piece of nouveau riche kitsch by the architectural historian David Gebhard. Although we probably did not launch the whole movement, we may have made it respectable. My late lamented friend Peter Banham—by far the most interesting architecture critic of my time—liked to tease me by insisting that the *Architectural Forum* had been the first publication to use the term.

However that may be, postmodernism in the U.S. was simply the latest manifestation of that old American malaise: a vast inferiority complex in all matters cultural and historic. Here was a country with a tradition of enormously innovative industrial and commercial building—a tradition that inspired every modern European architect from Le Corbusier to Mies to Mendelsohn and Neutra—and *its* architects seemed totally unaware of that tradition, and compulsively created absurd structures like faux-Gothic skyscrapers and faux-Renaissance railroad stations and faux-medieval factories and other embarrassing manifestations of nouveau riche insecurity. Here was a country with a tradition of cast-iron prefabrication developed by the likes of James Bogardus, of space frames like those designed and built by Alexander Graham Bell, of bridges like those built by the Roeblings, of skyscrapers like those built by Louis Sullivan, and of enormously innovative spatial and structural concepts of the kind designed and built by Frank Lloyd Wright—and its yuppie universities and their academics promoted unalloyed kitsch, the sort of kitsch that seems to come naturally to the nouveaux riches and their offspring. The whole thing was more than a little mystifying to many of us: what on earth had happened to American architecture—to an art and a discipline that had, in the previous twenty years or so, produced such extraordinary artists as Paul Rudolph, I. M. Pei, Richard Meier, and many more?

The answer was perhaps more obvious than it seemed at first: after a brief joust with radicalism, the schools of architecture—especially those at yuppie universities—began to produce new generations of elitist architects who instinctively knew which side their bread was buttered on. Their future clients, obviously, were likely to be the rich; and the rich, in America, especially, and in the second half of the twentieth century, were almost uniformly men and women of little education and no taste. So the way to make it in the American capitalist world was to become the chosen architects of the new elite—the chosen architects of a new vulgarian upper crust.

It was a very different view from that held by those of us who had come out of school in the 1940s, and by those whom we admired. We simply assumed that architects in an egalitarian society existed in good part to help make that society as good a place as possible for all, regardless of class. But this seemed to have become an old-fashioned notion. The architects who now emerged from yuppie universities had decided—or had been led to decide—that architecture was once again an elitist profession. After a brief involvement with the peace movement at Yale during the Vietnam War, most of its "activists" lost interest in social justice *the moment Nixon abolished the draft*—i.e., as soon as the fighting and dying could be left to the underprivileged!

And shortly thereafter, it seems, a new generation of architects began to reorient themselves ideologically. Suddenly, ironic condescension toward the slobs who made up the majority of their fellow men and women became the dominant attitude. Ironic name architects designed buildings in the shapes of private jokes that would leave their fellow Yalies rolling in the aisles, but possibly failed to amuse the ordinary people condemned to live and work in (and pay for) those private jokes. Other name architects—descendants from a long and distinguished line of buttonhole manufacturers, one imagines—spent much of their time promoting themselves by promoting their own "style": one became a specialist in crypto-Egyptian kitsch; another became known for his clothes (he became addicted to Savile Row tailors, because Philip Johnson had his suits made there—and because he, the name architect, thought these suits would make him look like Fred Astaire!); and still others became known for producing buildings done in a glittering, so-called Art Deco manner than which there is almost nothing more vulgar—mid-cult American nouveau riche kitsch, circa 1930! One of these "Nouveau Deco" architects, who had once been a student of Mies, announced that his former teacher would have approved. Since Mies by this time was conveniently dead, there was little danger of contradiction.

The postmodernists had their flacks in newspapers and popular magazines, and for a simple reason: if you are required to produce something new, something different, even something shocking—day after day, month after month—well, then, anything will do for a cover or a headline. And there was nothing quite so useful to an architecture flack as an architect willing to supply something new, different, or shocking at frequent intervals. I once told Philip—who was very good at this game—that his next skyscraper would have to be something X-rated, perhaps a giant dildo; nothing less would do. "You're too late," he said. "I just did one, in Denver. Go and see for yourself." I did, and he had. It was about forty stories tall, as I recall.

The postmodernists considered themselves brothers and sisters under Bob Venturi's skin, and they certainly shared some of his expressed contempt for modern architects of an earlier generation, whom no one had ever accused of designing an ironic building. Although much of Venturi's own work was "flat-modern"—that is, deliberately boring—he and his associates did, occasionally, lapse into postmodernism. For reasons having to do with such absurdities as Prince Charles's crusade against modern architecture, Venturi & Co. were selected to design the new Sainsbury Wing for the National Gallery of Art on Trafalgar Square, in London. The result—another one of those works dripping in irony—was described by one British critic as having a little too much "tugging at the forelock, if you know what I mean." The American critic Hilton Kramer was rather more devastating: "The Sainsbury orders up a veritable smorgasbord of showy historical reference. . . . Why it was thought appropriate to commission the author of *Learning from*

Las Vegas . . . to create a setting for the work of Giotto, Raphael, Leonardo, van Eyck, Uccello, and Piero della Francesca, must forever remain a painful object of inquiry for anyone charting the course of Western civilization. . . . Venturi has brought to [this] design a sensibility in many ways akin to Andy Warhol's: parody and charade, camp appropriation and ironic quotation, facetious pastiche and allusive drollery. . . . the result is unrelieved ersatz and contrivance." And Kramer then delivered the coup de grace: "The mind that designed [the Sainsbury Wing] is irredeemably hostage to architectural one-liners, and the butt of every joke is the art which this building was meant to enhance."

I don't think I would have gone quite so far, but Kramer's trenchant comments perfectly describe the pretentious arrogance of American postmodernism and its yuppie practitioners. A critic writing in the London *Architectural Review* used the term "mediocre slime" to describe the postmodern vulgarians and their works. He had it precisely right.

Europeans, being blessed with the ever present evidence of great architecture left over from many earlier times, recognized the exercises of American postmodernists for what they were: pitiful evidence of a cultural insecurity quite unjustified by the facts. And although some European academics, like their American counterparts, seized upon these pitiful exercises as opportunities for more interminable gobbledygook, most of those in Europe who really knew how to build tended to ignore the latest lapses in American taste. Only a few decided to emulate American postmodernism, presumably because they felt that Americans must surely know what "sells," and what sells in the U.S. would surely sell in Europe as well. (The Japanese never really understood American postmodernism; and the few Japanese copies of postmodern kitsch are charmingly innocent and silly. . . . Or else they simply understood it too well!)

Postmodern architecture, as a sales tool, was quite effective: Philip's AT&T Building, in Manhattan, certainly sold plenty of telephones, at least as effectively as the Chrysler Building, in its time, presumably sold plenty of Chryslers; but the AT&T Building did an even better job of selling Philip Johnson. The lesson was not lost upon architects, in the U.S. and elsewhere, who were understandably interested in promoting themselves—and on clients everywhere who were interested in using architecture to sell their products or their service. So, thanks to the postmodernists, archi-

tecture was becoming a sales gimmick; and much American architecture was becoming a laughingstock in the more civilized
world—on a par with the work of Albert Speer and the work of
Stalin's court architects, which, in fact, it closely resembled.

But in the U.S., postmodernism was the "hot button." Architecture flacks in newspapers and magazines, and in academia, promoted the most grotesque examples of kitsch as sophisticated
expressions of some new populist concerns and denounced the pioneers of modern architecture as "boring" and "utopist." It became
increasingly difficult for architects of character and conviction to
survive in the American marketplace; and several firms, like Skidmore, Owings & Merrill, which had made architectural history
with the work of Gordon Bunshaft, Walter Netsch, and others, became schlockmasters on a par with all other "hot button" artists
ground out by Yale and similar elitist institutions. It was a very
tough time for America's finest architects—people like Paul
Rudolph, I. M. Pei, Ed Barnes, Craig Ellwood, and others. Unless
they played ball with the flacks, they were written off as passé.

In retrospect, I think we might have been more critical in our magazine of this insidious corruption of American architecture. For a
long time, we simply ignored what was happening in the world of
"playboy architecture," as the Swiss historian Siegfried Giedion had
labeled it in an article in the *Forum*. Instead, we published everything that we considered significant and first-rate: Lou Kahn's Salk
Institute in La Jolla, Peter Harnden's houses in Cadaques, experimental urban housing developments in Barcelona, New Delhi,
Montreal, Nimes, and London, Kenzo Tange's cathedral in Tokyo,
a new City Hall in Toronto, some extraordinarily innovative iron-
frame buildings by Peter Ellis constructed in Liverpool in the early
nineteenth century, and B. V. Doshi's sensitive structures in Ah-
madabad, India. When Le Corbusier died in August 1965, I felt we
should devote an entire issue of our magazine to the life and work
of this extraordinary artist—and so Peter Bradford, a very talented
graphic designer, and I put together a special issue of the *Architectural Forum* that was probably unique in concept and design.

We published everything that might "astonish" our readers—and
often ourselves. I was intrigued by the early high-tech experiments
of the British Archigram group—Plug-in Cities, Walking Cities,
cities in outer space, and other sci-fi cartoons; and we published all

of their wonderfully imaginative futurist dreams, and some of the things that had inspired them: "floating cities" in the Gulf of Mexico and in the North Sea that served (or had served) as oil rigs or antiaircraft battle stations. We published the fantastic concrete fortifications built along the Normandy coast by Hitler's armies. And we published the wonderful structures in the Space Center at Cape Kennedy—because all of these, I felt, were possibly indicative of a new and visionary architectural language, likely to become that of another century and another world.

And we published highly critical articles, including articles critical of ourselves: We went back for another look at a huge public housing project in St. Louis known as Pruitt-Igoe, which the *Architectural Forum* had extravagantly praised when it first opened in the 1950s—and we, in effect, reversed ourselves and confessed to having been totally wrong. (Virtually all the buildings were subsequently dynamited!) We criticized LBJ's "Cut-Rate Revolution" when his administration cut back drastically on its promising Demonstration Cities Program, and we criticized IBM, which had been a patron of good architecture after Olivetti, its chief competitor, pointed the way—and which had recently reversed its commitment to first-rate design. We published Christopher Alexander's essays entitled *A City Is Not a Tree*—which challenged some of the basic concepts of urban planning and design in as dramatic a way as Jane Jacobs had challenged them five years earlier—and we published every significant new (and old) architectural manifestation that intrigued and excited and amused us. When a new book appeared on the early twentieth-century pioneer Adolf Loos, I persuaded Richard Neutra to review it for us, remembering that Neutra had often talked to me about his early days in Loos's office. (It was an extraordinary and touching review.) And when the first book appeared on Philip Johnson's own work as an architect, I asked my friend Joe Passonneau—the former architecture dean at Washington University in St. Louis, who had been a student at Harvard when Philip was a student there—to review it. "I think Philip is the only one qualified to do that," Joe told me—and so I talked Philip into reviewing his own book for us. (He liked it.) We even published the work of some of my less favorite architects—for example, Fritz Kiesler's "Shrine of the Book" and "Sanctuary for the Dead Sea Scrolls" in Jerusalem—and we published some of Sybil Moholy-Nagy's most opinionated prose, thus irritating everyone within earshot including those who, like myself, adored her some of the time. And, one day, when I saw an article on modern architecture and urban housing by Norman Mailer, of all people, I invited him and Vincent Scully to slug it out in our pages. They did, quite wonderfully—and when I ran into Mailer in Provincetown a few months later, he told me that he thought Scully was a better writer than he. "But I know more about architecture than he does," he added. He may have been right on both counts.

We had been producing a new *Forum* for close to two years when there was a tragic event: Stephen and Audrey Currier, who had been unfailingly encouraging and supportive and enthusiastic, were suddenly lost in an airplane crash and presumably killed. They had chartered a plane in San Juan to join their children in St. Thomas, and the plane apparently crashed into the sea. There were rumors of all sorts—even rumors of kidnapping by Castro agents (Audrey was the daughter of David Bruce, a charming former ambassador to France, West Germany, China, and probably every other nation on earth, and some people speculated that Castro's agents had kidnapped her to pressure the U.S. government to mend its ways). Others thought that the Curriers' chartered plane might have been accidentally shot down by an American antiaircraft battery located on an island halfway between San Juan and St. Thomas. In any case, no trace was ever found of the plane, its pilot, or the Curriers.

CHAPTER TWENTY-FOUR

■ In retrospect, the 1960s, for me and other architects, were not only a decade in which all kinds of ideas were challenged and all sorts of people and institutions came under violent attack; it was also a period in which we lost some of the best of friends, acquaintances, and others who had long inspired us. Just before the start of the decade, we lost Frank Lloyd Wright at a ripe old age—and then shortly thereafter, Eero Saarinen at a mere fifty-one. A few years later it was Le Corbusier, who died of a heart attack while swimming in the Mediterranean near his little studio on the Côte d'Azure; and then it was Walter Gropius, and then Mies, that pure and gentle soul. And there were all those remarkable public figures who had made us feel that a better world was just possibly within reach. And now there were the Curriers, who had been kind and supportive friends.

Fortunately for us at the *Architectural Forum,* the Curriers had provided for the continued existence of Urban America and of our magazine, and so there seemed to be no immediate threat to our economic survival. Still, we were quite shaken, and under no illusion that we would not be under pressure, before long, to become completely self-supporting—not an easy task in a declining economy, and in an industry whose potential advertisers were not renowned for their vision or, for that matter, for their literateness. Our task was not made much easier by the fact that the business types we had inherited from Time Inc., unlike our editorial staff, seemed not especially effective: our new publisher, who was put in charge of such matters as advertising and circulation, was a nice man whose prior expertise had been solely in getting the magazine printed. He seemed lost in the areas where we needed most help, as were some of the people he brought with him from our days in the Luce organization. So while we were doing a pretty spectacular job editorially, we had very little support from the business half of the magazine.

Still, our competitors, whom we tended to ignore because they seemed so uninteresting, were apparently scared out of their wits by the *Architectural Forum:* the publisher of one of those other magazines sent a letter to potential advertisers telling them that we were a gang of communists, and that advertising in our pages would be an un-American act! People had called me a good many things in the past, but never before had anyone noticed that I was subversive. . . . We didn't take this sort of thing very seriously—and perhaps we should have: in Nixonland, not many people—especially manufacturers of asbestos shingles or asphalt tile—were willing to be labeled "un-American"!

Despite our advertising problems, we persevered and won all sorts of popularity contests among our readers. We kept on producing rather wonderful stories and rather wonderful special issues of our magazine, "astonishing" our readers and ourselves and supplying the more popular presses, especially *The New York Times,* with innumerable leads to lively stories—which the latter then proceeded to appropriate without credit to our writers and other contributors. We kept on winning all sorts of medals and plaques and certificates of singular hideousness for editorial excellence. (The medals and plaques we would distribute, at Christmastime, to assorted impressionable lovers, relatives, and children.) Meanwhile we had moved into the old Steinway Building on West 57th Street (and I designed our new offices); and I had also managed to resume my architectural practice, this time in partnership with Jim Baker, a former student of mine at Yale. The architectural offices Jim and I found were in three beautiful, two-story-high, skylit studios on the top floor of Carnegie Hall—studios originally built to house rehearsal spaces for dancers, musicians, and singers, and still largely inhabited by those lovely people. Although the long-range prospects for the *Forum* were obviously tenuous, the present seemed pleasant and bright.

For various reasons, I was spending a fair amount of time abroad—in Canada, in Europe, in India, in Australia, in the Middle East, and in Japan—looking for buildings and projects to publish, talking to people with interesting ideas, and attending conferences that might produce grist for our editorial pages. I had begun to write a regular column called "Cityscape" for *New York* magazine, and continued to do so for seven or eight years. *New York* had been resurrected by my old friend Clay Felker; and I realized one day that the only trained architect aside from myself writing this sort of criticism regularly for the popular press in the U.S. was Bob Campbell, a friend who wrote and still writes regular and excellent reviews for the *Boston Globe*. Meanwhile the better-known architecture critics—the "tastemakers," as Russell Lynes once called them—were listened to by their readers with bated breath and vast respect, neither of which was exactly justified by their qualifications.

I spent a great deal of time in West Berlin—invited there partly because I was able to communicate in German as well as in English. There were international conferences in Berlin attended by people like Philip Johnson and Lajko Breuer and others from various parts of the world who would later leave their marks upon the international scene—people like Matthias Ungers, a Cologne architect whose work impressed me greatly, and whom I therefore recommended for the chairmanship in architecture at Cornell, and some of the Grand Old Men of earlier years, like Mies and Scharoun and Walter Gropius. It was still a rather small circle of people—although a new generation of modern architects was beginning to make itself heard and seen: "Team Ten," with people like Ungers, the Smithsons, Aldo Van Eyck, Bakema, Hans Hollein, Shadrach Woods, and others, was trying to fill the void left by the demise during World War II of CIAM (International Congress of Modern Architecture). But although, or perhaps because, the Modern Movement was still carried forward by a relatively few people in Europe, Asia, and the Western Hemisphere, we all knew one another and kept in close touch.

There were some memorable occasions: in 1968, when Mies van der Rohe's New National Gallery was dedicated in West Berlin,

Mies was too sick with arthritis to attend—or so his doctors and lady friends insisted. (Mies's grandson and associate, Dirk Lohan, did attend and checked it all out just as carefully as Mies would have done it.) I went with my friend Craig Ellwood, and we were enormously impressed by this extraordinary building—Mies's last major work, as it would turn out, before his death. I had seen all his buildings in the U.S. and in Canada, of course, and I had seen what remained of the Tugendhat House in Brno, Czechoslovakia; but the Barcelona Pavilion had not yet been reconstructed, and some of his early, pre-Hitler buildings seemed inaccessible. So the New National Gallery represented Mies's return to his homeland, and Craig and I were rather sad that the old boy had been unable to attend the dedication. Upon my return to New York, I called Mies and he must have spent an hour on the phone from Chicago cross-examining me on every single detail, and chuckling to himself when I told him how much we had admired this beautiful pavilion, how much good it would have done him to have been there. I think it was the last time he and I talked.

Although I was not aware of it at the time, I now realize that something rather unfortunate had been happening to architecture in the U.S. during the years following World War II. While the Modern Movement, in the twenty years between the two wars, had been totally committed to the improvement of the human condition in a world that was becoming very rapidly urbanized and even more rapidly overpopulated, modern architecture in the wealthiest country on earth became increasingly the earmark of the very rich. The best modern buildings constructed in the U.S. after 1945 were almost invariably such glistening corporate headquarters as Gordon Bunshaft's Lever House in Manhattan and his equally splendid headquarters for the Manufacturers Trust Bank, for Pepsi Cola, for Union Carbide, and for countless other corporate giants. Bunshaft's fine downtown office buildings were followed by even finer monuments to corporate America by Mies van der Rohe, by Eero Saarinen, and by several other modern American architects of similar reputation. More and more frequently, as time went on and downtown became associated with danger, these sumptuous headquarters were located in suburban Gardens of Eden far removed and carefully insulated from our problem cities and their poverty, crime, and physical decay. The Modern Movement—once dedicated to the ideals of an egalitarian democracy—had suddenly become the symbol of American capitalism at its most exploitative; and virtually no modern architect of any reputation was involved in such mundane problems as housing for the poor or even for those of low-to-middle income. In fact, since the banks controlled the construction of such housing with their iron fists (and mortgages), very few architects could afford to get involved in those areas of concern. The few who tried often bankrupted themselves and had to pursue more profitable commissions—i.e., those offered by the rich.

The design and building of inner cities was similarly controlled by bankers, and very few downtown structures were built that were not expected to be highly profitable—which meant that most downtowns became office ghettos surrounded by miserable slums or parking lots, or both. Only suburbia seemed to present profitable residential and related opportunities for banks and for the developers the banks liked to finance; and so architects in the U.S. found themselves increasingly drawn into areas of concern far removed from the issues that originally motivated the Modern Movement.

It is astounding how rapidly the architectural profession in the U.S. lost virtually all interest in the creation of urban prototypes. It was only a few decades earlier that Le Corbusier and Mies and Gropius and Breuer and innumerable others had spent much of their time drawing up plans for "ideal cities" that were supposed to demonstrate how the Modern Movement could help deal with twentieth-century problems—creating healthy and beautiful urban centers for all humanity. No one had paid those architects to spend thousands upon thousands of hours drawing up these proposals for ideal communities in ideal societies; they considered such work an absolutely essential part of their commitment to mankind—a challenge which they faced with excitement and imagination and artistry.

Such idealism, after World War II, virtually became a joke in most architectural circles in the U.S.—and I found nothing quite so sickening as the arrogant contempt displayed for the idealism of such wonderful artists as Le Corbusier and Mies by the graduates who began to emerge from yuppie schools of architecture, preening themselves in preparation for their impending service to the rich. Only Philip Johnson, among all the "observers" of the architectural scene, was honest enough to call a spade a spade, and to call the new generation of architects "whores." Being totally without illusions—both about the idealism of the years between the World Wars, and about the avariciousness of American capitalism—he enjoyed shocking his contemporaries by telling the unvarnished truth. Which incidentally included the fact that he, Philip, considered himself a whore, too—a perfectly honorable profession, in his view.

Although Philip's own work tended to be rather uneven, he produced much better buildings over the years than he has been given credit for. Even in his first decade as a practicing architect, while he was still completely mesmerized by Mies, he designed and built a series of houses that were much better than those done during those same years by his former fellow students at Harvard, and better than some of Mies's own: in addition to his own famous glass house in New Canaan, Connecticut, Philip did some houses—usually for rich friends—that were beautifully detailed, beautifully proportioned, and in beautiful taste. He had two very talented associates in those days—Landis Gores and later Richard Foster—who contributed considerably to the quality of Philip's work. But he deserves much greater credit than he would later receive, especially from those who were bitterly jealous of his popular successes.

Admittedly, Philip enjoyed playing the role of mentor to some young and often dubious "talents"—recent graduates of elitist schools who were willing to fawn to obtain his patronage; and he became, if not a "kingmaker," then a "princemaker" to one or two new generations of architects who often and effectively managed to exploit his generosity. In some instances, he did lend support to exceptional talent; on other occasions, I suspect, he enjoyed endorsing patent frauds if only to infuriate someone he liked to infuriate. And I suspect—no, I am certain—that Philip deeply harbored a high degree of contempt for the nouveaux riches in America, and that he often felt they deserved the sort of kitsch architecture being promoted by elitist schools.

But he was certainly not responsible for the corruption of some of the architectural profession in the years after World War II. Admittedly, it amused him to observe it all; but although his influence was considerable, it was hardly broad enough to corrupt more than a handful of Yalies. My gentle former employer, Louis Kahn, once said to me that he thought Philip was "profoundly evil." I thought Lou was crazy, and told him so. Philip could be a very naughty boy, all right; but he was always amusing, often even self-effacing, and never for a moment boring—and so many of his contemporaries found him infuriating. I confess that I never did: I considered him much more interesting than I did most of those who liked to attack him and his works.

In truth, it didn't take Philip Johnson to corrupt American architecture. The American cultural and political scene was becoming so thoroughly corrupt, all by itself, that nothing seemed likely to stop the process of decay.

Beginning in the 1970s, American society in effect ceased being a democracy and rapidly turned into an undisguised plutocracy: elections were routinely bought or skewed by the very rich, employing enormously expensive and increasingly sophisticated electronic devices developed in media advertising to lie, cheat, and distort the truth. Decisions that would dramatically change the shape of our man-made environment were made, almost exclusively, by and for the benefit of the very rich; and virtually all the humanistic concerns that, in the years of Franklin Roosevelt and others, had shaped some of our cities and suburbs, and the quality of their social and cultural amenities, began to be abandoned. Such decisions were now made almost invariably to serve the very rich and to satisfy their seemingly insatiable greed.

Less and less subsidized housing was being built for the poor and those with lower incomes; less and less money was spent to create healthier and happier urban environments, or better schools and universities, or better health facilities. The principal criterion determining the shapes of our cities and suburbs was profit. If it would enrich the already wealthy to destroy the centers of our cities and to replace viable communities with high-rent office ghettos—well, then those communities were destroyed. If it would further enrich the already wealthy to replace small-scale neighborhood stores with vast shopping malls—well, then those family-owned stores would be made to bite the dust, and the streets and neighborhoods that had once clustered about them would bite the dust with them. And if inconvenient zoning or other planning regulations stood in the way of the construction of monstrous blockbusting clusters of skyscrapers—well, then politicians could always be bought to rescind and revise the offending zoning or planning rules and open the way to the bulldozers.

Increasingly, architects in America simply became the handmaidens of those who were exploiting the public realm to enrich themselves. In centuries dominated by popes and princes, architects had always served the rich and powerful. But it had seemed to some of us that this had changed with the advent of participatory democracy—and indeed it had, for a brief period of time: the architectural profession had ceased to be a service to the elite and had, in the views of many of us, become an art and a profession in service to all of humanity.

Clearly we were wrong. Many of the young architects who came to the fore in the 1960s had obviously decided that their own best interests were on the side of people who could afford to commission $10 million vacation houses in Aspen, Colorado, or else monuments to their own egos: for example, so-called museums that were quite unsuitable for the display and study of art, but eminently suitable to feed the egos of buttonhole manufacturers (who would donate the monuments to grateful communities—and take generous tax deductions for their donations). Not coincidentally, the egomania of the name architects involved was similarly fed: they made absolutely certain that the image projected by the monument's facade would spell out, unmistakably, the name of the architect responsible. Such imagery, or self-advertising (viz., Robert Venturi's "decorated sheds"), became much more important than the manner in which the "decorated shed" might serve those who had to live and work inside it. . . . Unless, of course, the occupants also paid the bill, in which case their satisfaction did become a matter of some concern.

The kind of architecture that was being produced to feed the egos of nouveaux riches clients (and of their pet architects) thus became, increasingly, the product of "marketing." Major architectural offices in the U.S. were suddenly dominated by "marketing experts" rather than designers, and the nature and quality of the design that was being produced by the hired help was clearly attuned to the needs of self-promotion, rather than the needs of, for example, the human race.

The manner in which this corrupted the quality of architecture is easily described: Every architect knows that virtually *no* two determinants that shape any given buildings are ever likely to be identical: *no* two sites are exactly the same; *no* two users are identical (with identical likes and dislikes); *no* two building programs or budgets are ever identical; and *no* two architectural contexts—that is, the ways in which a new building might or should relate to its neighbors—are ever exactly the same; and so on. Yet, more and more buildings seemed to ignore such considerations as site, context, program, or user; instead, more and more buildings seemed to advertise, above everything else, the name of the architect: if a building looked as if it had been rather severely damaged in a recent earthquake, everybody who was aware of what was what (and latest) in the world of architecture knew that this was the work of Name Architect A; if a building seemed to be constructed largely of chain-link fencing, every cognoscente knew that this was the work of Name Architect B, who was also famous for building junk, and occasionally giant fish; if a building had been stenciled with crypto-Egyptian logos, you knew, instantly, that this was the work of Name Architect C, who was also known for enhancing his buildings with Bad Art; if a proposed building seemed to teeter on fragile stilts and otherwise ignore the laws of gravity (and several other laws as well)—well then, if you knew anything at all about architecture on the cutting edge, you could bet your life that this was the latest project by Name Architect D: mercifully unbuilt, of course, and probably destined to remain so. What was being "marketed" here in the name of architecture was in fact nothing more than exterior decoration—image-making to benefit the key players in a market-driven culture.

Architecture critics in the various media were an essential part of this marketing effort. Most of them had no experience in the design and building of buildings, but all of them knew that their livelihood depended upon discovering something new, something different, something outrageous, possibly even something shocking—every day or week or month. And so the "marketing experts" among a new generation of architects supplied just that—fodder for the critics. The critics responded with effusive gratitude, and so it became increasingly difficult for architects who were a little more interested in quality than in novelty to have their work published. As a result, throughout the 1970s and well into the 1980s, many of the best architects in the U.S. had a hard time surviving, and some of them succumbed to "market forces" and started to design schlock buildings to keep their associates and themselves from going under.

Architecture was not the only art in which "market forces" played havoc with quality. "Market forces" also promoted schlock painters and sculptors in lieu of first-rate ones (whose work was not "different" enough); and even American playwrights, like Arthur

Miller, found that their best work was being performed on London stages rather than on Broadway because the New York stage had became totally "market-oriented."

Under the circumstances, the *Architectural Forum* performed rather nobly, publishing only buildings and projects and ideas that were of the highest quality rather than of the most outrageous novelty. We did publish Bob Venturi's and Denise Scott Brown's ruminations, even though most of us thought they were more than a trifle bizarre and more than a little condescending. But we steered clear of "market-driven" architecture, most of which struck us as being vulgar and irrelevant. Instead, we published some of the most advanced "metabolist" architecture being produced in Japan by people like Kurokawa and Tange—including Tange's fantastic 190-foot-tall "crankshaft" office tower in Tokyo for the Shizuoka Newspaper Company, and his Yamanashi Communications Center in Kofu; we published some of Harry Seidler's perfectionist work in Australia, including his "Circle in the Square" (Australia Square, that is) in Sydney; we published Mies's New National Gallery in Berlin, of course, and Jim Stirling's History Faculty in Cambridge; and we published Riccardo Morandi's breathtaking concrete bridges in Italy. There was a great deal of good and serious architecture being produced abroad, even if most American architects seemed to have gone bonkers, and we published everything that we could find that met our standards.

We published a great deal more, of course: I think the *Forum* may have been the only architectural magazine in the U.S. that produced serious and searching criticism in those years. We "revisited" Pietro Belluschi's quite remarkable 1948 Equitable Building in Portland, Oregon, examining—twenty years after the fact—how well it had stood up. My associate Ellen Perry Berkeley, one of the most perceptive writers on architecture I know, wrote a long article in August 1967 attacking Paul Rudolph's Art & Architecture Building at Yale—a building that all of us had admired greatly when it was completed half a dozen years earlier, but that had apparently angered many of the students and teachers working in it, who regarded it as elitist and felt it was not designed to meet their needs; and it was being hideously vandalized. I was reluctant to publish something that might damage my friend Paul's reputation, especially since I considered him (and still consider him) the most talented architect of my generation in America; but the issues raised by the building seemed so pressing and so serious that we had to take a stand. (Paul wouldn't speak to me for about ten years after the article came out, and he speaks to me only very cautiously today.) And we published a wonderful photographic essay by Charles Eames on Eero Saarinen's General Motors Technical Center (about twenty years after the fact, also), and a highly critical piece comparing the 1931 McGraw-Hill Building, in Manhattan, by Raymond Hood, with the 1972 McGraw-Hill Building in Rockefeller Center, by a very nice architect who shall here remain nameless—and we minced no words.

But, mostly, we continued to publish the most "astonishing" work we could find, and we published it in ways that were often memorable. We published Alexander Liberman's sculpture in 1963, long before many people knew of it; we published an issue on New York with a cover photo of a "Battery Park skyline" constructed entirely out of souvenirs. We published John Johansen's own work—particularly his Morris Mechanic Theater in Baltimore and his wildly Constructivist Mummer's Theater in Oklahoma City— and we asked Johansen to write articles for us on such things as the floating mining towns in the Gulf of Mexico, and the futuristic structures at Cape Kennedy—all of which related closely to his own architectural work.

In fact, I can think of nothing of any interest that was built or imagined in the areas of architecture and related arts that we did not publish—from Frank Lloyd Wright's last work, to a madhouse called "Xanadu" in Calpe, by Bofill Arquitecto, to the first and last days of Wright's Imperial Hotel in Tokyo (demolished on February 28, 1968), to a Berber village south of Tunis and a beatnik village of geodesic domes made of flattened-out pieces of automobile bodies. (The village was called Drop City, and was located twenty-five miles from Trinidad, Colorado.) I have not the remotest idea how we managed to stay on top of so many wildly improbable stories, but I recall distinctly that we had a great deal of fun keeping in touch with our innumerable and informal "correspondents," and milking them dry of information on almost anything under the sun.

Meanwhile the other architectural magazines published all the predictable schlock produced by market-oriented name architects, most of them postmodernists. And most of those buildings were constructed in the U.S., using building materials manufactured by

American advertisers, who were not especially thrilled to see our enthusiastic and colorful publications of work done in Asia, Europe, Latin America, Australia, and just about anywhere else where postmodern kitsch had not taken hold and where "ironic architects" and other practical jokers were not paid very much attention.

In short, we became increasingly unpopular among advertisers—while our popularity with our readers seemed to rise by leaps and bounds. The result was fairly predictable; and Urban America, increasingly strapped for funds, decided to divest itself of the *Architectural Forum* and transfer its title to a commercial publisher who seemed to share our ideals. Alas, this turned out not to be the case, and in 1972 I decided to resign as editor of the *Architectural Forum*—and the entire editorial staff resigned with me. We had found a sponsor willing to support us in starting a new magazine, and so we decided to do just that.

We were obviously crazy—the U.S. was enjoying one of its periodic recessions, but we didn't know it: we knew we were pretty good, and the world of architecture seemed to agree; and so we decided to start a publication that would be devoted to all the design arts everywhere. We called it *Architecture Plus,* in memory of that remarkable supplement produced by and for the old *Architectural Forum* in the 1930s by Howard Myers and Paul Grotz: a supplement that Howard and Paul had named *PLUS,* and which, in its four spectacular issues, introduced the *Forum's* readers to what was then the international avant-garde in all matters of design.

The first issue of *Architecture Plus* appeared in February 1973, and it was an instant success: Paul had insisted that he didn't want to be its art director—he claimed he was too old, or something equally ridiculous—and so I appointed him editor-at-large over his protests: neither he nor I knew what that meant, except that we would have adjoining offices. I decided that Charlotte Winter, a wonderful graphic designer, would make a splendid art director—and fortunately for me, she accepted. She was a thin little witch who snarled at most of us most of the time, and whom all of us adored—for both her incredible perfectionism and her enormous imagination. Since we needed a managing editor, and since I felt the only person who knew what was going on in our operation day after day and year after year was a lovely lady called Ann Wilson (who had been my predecessor's secretary at the *Architectural Forum*), I decided to appoint her managing editor. It turned out to be the most brilliant move I ever made. There were several others who had left the

Forum and come with us to start *Architecture Plus:* Ellen Perry Berkeley, Marguerite Villecco, Virginia Dajani, Marie-Anne Evans, and others. Stanley Abercrombie, a practicing architect who had done a very interesting review that I saw in the *Wall Street Journal,* of all places, joined us. And we assembled an impressive crew of contributing editors, both in the U.S. and abroad, and they proved to be a significant resource. Everything began to look very promising.

Architecture Plus lasted for two years; and although the financial pressures took their toll on all of us, we had a wonderful time—and so, it seems, did a good many of our readers. In the end, alas, the recession wiped us out—that, and our blatant disregard for the demands of potential advertisers. Some of us were still imbued with Harry Luce's determination to keep Church and State rigorously separate. In fact, most of us believed that anything we published that would irritate an advertiser was, ipso facto, worth publishing.

So we ran stories on widely publicized "miracle products" that tended to fail when subjected to the test of time. We ran stories on buildings by widely publicized architects (and/or developers) that seemed to be perilous to the health of their occupants. And we ran stories that exposed the venality of politicians who claimed to be troubled by the environmental crisis, but whose principal concern seemed to be with matters closer to their own luxurious homes. . . .

But our favorite stories were those that dealt with the art of architecture and design, and with strange and often wonderful manifestations of that art. I suspect that what really did us in, in the end, were two stories that I liked a great deal. One was a picture essay on "The Kites of Guatemala," by the photographer Hans Namuth. Hans had taken some spectacular pictures of those huge and colorful wood and paper kites that are flown over the graves in Guatemalan cemeteries on *El Dia de los Muertos* (November 2), to celebrate the memory of the dead on All Saints' Day. We published six pages of Hans's snaps in dazzling color, and gave him the cover, too. And then, in another issue we outdid ourselves, and published an even more colorful story on the sixty-acre estate of the artist Alfonso Ossorio, in Easthampton, Long Island.

Alfonso and I had been friends for many years, and so he permitted our photographer, Norman McGrath, to invade this vast sanctuary and record what only a few visitors had ever seen: probably the most bizarre assemblage of art, crafts, and outrageous memorabilia of every conceivable time and place to be found in this or most other hemispheres. The documentation was complete and included such items as a massively decorated Turkish shoeshine stand as well as paintings by Jean Dubuffet, Jackson Pollock, Clyfford Still, Willem De Kooning, Max Ernst—plus, needless to say, hundreds of drawings and paintings by my enormously productive friend. "Ossorio's house," I wrote in the accompanying text, "is a sunburst of some new Dadaism, a wild storehouse of everything from the most beautiful painting Jackson Pollock ever painted, to the most bizarre works of religious fanatics and other, inspired lunatics." Among the works that I listed was a "glass cheese bell under which is displayed what appears to be a stuffed infant." I also reported a little brown Junior Jesus, a rather generous collection of human and animal skulls, and a couple of live African grays (parrots) that frequently said things like "Here today, gone tomorrow."

Our actual and potential advertisers had already, of course, been taking it on the chin for many, many months and years—but it was very likely the stuffed infant under the cheese bell, the little brown Junior Jesus, and those human and animal skulls that proved to be the last straw. And so we went down, in a blaze of glory—a band of brothers and sisters, a happy few who together left a fairly indelible mark. "Here today," as Alfonso's parrots liked to say. "And gone tomorrow."

But not quite: John Dixon, who had been with us on the *Architectural Forum,* became editor of *Progressive Architecture;* Don Canty, who had joined us from San Francisco, became editor of *Architecture* magazine; Stanley Abercrombie and Ann Wilson took over a magazine called *Interior Design;* and Ellen Berkeley, Margot Villecco, Virginia Dajani, and others who were part of those "happy few" are writing, editing, and "astonishing" their fellow men and women in different ways. I think they all learned something from those years. I know I did.

CHAPTER TWENTY-FIVE

■ Postmodernism died sometime in the 1980s, although vestiges of kitsch and neoklutz and other nouveaux riches lapses in taste continued to surface now and then in places like Washington, D.C., a city almost totally devoid of culture. But market-oriented architecture, and the flacks who were employed to promote it, desperately needed something "new," something "different": after all, once you have seen an ironic Palladian skyscraper you may not want to see another one for a month or two, if ever.

Since American architecture critics, by and large, had little knowledge of architecture, they searched for "novelty" and "differentness" in all sorts of places—and suddenly discovered Le Corbusier! And Mies! and Aalto! And Frank Lloyd Wright! And even Loos, and Schindler, and Chareau, and Asplund, and even Scharoun! Could Breuer and Gropius and Neutra and Mendelsohn be far behind? Fortunately for the critics, these rediscovered stars had all been born about 100 years ago, so it was possible to have a Mies centenary or a Corbu centenary to match your editorial schedule.

But rediscovery is a one-line joke, editorially speaking. Something *really* new and different was needed—or, at the very least, something that most of the market would not instantly recognize as a rehash of things past.

And so, after postmodernism had bit the dust, Deconstructivism was floated by the marketeers. Everybody who remembered the Russian Constructivist architects and artists of the years after 1912 (or thereabouts) was by this time conveniently dead—except for Philip Johnson, and his lips were sealed in a fixed smile. And so a "new style" could be safely invented, and safely promoted to satisfy the requirements of the market.

There were plenty of architects who were willing to sell the new style: some of them, in fact, had designed vaguely "Deconstructivist" buildings in earlier years—or at least buildings that ripped off such early de Stijl masterworks as Gerrit Rietveld's 1924 Schroeder House, in Utrecht. These Decon name architects were good at marketing: some of them, in fact, had made their reputations solely on the basis of unbuildable house projects that served as subjects for beautiful monographs published by the vanity presses. Others had spent much time on lecture circuits, promoting themselves and their totally new "style" in thousands of ill-chosen words, all of them multisyllabic and most of them unintelligible. The new style was outrageous, since the projects advanced in its name were unbuildable; it was very chic, since Deconstructivist buildings were sure to be monstrously expensive (if at all buildable), and America's nouveaux riches had always equated high cost with good taste; and the new style was "plenty ironic," since any Deconstructivist building, even if temporarily propped up, would be certain to collapse shortly thereafter, thus killing at least some of the occupants and bystanders.

In other words, it was a terrific style. Most Decon projects were, in fact, very ordinary boxes to which the name architect had attached enormous faux structures—girders and columns and beams and other interesting decorations that held up absolutely nothing, were enormously expensive to build, and violated the laws of gravity in every respect. In short, Deconstructivism was a toy—a piece of giant, nonsense-sculpture affordable only to the superrich.

In the forefront of those who promoted this nonsense were certain elitist schools of architecture whose professors were in need of interesting dissertation subjects, and therefore in constant search for esoteric subject matter. Since most of those schools were staffed by people who had never constructed anything much more elaborate than a kitchen window, it was understandable enough that they were drawn to a style that favored unbuildable structures. In any event, the academics provided the theoretical underpinnings for a style that was really in need of something just a little more . . . substantial. The Museum of Modern Art, at Philip's behest and with a major assist from a very serious Ivy League professor of double-linguistics, presented the new style—Deconstructivism—and thus gave it a stamp of legitimacy. Even though Sir Isaac Newton might disagree, the Museum of Modern Art decided that unbuildable architecture was a legitimate concern for our world. Even Jacques Derrida, the philosopher and rather reluctant patron saint of Deconstructivism, seemed to think that architecture was supposed to stand up. "What a silly idea!" said one of the name architects identified with the new style. "How ironic!"

Deconstructivism has one quality to commend it: it does, at least, *seem* to concern itself with structure, even if only by implication. The fact that Deconstructivist structures tend to deconstruct was predictable enough: schools of architecture, in the U.S. anyway, seem to be operated largely by people who talk interminably and unintelligibly, and know almost nothing about the way buildings are built.

Largely, but not exclusively. After my various magazines (unlike my buildings) deconstructed, I was asked to come to Boston and to head the School of Architecture at the Boston Architectural Center. I spent four years there; and while I was unprepared for some of the Byzantine politics of the academic world, I was thrilled by the quality of the school and its innovative programs. Here was a place in which young people could study architecture while actually working on construction sites or in architects' offices during much of the week; and their teachers, in the school's studios and classrooms, were practicing architects from the Boston area who wanted to transmit some of their enthusiasms and expertise to young people who could not afford to study at yuppie universities. It was and is a wonderful place—a place in which architecture for the real world is taught by people who know what they are talking about.

After four years, there was an opportunity to teach at a conventional school in Washington, D.C. For various personal reasons, I accepted. It was perhaps a mistake to do so, but it was an instructive mistake nonetheless. In that typical school, most of those who taught—and talked and talked, and talked and talked—knew very little about the realities of architecture, and seemed to care even less. And the students who graduated from this school, and from many schools like it, were quite unprepared to face the real world of architecture. All they were ready to do, after having been exposed to years of interminable and incomprehensible verbiage, was to talk and talk, and talk and talk. They were hardly prepared to design a building that might, just possibly, not fall down.

But then, Mies liked to say (on the very rare occasions when *he* talked) that it took a young person about ten years of practical work in construction before he or she could be trusted to design a building. It took Mies about thirty years of work—some of it as an apprentice to his father, a stonemason—before he knew how to design the Barcelona Pavilion.

·   ·   ·

Rehabilitation Center, Binghamton, New York. The extension of our building into the landscape was of major importance. (Norman McGrath)

I am an architect, and I have designed and built about fifty buildings and similar structures. I am not a postmodern, or premodern, or Constructivist, or Deconstructivist architect; I am a modern architect.

I believe that architects, in a free and democratic society, are responsible to *all* their fellow citizens, not only the rich. I believe they must fulfill that responsibility by, first, learning their trade; second, concerning themselves with those problems faced by their fellow men and women that can be solved—at least in part—by architectural means; and, third, doing their work with as much art as they are capable of summoning to those tasks.

It is really very simple; and fortunately for all of us, there are a few architects working in different parts of the world who continue to uphold the standards of Mies and Wright and Le Corbusier: Paul Rudolph and Ieoh Ming Pei in the U.S., Herman Hertzberger in Holland, Fumihiko Maki and Tadao Ando in Japan, Roland Rainer in Austria, and many, many others who are not at the moment chic

Another view of the same building, designed jointly by me and James Baker and completed in 1975. It is a large community center in which rehabilitated mental patients learn to return to a more normal existence. (Norman McGrath)

Ford Foundation Theater Project, ca. 1968. An experimental off-Broadway theater designed to be used with almost unlimited flexibility. My associate was the theater designer David Hays. (Gil Amiaga)

or otherwise newsworthy, but who will undoubtedly be rediscovered when today's critics run out of superstars.

There are, in short, a number of very, very good people doing very, very good buildings that serve humanity and art in roughly equal doses. There is no need to despair just yet.

But it is a close call. Ever since the early 1980s, when the treasure of the United States began to be stolen by the rich and superrich and their hired guns, this country has ceased to function as an egalitarian democracy. Its government, with which I became quite familiar after twelve years in Washington during the years of the Reagan-Bush plutocracy, was bought long ago. The people's "elected" representatives are put in power by hundreds of millions of dollars spent, year after year, to buy media time, to finance lobbies, to pass laws that will further enrich those who have already stolen us blind: while most people's taxes went up precipitously in the years after 1981, the three-tenths of 1 percent in the U.S. who

322

After the Ford Foundation Project was exhibited and published, Vanderbilt University asked me to design a new Drama School based on our concept. David Hays, Brian Smith, and I then built this flexible theater (plus other facilities), using the neo-Gothic shell of a 1917 building on the campus.

Another view of the multilevel Vanderbilt theater. All seating and all lighting are movable, and various interlocking levels can be used by the audience, or the performers, or both. The entire audience/performance area has a stainless-steel wire grid suspended above it, and stagehands can walk on this post-tensioned grid and operate all lighting and other mechanisms from any position.

declared an annual income of $200,000 and more—much, much more—were earning a total of $400 billion, and had their taxes cut in half by a grateful Reagan-Bush administration and its fellow profiteers in Congress.

The battalions of lawyers, lobbyists, politicians, and other beneficiaries of this generosity are, in fact, our new patrons of architecture and of the other arts in the U.S. today. Their almost uniform lack of culture, of ethics, and of basic education shapes the quality of our man-made environment, and the quality of much of our intellectual environment as well: museums and their boards of trustees are ladders for social climbing, and so are building committees in every field that usually consist of potential donors in search of a large tax deduction, and in search of an even larger nameplate on the building about to be dedicated to their present and future fame. The art of architecture, in short, has been largely corrupted to serve the egos and the pocketbooks of the superrich, rather than the 99.7 percent who thought they were living in an egalitarian democracy; and far too many practitioners of architecture have been corrupted in the process.

Our cities—God help them!—reflect the values of the three-tenths of 1 percent: downtowns are designed (by bankers) to make vast profits for the builders of giant office blocks—while the rest of downtown real estate serves as parking lots or as hovels for the wretched poor; suburbia (also designed by banks) is for those who have fled the desolation and violence of downtown before and after dark.

For those who spout balderdash about "urban design" and other pieties I recommend an extended visit to an "edge city" known as East St. Louis, Illinois. Actually, a brief visit will do.

East St. Louis, Illinois, is an unmitigated horror show. It looks, roughly, like Dresden after the massive air raids at the end of World War II: blocks upon blocks of burned-out and collapsed buildings, most of them now bulldozed; potholed streets, boarded-up storefronts, broken glass, drunken and drugged bodies strewn about, no street signs, no streetlamps, few trees, weeds and trash everywhere. On the edges of East St. Louis, Illinois—those "urban edges" that yuppie theoreticians like to talk and talk and talk and talk about— there are further wastelands: industrial plants that once offered thousands of jobs and are now in ruins, no longer even protected by chain link fencing, inhabited only by rats and occasional addicts.

There are no cops in sight. In the U.S. today, there are more privately paid security guards than publicly funded police—because the three-tenths of 1 percent want to guard what they have acquired, and know where to buy that protection. There are plenty of expensive doctors and expensive hospitals and luxurious private schools to serve those who can afford to pay; but not very much of anything in those departments for the 99.7 percent. I am not sure there are any hospitals in East St. Louis, Illinois; one suspects that death comes rather quickly in that trash can of American capitalism. There are some public schools. The kids that bother to attend come armed to the teeth. It is all frightfully ironic.

East St. Louis, Illinois, is the reality of American free enterprise today. Admittedly, it is not the whole story; but it is a very large part of the whole story, and it is an unforgivable disgrace.

It is an unforgivable disgrace especially when read against the arrogant verbiage spouted by the politicians put in power by the three-tenths of 1 percent—the verbiage addressed not only to the American electorate, but especially to the rest of the world, some of it just emerging from a totalitarian nightmare and looking desperately for guidance toward an egalitarian democracy. That "arrogance of ignorance" that Chesterton spoke of is only a part of the official American story—for most of the story, today, is one of arrogance of those who think they've got away with it. It is the arrogance of irony.

What does any of this have to do with architecture? I think Le Corbusier and most of his contemporaries gave the answer in their own work—work which attempted to create alternatives to an unjust, unequal, unfair social order and to the cities and countrysides shaped by elitist forces.

Some of us were inspired by the idealism and selflessness of those valiant few, those artists who practiced architecture in the service of all. Despite the corruption of so much of our profession, despite the vulgarity of yuppie architecture, despite the growth of elitist schools, despite the ubiquity of vulgarian clients and of name architects busy toadying to them, and despite the high price paid by some of the men and women who stuck to their ideals and their responsibilities—in spite of all of that, the memory and the evidence of what was accomplished by those valiant few is with us still, and continues to excite us.

It was marvelous to be alive when Utopia was young; and it will be marvelous again once the sham of the present has been washed away.

Not long ago, I spent some time in a miraculous little place called Thailand, and there I came across an object that seemed to me to represent an almost perfect work of architecture.

The object is known as a *ngob,* and it is a traditional farmer's or fisherman's hat that has existed in Thailand for centuries or, possibly, for thousands of years; and nobody (or ngobody) knows who originally designed it. In fact, most of my Thai friends never think of it as having been "designed"; so far as they are concerned, the *ngob* has been around forever, and it is as much a part of the Thai scene as palm trees or stalks of bamboo, from which, in fact, the *ngob* sprang.

A *ngob* consists of two separate parts, joined by two bamboo "needles": the first part is a kind of parasol; and the second is a basketlike cage inside the parasol that fits over the wearer's head.

The parasol is a lovely shell framed with a delicate, almost geodesic grid of bamboo and finished with wide palm leaves sewn to the structural grid. The shell is exquisitely curved to recall the outline of some kind of Buddhist shrine, and it does everything a regular parasol does, only better: it shades, it keeps out the rain, and it transmits a soft glow of light to the face beneath it. The rim of a *ngob* measures about eighteen inches in diameter, and the perimeter is defined by a ring of very thin bamboo. The structural "geodesic" grid that frames the parasol is laced to the exterior ring with fine string, usually red.

Within the outer shell or parasol sits a flexible cage or basket of sliced bamboo, and it has been designed to fit over the wearer's head. It will adjust itself to any size cranium, and fit very snugly around your skull. The cage is attached very simply to the inside of the parasol by means of the two long bamboo needles, and these are threaded through the crown of the hat on its inside to tie the two parts—the parasol and the basket—together. It sounds a little complicated, but it really couldn't be simpler in design. Because there is a lot of space inside this delicate structure, you get a wonderful

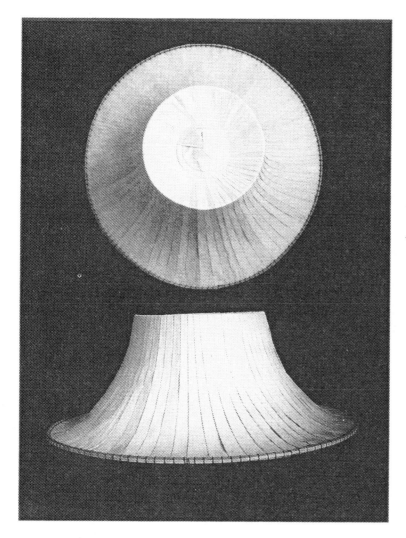

The Thai ngob—*one of the most perfect works of design to be found anywhere—can teach young architects most of what they really need to know. It is one of the lightest structures ever made, and one of the strongest; it is self-ventilating, water-repellent, shading, and self-adjusting. This sublime work of art has the form of a minimalist sculpture. It happens to be a hat made of bamboo and palm leaves, and it has existed for possibly thousands of years. (Louise Krafft)*

cooling breeze that wafts through your *ngob* and around your head.

After wearing a Thai *ngob* for a few days, I saw clearly that it was a perfect example of the interplay of all the elements that are essential to the making of great architecture and great design: its structure is minimal and flawlessly expressed, and covered by a skin that has been sewn to the supporting grid; its function—to shade, to protect from rain, and so on—is perfectly fulfilled; its shape is delicate and pure—as sophisticated as any Brancusi sculpture; it casts a glow of diffused light; the sound of raindrops on the palm leaves is music to your ears; and the sight of all this brings joy to your heart.

Buckminster Fuller used to talk about the economy of his structures—their performance per ton of steel or aluminum or concrete—and how little tonnage he employed to enclose how much cubage of space. Well, a typical Thai *ngob* weighs about zero ounces, and it doesn't leak the way some of our sophisticated structures do. So its performance, by Bucky's standards, is superior to that of many of today's high-tech structures. Not bad, in fact, for a primitive culture.

There are numerous farmers' and fishermen's hats in common

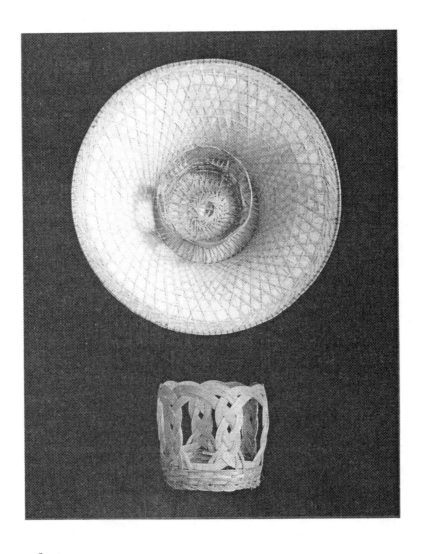

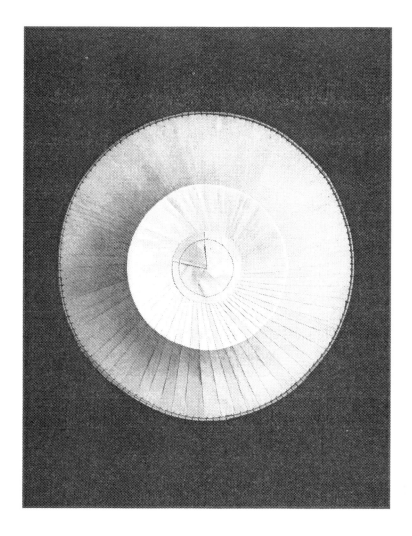

use throughout Asia; but I think the Thai *ngob* is superior to all of them—in form, in structure, in function, in light, in shade, and in the soft breezes that it generates. The Thai knew when they had a perfect thing, and they saw no reason to change it.

Wouldn't it be refreshing, I said to myself, to have a school of architecture, say, or a school of design in which students were introduced, on Day One, to the *ngob*—that absolutely flawless example of the interplay of form, function, light, texture, structure, and economy of means? That pure work of art and design—so modestly presented, so totally devoid of critical or academic double-talk? Wouldn't it be refreshing to start with something—as my friends and I did, not so very long ago—that is not postmodern, or Deconstructivist, not symbiotic, not ironic, not neo-neo-neo—something, in short, that simply is? And speaks for itself?

Wouldn't it be refreshing to start from scratch—to start from the First Principles that were once so crystal-clear?

INDEX

Aalto, Aino, 24, 198

Aalto, Alvar, 24, 100, 140, 198–203, 212, 223; Baker House, MIT, 198–9, 200 *illus.*, 201–2; furniture design, 172, 198, 202; at MIT, 100, 193, 198; Sanitorium, Paimio, 154

Abercrombie, Stanley, 315, 316

Addams, Charles, 214

Adler, Dankmar, 47, 100

Adler & Sullivan, 100

Agronomy Tower, Cornell University, 207

Ahmedabad, India, 255

Ain, Gregory, 131; exhibition house for MOMA, 142–3

Albers, Josef, 169

Albini, Franco, 174

Alexander, Christopher, 301

Alexander, Dorothy: Eckstein House, 186 *illus.*

Allen Art Museum, Oberlin, 294

Allen-Stevens Offices and Warehouses, Astoria, 187 *illus.*

American Abstract Artists, 115

American Institute of Architects (AIA), 277

American National Exhibition, 1959, Moscow, 220, 221, 228–48

Amerika Baut exhibition (1957), Berlin, 218–19, 221 *illus.*, 222–3, 226

Ando, Tadao, 321

Anshen, Robert, 102

Architects Collaborative, The (TAC), 63, 168, 277; dormitories at Harvard University, 168, 199, 201 and *illus.*, 277

Architectural Association (AA), 12

Architectural Forum, 20–6, 183–91, 215, 265, 269, 270, 272–8, 312–14; advertising, 304, 314; Blake at, 20–2, 44–9, 57, 71, 158–67, 171, 183–91, 266, 271–2, 314; ceases

Architectural Forum (cont.)
publication, 24, 282–4; circulation
and losses, 189–90, 281; cities, issues
devoted to single, 274–6; covers,
274–7, 287 *illus.*, 288 *illus.*, 289
illus., 313; Design Decade issue, 25;
editorial integrity of, 272–3, 278;
and Frank Lloyd Wright, 23, 45–9,
57, 164, 271–2; international
coverage, 279; and Perry Prentice,
160–6, 185, 186, 190–1; and
photography, 273; PLUS quarterly
supplement, 23 *illus.*, 24; promotion
of modern architecture and architects, 169, 177–9; published by
Urban America Foundation,
285–9, 300–2, 303–14; split into
two publications, 190–1, 217,
280–1
Architectural Record, 158, 217, 272, 283
Architectural Review, 11, 217, 271, 299
architecture: clients, 181, 182, 188;
corruption of profession, 307,
309–10, 317, 324–5; effect of
capitalism, private developers and
profit motive on, 196–8, 310–11,
317, 324; and humanistic concerns,
5, 13; minimalist, 96; modern,
146–8, 177–8; of 1980s, 13; opposition to modern, 119; and postwar
rebuilding of cities, 76, 102, 180;
regional movements, 106; schools
of, 28, 29, 144, 268, 297, 319;
symmetry in, 152–4; and the
wealthy, 307, 309, 310; *see also*
housing
architecture critics, 148, 154, 162, 181,
266, 278–9, 298, 305, 311, 317
Architecture magazine, 316
Architecture Plus, 212, 314–16
architecture publications, 184, 189,
217, 272, 277, 313; *see also specific
publications*
Armour Institute, 27, 28, 52, 91, 105;

see also Illinois Institute of Tech-
nology
Arp, Hans (Jean), 131, 169
Art Deco, 148
Art Nouveau, 130, 199
Arts & Architecture, 165, 189, 265
arts and crafts, 130
art scene: London, pre–World War II,
11; New York City, 1940s, 66–8, 70
asbestos, 273
Asplund, Gunnar, 30
AT&T Building, 299
Auditorium Building, Chicago, 100
Auschwitz, concentration camp, 79
Autobiography, An (Wright), 46–51
automobile design, 158
avant-garde, 24, 66, 146–8
Avedon, Richard, 211

Bacon, Edmund, 36, 87, 180
Baker, James, 304, 321
Baker House, Cambridge, 198–9, 200
illus., 201–2
Baldwin Hills, Calif., 33
Bangs, Jean Murray, 175
Banham, Peter, 296
Barcelona furniture, 174
Barcelona (German) Pavilion,
Barcelona Exposition, 55, 91, 154,
320
Barnes, Albert C., 39, 43–4
Barnes, Edward Larrabee, 60, 108,
144, 169, 217, 261, 262, 300
Barnes, Mary, 108, 128
Barnes Foundation, 39
Barr, Alfred H., Jr., 13, 106, 107, 109,
125–8, 133, 135; collecting for
MOMA, 126, 127, 128; death of,
126
Barragan, Luis, 68
Barry, Charles, 156
Barry, Iris, 128, 129
Bassett, Hood, 174
Bauhaus, 9, 24, 35, 137; closed under

Nazi pressure, 100; Dessau, 93, 137; Furniture Workshop, 9, 140; Weimar, 93, 137, 140

Bayer, Herbert, 169, 209, 217

Beaux-Arts Institute, New York, 28

beaux-arts tradition, 29, 43, 144, 155, 257

Beier, Annegret, 275–6

Belgioioso, Lodovico, 158

Bell, Alexander Graham, 296

Belluschi, Pietro, 312

Berkeley, Ellen Perry, 312, 315, 316

Berlin, 226–7; see also West Berlin

Berlin Diaries, 1940–1945 (Vassiltchikov), 86

Berlin Interbau; see Interbau Exposition

Bethesda Fountain, Central Park, 277

binuclear structures, 100

Birkerts, Gunnar, 260

Black, Misha, 11

Blackburn, Alan, 104, 106

Blake, Casey Nelson, 188 *illus.*, 278

Blake, Christina, 74, 154, 174, 188 *illus.*

Blake, Martha Howard, 73, 91, 123, 159, 173–4, 272

Blake, Peter, 7 *illus.*, 77 *illus.*; and American National Exhibition, Moscow, 228–48; and Amerika Baut exhibition, 218–19, 222, 223, 226; and *Architectural Forum, see* Blake, Peter, at *Architectural Forum;* and *Architecture Plus,* 212, 314; in armed services, 43, 62, 64–7, 70–84, 89, 173; buildings designed by, *see* Blake, Peter, buildings designed by; (Serge) Chermayeff, apprenticeship with, 11–15; "Cityscape" column for *New York* magazine, 305; in England, 3–19; family of, 3–4, 10; at Howe, Stonorov & Kahn, 36–7, 43; marriage to Martha Howard, 73; marriage to Petty Nelson, 123,

151; model for Pollock exhibition, 111 *illus.*, 112–13; at MOMA, 108, 113, 125, 129–31, 136, 157–9; partnership with J. Baker, 304; at Stonorov & Kahn, 30–6; teaching positions, 126, 319–20; at University of Pennsylvania, School of Architecture, 27–9, 31, 43

Blake, Peter, at *Architectural Forum,* 183–91; associate editor, 158–9, 160–7; free-lance draftsman, 20–2; junior writer, 44, 45–9, 57, 71, 171; managing editor, 266, 271–2; resignation from, 314; survey of American cities, 90–104; see also *Architectural Forum*

Blake, Peter, buildings designed by: Allen-Stevens Offices and Warehouse, 187 *illus.*; Blake House, Bridgehampton, 188 *illus.*; Eckstein House, Kings Point, 186 *illus.*; Ford Foundation Theater Project, 322 *illus.*, 323; Hagen House, Sagaponack, 185 *illus.*; Martinez House, Pound Ridge, 189 *illus.*; Pinwheel house, 116–18 and *illus.*; Rehabilitation Center, Binghamton, 320 *illus.*; Russell House, Bridgehampton, 182 *illus.*, 183 *illus.*; Temple Emanu-El, New Jersey, 187 *illus.*; thesis project (Pratt Institute), 157 *illus.*, 158; Tobey Barn, Amagansett, 184 *illus.*; Vanderbilt University Drama School, 323 and *illus.*; work discussed, 181–8 and *illus.*; work published, 218, 265

Blake, Petty Nelson, 117 *illus.*, 123, 151

Blake House, Bridgehampton, 188 *illus.*

Bofill, Riccardo, 289

Bofill Arquitecto, 313

Bogardus, James, 296

Bootham School, York, 6–8
Boston, *Architectural Forum* issue on, 275
Boston Architectural Center, School of Architecture, 319
Boston Globe, 305
Bradford, Peter, 288, 300
Brancusi, Constantin, 91, 179; *Birds in Space*, 101
Braque, Georges, 16, 115, 146, 179
Brazilian Pavilion, University City, Paris, 250 *illus.*, 259
Breger, William, 140
Breton, André, 66
Breuer, Marcel (Lajko), 9, 107, 140–2, 208–10, 212, 252–3; death of, 141; exhibition house for MOMA, 131, 137–40, 141, 142, 208; furniture design, 208; Geller House, 118; at Harvard, 10, 27, 28, 37, 60, 137, 139, 140, 144, 209, 262; IBM buildings, 253; Monastery and Abbey Church, 253; and Philip Johnson, 137–8; tubular steel and cantilever chair designs, 137, 140, 141–2, 174; UNESCO Headquarters, 140, 194, 195, 196, 253; Whitney Museum of American Art, 253
bridges, 312
British Archigram group, 300
Broadacre City, 52
Broadway Boogie-Woogie (Mondrian), 66
Brodovitch, Alexey, 209–12, 217, 272
Brooks, Charlotte, 124
Brooks, Jim, 122, 124
Brown, Denise Scott, 291, 295, 312
Brownjohn, Robert, 222
Bryn Mawr College dormitories, 255
Buchholtz Gallery, 115
Bunshaft, Gordon, 266, 300, 306; Lever House, 306
Burnham, D. H., 99

Burnham & Root, 100; Monadnock Block, 100
Burtin, Will, 72
Bush, George, 186, 322, 324
Butterfly chair, 172

Calder, Alexander, 23, 25, 67, 115, 179, 215
Callery, Mary, 104, 106, 192
Campbell, Bob, 305
Camp Ritchie, 72, 73, 79, 80, 81
Cantilever chair, 137, 142
Canty, Don, 316
Cape Kennedy, 301, 313
capitalism, 196–8, 307
Carlhian, Jean Paul, 155
Carmichael, Joel, 214
Case Study House, Los Angeles, 165
cast-iron prefabrication, 296
Castro, Fidel, 251, 279
Catholic University, Department of Architecture, 126
Central Intelligence Agency (CIA), 237–9
Centre Pompidou, Paris, 113
Cézanne, Paul, 44
chairs, 14,172–4, 203; Breuer, 137, 140, 141–2, 174; Eames, 173; Knoll, 171, 172
Chandigarh, India, 158, 205, 249, 272
Chandni-Chawk, New Delhi, 99 *illus.*
Chareau, Pierre, 66, 114
Chermayeff, Barbara, 13–16
Chermayeff, Ivan, 13, 16, 18, 220, 222, 275, 277, 287
Chermayeff, Peter, 13, 16
Chermayeff, Serge, 9, 10 *illus.*, 11–18; home of, 13; ICI laboratories, 15; industrial and furniture design, 14; at Institute of Design, Chicago, 93
Chicago, 90–101; *Architectural Forum* issue on, 274
Chicago Tribune Tower competition, 203, 256

Choay, Françoise, 220
Chrysler Building, New York, 35, 299
Church of the Autostrada, 279
CIAM (Congrès Internationaux d'Architecture Moderne), 11, 305
Circle in the Square, Sydney, 312
cities, 50, 51, 180, 324; reconstruction after World War II, 102, 180; *see also* Ideal Cities; urban congestion; urban housing; urban planning and design; urban renewal
City College of New York (CCNY), 39, 41
City Is Not a Tree, A (Alexander), 301
city planning, 42, 61, 145
Coates, Wells, 11, 18, 193
Cobb, Harry, 140, 145, 261
Columbia University, School of Architecture, 289
communism, 59, 61, 175
Communist International, 61
Communist Party, 22, 58, 59, 90
Complexity and Contradiction in Architecture (Venturi), 290, 291
concentration camps, 12, 61, 77, 79, 86
Congrès Internationaux d'Architecture Moderne (CIAM), 11, 305
Congress Hall, West Berlin, 224–5 and *illus.*
Constable, Rosalind, 70–1, 280
Constable Report, 71
Constantine, Mildred, 130
construction costs, 181, 182
Constructivism, 12, 22, 24, 35, 100, 146, 158, 318
contextualism, 204
Cooper, Louise, 163
Cornell University, 144, 163, 270; Agronomy Tower, 207
corporate headquarters, 306
Costa, Lucio, 250
Cox, Warren, 273, 274

Cranbrook Academy of Art, Bloomfield Hills, 144, 203, 256, 260
Cret, Paul, 28
Crown Hall, IIT, 97 *illus.*, 274
Crystal Cathedral, Garden Grove, 156
Cserna, George, 273, 274
Cuba, 251, 279
cubism, 146
Currier, Stephen and Audrey, 285–6; death of, 302, 303

Dacca, Bangladesh, 255
Dachau, concentration camp, 77, 79
Dailey, Gardner, 102
Dajani, Virginia, 315, 316
Dallegret, François, 286
Damora, Robert, 278
Daniel, Greta, 130
Death and Life of Great American Cities, The (Jacobs), 35, 180, 269, 290–1
de Carlo, Giancarlo, 286
Deconstructivism, 225, 262, 318–19
defense housing, 33, 34, 87–8
De Kooning, Willem, 115, 128, 179
Del Pezzo's, round table at, 213–15
Demonstrations Cities Program, 301
Dennis, Lawrence, 104
Derrida, Jacques, 319
Design, 288
de Stijl movement, 24, 35, 131, 142
Detroit, Mich., 101
developers, private, 196–8
Dewey, John, 39
d'Harnoncourt, René, 108–9, 129, 132
Dies, Martin, 59
Dietz, Albert, 229
Diller, Burgoyne, 110
Dinkerloo, John, 260
Dixon, John, 316
Dome house, Cave Creek, Arizona, 56 *illus.*, 57
Domus, 217, 271
Doshi, B. V., 300

Dragon, Ted, 124
Drew, Jane, 11
Drexler, Arthur, 112, 113, 159
Dreyfuss, Henry, 25
Drop City, Col., 313
Dulles, Allen, 82
Dulles Airport Terminal, Chantilly,
    Va., 204 and *illus.*, 205
Düttmann, Werner, 223, 226, 269–70
Dymaxion House (Fuller), 93, 96

Eames, Charles, 25, 102, 141, 168,
    193, 256, 260, 313; Case Study
    House, 165; films for American
    National Exhibition, Moscow, 220,
    229–30, 241, 242; furniture design,
    171, 173, 230; Organic Design
    Competition, MOMA, 203
Eames, Ray, 102, 165; films for
    American National Exhibition,
    Moscow, 220, 229–30, 241, 242
Eames chair, 173
East St. Louis, Ill., 324–5
Eckstein House, Kings Point, 186
    illus.
École des Beaux-Arts, Paris, 28
Edgerton, H. E., 23
Eiermann, Egon, 261, 272
Einstein, Albert, 44
Ellis, Peter, 300
Ellwood, Craig, 174, 189, 217, 261,
    268, 300, 306; South Bay Bank, 190
    illus.
Empire State Building, New York, 35
energy conservation, 160
Entenza, John, 102, 165, 189, 265
Equitable Building, Portland, 312
Establishment Underground (Ger-
    man), 78, 79, 88
Evans, Marie-Anne, 315
Evans, Walker, 273, 278; photogra-
    phy, 21 *illus.*
Expo '67, Montreal, 220–2, 264
Expo '70, Osaka, 220

Farnsworth House, Plano, Ill., 91, 153
    illus., 154, 251
fascism, 17, 58, 104–5
Felker, Clay, 305
film, 128, 229–30, 241
Fitch, James Marston, 25, 279
Florida Southern College, 252
Focus, 11
Folger Shakespeare Library, Washing-
    ton, D. C., 28
Ford Foundation Theater Project,
    New York, 322 *illus.*, 323
Fortey, Eastland, 10
Fortune magazine, 70, 161, 214, 266,
    271, 280
Foster, Richard, 308
Four Seasons Restaurant, New York,
    156
Frankenthaler, Helen, 220
Franzen, Ulrich, 140, 145, 169, 217,
    260, 261, 262, 268, 278; Agronomy
    Tower, Cornell University, 207
Franzen, Josephine, 278
Fry, Maxwell, 6, 9, 11
Fuller, Richard Buckminster, 93–5,
    96, 97, 215, 217, 328; geodesic
    dome for American National
    Exhibition, 228, 232, 240, 241, 246;
    U.S. Pavilion, Montreal World's
    Fair, 220, 221, 222
functionalism, 100
furniture design, 14, 202, 203; Aalto,
    198; Barcelona, 174; Bauhaus, 140;
    Breuer, 140–2; Knoll and Associ-
    ates, 171–4; Saarinen, 172, 173;
    Wright, 54 *illus.*
Futurism, 24, 146

Gabo, Naum, 12–13, 179
Gebhard, David, 296
Gebrauchsgraphik, 226
Geiger, David, 220
Geismar, Tom, 220, 222, 275, 277,

General Motors Technical Center, Warren, Mich., 204, 256, 259, 260, 291, 313

General Panel prefab housing system, 93, 95

geodesic domes, 96, 221

George, Phil, 242

German Pavilion, *see* Barcelona Pavilion

German Resistance, 78, 79, 88

Gestapo, 79

Getty Museum, California, 295

ghettos, 307

Giedion, Siegfried, 11, 101, 300

Gilbert, Cass, 294

Gittleman, Len, 277

glass, 130

Glass House, New Canaan, 143, 145, 149–55, 150 *illus.*, 152 *illus.*, 153 *illus.*

God's Own Junkyard (Blake), 291–3, 295

Goff, Bruce, 165, 217

Goldberg, Bertrand, 100

Goodwin, Philip, 128

Goodwin & Stone, 148

Gordon, Elizabeth, 175

Gores, Landis, 140, 145, 262, 308

Gorky, Arshile, 67, 113, 127, 262

graphic design, 128, 130, 180, 183, 222, 271, 275, 277

Graphis, 271

Greenbelt, Maryland, 33

greenbelts, 33, 34

Greenberg, Clement, 110, 127

Griffith, Jacqueline, 248

Gropius, Walter, 6, 9, 10, 22, 101, 107, 119, 202; Architects Collaborative buildings at Harvard, 63, 168, 169, 199, 201 and *illus.*, 277; death of, 303; at Harvard University, 10, 19, 27, 28, 37, 60, 137, 138, 139, 140, 199, 201, 262; Interbau Exposition, 223; and prefab housing, 95

Grotz, Paul, 21 *illus.*, 164 *illus.*; at *Architectural Forum*, 21, 23, 25, 48, 163–4, 183, 211, 212, 214, 217, 271–3

Guggenheim, Peggy, 110

Guggenheim (Solomon R.) Museum, New York, 191, 252 *illus.*, 252

Guimard, Hector, 130

Gutheim, Fritz, 46

Hagen House, Long Island, 185 *illus.*

Harnden, Peter, 72–5, 84, 85 and *illus.*, 86, 300

Harper's Bazaar, 209, 211

Harris, Harwell Hamilton, 102, 175, 193

Harrison, Wallace K., 192, 194

Harvard University, 137–8; (Marcel) Breuer at, 10, 27, 28, 37, 60, 137, 138, 139, 140, 144, 209, 264; dormitories, 168, 199, 201 and *illus.*; Graduate Center Complex, 168, 169; Graduate School of Design, 10, 19, 27, 28, 37, 60, 137–9, 140, 144, 199, 201, 209, 262, 264; (Walter) Gropius at, 10, 19, 27, 28, 37, 60, 137, 138, 139, 140, 199, 201 and *illus.*, 262; *Task* magazine, 59–60, 63; urban design conference (1960), 180; Urban Design Program, 87

Haskell, Douglas, 158–9, 162, 164, 168, 169, 185, 215–17, 270

Havinden, Ashley, 11

Hays, David, 322, 323

Hazen, Joe, 280, 282

Heckscher, Augie, 285

Hellman, Geoffrey, 214

Hepworth, Barbara, 11

Hertzberger, Herman, 321

high-rise buildings, 180

Hilberseimer, Ludwig, 97, 290; proposal for Ideal City, 98 *illus.*

Hiroshima, bombing of, 59

historic preservation, 61, 286–7
History Faculty, Cambridge, 312
Hitchcock, Henry-Russell, 13, 92, 106, 107, 132, 147–8
Hitler, Adolf, 18, 43, 46; assassination attempts on, 78, 79, 81, 82; ban on modern architecture, 9
Hitler-Stalin Pact, 59, 60
Hofer, Evelyn, 278
Hofmann, Hans, 67, 109
Holiday, 265
Hollein, Hans, 305
Holtzmann, Harry, 66
home fashion, 6
homelessness, 136
homosexuals/homosexuality, 132–4, 149
Hood, Raymond, 313
Hook, Sidney, 40
House & Home, 217, 280, 283
House Beautiful, 175
housing and housing projects, 34, 61, 147–8, 165, 166; defense, 33, 34, 87–8; low–cost, 50; mass-produced, 49, 136; for poor, low- and middle-income, 307, 309; for typical American family, 137, 139, 142–3
Houston, Tex., 101, 102
Howe, George, 35–7, 257; at Yale University, 36, 253
Howe & Lescaze, 35–6
Howe, Stonorov & Kahn, 36–7
Huxley, Aldous, 39
Huxley, Julian, 39, 40
Huxtable, Ada Louise, 130

IBA (Internationale Bauausstellung), 270
IBM, 261, 301
Ideal Cities, 98 and *illus.*, 216, 223, 269, 290, 307
Ideal Museum for a Small City (Mies van der Rohe), 112 and *illus.*
Illinois Institute of Technology (IIT),
91, 144; campus buildings by Mies van der Rohe, 91, 93, 100, 250; Crown Hall, 97 *illus.*
Imperial Chemical Industries (ICI), labs, 15
Imperial Hotel, Tokyo, 313
industrial design, 14, 25, 128, 286
industrialization, 102–3
inner cities, 307
Institute of Design, Chicago, 93; Moholy-Nagy at, 27, 28, 93; *see also* Armour Institute
intelligence operations, World War II allied, 75, 79, 80, 84
Interbau Exposition, West Berlin, 202, 223–6
interior design, 130
Interior Design, 316
Interiors, 67, 112, 159
International Style, 21, 22, 147, 148, 175, 266; term origin, 106
International Style: Architecture Since 1922, The (MOMA), 147
Italian Futurists, 24, 146
Ives, Norman, 129
Izenour, Steven, 291

Jackson, Martha, 124
Jacobs, Jane, 34–5, 42, 99, 196, 216, 269–70, 290–1; at *Architectural Forum*, 180
Japan, 46, 80
Japanese prints, 127
Jeanneret, Charles Edouard, *see* Le Corbusier
Jeanneret, Pierre, 174, 259
Jefferson, Thomas, 273
Jefferson Memorial Arch, St. Louis, 256–7 and *illus.*, 259
Jefferson Memorial Competition, 203
Jochum, Veronica, 87
Johansen, John, 140, 145, 189, 217, 261, 262, 268; Morris Mechanic

Theater, 313; Mummer's Theater,
313
Johnson, Lyndon B., 301
Johnson, Philip, 10 *illus.*, 104, 105
illus., 155–6, 168, 181–3, 268–9,
280, 298, 307–9; AT&T Building,
299; and Breuer, 137–8; competitors of, 205; Crystal Cathedral, 156;
Glass House, 143, 145, 149–55, 150
illus., 152 *illus.*, 153 *illus.*; and
Gropius, 132; at Harvard University, 138; Kline Laboratories, 156;
and Mies van der Rohe, 105–6,
156; and MOMA, 13, 105, 106,
108, 128, 130–5, 147–9, 156, 157,
159; and MOMA exhibition
houses, 136–8; Pennzoil Place, 156;
PPG Headquarters, 156; Seagram
Building, 156; University of
Houston, School of Architecture,
155
Johnson Wax Headquarters, Racine,
Wis., 23, 252
Judd, Donald, 181
Jumble Shop, Greenwich Village, 67,
68, 71

Kahn, Louis I., 36, 87, 168, 206–8;
Bryn Mawr College dormitories,
255; death of, 208; Howe,
Stonorov & Kahn, 36; Kimbell Art
Museum, 255; Library at Exeter,
255; Mellon Center for British Art,
253, 255; Olivetti building, 255;
Richards Medical Research Build-
ings, 15, 207, 208 *illus.*, 260; Salk
Institute, 15, 300; Stonorov &
Kahn, 30–4; Yale University Art
Gallery, 193, 253
Kalischer, Clemens, 273
Kandinsky, Wassily, 140
Kauffer, McKnight, 11
Kaufman, Edgar , Jr., 128, 129–30,
132–4

Kelly, Dick, 150
Kennedy, John F., 237, 267–8
Kepes, Gyorgy, 169, 180
Khrushchev, Nikita, 220, 228, 229,
236, 237, 243, 244, 245
Kiesler, Frederick, 67, 132, 193, 216,
301; Endless House, 216
Kiley, Dan, 260
Kimbell Art Museum, Fort Worth,
255
Kitchen Debate (Nixon and
Khrushchev), 229, 244–5
Klee, Paul, 17, 92, 179
Kline, Franz, 115, 122, 179, 215
Kline Laboratories, Yale University,
156
Knoll, Florence Shust, 171–4 and
illus., 256, 260
Knoll, Hans, 25, 66, 91, 171–5 and
illus.; death of, 174
Knoll (H. G.) and Associates, 171–4,
203
Koestler, Arthur, 61, 62
Komai, Ray, 183, 272–7
Kramer, Hilton, 298–9
Krasner, Lee, 68, 109, 110, 115, 122,
123, 124
Kresge Auditorium, MIT, 206
Kurokawa, Kisho, 260, 312

landscape, 55–7
Lawrence, D. H., 39
League of Nations Headquarters,
Paris, 120
Learning from Las Vegas (Venturi;
Brown; Izenour), 291, 294
Le Corbusier (Charles-Edouard
Jeanneret), 22, 69 *illus.*, 119, 132,
140, 148, 192–8 and *illus.*, 202, 212,
249–50, 254; Brazilian Pavilion, 250
illus., 259; Chandigarh city center,
205, 249, 272; Chapel at Ron-
champ, 249; and CIAM, 11; death
of, 303; and Interbau Exposition,

Le Corbusier *(cont.)*
  223, 225–6; League of Nations
  Headquarters, 120; monastery of La
  Tourette, 249; and (Tino) Nivola,
  68, 69 *illus.*; UN Headquarters, 68,
  120, 192, 194; Unité d'Habitation,
  6, 178 *illus.*, 193, 194, 197 *illus.*,
  249; Villa Savoye, 5; Villa Stein,
  154; villas superimposées, 6; Ville
  Radieuse, 5, 50, 51, 96, 180, 197,
  249, 290
Ledoux, Claude-Nicolas, 155–6
Lee, John, 76, 77 *illus.*
Leger, Fernand, 14, 24, 66, 67
Lescaze, William, 35–6
Levitt Houses, 139
Lewis, Whitfield, 10
Lewitt, Sol, 181
Libera, Adalberto, 259
Liberman, Alexander, 313
Lichtenstein, Roy, 220
Life magazine, 23, 71, 116, 123,
  160–1, 189, 265, 280
light and lighting, 53–5, 150, 151, 202,
  207
Lionni, Leo, 214, 217
Lippold, Richard, 169
Little, John, 122
Little (Francis W.) house, Minnesota,
  57
Lobmeyr, J. & L., 130
Lohan, Dirk, 306
London County Council, 10
Long, Huey, 104
Loos, Adolf, 301
Los Angeles, 101, 102
Loucheim, Aline, 205, 214
Lubalin, Herb, 275
Lubetkin, Berthold, 11
Luce, Henry, 21, 71, 160, 161, 162,
  185–6, 191, 281–4
luminism, 113
Lumsden, Tony, 260

Macdonald, Dwight, 58, 62, 104, 145,
  214
Machine Art, 198, 249
Magritte, René, 115
Mailer, Norman, 287, 302
Maki, Fumihiko, 140, 321
malls, 309
Man Ray, 115
Markelius, Sven, 120, 193, 223
marketing, 310–11, 317
MARS Group, 11, 18, 27
Martinez House, Pound Ridge, 189
  illus.
Masey, Jack, 218–22, 226–8, 230, 231,
  233, 235, 241, 242, 243, 246 *illus.*,
  248
Masey, Mary Lou, 246 *illus.*, 248
Massachusetts Institute of Tech-
  nology (MIT), 100, 101, 144;
  Alvar Aalto at, 100, 193, 198;
  Baker House, 198–9, 200 *illus.*,
  201–2; Kresge Auditorium, 204,
  206
Masson, André, 66
mass production, 136, 146, 165, 179,
  181
Matisse, Henri, 39, 44
Matter, Herbert, 109, 110, 124, 217;
  designs, 23 *illus.*, 24
Matter, Mercedes, 109, 124
Mauretania (ship), 74
Mayer, Albert, 158
McAndrew, John, 128
McCarthy, Joseph, 59, 170, 175
McCarthyism, 175
McGrath, Norman, 315
McGraw-Hill, 283
McGraw-Hill Building (1931), New
  York, 313
McGraw-Hill Building (1972),
  Rockefeller Center, 313
McQuade, Walter, 25, 163, 164, 266,
  270–1
Meier, Richard, 264

Mellon Center for British Art, Yale University, 255
Mendelsohn, Erich, 9, 14, 35, 103
Michelucci, Giovanni, 279
Mies van der Rohe, Ludwig, 15, 17–18, 22, 25, 91–3 and *illus.*, 95, 96, 97, 100, 119, 140, 148, 162, 192, 212, 250–2; at Armour Institute, 27, 28, 52, 91, 105; Barcelona furniture, 174; Barcelona (German) Pavilion, 55, 91, 154, 320; Crown Hall, IIT, 97 *illus.*, 274; death of, 303; Farnsworth House, 91, 153 *illus.*, 154, 251; *Ideal Museum for a Small City*, 112; IIT campus buildings, 91, 93, 100, 250; and (Philip) Johnson, 105–6, 137–8, 156; MOMA exhibition of work of, 105; New National Gallery, West Berlin, 251–2 and *illus.*, 305–6, 312; Seagram Building, 156, 223, 251; Tugendhat House, 91, 106; work misunderstood and criticized, 179, 293
Miller, Dorothy, 127
Miller (Herman) Inc., 172, 173
Mills, Mark, 56, 57; Dome House, 56 *illus.*, 57
minimalism, 96, 146
mining villages, Yorkshire, 7–8
Miró, Joan, 113, 115, 127, 169
Mock, Elizabeth, 128
Modern Architecture—International Exhibition (MOMA, 1932), 13, 105–6, 132
Modern Movement, 11, 21, 22, 103, 116, 266, 269, 293, 295; championed by Alfred Barr, 13, 126–8
modular design, 102, 181, 186 *illus.*, 199, 201
Moholy-Nagy, Laszlo, 24; death of, 93; and Institute of Design, 27, 28, 93
Moholy-Nagy, Sybil, 301–2

Monadnock Block, Chicago, 100
Mondrian, Piet, 66, 100, 131, 179
Montreal World's Fair, 220–2, 264
Moore, Henry, 11, 14, 127, 179
Morandi, Riccardo, 272, 312
Moreno, Hector, 272
Morris Mechanic Theater, Baltimore, 313
Motherwell, Robert, 66, 114–15, 179, 215
Moynihan, Daniel Patrick, 239
Mumford, Lewis, 42, 99, 132, 146, 148, 290, 291; articles criticizing modern architecture, 106–8
Mummer's Theater, Oklahoma City, 313
Museum of Modern Art, New York: and Alfred Barr, 125–8, 133, 135; Architecture and Design Department, 129–30; and avant-garde architecture, 146–8; "Cubism and Abstract Art" exhibition, 127; curatorial departments, 128, 129; and deconstructivism, 319; exhibition houses, 131, 136–43; Guimard exhibition, 131; "Hidden Talent Competition," 131, 132; internal politics, 132–4; *International Style: Architecture Since 1922* exhibition and catalogue, 147; and (Philip) Johnson, 13, 105, 106, 108, 128, 130–5, 147–9, 156, 157, 159; Lobmeyr exhibition, 131; Mies van der Rohe exhibition, 105; "Modern Architecture—International Exhibition," 13, 105–6, 132; "100 Useful Objects" exhibition, 134; organic design competition, 172–3, 203; permanent collection, 109, 126; Picasso exhibition, 109; trustees of, 147; West 53rd Street building, 128–9, 148; "What Is Happening in Modern Architecture" symposium, 106–8

music, 179, 181
Mussolini, Benito, 103, 156
Myers, Howard, 21–6, 48, 89, 160,
   161, 163; death of, 160

Nagasaki, bombing of, 59
Namuth, Carmen, 124
Namuth, Hans, 117, 118, 122–3, 124,
   214, 315
National Gallery of Art, Sainsbury
   Wing, London, 298–9
National Gallery of Art, Washington,
   D. C., 114
Nazi Germany, 43, 79
Nazism, 46, 58
Nelson, George, 160, 248; and
   American National Exhibition,
   Moscow, 228–30, 233 illus., 239,
   241, 242; at Architectural Forum, 21,
   25, 44, 47–9; and Frank Lloyd
   Wright, 47–9
Nelson, Paul, 132, 193
neoclassicism, 17, 22, 60, 103, 119,
   158
Nervi, P. L., 217
Neski, Julian, 266; collaborative
   designs with Blake, 182 illus., 184
   illus., 185 illus., 187 illus., 223 illus.,
   234 illus.
Netsch, Walter, 300
Neuffert, Erich, 193
Neutra, Richard, 102, 132, 193, 301
New Deal, 17, 33, 119
Newhall, Beaumont, 128
New National Gallery, West Berlin,
   251–2 and illus., 305–6, 312
New School for Social Research, 210,
   272
Newspaper Guild, New York, 90
New Yorker, The, 45, 106, 107, 214
New York magazine, 305
New York School, 114, 120, 127, 145
New York Times, The, 205, 214, 304
ngob (Thai hat), 326–30, illus. 327–9

Nicholson, Ben, 11, 27
Niemeyer, Oscar, 120, 193, 202,
   223
Niemöller, Martin, 77, 79
Nissen huts, 114
Nivola, Costantino (Tino), 67 and
   illus., 68–9, 120, 121, 213, 214
Nixon, Richard M., 59, 229, 243,
   244, 245, 297, 304
Noguchi, Isamu, 115
Nowicki, Matthew, 158, 205
Noyes, Eliot, 128, 145, 172, 261
nuclear energy, 41

Office of Strategic Services (OSS), 82,
   84, 88, 237
Olivetti, 301
Ossorio, Alfonso, 70, 113, 122, 124,
   315–16
Otto, Frei, 217, 224
Oud, J. J. P., 131, 132, 146, 148
Ozenfant, Amédée, 24, 132

Paepke, Walter, 93
Paine, Ralph Delahaye, Jr., 266, 271,
   280
Palladio, Andrea, 6
Pan-American Union Building,
   Washington, D. C., 28
Papadaki, Stamos, 214
Paris Metro, 131
Parsons, Betty, 70, 110, 115, 127, 215;
   Gallery, 111, 127
Partisan Review, 193
Passonneau, Joe, 262, 301

Patton, George S., 75
Pearl Harbor, attack on, 36
Peck, Cameron, 158
Pei, I. M. (Ieoh Ming), 140, 207, 217,
   260–2, 268, 300, 321
Pelli, Cesar, 260
Penn, Irving, 211
Pennzoil Place, Houston, 156

Pension Building, Washington, D. C., 274

Peressutti, Enrico, 158

Perret, Auguste, 193

Peterhans, Walter, 97

Pevsner, Nikolaus, 11

Philadelphia Bulletin Building, 37

Philadelphia City Planning Commission, 30, 87

Philadelphia Savings Fund Society Skyscraper, 35

Philipsborn, Martin, 80, 81, 88

photography, 128, 180, 210, 273, 274, 278

Picasso, Pablo, 14, 39, 44, 92, 113, 115, 127, 146, 179, 215, 250; MOMA retrospective (1980), 109

Pinwheel beach house, Long Island, 116–18 and *illus.*

Piper, John, 14, 16, 27

planned society, 34, 97–9

plug-in cities, 300

PLUS (quarterly), 164; covers, 23 *illus.*, 24

politics, 58

Politics (magazine), 62

Pollock, Jackson, 25, 68, 109–11 and *illus.*, 112–18, 121–4, 179, 212; death of, 121, 124; exhibition at Betty Parsons Gallery (1949), 111; and MOMA, 127–8; retrospective at Centre Pompidou (1983), 113

Pop Art, 270, 293

population, 98, 102, 146, 147, 166, 170, 291, 306

Portfolio (magazine), 211

Postmodernism, 148, 156, 171, 291, 295–300, 313; end of, 317, 318

Potter, Jeffrey, 122–3, 124

Potter, Penny, 124

PPG Headquarters, Pittsburgh, 156

Pratt Institute, New York, 144; School of Architecture, 157–8

pre-Columbian art, 132

prefabrication, 49, 93, 95, 96, 189

Prentice, Pierrepont Isham (Perry), 160–6, 185, 186, 190–1, 215, 216, 217, 280–1

Prestini, James, 100–1

Price Tower, Oklahoma, 252

Princeton University, 144

Progressive Architecture, 67, 214, 217, 272, 316

Pruitt-Igoe housing project, St. Louis, 301

Public Buildings Administration, Washington, D. C., 36

public housing, 61

Pugin, Augustus W., 156

Quakers, 6

Radburn, N. J., 33

Radio City Music Hall, 128

Rainer, Roland, 321

Rapson, Ralph, 174, 193

Rauch, John, 295

Rauschenberg, Robert, 220

Reagan, Ronald, 186, 322, 324

Reed, Henry Hope, 279–80

Rehabilitation Center, Binghamton, 320–1 *illus.*

Renwick Buiding, Washington, D. C., 274

Resor, Stanley, 105

RIBA, *see* Royal Institute of British Architects

RIBA Building, 11

Richards Medical Research Buildings, University of Pennsylvania, 15, 207, 208 *illus.*, 260

Rietveld, Gerrit, 100, 131, 146; Schroeder House, 318

Risom, Jens, 174

Ritchie, Andrew, 128

Robie House, Chicago, 154

Roche, Kevin, 260

Rockefeller, Nelson, 130, 142, 237

Rockefeller Center, New York, 35
Rockefeller family, 194
Roebling, John Augustus, 296
Rogers, Ernesto, 193
Root, John Wellborn, 100
Roosevelt, Franklin D., 309
Ross, Harold, 45
Rosset, Barney, 115
Roth, Alfred, 193
Royal Institute of British Architects
    (RIBA), 11, 12
Rudofsky, Bernard, 68
Rudolph, Paul, 140, 145, 169, 189,
    216, 261–5, 268, 300, 321; Art and
    Architecture Building, Yale Uni-
    versity, 263 illus., 312; at Yale
    University, 263
Russell, Bertrand (Diddy), 38–44, 59,
    61, 78, 178, 216, 290
Russell, Conrad, 38, 39, 40
Russell House, Bridgehampton, 182
    illus., 183 illus.
Russian Constructivism, 12, 22, 24,
    35, 100, 146, 158, 318

Saarinen, Eero, 25, 87, 101, 107–8,
    132, 151, 165, 203–6; death of, 204,
    205, 303; Dulles Airport Terminal,
    204 and illus., 205; furniture design,
    172, 173; General Motors Techni-
    cal Center, 204, 256, 259, 260, 291,
    313; Ingalls Ice Hockey Rink, Yale
    University, 204, 206, 259; Jefferson
    Memorial Arch, 256–7 and illus.,
    259; Kresge Auditorium, MIT, 206;
    TWA Terminal, Kennedy Airport,
    204, 206, 259; University of
    Pennsylvania dormitories, 259; U.S.
    Embassy, London, 204, 206, 257–8;
    Yale University dormitories, 258
Saarinen, Eliel, 144; Chicago Tribune
    Tower competition, 203, 256; and
    Cranbrook Academy of Art, 256
Safdie, Moshe, 264

Safire, William, 245
Sahl, Hans, 62
St. Louis, Mo., 101
Salk Institute, La Jolla, 15, 254, 300
Sanctuary for the Dead Sea Scrolls,
    Jerusalem, 301
San Francisco, architecture, 101, 102,
    190, 279
Sanitorium, Paimio, 154
Saulnier, Jules, 287
Scharoun, Hans, 193, 225, 226
Schenk von Stauffenberg, Claus, 78
Schindler, Rudolph, 102
Schinkel, Karl Friedrich, 154, 155
Schroeder House, Utrecht, 318
Scully, Vincent J., 169, 170, 302
Seagram Building, New York, 156,
    223, 251
Seidler, Harry, 140, 261, 262, 312
Sert, José Lluis, 67, 87
Shaw, George Bernard, 39
Shizuoka Newspaper Company office
    tower, Tokyo, 312
shopping malls, 309
Shrine of the Book, Jerusalem, 301
Shust, Florence, see Knoll, Florence
    Shust
Singh, Patwant, 288
Skidmore, Owings & Merrill, 169,
    261, 300
skyscrapers, 100, 296
Smith, Brian, 323
Smithson, Alison and Peter, 264, 305
Snow, Carmel, 211
socialism, 39, 97, 103, 145
social realism, 60, 170
Soleri, Paolo, 56, 57, 169, 189, 279;
    Dome House, 56 illus., 57
Sorenson, Abel, 30, 32
Soriano, Raphael, 102, 193
South Bay Bank, Manhattan Beach,
    190 illus.
Soviet NKVD, 82–3
Soviet Union, 12, 42, 103, 158;

American National Exhibition, Moscow, 228–48; invaded by Hitler, 59; and nuclear energy, 41
Spanish Civil War, 60
Spanish Republic, 12
Speer, Albert, 63, 167, 300
Spence, Patricia (Peter), 38, 39, 40, 42, 44
Speyer, James, 91
stained glass, 55
Stalin, Joseph, 22, 46, 167, 236, 237; purges, 42, 58, 61, 158
Stalinism, 17, 58, 60–3, 145, 170
Stam, Mart, 142
Stamos, Theodoros, 70
Stanton, Frank, 189
steel, self-oxidizing, 273
Steichen, Edward, 128
Stein, Clarence, 33
Stein, Gertrude, 5
Stein, Michael, 5
Steinberg, Saul, 68, 70, 214
Stirling, Jim, 272, 312
Stoller, Ezra, 217, 278
Stone, Edward Durrell, 128
Stonorov, Oskar, 30–6
Stonorov & Kahn, 30–4
structural expressionism, 207
Stubbins, Hugh, 224
suburbia, 307, 309, 324; sprawl, 33–4
Sullivan, Louis, 47, 100, 274, 296
Sun and Shadow—Sol y Sombra (Breuer), 209
surrealism, 66
Sussman, Deborah, 277
Swanson, Robert, 256
Swayduck, Eddie, 195–6
Sweden, 103
Sweeney, James Johnson, 23, 24
symmetry in architecture, 152–4

Taliesin East, Spring Green, 55 illus.
Taliesin West, Scottsdale, 12 illus., 28, 54 illus.

Tange, Kenzo, 193, 261, 272, 300, 312
Tanguy, Yves, 66
Task (magazine), 59–60, 63
Taylor, Adrien, 183
Team Ten, 305
Temple Emanu-El, New Jersey, 187 illus.
Thai ngob (hat), 326–30, 327–9 illus.
Thatcher, Madeleine, 21, 183
Thomas, Clara Fargo, 36
Thonet (manufacturer), 142
Time Inc., 21, 71, 160, 162, 185, 191, 215, 280, 282, 284, 287
Time-Life Building, New York, 20
Time magazine, 71, 161, 280
Times Square Tower, New York, 295
Time/Warner merger, 284
Tobey Barn, Amagansett, 184 illus.
traffic, 50, 51, 52, 180
Trotskyites, 58
Tucci, Niccolo, 214
Tugendhat House, Brno, 91, 106
Tunnard, Christopher, 14, 25
TWA Terminal Building, Kennedy Airport, 204, 206, 259

underground resistance, World War II, 77–9, 88
UNESCO Headquarters, Paris, 140, 194, 195, 196
Ungers, Matthias, 305
Union Carbide Building, 223
Union Party, 105
Union Station, Washington, D. C., 274
United Automobile Workers, Detroit, 36
Unité d'Habitation, Marseilles, 6, 178 illus., 193, 194, 197 illus., 249
United Nations Headquarters Complex, New York, 30, 192, 194
Unity Temple, Oak Park, 100
University of Houston, School of Architecture, 155–6

University of Pennsylvania: Richards Medical Research Buildings, 207, 208 *illus.;* School of Architecture, 20, 27–9, 31, 43, 144; women's dormitory, 259

University of Virginia, 273

Urban America Foundation, 285–9, 300–2, 303, 314

urban congestion, 50, 51, 52, 180

urban housing, 300; *see also* cities

urbanization, 147, 170, 178, 194; *see also* cities

urban planning and design, 11, 269, 286, 290; *see also* cities

urban renewal, 177, 180, 197, 198, 216; *see also* cities

U.S. Army, 65; 5th Armored Division, 75, 173; intelligence, 237

U.S. Embassy, London, 204, 206, 257–8

U.S. Information Agency (USIA), 218–21, 228, 235, 240

U.S. Pavilions, Montreal World's Fair, 220, 221, 222, 264

U.S. Space Center, Cape Kennedy, 301, 313

Utley, Freda, 40, 42, 61, 175

Valentin, Curt, 115

Valle, Gino, 254

Vanderbilt University, Drama School, 323 and *illus.*

van Doesburg, Nellie, 132

van Doesburg, Theo, 131, 132

Van Eyck, Aldo, 305

Van Eyck, Peter, 72–5, 84–5

Vantongerloo, Georges, 131

Vassiltchikov, George, 86

Vassiltchikov, Marie, 85–7 and *illus.*

Vaux, Calvert, 277

Venturi, Robert, 99, 170, 260, 290, 291–5, 312

Venturi & Co., 295, 298

Victory Boogie-Woogie (Mondrian), 66

Vietnam War, 269, 289, 297

Villa Savoye, Poissy-sur-Seine, 5

Villa Stein, Garches, 153

Villecco, Marguerite, 315, 316

Ville Radieuse (Le Corbusier), 5, 50, 51, 96, 180, 197, 249, 290

Vogue, 265

von Gaevernitz, Gero, 82, 83, 88

von Moltke, Freya, 81–3, 87

von Moltke, Helmuth James, 42, 43

von Moltke, Wilhelm Viggo (Willo), 30–1 and *illus.*, 32, 42, 44, 78, 164, 205, 260; in armed services, 43, 78, 79, 81, 87; at Harvard University, 37, 43, 87

von Schlabrendorff, Fabian, 80, 88

von Schnitzler, Frau, 91–2

von Trott zu Solz, Adam, 42, 78, 79, 85

VVV (publication), 66

Wachsmann, Konrad, 93, 95, 96, 97

Wakefield Gallery, New York, 70

Walking Cities, 300

Wallace, Henry, 145

Walsh Mansion, Washington, D. C., 274

Warhol, Andy, 220, 299

Warnecke, John Carl, 169

Washington, D. C., 274–5

Wassily chair, 140

Waugh, Evelyn, 6

Weber, Hugo, 92; sculpture of Mies van der Rohe, 92 *illus.*

Weese, Harry, 100, 169, 193, 217, 256, 260

Weidlinger, Paul, 217

Weimar Germany, 10, 12, 35

West Berlin, 76, 269–70; *see also* Berlin

"What Is Happening in Modern Architecture" symposium, MOMA (1948), 106–8

Wheeler, Monroe, 129

White, Stanford, 205

Whitney Museum of American Art, New York, 253
Wilder, Thornton, 226
Wilson, Ann, 314
Winter, Charlotte, 183, 211, 212, 272, 287, 314
Woods, Shadrach, 195, 305
World's Fair, Montreal (1967), 220–2, 264
World War I, 3–4, 38
World War II, 39, 60, 61, 64–88 *passim*, 136
WPA (Works Progress Administration) murals, 110
Wright, Frank Lloyd, 22, 53–7, 100, 119, 145, 175, 271; and *Architectural Forum*, 23, 45–9, 57, 164, 271–2; Broadacre City, 52; death of, 252, 303; Francis W. Little house, 57; furniture design, 54 *illus.;* Guggenheim Museum, 192, 252 and *illus.;* Imperial Hotel, Tokyo, 313; Johnson Wax Headquarters, 23, 252; light, use of, in work, 53–5; Mile High Tower proposal, 51; residential commissions, 50, 53; RIBA lectures (1939), 11–13; Robie House, 154; Taliesin East, 55 *illus.;* Taliesin West, 12 *illus.*, 28, 54 *illus.;* Unity Temple, 100
Wright, Henry, Jr., 25, 160
Wright, Henry, Sr., 33
Wurster, William Wilson, 101–2

Xanadu, Calpe, 313

Yale University, 14, 36, 144, 160; Art and Architecture Building, 263 *illus.*, 312; Architecture Department, 253, 256, 263, 264, 300; Art Gallery, 193, 253; dormitories, 258; Ingalls Ice Hockey Rink, 204, 206, 259; Mellon Center for British Art, 255
Yalta Conference, 76
Yamanashi Communications Center, Kofu, 312
Yamasaki, Minoru, 101, 258
Yorke, F. R. S. (Kay), 9, 11

Zachary, Frank, 211
Zeckendorf, William, 261
Zevi, Bruno, 140
Zion, Robert, 228, 233
Zogbaum, Betsy, 124
Zogbaum, Wilfred, 111, 124

Peter Blake was born in Berlin in 1920 and educated in England and the United States, to which he came in 1940. He served as a Combat Intelligence Officer in the U.S. Army in Europe during and after World War II, was trained as an architect, and has been associated with such pioneers as Louis Kahn in Philadelphia and Serge Chermayeff in London. In his own architectural practice, he was responsible for the design of a number of important buildings and exhibitions, winning awards in several international competitions. Beginning in 1950 he was on the staff of *Architectural Forum,* serving as its editor-in-chief from 1964 to 1972; from 1972 to 1975 he ran its successor, *Architecture Plus.* Blake has written for many professional and popular magazines, and has taught and lectured at museums, colleges, and universities in the United States and abroad. Among his books are *The Master Builders, God's Own Junkyard,* and *Form Follows Fiasco.*

Printed in the United States
R4534300001B/R45343PG134462LVX4B/2/A